Hajo Riesenbeck and Jesko Perrey
Power Brands

Hajo Riesenbeck and Jesko Perrey

Power Brands

Measuring, Making, and
Managing Brand Success

Second, revised, and enhanced edition

WILEY-
VCH

WILEY-VCH Verlag GmbH & Co. KGaA

Second, revised, and enhanced edition

All books published by Wiley-VCH are carefully produced. Nevertheless, authors, editors, and publisher do not warrant the information contained in these books, including this book, to be free of errors. Readers are advised to keep in mind that statements, data, illustrations, procedural details or other items may inadvertently be inaccurate.

Library of Congress Card No.:
applied for

British Library Cataloguing-in-Publication Data
A catalogue record for this book is available from the British Library.

Bibliographic information published by the Deutsche Nationalbibliothek
Die Deutsche Nationalbibliothek lists this publication in the Deutsche Nationalbibliografie; detailed bibliographic data are available in the Internet at http://dnb.d-nb.de.

© 2009 WILEY-VCH Verlag GmbH & Co. KGaA, Weinheim

Printed in the Federal Republic of Germany

Printed on acid-free paper

Typesetting   Kühn & Weyh, Freiburg
Printing and Binding   Ebner & Spiegel GmbH, Ulm
Cover Design   init GmbH, Bielefeld

ISBN: 978-3-527-50390-2

Table of Contents

Power Brands. H. Riesenbeck and J. Perrey
Copyright © 2009 WILEY-VCH Verlag GmbH & Co. KGaA, Weinheim
ISBN: 978-3-527-50390-2

Table of Contents

Interview with Chris Burggraeve: »New Models and Measurements to Stay the Number One Global Brand in the Digital Age« *315*

Why you should read this book

Brands. Is there any other topic in modern management about which so much has been published in recent years? The authors range from university professors to practitioners, advertising »gurus,« and consultants. On paper, their collected works would weigh many tons, leaving the impression that all aspects of branding have been covered in rich detail. Why then a book from McKinsey on brands?

The initial idea emerged in response to the concerns of many managers about the shortcomings of existing concepts and tools. At the one extreme, many texts are so theoretical that companies can't use them without major adaptations. At the other extreme, you find easy-to-read popular points of view on the world of branding that everyone can agree with, but which fail to offer practical tools or guidance. But the middle ground of a substantial yet pragmatic branding toolkit was nowhere in sight. In dealing with this concern over the course of many branding projects we have conducted, we became increasingly confident that we would be able to occupy this »white space« by covering the topic in a practical, realistic, and analytically robust way. Many McKinsey teams have developed effective instruments in their marketing projects, which we know help our clients to improve their understanding of the complex issues of branding, and to manage their brands more effectively. Some concepts and tools evolved through intense cooperation with leading academics and practitioners over some years – in particular, the concept of brand relevance, developed in cooperation with Professors Meffert and Backhaus of the University of Münster, and with our McKinsey alumnus Professor Marc Fischer of the University of Passau (formerly of the University of Kiel).

These concepts and tools have proven successful in many projects in completely different industries. The results motivated us to pull together McKinsey's diverse know-how on individual aspects of successful brand management into a holistic approach that top management could quickly grasp and apply. We also knew from discussions with our own McKinsey Editorial Review Board and external parties that brand management was a

Power Brands. H. Riesenbeck and J. Perrey
Copyright © 2009 WILEY-VCH Verlag GmbH & Co. KGaA, Weinheim
ISBN: 978-3-527-50390-2

hot topic on the top management agenda. The total amount of money potentially spent ineffectively and inefficiently is just too large to leave decisions on branding to lower-level specialists or third parties.

Brands are an increasingly important issue not only for top management, but also in top management's discussions with analysts. For many acquisitions, for example, the questions often revolve around how to handle the acquired brands. Which ones have high value? Which ones can be given up? And what potential for value creation can be extracted from the acquired brands? Some companies excel at exploiting the potential of the brands they acquire, as BMW has shown with the Mini brand, or Marriott with Ritz Carlton. Others simply kill acquired brands or let them fade away over time. We believe that these decisions should not be based on gut feeling or left up to luck. Instead, top management should have a fact-based, quantitative way to make brand decisions and to explain them to their stakeholders.

We saw this as a challenge, an ideal one for McKinsey. Our traditional strengths could be exploited: careful attention to detail, fact-based approach, analysis-driven recommendations, and systematic follow-up and control of impact. The challenge of applying this approach to brand management, where a belief in gut feeling and luck still largely prevails, beckoned irresistibly and drew us into what proved to be a highly motivating and satisfying journey.

When you take a closer look, you realize that marketing, unlike other management functions, really lacks great unifying breakthroughs. Marketing science has developed more and more into a niche field, where scholars talk to one another in their journals, while marketing practitioners have trouble understanding their theories or have simply stopped listening. Brand managers, on the other hand, along with advertising agencies and the media, have followed their own course. The media have all developed their own specific quantitative metrics. Brand managers can define their own market research so that the results will prove their hypotheses. Under these circumstances, it is no surprise that senior management's trust in marketing decisions has declined, reducing any willingness to spend increasing amounts on brands. Faced with increasing pressure for business performance and transparency, boards and investors expect clear plans and quantified results.

To meet these expectations and regain credibility, marketing and brand management need to demonstrate much greater professionalism: they need to take a more systematic and more quantitative approach to brand management. Power brands are just pure luck? That won't fly today. Brand success can be managed. This book will show you how. Our holistic approach, McKinsey BrandMatics®, provides senior executives with a complete framework for evaluating brand performance better, and gives marketing and brand managers a rich tool kit, illustrated with many examples, to manage brands more effectively. McKinsey BrandMatics® will help you make better brand decisions on the basis of data and facts and thus equip you to manage your company's brand success systematically.

When we published the first edition of this book for the German market in February 2004, our ambition was to get the ball rolling on systematic brand management in German-speaking countries. The examples and illustrations we chose were therefore very well known in those markets. We were thrilled by the book's success and many positive reactions from readers. After adding to and improving our concepts, we published the second German edition in August 2005. By then, many global clients were asking us for an English version. We therefore proceeded to adapt our book to global markets. In doing so, we have tried to choose brand examples known or readily understood around the world. *Power Brands* has German roots, but we are convinced that it will be useful in your home market as well. We know from many international projects that, as different as individual country markets may be, a unified global approach to the art, science, and craft of branding is the only way to manage the complexities of global brands successfully in a rapidly changing world.

Why even readers of the first edition should read the second edition

How rapidly things are changing becomes apparent when we take a look at some of the things that have happened since the first English edition of this book was published in 2007. That was only two years ago, and already the world of brand management is a different place:

Brands in motion. More than 50,000 international brands have been registered or extended since 2006, among them category-transforming product brands like Apple's iPhone or Nintendo's Wii, as well as brands that reflect differentiating consumer needs, like H&M's upmarket spin-off COS. At the same time, long-established brands, such as Chrysler, Jaguar, Puma, or The Wall Street Journal, have changed hands, and major brands, such as Cingular or Degussa, have vanished. Google, on the other hand, became one of the world's most valuable 20 brands in

2007, a mere nine years after its initial incorporation. The complementary trends of portfolio consolidation and needs differentiation have also spawned the creation of a new type of umbrella brand exemplified by Arcandor or Evonik in Germany. In sum, this dynamic makes Brand Portfolio Management an increasingly challenging enterprise.

Advertising is back. After the slump that started half a decade ago, advertising has come back with a vengeance. Global advertising spending is estimated to total some USD 480 billion in 2008, which exceeds the GDP of medium-sized national economies like Turkey, Belgium, Switzerland, or Sweden. The way this money is spent and allocated is also changing. Google, for example, has not only pushed the limits of online advertising, but also pioneered auction sales of classic above-the-line media space. In the same period, online advertising has increased by 50 percent globally, and mobile advertising has tripled. Print, on the other hand, has seen the dramatic rise of free papers. In Europe alone, there are now more than 120 free titles, up from 80 in 2006. In four European countries, the total circulation of free newspapers already exceeds that of papers that come at a cover price.

Digital marketing. Second Life may have come and gone, but Web 2.0 remains a major marketing opportunity for the foreseeable future. For example, active users of Facebook have increased tenfold since early 2006 and now total around 70 million. The online world has become a multiple-platform network of content generated by marketers, third parties, and consumers themselves. Much of this content is brand-related, be it branded entertainment (car makers' mini movies), product comparisons (mysimon or jellyfish), or consumer blogs (epinions). As a consequence, digital marketing holds opportunities for a wide range of branding applications, such as insights gathering, outbound communication, viral marketing, or a combination of all three.

Branded life. Brands increasingly evolve from sheer labels to clusters of experience, often spilling over into entertainment and art. Above the line, brands such as Pirelli, Audi, and Apple have started hiring feature directors, A-list actors, and mainstream musicians for their commercials. Below the line, brands are trying hard to create tangible and lasting impressions; examples include Volkswagen's, Mercedes' or BMW's flagship locations that are half museum, half amusement park. Fast-moving consumer goods companies do it, too; Beiersdorf has recently opened »Nivea House« as the brand's physical landmark in Hamburg, while Giorgio Armani built the »Armani Tower« in Tokyo in 2007, both of which feature spa-like environments and aspire to transform the consumer's interaction with the brand into a lifestyle experience. Ikea's CEO Anders Dahlvig put it even more bluntly: »We are trying to become like Disneyland.«

In reaction to these trends, many of which have shaped our recent consulting engagements, the first English edition of the book has been thoroughly revised and enhanced. In addition, key findings from McKinsey's latest knowledge-building efforts in the areas of marketing and branding have been incorporated. Apart from routine updates of facts and figures, cornerstones of this revision include:

- One of the world's most systematic studies to quantify the **bottom-line impact of creative advertising**, conducted by McKinsey in collaboration with the Art Directors Club.

- An all-new section on **customer segmentation as a strategic platform** that integrates a wide range of market insights to support brand management decisions.

- The latest insights into **consumer decision making**, including practical advice on what it takes for a brand to enter the consumer's consideration set.

- A new approach to translate brand image attributes into quantifiable, **concrete operational measures** from product and service definition to store design.

- The latest insights into **frontline optimization of reach, cost, and quality** at critical customer touch points from above-the-line communication to point-of-sale materials.

- New **executive interviews and case studies** providing best-practice examples from the forefront of B2C as well as B2B branding; featured brands include Nokia, Nivea, DHL, and the Kion Group.

We trust that even diligent readers of the first edition will find something new and helpful to guide and inspire them in coping with the increasing complexity and accelerating change in the world of brand management. They not only shape millions of purchase decisions and countless company decisions, but entire markets and the people who live in them; they also influence our perception and behavior, our self-esteem, our impression of others, and our value judgments. Put simply: brands shape people and markets alike.

Second edition acknowledgements

The first English edition of this book, originally published in early 2007, was well received by marketing practitioners, academics, and colleagues alike. Their positive reactions encouraged us to publish an updated and extended second edition. It incorporates a wide range of new tools, refined approaches, and recent insights rooted in the daily work of leading international companies, researchers, and consulting teams.

Because of this close connection to a global network of marketing practitioners, many individuals have contributed to the richness of the second edition. First and foremost, we are indebted and grateful to distinguished brand managers and experts at a number of leading international companies: Pieter Nota, Executive Board Member for Brands at Beiersdorf AG; Are Thu, Vice President Brand Strategy at Nokia; Tarja Stenvall, Director of Marketing Excellence at AstraZeneca; Jens Menneke, Head of Strategic Marketing at the Kion Group; Professor Sebastian Turner, Partner and Chairman of Scholz & Friends; and Wolfgang Giehl, Head of Brand Management at Deutsche Post World Net Group, were all kind enough to contribute new or updated interviews and inserts. Their contributions enrich the book with the latest thinking from the forefront of international brand management and will capture the attention of many readers.

We are also grateful to the companies that have granted us permission to reproduce their proprietary graphics and texts, among them Apple, Audi, BMW, Coca-Cola, IBM, Ikea, Nestlé, Procter & Gamble, Sixt, Sony, Starbucks, Unilever, Virgin, and Volkswagen, and also for their cooperation regarding case examples and other contributions. We also thank Jens Lorenzen for renewing his permission to reproduce his full-page illustrations that have been inserted between chapters.

Again, many colleagues at McKinsey helped make the second edition of *Power Brands* possible. The evolving BrandMatics® toolkit in general is built on the support and expertise of McKinsey's global branding leadership group: David Court, Mary Ellen Coe, Dave Elzinga, Jonathan Gordon, Jean-Baptiste Coumau, Claudia Meffert, and Thomas Meyer. Specifically,

Hemant Ahlawat, Christoph Erbenich, Harald Fanderl, John Forsyth, Maarten Schellekens, Vicky Smith, and Ansgar Hölscher all contributed to the development of new contents and updates in some way or another. The support of Nils Liedtke and Michael Egli was instrumental in bringing facts and figures up to date. We are also grateful to Ruth Balcombe, Terry Gilman, and Ivan Hutnik for their editorial supervision, as well as to Frank Breuer and Luisa Kaumanns for handling exhibits and illustrations. Publishing coordination and process management were in the capable hands of Marie Luise Cöln, Michaela Dülks, and Pia Verbocket at McKinsey and Jutta Hörnlein at Wiley-VCH.

Last, but not least, very special thanks to Thomas Meyer, our Senior Knowledge Expert for Branding and Marketing ROI, and to Cornelius Grupen, our Expert for Marketing Knowledge Development, for coordinating this project, as well as for updating and expanding large parts of the book.

Over the course of two German and two English editions, *Power Brands* and its German equivalent, *Mega-Macht Marke*, have, to some extent, become brands in themselves. We hope this new edition will inspire previous and new readers alike, help them to stay at the cutting edge of fact-based brand management, and act as a stepping stone for the creation of the power brands of the future.

Düsseldorf   *Hajo Riesenbeck*
November 2008   *Jesko Perrey*

First edition acknowledgements

The many positive reactions to the first two editions of *Power Brands* in German (entitled *Mega-Macht Marke*) encouraged us to publish a version more accessible to an international readership. For the English edition, we have updated and internationalized many examples, added new steps, and described advances in our thinking and further ranges of application.

Many people participated in the writing of this book. We would like to thank our advisors outside of McKinsey, Professors Klaus Backhaus and Heribert Meffert of the University of Münster, who not only contributed to the rich exchange of ideas between scholarship and practice, but also participated actively in the development of some individual concepts and instruments. We also thank our alumnus Dr. Marc Fischer of the Department of Innovation, New Media, and Marketing at the University of Kiel for his research and analysis and for his suggestions on the chapters about brand relevance. Furthermore, a special thank you to Professor Henrik Sattler of the University of Hamburg for his support in advising and coordinating the international market research on brand relevance.

We are also grateful to all of the companies that granted us permission to reproduce their proprietary graphics and texts, such as Audi, Beiersdorf, Deutsche Post World Net, Henkel, Katjes, Linde, Orange, Samsung, Skoda, Sony Ericsson, and Volkswagen, and also for their cooperation regarding case examples and other contributions. Our very special thanks to Chris Burggraeve at Coca-Cola and Professor Dr.-Ing. Wolfgang Reitzle at Linde for their stimulating and informative answers in our interviews, and to Dee Dutta at Sony Ericsson Mobile Communications, who shared his systematic and structured approach to allocating and evaluating marketing spending. We also very much appreciate the case example from the French telecommunications market contributed by Jean Baptiste Coumau, managing partner of Izsak Grapin & Associés and member of the Blue Ocean Network, and Emmanuel Josserand, professor at the University of Geneva and associate researcher at CREPA University of Paris Dauphine.

Many people at McKinsey helped make *Power Brands* possible: Jürgen Schröder, our partner colleague in Düsseldorf, contributed materially to the development of many of the tools we discuss, very often in collaboration with the University of Münster. Thomas Barta, Nicole Baumüller, Jens Echterling, Christoph Erbenich, Harald Fanderl, Tjark Freundt, Fabian Hieronimus, Ansgar Hölscher, and Patrick Metzler supplied valuable insights and examples from their consulting practice. Our expert researchers, Saule Serikova and Geoffrey Sherburn, devoted countless hours to researching and verifying individual brands and brand stories, with support from their colleagues in McKinsey Research & Information Services.

We also owe a special debt of gratitude to our colleagues Thomas Meyer, our European Branding Practice manager, and Mathias Kullmann for their great support in coordinating this project and in updating, internationalizing, and expanding the book. A very special thank you also to Ivan Hutnik, our editor, for his incisive questions, practical suggestions, and expert editing of our drafts. As for the first two editions, publishing coordination was again in the capable hands of Hella Reese, Rainer Mörike, and Daniel Münch. With their unstinting dedication and expert support, our assistants, Michaela Dülks and Denise Kranepoth, also once again helped us to advance steadily towards completion of the manuscript.

This third edition would never have come to be without the thoughtful and detailed comments we received on our very first drafts. We sincerely thank Winfried Wilhelm and Dr. Axel Born, both members of our Editorial Review Board, as well as Professor Heribert Meffert for their valuable critical examination and suggestions regarding the original manuscript of the first German edition. Very warm thanks for their support of this first international edition go to our partner colleagues in McKinsey's European Marketing Practice, Johanna Waterous and Yoram Gutgeld, and especially to Trond Riiber Knudsen, who has been advocating an international edition of *Power Brands* for a long time.

Finally, we want to thank Jens Kreibaum and his colleagues at our publishers, Wiley-VCH, for their enthusiastic and experienced support.

We wish our readers interesting discoveries, rewarding insights, and every possible success in implementing BrandMatics® and hope that sharing our experience will contribute to the creation and development of new power brands.

Düsseldorf   *Hajo Riesenbeck*
November 2006   *Jesko Perrey*

1.
What Brands Can Do, and What Makes Them Strong

What has led six companies to pay EUR 100 million each just to secure their place as a sponsor for the 2010 FIFA World Cup in South Africa? Why does Procter & Gamble spend over EUR 6.8 billion on advertising each year? What it is that made companies spend USD 480 billion on advertising in 2008? Why are some people willing to pay enormous sums for a Rolex watch or a Louis Vuitton bag? Why do consumers »google« information on the Internet, instead of searching for it? And how did matte-white in-ear headphones, the Apple iPod's trademark accessory, become the hallmark of urban trendiness all over the world?

The answer is simple: brands. Brands, as these examples show, are the true giants of the modern world of consumption, dominating the household budgets of consumers and the investment calculations of companies. They not only shape millions of purchase decisions and countless company decisions, setting prices and determining profits; they also influence our perception and behavior, our self-esteem, our impression of others, and our value judgments.[1] Put simply: brands shape people and markets alike.

1.1 What Brands Mean for Consumers and Companies

Brands are omnipresent. They address us directly in public and subtly in the most intimate spheres of our lives. They stimulate our desires and form the hubs in the network of goods that typifies advanced consumer societies. No one can escape their influence. They are the emblems of a global economy, reaching new markets well ahead of the rest of the economy and visible from much farther away than the turrets of any company's headquarters.

The message is clear: there is hardly a bank or an insurance company, a company in the automotive or telecommunications sector, a machine tools manufacturer, or a chemicals, electricity, or gas supplier that now ignores the growing importance of brands. Even public institutions such as the

Power Brands. H. Riesenbeck and J. Perrey
Copyright © 2009 WILEY-VCH Verlag GmbH & Co. KGaA, Weinheim
ISBN: 978-3-527-50390-2

armed forces, state pension providers, the EU, and even individual regions or cities have sat up and taken notice.

Brands shape our perception and our behavior

Perception is reality. It can also determine success or failure. Largely subconsciously, we pigeonhole people according to the car they drive, the clothes they wear, and the accessories they surround themselves with. We use brands as beacons in the flood of signals and information we are presented with. Take the launch event for the last Mercedes A-Class model: Christina Aguilera performs »Hello,« a hit written for Mercedes. Giorgio Armani and Boris Becker are among the guests; a famous television presenter is moderating the program. Coca-Cola, Red Bull, and Beck's provide the refreshments; and reporters from *Time, GQ, Paris Match,* and *Hello!* magazine take endless photographs for their forthcoming editions. Similarly, the new Fiat Cinquecento's introduction in the United Kingdom was hailed by pop phenomenon Mika performing live with the brand-new Cinquecento as his stage partner. The Cinquecento's Japanese launch in March 2008 was staged at the Italian Institute of Culture in Chiyoda, Tokyo, and featured an exclusive ivory-colored edition of the Cinquecento, handpainted by Tuscan artist Giuliano Ghelli. Lorenzo Sistino, head of Fiat Auto, said the model was specifically designed to help promote the brand's image in Japan.[2] Lancia went as far as prelaunching their new Delta model in Second Life to generate additional buzz for the real-world launch event. How can you resist such corporate seduction? Brands save us time in that we do not have to check, challenge, classify, or critically weigh up everything before we make a decision to act. They are »an established, unmistakable mental representation of a product or service in the mind of the potential consumer.«[3] This representation is formed at all the points where we come into contact with the brand, including the product itself, advertisements, and word-of-mouth (Figure 1.1).

Brands can mark class boundaries – or blur them. For some, owning a Rolex, a BMW, or a Louis Vuitton bag helps demonstrate, to themselves and to others, their membership in a particular social stratum. For others, brands can be used as a way of breaking free from their class shackles. Maybe they starved themselves to be able to afford that BMW – but once in the driver's seat, they moved into a different milieu.

Fig. 1.1: A holistic concept for brand management: Experience the brand at all customer touch points

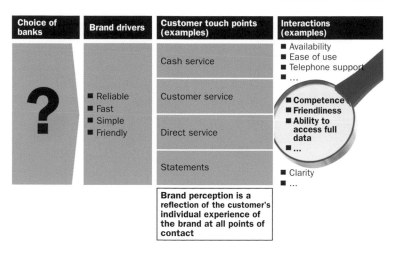

EXAMPLE: BANKING SERVICES

Choice of banks	Brand drivers	Customer touch points (examples)	Interactions (examples)
?	■ Reliable ■ Fast ■ Simple ■ Friendly	Cash service	■ Availability ■ Ease of use ■ Telephone support ■ …
		Customer service	■ **Competence** ■ **Friendliness** ■ **Ability to access full data** ■ …
		Direct service	
		Statements	■ Clarity ■ …

Brand perception is a reflection of the customer's individual experience of the brand at all points of contact

Source: McKinsey

Branding reaches ever more traditionally unbranded areas. Many formerly anonymous (i.e., no name) products or private labels (also referred to as »own brands,« »store brands,« or »house brands«) are giving themselves distinctive profiles by differentiating their value proposition and investing large amounts in publicity and uptrading. The previously clear-cut differences between branded, no name, and house brand products are blurring in the face of increasing competition for the consumer's affection and loyalty.

Over the past few years, some retailers have even started to promote their private labels with mass media advertising. In a print campaign, the French grocery chain E. Leclerc compared branded products with equivalent private labels. The main message was: »The branded product is available at E. Leclerc at the lowest price permitted by law. But you can get the same quality 30 percent cheaper when buying the private label«[4] (Figure 1.2). German coffee chain and general retailer Tchibo has teamed up with fashion designer Michael Michalsky to establish their range of sports apparel as a kind of budget designer label in its own right, »Mitch & Co.«

As a result, consumer spending on private label consumer packaged goods is rising quickly, having increased from USD 172 billion in 2000 to USD 246 billion in 2005 to account for 23 percent of total consumer pack-

What Brands Can Do, and What Makes Them Strong

Fig. 1.2: Private label advertising

Vendu chez E.Leclerc au prix le plus bas autorisé par la loi.	La qualité équivalente 30 %* moins chère.
Sold at E.Leclerc at the lowest price permitted by law	The same quality, 30 %* less expensive.

* Prix relevés par une société d'études indépendante en 2004 dans les centres E.Leclerc.

E.LECLERC

Source: E.Leclerc, Photo: Sébastien Lucky Studio

aged goods consumption in Europe.[5] In specific product segments (e.g., pet food or paper products) and countries (e.g., Germany or the United Kingdom), the share of private label products is even significantly higher.

Producers of branded products are taking this private label threat very seriously. When the German retailer Rewe launched a mass-media campaign for private label products, the German Brands Association was not very happy. »Rewe has to think exactly where it sees itself in the future,« said a representative. In the past, the Association saw Rewe as an ally of manufacturers of branded products in their struggle against discount retailers and their store brands. Other brands associations even go one step further and are no longer mincing their words. For example, the 2005 campaign run by the Austrian Branded Goods Association treats the competition with private labels literally as »a battle between good and evil.«[6]

At the beginning of 2008, the Austrian Branded Goods Association launched a new campaign, this time showing branded articles as desirable and attainable. According to the Association, the campaign – including TV, print, Internet, and over 10,000 posters – will be one of the largest the Austrian consumer will see in 2008.[7]

No product group is safe from encroachment by private labels. Even the safest, most established areas, where the newcomers were long powerless, are now reporting a dent in sales due to competition from private labels. Take tobacco products, for example, where private label brands have made little headway in Europe overall. The German market is the major exception. Here, while private label brands accounted for only 7.5 billion cigarettes in 1997, just five years later sales had topped 22 billion, an increase of nearly three times. In the two years following this, 2003 and 2004, sales fell dramatically across the market following increases in tobacco tax. But the losses were differentiated: sales of branded cigarettes fell by 22 percent, while sales of private label cigarettes dropped by just 14 percent.[8] The success of private labels should, however, not be interpreted as a sign that brands have lost their former power. On the contrary, it shows that brands have become increasingly important, even in areas previously thought immune to the lure of branding. As a consequence, manufacturer brands must gather their strength to hold their ground as they face new competition from former store brands.

Brands both need and fear publicity. In today's information society, our beliefs, thoughts, and behavior are more and more subject to external stimuli. Companies that do not communicate well across all channels, or that fail to publicize their company and brand profile, soon stop being noticed by consumers and ultimately disappear from the market. What is more, public opinion acts as an independent force and can praise a company or a brand to the skies one day and write it off the next. Such word-of-mouth, powerful as it may be, cannot be steered by the companies themselves.

In October 2006, Unilever's personal care brand Dove published the video »Dove Evolution« on the Internet, showing the transformation from an average woman to a billboard model and thereby criticizing its own industry for creating a distorted beauty standard (as part of their »Campaign for Real Beauty«). In less than a month, over 1.7 million people watched the video on YouTube. In addition, the video gained wide and extremely positive coverage by the media. Unilever estimated the media coverage to be worth over USD 50 million.[9] One year later, Dove published its new online video »Dove Onslaught,« showing a young girl followed by a barrage of commercials showing lingerie models or selling weight-loss products and TV reports about plastic surgery. The video ends with a piece of advice to all parents: »Talk to your daughter before the beauty industry does.«

Again, over one million people watched the video on YouTube and major media covered the video. However, this time the echo was not uniformly positive. The video prompted counterattacks by various bloggers who criticized Unilever for being hypocritical because their private label Axe/Lynx allegedly contributes to the very same problem with its advertising.[10] It turns out that in the peer-to-peer world of opinionated, user-generated content, brands may benefit, but also easily suffer from publicity. A few months later, more criticism ensued when it became known that celebrated airbrush artist Pascal Dangin had retouched the Dove ads showing supposedly natural women to cover up skin imperfections and digitally remove stray hairs.[11] Says Keith Pardy, Nokia's Senior Vice President of Strategic Marketing: »Brands are going to be made and destroyed on the Internet, and there's a whole set of new marketing rules for it. If you start playing games with people, they'll find out and eat you alive.«[12]

As the YouTube videos show, brand communication doesn't necessarily equate to advertising spend. The Spanish fashion chain Zara operates in a world where marketing spend generally amounts to 3 to 4 percent of sales revenue,[13] but it manages to do without any advertising at all. Zara's sole means of advertising is its highly styled stores, always located on the best city streets and designed by a sizable team of top window designers. Potential customers see the goods in the store windows as they walk through the city and hear the store recommended by satisfied customers – and no more is needed to sell fashionable items of clothing by the million. It works beautifully: Zara's sales revenues have grown on average 16 percent per year between 2002 and 2006 (faster than its heavily advertised archrival H&M). At the beginning of 2008, Zara had 1,347 stores around the world, including the Zara Home stores – 816 more than five years before.[14]

Jägermeister is another example of successful brand management without expensive mass-media advertising. A few years ago, after 20 years of being imported to the United States without hitting the big time, the German brand's managers decided to completely change Jägermeister's communication strategy. The brand started to target younger drinkers, particularly college students, and focused its communication on inexpensive, but targeted activities like the sponsorship of student parties and promotions in student bars. The result speaks for itself. Between 2001 and 2006, sales grew at over 30 percent a year, making Jägermeister the fastest growing imported liqueur in the United States.[15]

Companies and their brands: A special relationship

Brands can immunize. While a media push is often very helpful for a company, negative publicity can be very dangerous. Nevertheless, companies that have continually built and promoted their brands in a well-founded and fully rounded way can survive media attacks relatively intact. Thus a top brand like Coca-Cola can shake off an incident, such as the scandal over contaminated cans in Belgium in the summer of 1999, within a few weeks and without much further ado. Leading toy producer Mattel had to recall over 20 million toys between summer and autumn 2007 due to toxic lead-based paint and magnets that could be swallowed by children. Nevertheless Mattel still managed to exceed analysts' expectations in the fourth quarter of 2007, and increased sales by 4 percent and net profit by 15 percent compared to the fourth quarter in 2006.

Brands live and survive. The best product names can even survive attacks of quite a different kind. Entire companies can go under, yet their brands are not sucked into the depths after them. Maybach, the luxury car brand from the 1920s and a symbol of German quality engineering, all but disappeared in the Second World War. However, the heritage of the brand was so strong that it lived on and was revived by the Daimler-Chrysler group in 2002. Although it is far from being a volume brand by modern standards, since its relaunch Maybach has already sold more cars than during the first period from 1919 to 1941. By 2007, Maybach had a brand awareness of 53 percent in Germany, ahead of Aston Martin, the car driven by James Bond in some early installments of the series, as well as in the movie »Quantum of Solace.« Even without advertising, brands do not simply disappear. They can survive the drought like plants in a desert, waiting for the warm rain of fresh investments, to flower once again in abundance.

Strong brands are like living organisms. Their potential for adaptation and renewal seems almost unlimited. Strong brands such as Patek Philip (1839), Nestlé (1867), Heinz (1869), Coca-Cola (1886), Johnson & Johnson (1887), General Electric (1892), Maggi (1897), Mercedes (1902), Osram (1906), and Nivea (1911) have reached a legendary age and yet remain forever young. Market and brand leaders like McDonald's, Marlboro, and Nokia are just as much on everyone's lips today as Apple, IBM, or Microsoft. Classic brands such as Harley Davidson and the Mini or Sinalco can be revived and even attain new heights.

It is the brands that truly claim this longevity, not the companies themselves. After fifty or a hundred years, who can remember a company's

Fig. 1.3: Brand logos create distinctive mental images

Source: Nike, Apple, McDonalds, Lacoste

founders, its managing directors, the first board, or its core production plants or headquarters? But everyone knows the brands.

Brands generate strong impressions and powerful feelings. When consumers hear the name Marlboro or just see the red Marlboro box, they immediately associate it with freedom and adventure, the cowboy riding across the plains. Nike evokes similarly strong, if quite different, associations, with its images of athletics, performance, and lifestyle. The Lacoste crocodile immediately triggers thoughts of sporty luxury, or even the tennis court at Wimbledon, while McDonald's golden arches make many people's mouths water (Figure 1.3).[16]

Brands generate tangible value. Apart from creating strong impressions, brands also generate tangible value. They create price premiums, help to recruit the best talent, and save sales cost due to their inherent appeal to customers. Perhaps most important of all, companies with strong brands frequently outperform the stock market. A recent McKinsey analysis shows that a portfolio of 40 stocks, with their brands (or parent companies) being top ranked in *BusinessWeek*'s annual »Best Global Brands« report, has outperformed traditional benchmarks like the MSCI World or the S&P 500 index in seven of the last eight annual periods. From a total return to shareholders perspective, the MSCI World was outperformed by a more than respectable 17 percent since the *BusinessWeek* ranking was first published in 2000. (Based on stock price alone, i.e., when disregarding dividend, the gap would be even more dramatic.) With the exception of a single period (2004/05), top brands have beaten the stock market both in its bear and bull phases, especially since 2006. Brand strength, it turns out, is a reliable indicator of economic performance (Figure 1.4). This analysis is one of the first to avoid the self-fulfilling prophecy of assessing the *past* economic

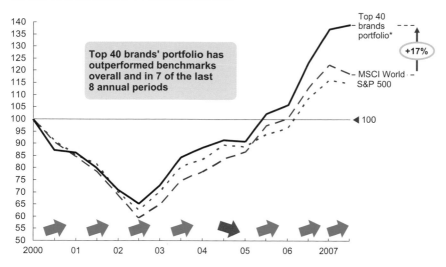

Fig. 1.4: Strong brands outperform the market
INDEX, TOTAL RETURN TO SHAREHOLDERS

Top 40 brands portfolio*

+17%

Top 40 brands' portfolio has outperformed benchmarks overall and in 7 of the last 8 annual periods

MSCI World
S&P 500

◀ 100

2000   01   02   03   04   05   06   2007

* Portfolio consisting of the 40 top-ranked listed companies, picked from Business Week's "BestGlobal Brands" report, published each summer since 2000. Stocks in local currency, equally weighted and adjusted every July 1
Source: Datastream, Business Week/Interbrand, McKinsey analysis

performance of strong brands. Since brand strength, to some extent, reflects past economic performance, top brands will come out as strong stock market performers almost by necessity. This effect is eliminated in the analysis by assessing stock market performance *after*, rather than *before*, the publication of the annual brand strength ranking.

Three factors determine the brand's perceived added value

As shown by many examples, three factors determine the impact of a brand as perceived by the consumer – and thus its value for a company (Figure 1.5).

1. **Information efficiency (the »time« factor).** Brands are information carriers. They say something about the provenance of the item, help with recognition, and provide us with orientation. They act as consumer beacons in the flood of signals and information, making it easier to gather and process information about a purchase option. Brands as carriers of information help save time.

2. **Risk reduction (the »trust« factor)**. Brands reduce the consumer's (subjective) risk of making a purchase mistake. Branded products promise consistent quality and a lower level of depreciation. Brands offer a safe choice, creating a basis of trust between the manufacturer and the consumer and then providing continuity in this relationship, e.g., continued predictability of the product benefit.

3. **Image benefit (the »identity« factor)**. Brands help consumers express who they are, contribute to self-esteem, communicate this to others, and enable them to claim allegiance to particular ideas or social groups.

The Volkswagen Golf brand (some models are badged »Volkswagen Rabbit« in North America) provides a good example of these three components of added value. For decades, the Golf brand has been a constant, almost universal presence on the roads of Europe and the US coastal states. The Golf brand bundles together everything that the consumer needs to know about the vehicle. Reliable quality and solid construction combined with decent prices in the used-car market limit the risk in buying a Golf. Combining a well-balanced drive with time-tested reliability and resale value, the Golf is a widely accepted safe choice for all but the most expressive drivers (in North America, the Golf has a slightly younger and sportier image). However, the difficulties faced by the more recent larger and pricier Golf models in defending their position in the market show that even strong brands can face challenges; the strengths of the brand have not transferred automatically to the new models.

The Golf is typical of the current challenge. Today, even the strongest brands must make headway in turbulent waters. Two trends can be observed: on the one hand, the number of registered brands is increasing dramatically. In 2007, there were nearly twice as many internationally registered trademarks worldwide as there were 10 years before.

The dramatic expansion in the number of brands has inevitably given the consumer almost too much choice. Over the past 15 years, both the number of products advertised on German television and the number of brands available in a large supermarket have tripled, the latter having risen from 15,000 to over 45,000. On the other hand, in consumer goods there is greater concentration, with fewer manufacturers and a greater focus on core brands. Despite having a portfolio of around 300 brands, Procter & Gamble still finds that the 41 largest brands account for over 90 percent of the company's profit. Only those largest brands and some selected promising brands in emerging markets are allowed to increase cost; all other brands have to maintain or decrease their expenditure. Procter & Gamble's competitor Unilever even reduced its brand portfolio from some 1,600

Fig. 1.5: Brands fulfill three basic functions

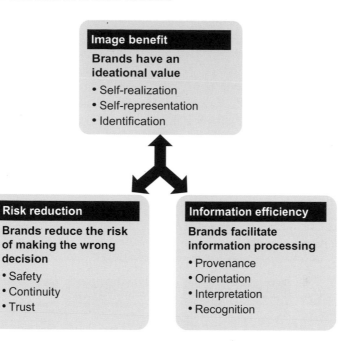

Image benefit
Brands have an ideational value
- Self-realization
- Self-representation
- Identification

Risk reduction
Brands reduce the risk of making the wrong decision
- Safety
- Continuity
- Trust

Information efficiency
Brands facilitate information processing
- Provenance
- Orientation
- Interpretation
- Recognition

Source: MCM/McKinsey

brands in 2000 down to 400 core brands in 2005. So, despite the overall proliferation of brands, the leading companies are thinning out their brand portfolios and are focusing only on the brands that are strong enough to face tomorrow's challenges. For brands, it is quality that counts.

To complicate the situation even further, proliferation is by no means limited to brands proper. The number of distribution channels, consumer touch points, and marketing messages is constantly increasing. At the same time, complexity is increasing on the demand side as well. Partly driven by the wide variety of available options, consumer choice is harder to predict than ever. For many consumers, it's coffee-to-go in the morning, fast food at lunch, and a three-course dinner at a fancy restaurant in the evening. But at the weekend, the same person may go for a healthy breakfast with wholegrain cereal and fresh fruit from an organic food store, no lunch at all, and a late-night microwaved TV dinner after a long day on the road, driving back from the in-laws. Old patterns no longer apply in the world of proliferation. The polarization effect can be seen across industries; consumers are both trading up (and prepared to pay premiums for products they emotionally relate to) and trading down at the same time (and looking for savings on products that they don't feel passionate about) (Figure 1.6). While a business traveler will often fly with major airlines booked through a trusted ticket agent, the same person will book cheap tickets online from no-frills carriers for private travel. As a result, companies that find themselves stuck in the middle are facing increasing challenges and are showing much lower growth rates than both the premium and the no-frills providers. Alex Myers, Senior Vice President for Western Europe at Carlsberg, summarizes the dilemma, »Historically, brewers have been big in the middle of the market. Now there is a polarization between the top and the bottom, and the risk is getting stuck in the middle.«[17]

Fig. 1.6: Polarization effect
Net sales growth (compound annual growth rate), 1998 - 2005
Percent

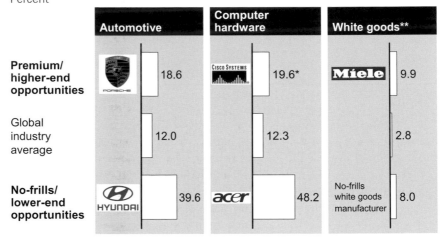

* 1998 - 2004 CAGR for Cisco
** 1998 - 2003 data was used, later data was not available for Miele
Source: Global Vantage, Bloomberg

What Brands Can
Do, and What
Makes Them
Strong

Tougher times require more effective brand management tools

In this environment, efficiency is more important than ever. The good news is, that proven tools and approaches are available to fine-tune branding investments for the highest possible impact. »Scatter losses« of 50 percent or more are by no means a law of nature. Rather, they are the result of insufficient analysis, shaky methodology, and dubious strategies.

It's no longer only the advertising gurus who dominate the scene with their creativity. Admittedly, creativity helps to increase advertising effectiveness; consider the findings from a recent analysis by McKinsey and the Art Directors Club on the success of creative campaigns in the next section (editorial insert by Sebastian Turner). But brand managers cannot do without deep customer insights and thorough market analysis to complement creativity. After all, investing in brands is in many ways similar to other investments. Who would invest in a production facility, a research and development center, or a new head office without first examining the necessary commercial and financial groundwork to make a clear assessment of the probable payoff?

A shift towards a more professional approach to marketing and more efficient processes has been gaining pace recently. A literature search of the international journals reveals that more than 5,000 articles on branding have been published in the past five years alone.[18] Despite this flood of academic and practice-oriented publications, the right tools for effective and efficient brand management are still under debate. Experts are currently analyzing the basic factors underlying brand power, how best to describe them, and what their precise functions are for consumers. They are also looking into what makes brands strong, and what makes them weak.

While this debate continues, McKinsey has developed its own approach called BrandMatics®. This book uses this approach to reveal how companies can measure, make, and manage brands effectively without throwing creativity overboard.

1.2 The Secret of Strong Brands

What makes a brand strong? What distinguishes Marlboro from Camel, Nokia from BenQ Mobile, and Giorgio Armani from Pierre Cardin? One answer that is commonly given to this question is that a brand becomes dominant and full of life when everyone in its target group has internalized it as »well known.« Though this might be a very common assumption about what makes a brand successful, it fails to distinguish the great brands from the also-rans.

Brand awareness, and the often corresponding high scores for brand recognition in market research evaluations, is not enough in itself to secure a place among the front-runners. Such indicators, however popular they are, actually say very little about consumers' buying preferences. BenQ Mobile, for example, was probably never more widely known than at the time when it went out of business in early 2007. Market share and profit margins are far more revealing when it comes to describing a brand's position. Companies that achieve a bond with buyers and produce customer loyalty that cannot be matched by the competition are the brand winners. The right strategy for brand management can be summed up in a single, simple sentence: strong brands need buyers – and repeat buyers.

Coca-Cola is a good example, Coca-Cola drinkers are particularly loyal to their brand. In Germany for example, 52 percent will only drink »their Coke.« By comparison, just 10 percent of Pepsi drinkers will drink only Pepsi-Cola.[19] This one fact is enough to indicate the relative strength of those two major cola brands in that market. Pepsi's endless celebrity endorsements, including Britney Spears, Michael Jackson, and David Beckham (to name but the most prominent), may have increased the public's general attention, but have failed to turn around drinkers' choices in many markets. Although Coca-Cola's market share has slipped, it is still the world's leading carbonated cola. Specifically, Coca-Cola is far ahead of Pepsi in much of Europe and South America.[20]

Three elements of success: The trinity of *art*, *science*, and *craft*

For management, the strongest indicators of brand success are market presence, profitability, and customer loyalty. Companies that want to ensure this sort of brand strength for the long term need to achieve a harmonious blend of three elements underlying good brand management: *art, science,* and *craft*.

The *art* is in endowing the brand with a superior brand proposition, keeping it consistent yet up-to-date and executing it as creatively as possible. The *science* is measuring and understanding the brand's performance. The *craft* is managing the brand rigorously in all its individual aspects throughout the organization.

Naturally, brands do not have to attain perfection in all three areas in order to be strong. Inevitably, companies have different approaches, as well as different strengths and weaknesses. Nonetheless, however well a company masters an individual element, this will be of little use unless the brand achieves a minimum standard in the other two elements as well (Figure 1.7).

We will now look at each element in some depth. We will start with the *art* of the brand, as this is the most familiar and widely accepted aspect of brand management, before moving on to the *science* and the *craft*.

Art: Superior content generates emotions

First, brands must have the right content in order to appeal to customers and to generate demand. They need to move us emotionally so that we find them appealing. They need to appear trustworthy in their claims. Companies, faced with the challenge of choosing the right attribute from among a mass of similar-looking technical and non-technical features, hardly know where to start. Should they focus on rational elements, or on the more emotional elements that they think will speak to customers' feelings?[21]

In fact, strong brands always do both, although the balance between the two varies. There are hardly any strong products or services that are not at least as good as the competition in their rational elements, and they are usually better in one or two attributes. At the same time, real brand champions, Marlboro, Nike, or Porsche, for example, show champion-like qualities in their emotional elements, too.

Nivea is another good example. Every Nivea product features a rational product benefit and backs this claim up with research and information. This approach goes back to its introduction in 1911, when Nivea produced the first long-lasting oil-in-water emulsifier that was not based on animal and vegetable fats and so would not go rancid. This scientific approach continues. The company's research center employs over 150 dermatological and cosmetics researchers, pharmacists, and chemists. Today, according to the company, Nivea Visage DNAge products contain a »combination of Folic Acid and Creatine to protect the skin cells' DNA against future external damage«; their Anti-Wrinkle & Firming Creme features a »unique patent-pending antioxidant complex, including Vitamins A & E and sunscreen (SPF 4)«; while the Nivea for Men Revitalizing Lotion Q10 has a »combination of Vitamin E and SPF 15« to help protect against UV rays.

The rational product benefits are not just displayed on the packaging, they are also backed up by numerous product tests and, even more importantly, by the trust placed in them by large numbers of customers. Since 2005, Nivea has won the award as the most-trusted skin care brand by Reader's Digest every single year in every one of the 16 participating coun-

Fig. 1.7: Three elements underpin excellent brand management

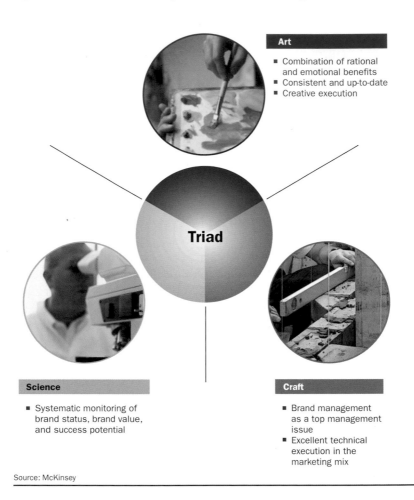

Art
- Combination of rational and emotional benefits
- Consistent and up-to-date
- Creative execution

Triad

Science
- Systematic monitoring of brand status, brand value, and success potential

Craft
- Brand management as a top management issue
- Excellent technical execution in the marketing mix

Source: McKinsey

tries. At the same time, the brand is positioned in a clearly emotional way as a »gentle care« brand, supported by soft-focus photos and carefully chosen images that build a consistent identity, closely tied to central values of the blue »aura,« true values, and a code for genuine »close to touch« human togetherness. The product's appeal is thus aimed equally at customers' emotional and rational sides; this is what gives the brand its competitive advantage (Figure 1.8).

Fig. 1.8: Nivea: Appealing to emotions and reason simultaneously

Energy Fresh Deodorant
New Zealand 2007

Visage Anti-Wrinkle Q10 Plus
United Kingdom 2008

Body Good Bye Cellulite
United States 2008

Source: Beiersdorf AG

This combination of emotional and rational elements is also part of the brand appeal of luxury goods, even though these are commonly perceived to be purely emotional. For Louis Vuitton products, for example, the customer's self-profiling plays a major role in the purchase and justifies the price difference compared with competitor products. At the same time, however, the materials used in the product are very high quality: the finest leather, tanned by hand (using plant extracts), and water- and scratch-resistant. It is this combination of quality (rational) and prestige (emotional) that is fundamental to the brand's strength.

Audi is another example of a brand that successfully blends rational and emotional elements. The brand stands for technological leadership as well as emotional appeal. Audi's technological assets, condensed in the claim «*Vorsprung durch Technik*» (»Advanced engineering«), include the permanent all-wheel drive »Quattro« technology (a major factor in Audi's longstanding success in the World Rally Championship), the TDI diesel engine concept pioneered by Audi engineers to wide acclaim in the late 1980s, and the FSI injection technology derived from successful trials in motor sports. On the emotional side, recent milestones along Audi's development towards more progressive design include the introduction of »halo« cars such as the company's first modern convertible in 1991, the immensely successful TT model in 1999, and the launch of the R8 mid-engine sports car in 2006. As a consequence, the Audi brand radiates both technological excellence and technological sex appeal. As a result, after years of playing

What Brands Can
Do, and What
Makes Them
Strong

catch-up with brand leaders BMW and Mercedes, Audi secured the top spot in the half-yearly AutomarxX survey by Germany's motoring organization ADAC December 2006 and has retained it ever since.[22]

At the same time, emotional positioning alone will not make a brand strong if rational benefits are missing. Apparel manufacturer and retailer C&A faced this problem in the early 1990s with its television and cinema commercials (including its Daydream campaign). The commercials appealed greatly to the young target groups and even won industry awards, but the reality in the stores was different. Large rummage tables with cheap T-shirts and other bargains conflicted with the emotional world depicted in the commercials in terms of store design and product presentation. Potential customers were so disappointed that they seem to have avoided the shops for a long time afterwards. C&A managed to resolve this problem at the end of the 1990s. It did so by refocusing on the brand's traditional core positioning and values. This change in focus in its campaigns has seen C&A become increasingly successful in attracting its target group of families with below-average to average incomes back into its stores. As a result, the company is managing to hold its ground.[23]

For consumers, emotional advertising without a rational basis is like a vacation brochure's misleadingly attractive pictures. This is ultimately a form of advertising that can have a negative impact.

Art: Modern creativity and consistency are no contradiction

Strong brands are consistent, preserving and maintaining their brand names. They do not make constant changes to their positioning, their target group, or their image. At the same time, strong brands innovate constantly, building on the brand promise.

At first sight, being both consistent and innovative might appear something of a contradiction. Nivea provides a good example of how a brand can be both highly innovative while always remaining consistent with its brand values. Nivea Creme's distinctive packaging, a blue container with the Nivea name spelt out in prominent white script, is a vital part of this. Today's packaging has a long pedigree and can be traced back to 1924, when the distinctive blue container was first introduced. Just as important is that Nivea's brand promise from its introduction has been that of providing high quality and gentle skin care at a reasonable price, using a straightforward approach. It is this reputation for dependability and trustworthiness that has stood the company in good stead throughout the decades. At the same time, Nivea has innovated constantly. As far back as the 1930s, Nivea introduced sunscreen into its product range. Since then there have

What Brands Can
Do, and What
Makes Them
Strong

been regular product innovations, with a large expansion in products from the 1980s onwards. Today Nivea's products include specific care products for different skin types, shampoos designed for various hair types, and products for men as well as women. All these innovative products are distinguished not only by their packaging, but also by Nivea's brand values of gentle care. Nivea's consistent innovation and brand promise are well recognized in the industry, and Nivea has won many international prizes for its products, including the 2006 Beauty Glammies Award in Greece for Nivea Visage DNAge and the 2007 New Best Product Award in Canada for Nivea Lip Care Effect Q10 Plus.

Let's look at an industry many would say is dominated by engineering and rational buying factors: cars. BMW's well-known and successful brand promise of »The Ulimate Driving Machine« has been at the heart of the brand since the 1960s and has made a large contribution to BMW's global success. »Our brand delivers performance and sportiness. That's our brand promise,« the company board was quoted as saying in early 2008. In 1962, BMW launched the 1500, a dynamic compact sedan with front disc brakes and independent suspension. This innovative specification cemented BMW's reputation for fast sports cars, especially when the car won races in motorsports. Since the 1970s, BMW has been building its M models as especially powerful cars. After the launch of the M1 in 1978, BMW started to create extra sporty versions of the (already sporty) regular BMW vehicles. Not surprisingly, the M model of the 3-Series is the most successful motorsports car in the world, having won more than 1,500 races over the past 20 years. More important, BMW has pledged never to introduce a car that does not fulfill the brand's promise of performance and sportiness. Therefore BMW decided not to launch a minivan. »The more sporty you make it, the less room you have. But as we continued to work on it, it involved too many compromises, and we felt it wouldn't be a BMW in its own right,« said a BMW executive. Even BMW's way of communicating the improvement of the carbon footprint of its fleet still incorporates the promise of sportiness (»Efficient Dynamics«). Commercials highlighting the fuel efficiency of the latest BMW models make sure to point out a BMW is sportier than most. This combination of a consistent message and constant innovation has led to global success for the company. In the United States, for instance, sales have increased at a compound annual growth rate of 12 percent since 1991.[24] Compare the example of Skoda's decision not to introduce a convertible for consistency's sake. Despite the considerable revenue potential, management decided against it because a convertible would unavoidably be more expensive and more extravagant than a sedan and, hence, contradict the Skoda brand's no-nonsense promise of solid quality at attractive prices (see section 3.2).

The contrasting example of Pontiac shows what can happen to a brand that is not consistent. In the 1950s, Pontiac started to focus on young and performance-oriented drivers and managed to climb to third place in car sales in the United States. Over the next 20 years, Pontiac continued along this path with the launch of sporty models like the Firebird and the GTO, which became an icon for power and performance and was instrumental in starting the »muscle car« era in the United States. But when insurance and fuel costs increased at the beginning of the 1970s, Pontiac shifted towards a positioning that included safety and economy by decreasing the power of its engines and by launching models like the Astre, the brand's first venture into the fuel-economy category. Pontiac tried to be all things to all people. As a result, the brand image became fuzzy and satisfied fewer and fewer customers. In the 1980s, Pontiac refocused its positioning with performance as the core attribute, supported by the redesign of the Firebird in 1982 and the launch of the Fiero in 1984. This »back to the roots« approach was rewarded by car buyers almost instantly. For the first time in more than a decade, Pontiac was the number three brand in the United States. The median age of its buyers dropped from 46 in 1981 to 38 in 1988. More recently, Pontiac got off track again by launching a range of cars out of line with the brand's performance promise, including minivans and family SUVs. But what was even worse, the brand continued to claim it was first choice for performance-oriented customers, when in fact its products could not fulfill this promise. Models offered aggressive styling, but lacked actual performance. This was partly due to the fact that Pontiac's models often used the same engines as other, less performance-focused General Motors brands. Between 2000 and 2007, Pontiac's sales decreased by over 40 percent. Of course, there are always multiple factors at work when it comes to sales development. Products, prices, dealers, competitor moves, and external factors such as the 1973 oil crisis may well have been at least as influential as Pontiac's brand identity in the case in question.

Another example of the advantages of consistency is that of Coca-Cola. While Coca-Cola has always stuck to its classic curly logo and the color red, Pepsi has changed its logo nine times since the brand was created. Perhaps the most radical change was that made in 1998. With a budget of USD 500 million, Pepsi changed its colors from red, white, and blue to just blue. The reason given by the company for the redesign was that the old logo was not distinctive enough and that it was imperative that Pepsi distinguish itself from Coca-Cola.[25] In 2003 the next update occurred, aimed at stressing

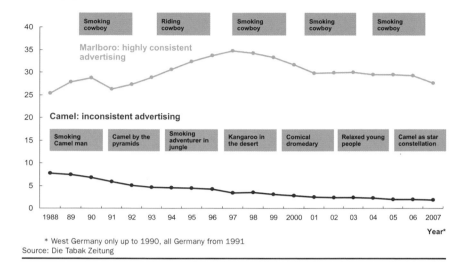

Fig. 1.9: The cowboy is constant – The camel wanders
Share of branded cigarette market
Germany, percent

Smoking cowboy	Riding cowboy	Smoking cowboy	Smoking cowboy	Smoking cowboy	

Marlboro: highly consistent advertising

Camel: inconsistent advertising

| Smoking Camel man | Camel by the pyramids | Smoking adventurer in jungle | Kangaroo in the desert | Comical dromedary | Relaxed young people | Camel as star constellation |

1988 89 90 91 92 93 94 95 96 97 98 99 2000 01 02 03 04 05 06 2007

Year*

* West Germany only up to 1990, all Germany from 1991
Source: Die Tabak Zeitung

the brand's youthful image. Yet in the vast majority of markets, these continuous makeovers have neither helped it catch up with Coca-Cola nor ensured it a better brand image.[26]

Marlboro has shown nearly the same persistence as Coca-Cola. Since Marlboro's makeover by Leo Burnett in the 1950s, it has never questioned its positioning as a cigarette brand associated with freedom and adventure. The image of the cowboy (since 1963) and the Marlboro red (since the 1950s) has remained constant over a very long period, while the contents of the advertising campaigns have been adjusted many times in line with current fashions, and new innovations in cigarettes have been used to refresh the brand. The umbrella brand name Marlboro was only extended with the launch of Marlboro Lights in 1986. In 1994 Marlboro Medium was introduced, and today there are additional product extensions such as Marlboro Menthol, Marlboro 100, and Marlboro Blend 29 (Figure 1.9).[27]

Outside the United States, where there has been somewhat greater consistency, Camel, the number two brand, has changed its positioning constantly over the same period. In Germany, for example, it has moved from the Camel man as an adventurer with a hole in his shoe in the 1970s and 1980s to the leather-clad toy camel in the 1990s, to the image of the relaxed young professional between 2001 and 2004, and finally back to the camel.

What Brands Can
Do, and What
Makes Them
Strong

The image of the brand has been altered so many times that it has become almost devoid of meaning. Today, while Marlboro controls 19 percent of the European market, Camel has a share of slightly less than 5 percent.[28]

The importance of consistency is shown in the results of a survey conducted in late 2006 among 300 marketing experts as well. When asked about the aspects of successful branding in an open-ended question, the experts rated consistency the most critical aspect by far with 38 percent of all answers.[29]

However, consistency is not to be confused with stagnation; without the courage to change, brands that were once weak or undifferentiated – like Puma, Audi, and Burberry – would never have managed to become the premium brands they are today. Samsung Electronics is another good example of a brand making the journey from a mass-market image to a quality brand, a transition that requires careful management of brand positioning – and a great deal of patience.

Until well into the 1990s, the Korean electronics manufacturer Samsung earned its way by producing cheap Samsung-branded products, and by acting as a third-party manufacturer of components or entire devices for premium brands such as Sony.[30] The transformation began at the end of the 1990s. This was prompted by the Asian financial crisis, which led to staff reductions of around a third and the realization that, as an increasingly high-wage country, Korea would soon no longer be able to compete with China in the mass-market segment. As a first step, management established a global marketing function, thus underlining the importance of marketing for a company that had previously been dominated by an engineering mentality. Next, Samsung supported the development of the brand by bundling marketing activities across the company, stopping the production of cheap products in many countries, and concentrating instead on innovative digital products with exclusive design. While its competitors were still clinging on to cathode ray tube technology for television sets, for instance, Samsung made the strategic move into new digital technologies such as liquid crystal displays and plasma screens. This helped it overcome its image as a budget manufacturer, and move into the category of premium manufacturer. At the same time, the company tried to strengthen the emotional promise of the products and raise the brand's profile. As part of this strategy, Samsung became a leading sponsor of major sporting events, such as the soccer World Cup and the Olympic Games, and paid EUR 73 million to have its name displayed prominently on the chests of the London soccer club Chelsea.[31]

What Brands Can
Do, and What
Makes Them
Strong

Today, the results of this transformation are evident. The company's claim to be »leading the digital convergence revolution« is reflected at the product level; Samsung developed the first-ever speech recognition phone in 2005, launched the world's first Blu-ray Disc player in 2006, and released the world's thinnest liquid crystal display (a mere 0.82 mm) in 2007.[32] At the brand level, Samsung not only manages to increase its brand value continuously, which – according to Interbrand/*Business Week's* ranking – has doubled in five years to reach USD 16.9 billion in 2007, but is also trying to strengthen the emotional elements of the brand in order to develop it further. In an interview with *Business Week*, Samsung's Global Chief Marketing Officer Gregory Lee stated: »In the past, our communication was all about the product. There wasn't a real story to it. We are really trying to tell a story about how it fits into consumer lives in our newer communications.«[33] To accomplish this, the company launched a new advertising campaign – »Imagine« – in 2005 to accelerate their transformation into a truly premium brand. The earnings from the first quarter of 2008 confirm the success of the new approach. Samsung's overall profit is up 37 percent from the first quarter of 2007. But more important, there was a shift from the company's traditional semiconductor component B2B business towards consumer sales of devices, such as mobile phones, liquid crystal displays, and television sets.[34] This shift lends further momentum to Samsung's aspiration to break free from its past as an original equipment manufacturer to offer upscale products that are bought not only for their functionality, but also for their appeal as branded items.

Art: Creativity doesn't necessarily mean winning prizes

In addition to ensuring that the brand has superior content and stays up-to-date (while consistent), a very important aspect of the *art* of brand management is the creativity of its communication. As a source of creative ideas, the advertising industry has always been an important partner to brand management. Today, however, in a society flooded by multimedia, many believe that advertising is no longer as effective as it once was. As a result, many companies are questioning the service offered them by advertisers, and greater financial discipline is being brought into marketing, moving it into line with other functions in terms of measuring profits and losses. The demand is that advertising must deliver measurable results.

Plainly, some brands do manage to achieve consistent competitive advantage by means of superior creativity in their communication; they know exactly where to place the bait so that the fish will bite. Strong brands are highly effective in the way in which they use creative campaigns to distinguish themselves from the competition, to strengthen their brand image, and thus ultimately also to generate correspondingly high sales. Examining the advertising used by brands over many years reveals a number of particularly successful long-lasting examples: Lucky Strike's minimalist approach limited to the packaging and a witty headline, Red Bull's unique scribbles, and Sixt's smart and often provocative advertising tag lines.

Creativity can take different forms, as the results of the »creativity in advertising« study show (compare the insert on creative advertising on the next page). Often, really effective creative advertising contains something that might be irritating, provocative, or funny, whether in pictures or in words, as the aforementioned illustrate. Many other major brands take a less radical approach, however, and are no less successful for it. For brands such as Nivea, Beck's, and Marlboro, creativity is primarily about constantly renewing a consistent brand in as simple and catchy a way as possible, occasionally introducing new elements to revitalize the message. This ensures that the brand remains up-to-date over the years and, although it may appear less original to the judges of creativity contests, it often delivers higher dividends.

Even if the advertising industry has stopped focusing exclusively on creativity, prizes remain as important as ever. One of the most respected advertising awards worldwide is the Effie, which recognizes ideas that work commercially. Mary Lee Keane, executive director of the Effie Awards says, »Effie winners share the honor of finding the perfect combination of strategy, creativity, and media to resonate with consumers« (Effie press release).

Bartle Bogle Hegarty's campaign for Unilever's Vaseline brand »Keeping Skin Amazing« won the global top prize in 2008. The campaign repositioned Vaseline as the skin authority in 15 countries and led to double-digit growth for the brand, which had suffered a 30-year share decline.

The Global Golden Effie in 2007 was awarded to Cayenne Communication for their campaign »It's Playtime« for Canon's EUR 1,000 single-lens-reflex camera EOS 350D. The big idea was to position the product not as a professional tool, but as license to play, a toy for adults to explore the world. As a result, Canon's sales in the segment grew by 135 percent and its market share increased by nine percentage points while its main competitor, Nikon, lost twelve percentage points.[35]

Jim Stengel, the former CMO at Procter & Gamble, is another firm believer in the significance of advertising awards. At the 2008 Cannes Lions awards ceremony, he said: »There is a correlation between awards for creative advertising and an increase in market share.«[36]

Art meets Science: Creative Advertising Examined

by Professor Sebastian Turner. A partner and supervisory board member at Scholz & Friends as well as a board member of the Art Directors Club for Germany (ADC), Sebastian Turner teaches at the Berlin University of the Arts.

Who doesn't like creative advertising? Think of Dove's Campaign for Real Beauty. For perhaps the first time ever, Unilever's skin care advertising featured real-life women, complete with their curves and imperfections, rather than the skinny models we have come to take for granted in print advertising and on billboards. Who wouldn't give this unusual sight a second look? The Campaign for Real Beauty is nothing short of a show stopper. It surprises, amuses, and inspires. In short, it's creative advertising.

We all love it, remember it, and tell our friends about it. But does creative advertising work? Everybody knows recall isn't everything. Some go as far as claiming creativity doesn't matter at all. The head of marketing at a major fast-moving consumer goods company says, »Creativity is irrelevant at best. Often, it is downright harmful to advertising success.« Traditionalists focus on making sure advertising content and messages are tailored to the brand, the product, and the target group in question. For them, »content fit« is much more important than creativity. Campaigns based on this belief may sometimes come across as conventional, but often have credibility on their side.

But can there even be a winning strategy irrespective of the industry? McKinsey, the Art Directors Club of Germany, and the Berlin School of Creative Leadership have teamed up for a pilot effort to quantify the success of German marketing campaigns. Some one hundred television commercials submitted for the 2005 GWA Effie award have been examined; advertising recall and changes in market share were used to measure their respective psychological and business impact. The findings are likely to surprise the »purists.« In fact, both types of advertising – creative and conventional, content-fit focused – work. But not for any product, and not always in the same way. The more creative a campaign, the higher the likelihood that the featured product will sell. But at the same time, not all successful campaigns are particularly creative.

Advertising success can be measured

Despite the best intentions, most past attempts to measure advertising success have been controversial, simply because there are no widely accepted, objective indicators. This is especially true for the creative quality of campaigns. Creativity is typically assessed by jury votes that many would say are mostly subjective. The ADC/McKinsey study has chosen a different course. To determine the relative importance of creativity and content fit, a set of five criteria each was used, as shown in the checklist in Figure 1.10.

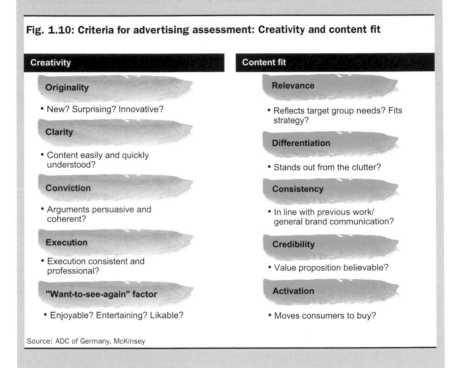

Fig. 1.10: Criteria for advertising assessment: Creativity and content fit

Creativity	Content fit
Originality	**Relevance**
• New? Surprising? Innovative?	• Reflects target group needs? Fits strategy?
Clarity	**Differentiation**
• Content easily and quickly understood?	• Stands out from the clutter?
Conviction	**Consistency**
• Arguments persuasive and coherent?	• In line with previous work/ general brand communication?
Execution	**Credibility**
• Execution consistent and professional?	• Value proposition believable?
"Want-to-see-again" factor	**Activation**
• Enjoyable? Entertaining? Likable?	• Moves consumers to buy?

Source: ADC of Germany, McKinsey

Using these criteria, all advertisements submitted as Effie contenders were assessed on a scale from 1 (poor) to 5 (excellent). A panel of art directors, including the author of this insert, assessed the creativity criteria, while a group of McKinsey marketing experts, including the authors of this book, analyzed each advertisement's content fit. This assessment was then tested for correlation with advertising recall and post-campaign changes in market share. Audi's »Tomorrow has arrived today« brand campaign came out as the most creative campaign with a score of 4.7. Lenor's »Poetry« commercial for their fabric softener, a classic spot focusing on the product features »softness« and »freshness,« only achieved a creativity score of 1.5 (Figures 1.11 and 1.12).

Fig. 1.11: Audi's "Tomorrow Has Arrived Today" campaign

1 = poor
5 = excellent

Pure creativity – Example: Audi

© Propaganda GEM - 2004

- Highly creative – highly unique in execution and media selection (cinema), clearly differentiated from other automotive advertising
- Weaker content fit – the key message (new design of front) not explicitly communicated; limited link to current models
- Very high recall – latent communication of key attribute "innovative" works well and engages emotionally

Creativity*	Content fit*
4.7	2.2
Individual dimensions	**Individual dimensions**
Originality	Relevance
4.8	1.9
Clarity	Differentiation
4.3	3.2
Conviction	Consistency
4.2	2.5
Execution	Credibility
4.4	2.5
Want-to-see-again factor	Activation
4.5	2.9

* Weighted average of individual dimensions
Sample: 100 German TV campaigns from 2003 to 2004
Source: ADC of Germany, McKinsey

Fig. 1.12: Lenor's "Poetry" campaign

1 = poor
5 = excellent

Pure product benefit – Example: Lenor

- Low creativity – message and execution not very original (well-known portrayal of nature/green meadows)
- High content fit – focus on key product features "softness" and "freshness"
- High economic success – believable communication of product benefit and high degree of consumer activation led to significant market share increase while campaign was on the air

Creativity*	Content fit*
1.5	4.3
Individual dimensions	**Individual dimensions**
Originality	Relevance
1.5	4.1
Clarity	Differentiation
3.2	4.3
Conviction	Consistency
2.4	4.8
Execution	Credibility
2.2	3.9
Want-to-see-again factor	Activation
1.5	4.0

* Weighted average of individual dimensions
Sample: 100 German TV campaigns from 2003 to 2004
Source: ADC of Germany, McKinsey

Things looked different, however, as far as content fit was concerned. Thanks to its product focus and inherent consistency, the Lenor spot came out on top with a score of 4.3. Yakult's yoghurt commercial and Hipp's baby food spot achieved similarly respectable values for content fit. Because of their comparatively low profile, these campaigns were less well recalled than the highly creative spots, but performed equally well in terms of economic impact.

Although both highly creative and, in terms of content fit, highly relevant campaigns can be economically successful, there are some notable differences (Figure 1.13). While successful creative campaigns come mostly from the automotive industry, the campaigns that succeed thanks to their content fit were typically created for FMCG companies such as Lenor or Hipp. A similar category bias can be observed among the low performers. Many of the advertisements that the jury's verdict sent to the »Boring losers« corner came from financial institutions. Their messages are often abstract and hard to bring to life, which frequently leads to less exciting and less appealing spots. As a consequence, these campaigns also have lower sales impact.

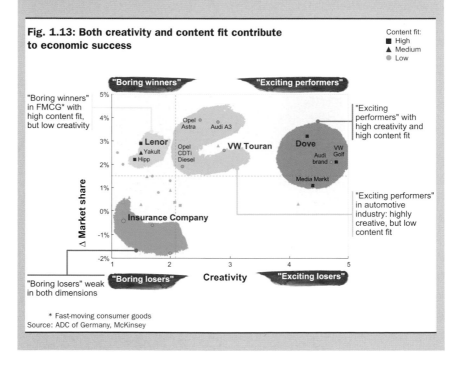

Fig. 1.13: Both creativity and content fit contribute to economic success

Content fit:
■ High
▲ Medium
● Low

"Boring winners"

"Exciting performers"

"Boring winners" in FMCG* with high content fit, but low creativity

"Exciting performers" with high creativity and high content fit

Opel Astra
Audi A3

Lenor
Yakult
Hipp

Opel CDTi Diesel

VW Touran

Dove
Audi brand
VW Golf

Media Markt

"Exciting performers" in automotive industry: highly creative, but low content fit

Insurance Company

Δ Market share

"Boring losers" weak in both dimensions

"Boring losers"

Creativity

"Exciting losers"

* Fast-moving consumer goods
Source: ADC of Germany, McKinsey

What Brands Can Do, and What Makes Them Strong

As a general rule, one could say that the more emotionally charged the product, the more creative the campaign should be. This is especially true for high-involvement products characterized by long life cycles and high purchase prices: cars, watches, jewelry, or high-end consumer electronics. By contrast, fast-moving everyday products and items with low ticket prices typically derive a high sales benefit from campaigns with a good content fit. We will find this differentiation substantiated once we look more closely at three categories with very different involvement values: cars, short-lived consumer products, and financial services. Despite the differences, the analysis also shows that creativity almost always leads to success. In Figure 1.13, you will find the bottom right »exciting loser« quadrant almost empty. In other words, there are next to no highly creative campaigns that are not successful. Other things being equal, creativity is an advertiser's best bet.

Automotive advertising: Pure creativity

The German car industry thrives on emotional benefits, and creativity is the instrument of choice to make them come to life. The price of a new car is so high that buyers will have the basics covered anyway. Most of them are sure to research features, fuel economy, resale value, and the like by studying catalogs, checking test results, and visiting the dealer lot. This makes it imperative for automotive advertising to appeal to the heart and soul rather than reason. It must strive to generate desire by conveying emotional benefits: freedom, power, luxury, or simply »fun to drive.« This makes the creation of successful automotive advertising a real and present challenge for advertising executives. Compared to other industries, an above-average creative effort is required to make a given brand or model stand out among its competitors. Small surprise automotive advertising is considered the hallmark of creativity; car campaigns have long dominated the advertising award scene. The Cannes Golden Lion, seen by many as the equivalent of the Oscar for creative advertising, has been awarded to car manufacturers such as Volkswagen, Honda, Mercedes, and Mini in recognition of their leading positions among the most creative advertisers in the world. According to the Gunn Report, an independent publication listing award winners from multiple such competitions, Volkswagen has consistently come out as one of the most creative global advertisers in past years.[37] This study underpins the economic payoff of creative excellence in the automotive industry.

Creativity, however, is not the only success factor, not even in automotive advertising. Especially in the budget segment of the market, most buyers make their decisions largely based on rational benefits. They want to see their buying factors reflected in advertising campaigns: small on the outside, yet roomy on the inside, and high mileage per gallon. In other words, low- to mid-range cars call for advertising with high content fit, ideally combined with creative delivery, of course, since nowadays even an affordable compact car needs to be more than just a vehicle. It remains to be seen whether the current trend of eco-advertising focusing on rational benefits like fuel efficiency and low carbon emissions will change the way automotive advertising works.

Soap and snacks: Up close and personal with the customer

Content fit is what matters most in the fast-moving consumer goods category. Very few people develop emotional ties to their detergents or groceries. And because of the relatively low ticket price, most customers rarely use sources other than advertising for information gathering. As a consequence, fast facts are what counts in this area. Successful campaigns convey the brand's or product's value proposition clearly and believably; examples include »softness« and »freshness« for the fabric-softener category Lenor competes in, or »health« and »well-being« for prospective buyers of Yakult dairy products.

But even in this category, creativity can certainly tip the scales. One of the most prominent examples is Dove's legendary Campaign for Real Beauty mentioned above. Unilever's idea to go against long-established beauty stereotypes and have the company's skin care products endorsed by »girls next door« rather than skinny models was a surprise hit in the category. Recent allegations that extensive retouching was done in the final stages of post-production didn't harm the campaign's basic appeal. The Campaign for Real Beauty remains a prime example of how to combine creativity and content fit. It was doubly rewarded, not only with considerable industry buzz, but also with a high economic payoff (3.0% growth in market share as shown in Figure 1.13) (for details, see section 2.2 on brand communication at Dove). So the answer to the question raised above is: yes, creative advertising does work. By and large, it is effective advertising, even in allegedly rational categories such as fast-moving consumer goods.

Fig. 1.14: Dove's "Campaign for Real Beauty"

Creative and coherent – Example: Dove

Creativity*	Content fit*
4.3	4.6

Individual dimensions	Individual dimensions
Originality	Relevance
4.5	4.1
Clarity	Differentiation
3.8	4.8
Conviction	Consistency
4.1	4.8
Execution	Credibility
4.5	4.0
Want-to-see-again factor	Activation
4.2	3.9

- High creativity – outstanding, innovative campaign idea (real women instead of models)
- High content fit – advertising message highly relevant to target group and differentiating in beauty category
- Clear economic success – unconventional approach with high activation impact lead to significant market share increase while campaign was on air

* Weighted average of individual dimensions
Sample: 100 German TV campaigns from 2003 to 2004
Source: ADC of Germany, McKinsey, Picture: Unilever/Dove

Financial services: Make it snappy

There is no disputing the fact that banking and insurance are among the more challenging advertising subjects. The reason is that when choosing financial products and services, customers apply a combination of emotional buying factors, such as the need to feel safe, and rational factors, such as achievable rate of return. To make things even more difficult, most messages in this industry are fairly complex to begin with; they require both explanation and clarity to get the customer's attention.

As a consequence, the demands on creativity and content fit are equally high in financial services and present a major challenge, as the poor performance of many financial advertising campaigns in this study shows. Only Allianz stood out with its original and appealing way of packaging the touchy subject of retirement funds. Thanks to the unusual and surprising image of young soccer fans having a nice cup of tea, their campaign »It pays to stay alive« cut through the cliché of the contented retiree. It was rewarded with significant market share growth while the campaign was on the air.

Bottom line: Mix and match!

What are the practical implications of these findings for day-to-day brand communication planning and campaign management? The analysis conducted by McKinsey and the ADC yields three guiding principles:

(1) Content fit and creativity both have a substantial impact on advertising success. Even the biggest budget can't make up for a weak campaign that misses out on both dimensions.

(2) The appropriate mix depends on the category. Emotional products call for highly creative advertising, while for fast-moving goods a high content fit is a necessary condition for success. That said, higher creativity almost always translates into higher impact regardless of the product category.

(3) The biggest hits among advertising campaigns tend to combine creativity and content fit.

Once and for all, this study refutes the misconception that advertising can only be either of two things: innovative or informative, noticeably different or optimally adjusted. It's the appropriate mix that makes successful advertising. The criteria identified in the analysis will help to find the right proportion of creativity and content fit in a given situation, and will help to make advertising success more predictable. If they get it right, advertisers will walk away with real returns – and real beauty.

Science: The challenge of accurate measurement

The second element of good brand management is *science*. Most marketing managers and agencies use primarily, or even exclusively, brand awareness and advertising recall to measure the success of their brand management. But experience shows that this is an insufficient basis to assess the specific strengths and weaknesses of a brand. In some cases, such limited measurement can even create the illusion of a healthy brand, when in fact the brand is in trouble. The way out is to expand the toolbox of brand metrics, and to leverage it more comprehensively in brand management.

Despite recent innovations in brand measurement, advertising tracking instruments used for confirming the value of advertising investments still tend to focus on the level of awareness and recall. Determining that the brand enjoys a high level of awareness and recall can all too easily lead to the conclusion that the investment is well spent and the brand is strong. But often this is a false inference. This problem can be seen in teaser campaigns, for instance. Companies have wasted millions on advertising aimed to attract attention to a brand before it actually appeared on the market, or in situations where general brand awareness was of little relevance to a company's success. Take Evonik Industries for example. Evonik is the new name for the German RAG (»Ruhrkohle«), which was renamed after spinning off its former mainstay, coal mining. The company worked on the new name and the launch campaign for almost two years, but never disclosed anything. Halfway into the relaunch, Evonik found they had prematurely struck a sponsorship deal with Borussia Dortmund's soccer team worth EUR 12 million in licensing fees. Since they were not ready to launch the brand, they put a simple exclamation mark on the players' shirts for two seasons. A few weeks before actually introducing their new name, Evonik started a mass-media teaser campaign that showed creative images (such as an elephant stuck to the side of a building) and the question »Who is doing this?« In September 2007 the company gave the answer, »We are doing this. Evonik Industries.« Evonik spent over EUR 20 million on advertising within one month to make the brand known and establish »innovation« as its core promise. It is questionable whether this level of mass-media investment is justified for a B2B-focused company that generates two-thirds of its revenues from its chemical business unit. The objective of the mass-media campaign was therefore not to sell, but to generate attention for the company's upcoming initial public offering. However, a few months later, Evonik announced it would postpone the initial public offering at least until 2009. It remains to be seen whether Evonik will ever achieve its branding objectives, or what those objectives even are. But simple brand awareness is obviously an insufficient metric in a complex situation such as this, where multiple stakeholders are involved.[38]

The experience of E.ON was similar. Arising out of the merger of Veba and Viag in June 2000, E.ON needed to establish itself both as a corporate brand and as a product brand for electricity. When the campaign started, it only showed a red screen accompanied by dramatic music. After two weeks, the brand name E.ON and the nametag »new energy« appeared. Another three weeks later, E.ON started to position itself as an innovative brand by showing new energy products like the possibility to switch off your light from a distance via a hotline. Finally, E.ON launched its »Mix it, baby« spots with Arnold Schwarzenegger, introducing a product that allowed the consumers to create a personal energy mix by choosing from several energy sources like wind or water. From a corporate branding point of view, the E.ON campaign was successful. E.ON certainly was able to strengthen awareness of its corporate brand among corporate stakeholders, for example, the capital markets. From a product marketing perspective, however, the success of the advertising in financial terms was, not unsurprisingly, modest.

The »Mix it, baby« part of E.ON's campaign initially won great plaudits for its creativity. But in terms of product marketing and branding, it did not produce the desired results. Only just over a thousand customers switched to E.ON as a result of the campaign, which cost the company an estimated EUR 22.5 million for product advertising alone (resulting in an acquisition cost of around EUR 20,500 for each new customer).[39] Given an average annual revenue of approximately EUR 600 per customer, this campaign could never pay for itself, even if customers remain loyal to E.ON for the rest of their lives. Yet the E.ON brand was considered strong because it achieved a high level of brand awareness within a short time. Just four months after its launch, market research showed aided brand awareness of 93 percent and unaided advertising recall of 66 percent. Fifty percent of Germans knew the »On« slogan, and 85 percent knew it came from E.ON.[40] The problem wasn't recall, the problem was revenues. McKinsey analysis shows that the brand is, in fact, not an important driver in the purchasing process for electricity. It is a low-interest product. As a consequence, content fit of the communication is far more important than creative advertising campaigns. The providers need to communicate clear benefits like »low-price guaranteed« instead of the emotional or innovative appeal of their brands. Again, focusing on brand awareness or advertising recall is insufficient to uncover this causal relationship between corporate image and consumer purchasing behavior.

The German power sector appears to have learned from E.ON's failed trial; in 2004, the sector invested a mere EUR 52 million in traditional advertising, just over a fourth of the level of five years earlier. German energy providers are only now regaining confidence when it comes to brand communication and spent EUR 101 million in 2007. But this time, they are placing far greater emphasis on connecting the advertising to relevant products and benefits offered to specific target customer segments. A good example is E.ON's subbrand e-wie-einfach (e-like-easy, or s-like-simple to be precise), launched in February 2007. If you look only at the awareness e-wie-einfach managed to generate for the new brand (a meager 36 percent in January 2008), you might think it is a failure. But thanks to its more targeted and more rational positioning, the brand won over half a million new customers in less than a year. Although about half of these are in-house switchers from other E.ON subsidiaries, the remaining 200,000 first-time subscribers exceed the company's original target of 100,000 new customers in year one by 100 percent. In total, e-wie-einfach attracted one

What Brands Can
Do, and What
Makes Them
Strong

fourth of all consumers who switched energy providers in Germany in 2007. It seems E.ON originally fell prey to the first-mover curse: after the deregulation of the German energy market, they paid a high price to bring about a change in consumer mindset, the effects of which are becoming visible only now. Says Matthias Kurth of the Federal Network Agency, Germany's energy and telecommunications regulatory body, »It took some getting used to for consumers, but these days they are well aware of the possibility to switch providers.«[41]

To sum up, the success of e-wie-einfach is driven by two factors. Firstly, brands like e-wie-einfach (and its competitors) are reaping the benefits of a mindset change initiated years ago. Secondly, E.ON has shifted the focus of its marketing campaigns from pure brand awareness in the general population, built on emotional appeal, to serious consideration among likely switchers, brought about by clearly communicated rational benefits like »hassle-free« and »affordable.« The promise of simplicity that is built into the e-wie-einfach brand turns out to be more relevant to consumer decision making in this category than the vague appeal of a heavily advertised, celebrity-endorsed brand awareness building. Unlike a watch, a pair of sunglasses, or a car, an energy provider contract is not something you are seen and associated with. Therefore what those consumers who are willing to switch in the first place are looking for in an energy provider brand is a credible and fail-safe promise of the lowest rates and the least amount of trouble. But this also means that a brand's sheer high profile is at best irrelevant, if not harmful; expensive advertising may be taken as a sign of expensive tariffs (the different functions of a brand are discussed in more detail in section 2.1).[41]

Strong brands generate strong sales and profits. They need buyers, repeat buyers, and a price that ensures they will continue developing and bringing in revenue. Accordingly, the tool used for measuring the brand needs to be one that is able to dissect brand performance in terms of its impact on the bottom line and not just its effect on consumer consciousness.

Even the notoriously advertising-savvy automotive industry sometimes misses the mark. Assuming attention was what would help them conquer the compact car category in Germany, Toyota focused on generating the maximum amount of advertising noise prior to the introduction of the Auris. In March 2007, Toyota launched its new model with the largest outdoor advertising campaign in German history. Toyota spent over EUR 30 million in March alone (EUR 43 million in 2007) to present the Auris on over 200,000 billboards in 82 major cities, more than 60 percent of all available billboards in Germany. Although Toyota achieved an impressive 300 million advertising impressions in one month, it turned out 85 percent of all viewers were not even interested in buying a new car. With 18,561 cars sold in 2007, less than 10 percent of its main competitor, the Volkswagen Golf, the Auris fell far short of Toyota's expectations. The company ended up spending EUR 2,334 per Auris on advertising. This amounts to 15 percent of the car's starting price (EUR 15,500). It is also more than six times the amount Volkswagen spent per car in 2007 (EUR 354).[42]

The main lesson from these examples is that any measurement focused on awareness does not provide sufficient insight into whether the advertising investment will translate into a tangible payoff for the company. If you look only at brand awareness, you remain in the dark as to whether the consumer is clear about the product benefits and, if they are clear, whether these benefits are relevant to consumer purchasing behavior. To get closer to measuring advertising impact on actual purchase decisions, what brand managers need is a measurement approach that helps them understand how advertising can promote the emotional and rational benefits of the brand itself.

Naturally enough, measuring brand strength will always take brand awareness as its starting point. But high awareness is only the start for a strong brand; though a prerequisite for success, high brand awareness is not enough in itself to make a brand truly strong. For this to happen, consumers must also be familiar with the contents of the brand in terms of the product or service offer, and the target group must be willing to give greater consideration to the brand than to its competitors when making purchase decisions. In other words, the brand must perform well along the entire purchase funnel (see section 2.4 for details on the purchase funnel).

This is not to say that a strong brand performs equally well at each stage of the purchase funnel. It is rare that a brand outperforms the competition at every stage, from initial awareness right up to brand loyalty; most brands reveal slight weaknesses at one stage or another. Nevertheless, for strong brands these weaknesses are rarely severe.

Accurate measurement of a brand's relative strengths and weaknesses in the brand purchase funnel is the starting point for making further improvements to the brand. Nivea is an example of a brand that has strengths throughout the funnel. Nivea is today one of the leading cosmetics brand in Europe and a world leader in skin care, as well as in many other personal hygiene segments, such as baby care, sun care, and deodorants. Brand awareness for Nivea Creme is very high; in Germany, 85 percent are aware of the brand, 48 percent say they like it, and, most importantly, 39 percent use it regularly.[43] This funnel performance has been rewarded by Nivea's global sales increase by five times since 1990, reaching EUR 3.1 billion in 2006.[44] At each stage, Nivea's brand managers measure the brand's success in the funnel, dissecting every aspect of the indicators, reinforcing positive trends, and taking immediate action to compensate for even the slightest negative change.

Good brand managers look below the surface at their brand's strengths and weaknesses. They make detailed measurements using objective standards and constantly hone their measurement techniques. Companies such as Procter & Gamble, Henkel, and Unilever spend millions of euros each year on market research, and the heads of their market research departments are some of the best-known experts in the field; top management listens to them before making decisions.

Craft: Brand management is CEO business

Ultimately, brands can only survive if their management is first class. Such excellence requires continuity and a steady hand. This usually means the leadership of one person who has the depth of experience to ensure that the brand core remains unchanged over years (better still, decades) while being kept up-to-date through innovation and advertising. At Apple for instance, every new product design and every global advertising campaign has to be personally approved by the CEO Steve Jobs. Moreover Steve Jobs even represents some of the core attributes of the brand (cool, individualistic, revolutionary, different, creative) in his personal appearance. The more senior the manager, the more likely that the brand management will be successful. Two of the best examples of how to do this well come from Puma and Porsche, which are seen as the most successful turnarounds in Germany over the past 20 years. When Jochen Zeitz became CEO of Puma in 1990, he made brand building the corporate priority number one, taking the leading role himself. In a recent interview with the *Sunday Times*, Zeitz said that he made re-positioning the Puma brand his top priority in the 1990s: »I said let's become premium. Let's bring fashion and style into play.«[45] Wendelin Wiedeking, CEO of Porsche since 1992, believes that brand management is a key part of his job: »A company's brand is like its crown jewels, and it requires the same care. You don't keep hauling them out and you don't wear them on every occasion, but you have to remember that they are there and need careful cleaning and looking after.«[46]

These are words that many an advertising agency would do well to listen to. Too much tinkering is more likely to damage the brand than enhance it. Deciding what will add to the brand's strength and what will not is a top management decision. The Smart car did not fit the Mercedes-Benz image,

What Brands Can
Do, and What
Makes Them
Strong

so it was better to choose a new brand name. Nivea can offer shampoo and perhaps nail polish besides its creams and care products, but it should not offer a household detergent. The core of the Porsche brand will always be in its sports cars, even if certain models, such as the Cayenne or the upcoming Panamera, may succeed in breaking down category barriers.

The CEO or other chief caretaker of a brand must have internalized the brand core in order to be able to manage the trade-off between generating additional revenue potential and weakening the brand. Brand management is a top management issue – it should not be delegated to product managers, external agencies, or another third party.

Craft: Using the brand's strength to its greatest extent

Besides requiring an experienced guiding hand, craft also means translating the power of the brand concept into a reality on the street. In a word: execution. Companies with strong brands ensure attention to detail.

Take McDonald's, for example. The company unfailingly achieves the same quality in its products in every McDonald's restaurant and in every country in which it operates. It insists on perfection in every detail and on scrupulous adherence to fixed standards and documentation in each stage of the process, from selection, purchasing, and processing of raw materials, right up to the preparation of individual products. To ensure that all staff members are aware of these operating standards, McDonald's managers around the world are trained in special »Hamburger Universities« where they learn the basics as well as the latest developments.

McDonald's ensures that all raw materials and ingredients are subject constantly to almost obsessive visual, physical, chemical, microbiological, and nutritional checks. Suppliers, like the restaurants themselves, work according to the HACCP principle (Hazard Analysis and Critical Control Point), a risk analysis method for production processes originally developed by NASA to protect astronauts from the risks of food poisoning.[47] All McDonald's products have sell-by times (not dates), after which they are disposed of. Fries must be sold within seven minutes of frying, and hamburgers can remain on the prewarmed sales racks for a maximum of ten minutes. After this, the food is thrown out. Another factor in McDonald's success is the speed with which customers are served. McDonald's prescribes, down to the second, exactly how long different operations should take. A Big Mac bun, for example, is toasted for exactly 35 seconds and no longer.[48]

McDonald's beats other fast-food providers in the areas of product quality and speed. In other areas, such as restaurant decor, friendliness of service, and location, McDonald's does not have a decisive edge over the competition. It doesn't need to. McDonald's corroborates the statement made earlier: a strong brand needs only one or two outstanding attributes in its rational product benefits in order to hold its own against the competition. In its remaining attributes it doesn't need necessarily to be better, but neither should it have any significant disadvantages in the eyes of the target group.

Nokia also executes its brand strategy excellently. Jorma Ollila, former CEO of Nokia, said: »Why have we been a successful company? If you want a simple answer, it is getting the balance right between innovation and execution. In a technology business you need a tremendous amount of innovation, but with these volumes and growth, you need to execute or it will kill you. So, it is balance. I think we have done this better than anybody else.«[49] Nokia's success arises from the fact that it focused on getting not only its product and brand right, but its production and distribution as well.

The company takes its customer insight functions and knowledge gathering very seriously. »Our approach is all about putting people at the heart of the way we design and market products. First we observe, then we design. We have teams of anthropologists, ethnographers, psychologists, and consumer insight experts observing and understanding people's behavior. Their insights are used to shape our research and development and design focus. People don't buy features. What they are after is benefits,« explains Keith Pardy, Nokia's Senior Vice President of Strategic Marketing. Within a few months, Nokia demonstrated that it was able to respond to customer needs. In the first half of 2005, Nokia's market share recovered visibly.[50] Within the 10 years from 1997 to 2007, Nokia was able to double its global market share from 19 percent to 38 percent.[51] These days, Nokia thinks of itself as a fast follower that excels not so much at cutting-edge research and development, but at selecting, refining and communicating innovations that matter to the company's target groups. Says Are Thu, Vice President Brand Strategy at Nokia: »Nokia's brand promise is of ›very human technology helping people feel close.‹ [...] The way we summarize it in one line is ›connecting people in new and better ways,‹ which is a powerful filter for us to put against the technology.« Are Thu admits that it can be a bit of a »culture clash« to try and make development engineers adopt a consumer mindset, but thinks it's worth it to come up with relevant value propositions for a wide variety of audiences: »I want the grandmas, my mom, to upgrade to a camera phone« (also see the interview at the end of chapter 2). Figure 1.15 takes some examples from Nokia's product portfolio of the past 10 years to show how device and feature development has consistently reflected specific consumer needs.

The Porsche 911 is one of the world's most successful car brands. Porsche has shown outstanding execution in the brand, positioning the product for that small segment of the market that values well-above-average acceleration, a sporty chassis, and unique design. Porsche has implemented this positioning in the 911's development from the design phase right up to vehicle testing. The concern for detail is particularly noticeable in the design. The typical Porsche boxer engine (featuring horizontally opposed cylinders) should sound »powerful, somewhat metallic in places, unmistakable, but always pleasantly sonorous and restrained.« This sound is monitored by no less than 50 engineers in Porsche's acoustics and vibration technology section. They listen not only to the six-cylinder engine but to wipers, blinkers, door locks, and light switches as well. The sound technicians check every moving part and correct even the slightest dud note. Every 911 has the distinct 911 sound.[52]

Fig. 1.15: Nokia: Consumer needs are driving product development

1998	1999	2003	2005	2008
Nokia 9110 Communicator First handheld telephone supporting mobile image processing	**Nokia 7110** First WAP mobile phone for basic online applications	**Nokia 6800** First mobile phone with folding screen and keyboard	**Nokia N95** Unique 2-way slide for fast transition from computer to multimedia player	**Nokia N810** Innovative handheld mobile Internet tablet with GPS
Mobile computing capability for professionals	Basic **Internet access** on the go for everybody	A phone that **fits in your pocket**, but still allows **easy typing**	Minimize number of devices carried: phone, PDA, iPod **in one device**	**Near-desktop computing power** for heavy users on the go

Consumer needs

Source: Nokia   * WAP = Wireless Application Protocol

What Brands Can
Do, and What
Makes Them
Strong

Excellent execution is not necessarily limited to the product. Price, sales channel management, and details of communication can form key characteristics in strong brands. For the discounter Aldi, for example, price is the key; this is the competitive advantage that has made the brand strong. Right from the outset, Aldi stressed that every article they sold was cheaper than the equivalent elsewhere.

Aldi has turned simplicity of execution into a guiding principle, from its spartan stores to its narrow assortment of around 750 products. Logistics costs play a role in the renting of new branches: the stores must be accessible for articulated trucks and the aisles wide enough for maneuvering pallets. Aldi's stores are usually located either on side streets near high-traffic areas, or on the edge of town where there are good parking facilities and low rental costs. The comparatively narrow assortment of goods ensures simplicity in buying and handling, and the scale advantages give bargaining power in negotiations with suppliers. Aldi also keeps labor costs down by reducing management to an absolute minimum and having notoriously low-headcount central functions.[53]

The rapid rise of Lidl, Germany's second-largest discounter, is challenging Aldi in its market leadership. Lidl has copied many basic business processes from Aldi, but offers a wider assortment of products, with some 1,200 different stock-keeping units, including substantially more branded articles than its competitor. At the end of 2007, Lidl surpassed Aldi for the first time regarding the number of outlets in Europe. In response to this, recently Aldi has also started stocking branded articles such as Ferrero's Kinder Country, Mars, or Bounty.[54]

One brand that has always been excellent in every aspect of execution is Coca-Cola. As early as 1923, the then-CEO Robert Woodruff made execution a key part of the brand by announcing that Coca-Cola should always be »within an arm's reach of desire.«[55] Coca-Cola has stuck to this motto, implementing it around the globe with great attention to detail.

To realize this objective, Coca-Cola has developed new sales channels systematically: in addition to traditional food retailers, gasoline stations, and kiosks, it targets major sporting events and the like. Any remaining gaps in distribution are closed by means of vending machines; there are some one million of them in Japan alone, for example.[56] Coca-Cola continues to develop and perfect these machines, some of which feature the very latest technology, for example in allowing customers to pay by using their mobile phones.

Similarly, Coca-Cola's supply chain management is excellent: the product is always available in every sales channel. This is a critical competitive

What Brands Can
Do, and What
Makes Them
Strong

advantage for an impulse drink such as Coca-Cola, which needs to be available whenever the customer wants it. The product quality is reliable, the packaging is constantly being improved, and the brand has an enormous emotional appeal.[57]

It is top management's job to ensure that day in, day out, the core elements of the brand retain their quality in every aspect. This is no easy task, of course, and things can go seriously wrong, as was demonstrated by the infamous Howard Schultz Starbucks memo, which was leaked to the public in 2007. Schultz had bought the Starbucks chain in 1987, then only a medium enterprise, and transformed the company into a global coffee shop chain with more than 15,000 stores today. In 2000, he stepped down as CEO and became Chairman. In 2007, Schultz had seen enough of what he called »the commoditization of the Starbucks experience.« In a memo to the top leadership group of the company, he criticized a series of decisions that had seemed right on their own merit, but, in sum, diluted the Starbucks brand. For example, the introduction of automatic coffee machines increased the speed of service and efficiency, but destroyed much of the romance and theater that was in play with the old machines. Moreover, the height of the new machines blocked the line of sight the customer previously had to watch the drink being prepared, and made eye contact with the barista near impossible. The introduction of flavor-locked packaging clearly improved the quality of the fresh-roasted bagged coffee, but at the cost of the loss of aroma filling the premises, the perhaps most powerful non-verbal signal Starbucks had in its stores, a signal that stood for tradition and heritage. The streamlining of store design increased economies of scale and satisfied the financial side of the business. However, the stores lost their former soul, the warm feeling of a neighborhood store, and instead seemed increasingly like just a random chain of stores. Finally, the increasing number of merchandising articles, such as music CDs, took Starbucks even further away from its heritage as a coffee shop. »In fact, I am not sure people today even know we are roasting coffee. You certainly can't get the message from being in our stores,« Schultz wrote. Less than 12 months later, Schultz returned as CEO to help the company to refocus on the original Starbucks experience. One of his first decisions was to stop selling hot breakfast sandwiches. These sandwiches accounted for revenues of around USD 500 million for the company. But on the other hand they made the stores smell like cheese factories, and the baristas felt like they were working in a fast-food store. »The decision and the courage it takes to remove something when there's pressure on the business – like the sandwiches – is emblematic that we're going to build for the long term and get back to the roots and the core of our heritage, which is the leading roaster of specialty coffee in the world.«[58] Most recently, Starbucks ordered all-new espresso machines from Thermoplan, a relative newcomer in a category long dominated by traditional Italian manufacturers. Thermoplan's USP: the coffee is ground individually for each cup of espresso. What is more, the machines are much lower than the current models, making customer-to-staff eye contact possible again. Schultz says the new machines are meant to bring back some of the old charm: »Once again, it will be all about the coffee.« James Alling, responsible for the company's overseas business as President of Starbucks International, sums up the brand management challenge as follows: »There's always going to be someone selling okay coffee at a low price. It's our job to make sure Starbucks is more than okay coffee.«[59]

The secret of brand success: The brand trinity

Strong brands develop and prosper by achieving a harmonious trinity of *art, science,* and *craft*, whatever their particular focus. High-powered brands need powerful content – in both emotional and rational terms – and an image that remains consistent over many years without ever becoming outdated. Top brands maintain and develop their strength by tracking their status continuously according to qualitative criteria, such as their image, and quantitative indicators, such as market share and customer loyalty. Strong brands are also executed in a consistent and effective manner, as reflected in the marketing and through the actions of the entire organization, from CEO to the front line.

Only a few brands have been able to achieve this balance and maintain it over the longer term. Top brands do not usually excel in all three disciplines, as already mentioned. Instead, they tend to have one or two areas where they really shine, and they keep plowing away at the other areas.

Ikea: Brand trinity, Ingvar's way

Ikea, the largest furniture retailing chain in the world, provides another good example of how it is possible to produce harmony in the trinity of *art, science,* and *craft*. As of early 2008, the Swedish furniture empire operated more than 242 home furnishings stores in 24 different countries (273 stores in 40 countries if one includes franchised stores) and had revenues of EUR 19.8 billion in 2007. Around the globe, Ikea still stands for the concept launched by founder and owner Ingvar Kamprad in the 1940s: furniture and home accessories that combine function and design at affordable

Fig. 1.16: Ikea: Expertly developed into a global brand

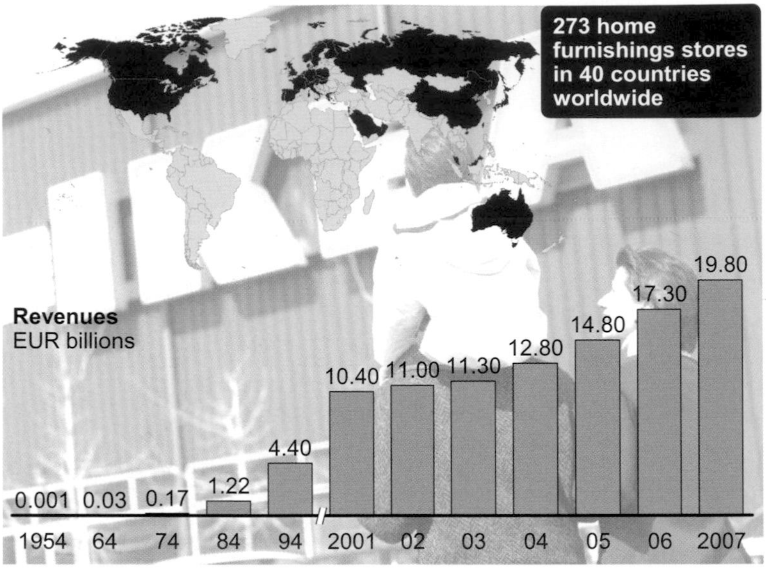

273 home furnishings stores in 40 countries worldwide

Revenues
EUR billions

1954	64	74	84	94	2001	02	03	04	05	06	2007
0.001	0.03	0.17	1.22	4.40	10.40	11.00	11.30	12.80	14.80	17.30	19.80

Source: Inter IKEA Systems B.V.

prices (Figure 1.16). What is it that makes Ikea so successful? It is a unique combination of the three pillars of successful brand management: *art, science,* and *craft*. Ikea excels in all three areas, with a particular spike in the »art« department. The combination leads to a unique, almost cult-like relationship between the brand and its customers, a deep attachment rivaled by perhaps only a handful of other brands. Ikea reports it had 583 million customers in 2007. This is a magnitude achieved by very few companies and certainly by no other furniture retailer. Let's look at the three components in some more detail to find out how Ikea does it.

Art: Creative communication leads to emotional appeal. Since 1985, the company's campaigns have spotlighted ingenious solutions using Ikea products. When launching new stores in Tokyo, Ikea ran a major outdoor campaign in the city center and near the stores. Among other things, Ikea built 14 small »Ikea 4.5 museums.« In an area measuring just four and a half tatami mats (around 7.5 square meters) – slightly smaller than the standard room size in Tokyo – Ikea showcased how to make the most of small rooms by using Ikea furniture. The campaign led to a new record in store visitors and was awarded a Cannes Golden Lion in 2007.

What Brands Can
Do, and What
Makes Them
Strong

In Germany, Ikea uses a more emotional communication strategy. In its 2007 brand campaign, Ikea created a fictional town to illustrate the almost unlimited possibilities that come with the company's flexible, multi-purpose products. The campaign not only achieved great results in terms of recall, but created real impact by increasing the number of store visitors by 9 percent compared to the same period in the previous year, and by making Ikea the number one choice in 37 of 40 regions. In the previous »Started living yet?« campaign, Ikea depicted home decoration as a lifestyle activity. The slogan they came up with has already become an advertising classic and won the agency, Weigert Pirouz Wolf, a silver Effie in October 2004.[60] Today, Ikea is the best-known home furnishings brand in Germany, with current brand awareness at 87 percent (up from 77 percent four years ago). Other brand funnel measurements are similarly healthy; 47 percent of consumers say they are likely to make a purchase; the industry benchmark.[61]

Ikea's most important tool for building relationships with its customers, apart from the stores themselves, is its catalog. Some 191 million copies of the catalog are printed worldwide in 56 different editions and 27 languages. In most countries, this circulation is rivaled only by Harry Potter and the Holy Bible.[62] Most recently, Ikea has introduced the unique concept of a personalized catalog. Customers have their pictures taken at one of the stores, and pick up a copy featuring themselves, rather than a random model, in the living room shots. It brings customers back into the stores, and it creates a deep personal connection to the brand. The personalized catalog is yet another example of how Ikea's communication conveys the impression that the brand has a lot more to offer than just decently priced pine furniture. The message conveyed is that Ikea is a lifestyle brand, that its products are attractive and stylish, and that they enrich people's lives.

Science: Systematic consumer research ensures fact-based brand management. Ikea engages in extensive market research to ensure the brand meets consumers' needs at key touch points, such as the product and store experiences. Partnering with AC Nielsen, Ikea explores what it calls the »three moments of truth« in its research: the shopping planning in the consumer's home, the core brand experience at one of the Ikea stores, and the product experience back at home. Using a wide range of observational techniques, Ikea aspires to generate the type of insights that enables the company to develop inventive interior decoration solutions that actually *solve* consumers' problems, rather than (just) pieces of furniture. One example are the extensive store design tests conducted by the company to ensure customers are guided so that they get to see the entire assortment. Says

Wim Neitzert, former Head of Ikea Southern Germany: »We tested what happens when we let customers roam freely in the store. They made straight for the exit, missing the bulk of our floor space. Also, 40 percent of the shoppers never get to the second level in a traditional store. That's why we make them *start* on the second level.« Products are also thoroughly tested to ensure their quality and generate improvement ideas. For example, children's furniture is deliberately pressure-tested in the rough environment of child-care facilities.

Consumer feedback management is another area in which Ikea adheres to strict and systematic standards to ensure continuous input on the quality of its products, stores, and services. To get consumers' help in the area of product innovation (and foster loyalty at the same time), Ikea runs design contests (»fiffiga folket«). The winning designs are made into prototypes. As far as the store experience is concerned, consumers are rewarded with food vouchers for their improvement ideas, the best of which are presented directly to the store manager. On a broader level, shopper insights derived from cash registers (where shoppers are asked to give their ZIP codes) and, more importantly, the »Ikea family« loyalty card, are pooled and leveraged systematically. Partly thanks to targeted offers based on these insights, Ikea generates more than half of its total revenue with non-furniture items, including small design items, as well as food and snacks. One of the insights behind the revenue mix is the low purchase frequency of larger items Ikea detected in the shopper data. But even when their apartments are fully equipped with the necessities, shoppers can be lured to come back for smaller, more decorative items, or for the sheer experience. Says CEO Anders Dahlvig: »We are trying to become like Disneyland.«[63]

Craft: Consistent global brand promise, carefully adapted to local needs. At Ikea, brand management is all about consistency. The store experience (size, number of stock-keeping units, corporate identity, and color scheme) is largely standardized globally. The same is true for the product lineup. Says product developer Tomas Lundin: »A product must do well in all countries to be successful.«[64] The catalog, however, can be more easily and cost-efficiently adapted to make Ikea come across as a company that thinks globally, but acts locally. Although produced in Sweden for all countries, the props reflect local peculiarities. Television sets in the American edition are bigger than anywhere else, while the Chinese edition features kitchen supplies with Chinese *kaishu* characters.

To ensure a stream of consistently well-designed and innovative products, Ikea shares the common language and standards of its »design culture« even outside the organization, especially with its supplier community.

What Brands Can
Do, and What
Makes Them
Strong

Innovative designs and materials are consistently requested and rewarded to ensure a steady influx of simple, reliable, and profitable products. Ikea summarizes its brand promise as follows: »To offer a wide range of well designed, functional home furnishing products at prices so low that as many people as possible will be able to afford them.«[65]

Ikea's version of the brand trinity of art, science, and craft is so successful that it is even spinning off its unique approach to a new category. In 1996, Ikea set up a joint venture with the building company Skanska with the aim of building apartments and houses. For decades, Ikea had been providing furnishings for homes, so it seemed logical to start building the homes, too. BoKlok (Swedish for »smart living«), as the joint venture was called, set itself the task of developing living spaces that were of high quality, yet affordable. Priced competitively at around EUR 150,000 per unit, more than 1,000 houses are built every year in Scandinavia. Who knows what's next?

Strong brands can survive occasional mistakes

Trying to maintain the consistency of a brand at the same time as keeping it up-to-date is a tall order, and managers sometimes make mistakes. But consumers forgive strong brands for such mistakes if they are corrected quickly and in full: brands can, in fact, immunize at least against minor to medium hiccups in corporate conduct. A classic example is that of New Coke in the 1980s. In the attempt to counter falling market shares and consumers' preference for Pepsi-Cola in taste tests, Coca-Cola's management decided, in what was in retrospect surely a moment of madness, to change the recipe of Coca-Cola, a closely guarded secret that had remained unaltered for 99 years. After extensive testing, the company believed it had come up with a mixture that people would prefer to both Pepsi-Cola and traditional Coca-Cola. The results of consumer acceptance tests looking into the psychological aspects of a new Coke were also positive. Thus in April 1985, the company decided to break all taboos and launch New Coke, spending a suitable amount on advertising, of course.

To say that New Coke was something of a disappointment is probably a masterpiece of understatement. The financial writer Stuart Crainer described it as »the marketing mistake of the century.«[66] The disaster took its course, accompanied by a storm of protests from customers. »It's as if God had dyed the grass pink,« complained a Coca-Cola fan. The company had to deal with up to 8,000 calls of complaint each day and was

What Brands Can
Do, and What
Makes Them
Strong

bombarded with tens of thousands of letters of protest. Coca-Cola was taken by surprise by this massive rejection of its product but soon took appropriate remedial steps: it admitted to making a mistake and asked its customers for forgiveness. Within three months, in July 1985, the old Coca-Cola was reintroduced under the name Classic Coke and enjoyed a massive comeback. New Coke was still supplied to retailers, but its market share plummeted until it was finally dropped by the company. The big surprise for many was that the New Coke affair did not inflict any serious damage on the company's sales: between 1984 and 1985 sales rose by 7 percent. Coca-Cola had inadvertently proved that no brand is stronger.

It is not only Coca-Cola that can survive shooting itself in the foot. Mercedes-Benz shows how a strong brand can overcome even the most spectacular public relations disaster. In November 1997 the company had assembled journalists from the Swedish automobile journal *Teknikens Varld* to watch its brand new A-Class compact perform the 50-meter slalom-shaped »Avoidance Maneuver Test,« commonly known as the »elk test.« At 60 kilometers an hour, watched by television cameras and with journalists aboard, the A-Class teetered on two wheels and then turned over. One of the journalists was injured. Soon the television footage was being broadcast around the world, and the A-Class had been labeled unstable and unsafe. New deliveries of the A-Class were suspended until February while engineers considered the situation. In just 19 days, Mercedes announced a plan and a timetable by which to set the problem aright. The introduction of an »electronic stability program« (ESP) cost Mercedes a little more than EUR 80 million. Within two months, the number of positive articles about the A-Class's stability had overtaken the negative. Brand perception for attributes like high safety standards or high reliability did not even suffer during October and December 1997. Up to 95 percent of sales targets for the first year were achieved even though delivery was stopped for a few weeks. During the whole product life cycle of seven years, Mercedes sold 1.1 million cars of the A-class model. For any lesser brand, failing the elk test so spectacularly would have inflicted severe, long-term damage. For Mercedes, there was no lasting damage to its reputation for producing well-engineered cars.

Companies also make mistakes with business-to-business brands, but even here the strong brands survive. In 1994, a calculation flaw came to light in the Intel Pentium chip, which according to Intel advertising was the best on the market. Thomas Nicely, a professor of mathematics at Lynchburg College, Virginia, had noticed that his new PC, fitted with an Intel Pentium processor, made rounding errors from the fifth digit onwards, even when making simple divisions. He complained to Intel straight away, but the company's reaction was dismissive. It said that it saw no grounds to take action, since the rounding error would be a problem for only a few specialists and thus not significant for the average user.

That this position wasn't sustainable should have been immediately evident to Intel. Intel's response provoked Professor Nicely to vent his anger publicly on the Internet at the end of October 1994. This led to over 10,000 further responses, all of which expressed outrage at the calculation flaw on Intel Pentium processor. The problem was discussed in more than 20 chatrooms, and soon a parody of Intel's co-branding slogan was making the rounds: »Intel inside. Can't divide.« The stakes rose and soon news media from around the world were reporting on the plight of the dumb chip.

Somewhat surprisingly, Intel was still unwilling to listen. Andy Grove, CEO of the computer chip giant, even went so far as to demand that customers prove they were carrying out such advanced mathematical calculations before he would replace the faulty chips. This led to practically full-scale mutiny against Intel.

The problem escalated still further in early December 1994. Computer giant IBM, then one of Intel's major clients, announced that it would replace all personal computers fitted with Intel Pentium processors and that from now on no computer would leave IBM's production sites with the faulty chip fitted. The stock markets were not slow to react; within minutes Intel's stock fell dramatically, reaching the point where trading was temporarily suspended. To top it all, the *New York Times* awarded Intel a Consumer Deception Award. After having made a mountain out of a molehill, a few days before Christmas 1994, Intel finally reacted. Three board members publicly apologized to customers and offered to replace all processors free of charge, no questions asked.[67]

The most surprising thing was that following these events, Intel's sales did not ultimately suffer: between 1993 and 1995, sales revenue almost doubled from USD 8.8 billion to USD 16.2 billion.[68] The lesson is clear: strong brands like Intel can even compensate for (temporary) poor management.

Strong brands that get the trinity of *art, science,* and *craft* right have such power over customers that, in extreme cases, they can even function successfully without any research and development, production, logistics, or sales of their own. Branded companies such as Red Bull, Adidas, and Porsche can ignore certain parts of the value chain altogether, outsourcing certain steps to third parties without damaging the perception of the brand.

Red Bull, for example, has concentrated from the very beginning on the concept of the drink and its communication. The company does not own a single bottling plant, warehouse, or delivery truck. The fruit juice company

What Brands Can
Do, and What
Makes Them
Strong

Rauch, based in Rankweil in western Austria, takes care of worldwide production, and forwarding agents transport the product to the various national distribution companies.[69]

Similarly, the Adidas brand is so strong that consumers aren't worried about how the shoes are produced. This enabled Adidas to switch its production strategy in order to copy that of its major competitor Nike, which since its creation in 1962 has never owned its own production facilities and has had all its goods produced in Asia. »We don't need production expertise,« said CEO Herbert Hainer.[70] To minimize production cost, Adidas outsourced over 95 percent of production to independent third-party manufacturers, primarily located in Asia. As a consequence, in 2007 only 6 percent of all employees worked in production, compared to 27 percent in 2001 when Hainer took over.[71]

It is undoubtedly the case that brands such as these are highly valuable assets, but for those struggling on the periphery the question remains: How does one develop a strong brand? The remaining chapters set out the right approach to brand management, analyze what makes a strong brand strong, lay out the tools that managers will require for a full understanding, and look at the ingredients for success in developing a strong brand.

1.3 McKinsey BrandMatics® – Mastering Brand Management

More myths surround the process of creating and developing a brand than any other area of business management. This is because the art of a brand flatters the consumer, appeals to the emotions, and develops a resonance that it is hard to quantify. Indeed, the wit, originality, and imaginativeness of successful brands such as Red Bull, Apple, and Nike show the importance of the intuitive and the creative. Strong brands are able to create their own myths. Iconic brands such as Chanel have even been immortalized in the works of artists such as Andy Warhol (Figure 1.17).

Nonetheless, despite the undoubted importance of art, strong brands are seldom developed by art alone but by a careful mix of art, science, and craft; the role of science and craft in this mix often being underestimated. Take Red Bull, for example, a brand with strong appeal to the younger generation. Science played a vital role in developing a detailed understanding of the brand's market appeal to target groups; craft was central too, in ensuring outstanding execution and consistency in the management of the brand.

Fig. 1.17: Example of "branded" artwork: Chanel

Source: The Andy Warhol Foundation, Inc./Art Resource, NY

The story of Red Bull is illustrative of how art, science, and craft combine. Dietrich Mateschitz, the founder of Red Bull and former marketing manager of Blendax (later acquired by Procter & Gamble), spent five years developing his idea for launching a sweet, caffeinated beverage. His idea was to introduce a pick-me-up of the type he had come to know and appreciate during his travels in Asia. The brand concept was carefully planned. He developed every process in detail, from packaging to communication. Mateschitz then ensured the precise coordination of all the processes before launching and distributing the beverage in its first market, Austria, in 1987.

He was equally meticulous in introducing the drink in each subsequent market. Each national market was divided into »cells,« in which the goal was to make consumers aware of the new product within three to six months. The initial customer base was sought out and developed by specially trained teams that focused on locations where the young congregate, such as universities or clubs and bars. Once a loyal customer base had been developed in this manner, wide-scale distribution followed, typically two to three months later, using all the normal distribution channels, with a slight preference for restaurants over food retail. Only then did classic advertising begin, focusing primarily on cinema, television, and radio.

The focal point of the Red Bull communication was and remains the product itself, with its clear positioning: stimulation of mind and body. The design and color scheme of the drink cans reflect the product's positioning and demonstrate the meticulousness of the brand's planning. Some 100 different draft designs were commissioned before the final ones were chosen.

The intention of the final design is carefully thought out. The bull embodies strength, courage, and stamina. Cold colors, blue and silver, were used to represent the intellect, while hot ones, red and gold, were used to symbolize emotion. On the Red Bull Energy Drink, the logo is rounded out by the claim, »vitalizes body and mind.« This claim was reinforced with the slogan »Red Bull gives you wiiings!« This catchy motto is designed to convey individuality, innovation, fun, and agility and thus promote the emotional values of the brand.

Red Bull's advertising creativity is kept direct, simple, and fun using cartoon sketches that, through their humorous depiction of a bull, have achieved a high degree of consumer recognition. New motifs and ideas for advertisements follow the same design principles, ensuring that the product remains unmistakable for its market.

Red Bull has gone well beyond traditional media in many aspects of its campaigns. Nowhere is this better exemplified than in its sports event Red Bull *Flugtag* (or »Flight Day«). These events are an innovative and creative form of marketing that supports the claim »Red Bull gives you wiiings!« Teams have to build and fly their own aircraft. What constitutes an aircraft is left to the imagination of the teams participating in the event. The teams are judged on three criteria: distance, creativity, and showmanship. The first Red Bull *Flugtag* took place in Vienna, Austria, in 1992. Since then, more than 70 events have been held around the world – from Wellington, New Zealand, to San Francisco, California, – attracting huge publicity and up to 300,000 spectators each time. By 2007, Red Bull achieved sales of more than 3.5 billion cans (Figure 1.18). Red Bull succeeded in achieving high brand recognition and market success through a well-measured combination of art, science, and craft.

There is no question that the creativity of advertising agencies is crucial in brand management – and will remain so for the foreseeable future. But their creativity needs to be applied in the context of the science and craft of brand management, and not independently of them. For many companies, accepting this simple fact requires stepping back from their current way of doing things, and it involves a complete readjustment of their brand management approach. It is senior management who must set this course.

It is clear that management, in its desire to integrate the creative aspect of brand management with its other management processes, is looking beyond market research institutes, and turning increasingly to academia and strategic management consultants. Until now, there has been little light even here. Instead, management is presented with a nearly incomprehensible jungle of concepts that all make the claim that they lay bare the economic value of the brand without producing the necessary transparency.

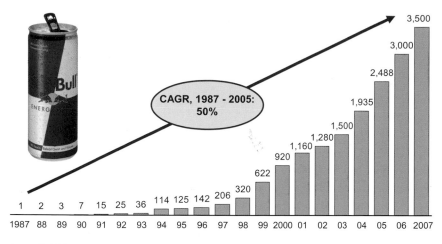

Fig. 1.18: Red Bull: Painstaking planning gave the brand wings
Red Bull unit sales
Cans, millions:

CAGR, 1987 - 2005: 50%

| | 3,500 |
| 3,000 |
| 2,488 |
| 1,935 |
| 1,500 |
| 1,280 |
| 1,160 |
| 920 |
| 622 |
| 320 |
| 1 2 3 7 15 25 36 114 125 142 206 |

1987 88 89 90 91 92 93 94 95 96 97 98 99 2000 01 02 03 04 05 06 2007

Source: Red Bull

That this situation should prevail today is somewhat surprising. Whereas top management is used to receiving concrete facts and figures for revenues, returns, capital ratios, costs, volumes, and productivity every Monday from virtually all areas of its business, branding has so far been the exception to the rule. This handicaps sound decision making and alienates top management from the management of one of the most vital components of success – the control of the brand. This is something we seek to redress here.

We believe that top management requires the integration of art, science, and craft for systematic, fact-based brand management. This requires creating a degree of transparency that has so far been lacking in the branding world. This transparency is essential if executives are to base their brand management decisions on sound foundations. The following chapters present a holistic approach to brand management. This includes systematic, qualitative indicators (e.g., brand image) and quantitative ones (e.g., revenue potential). We refer to this approach as BrandMatics®, as it provides a systematic framework for brand management. In the following pages, the individual tools and detailed concepts are organized into three topic areas: measuring, making, and managing power brands.

53

What Brands Can
Do, and What
Makes Them
Strong

Measuring brands

When setting out to measure the brand, the starting point should always be a thorough survey of the current perception of the brand, from the point of view of both established customers and potential new customers.

The *Brand Relevance Calculator* provides answers to the often-neglected (but critical) question of whether and to what extent it is worthwhile to develop and invest in brands in a certain sector.

The *McKinsey Brand Diamond* is a framework for conducting a complete (image) analysis of all of a brand's emotional and rational benefits to reveal what the brand represents to customers and non-customers.

The *Brand Purchase Funnel* gauges the strength of the brand in comparison with competing brands, from the point of the initial awareness of the consumer to that of repeat product purchase by loyal customers. This analysis provides information for the refinement of the brand. It also helps to identify which brands in a brand portfolio will be the most effective in reaching a target group of customers.

Using the *Brand Potential Approach,* brand managers can quantify the brand sales potential embedded in the purchase funnel and reallocate their brand investments in order to tap this potential.

Making brands

Building on the results of the brand diagnosis, the next step is to identify what actions need to be taken to build the brand.

First, the *Analysis of Brand Drivers* helps identify those factors and customer needs that distinguish strong brands from weak ones in the purchase funnel. This defines the strategic direction and the initiatives that need to be taken to grow the brand. In most cases the fundamental *Brand Promise* will need to be adjusted (or even completely reformulated) to take account of the brand's current weaknesses. Of course, for this process to be effective in growing the brand, the brand promise needs to be anchored in the actual capabilities of the company's operating units (rather than those that the company might wish for).

The next step is to engage in *Brand Driver Disaggregation*, and create a Matrix of Options for Action. This step translates abstract brand elements into practical and understandable terms, for instance, for the creative brief. Techniques such as pathways analysis help ensure that the brand is manageable within the company.

Brand Portfolio Management: While the professional management of a single brand requires the right mix of *art, craft,* and *science,* the task of managing an entire portfolio of brands is substantially more complex. However, with the support of some selected portfolio instruments, the Brand-Matics® approach can also be used for systematic and successful Brand Portfolio Management.

Many brands appeal to their customers in a primarily rational manner and thus appear relatively unattractive emotionally from a customer's point of view. To overcome this weakness, the *Brand Personality Gameboard* provides an analytically grounded and almost playful tool for building or expanding the brand personality, especially with the help of suitable celebrity endorsements and testimonials.

Managing brands

Even a brand with a well-defined brand promise can fail, however, if it is not established consistently across all the relevant stakeholders within and outside the organization. A positive brand image is created through the individual's experiences of the brand on a daily basis. This image will only become anchored in the customers' minds if it is consistent over a long period. The *Brand Delivery Approach* provides a systematic, three-step approach for creating a brand mindset in the organization, for translating the brand promise into concrete actions along all the customer touch points, and for ensuring its longer-term institutionalization.

Once the desired brand promise has been defined and translated into a suitable touch point strategy, the new or improved brand content will need to be put in place. This requires identifying the optimal budget and suitable media – the basic concept of *Marketing Return on Investment.*

The *Brand Cockpit* then ensures that the main criteria for brand success are continually measured and assessed. If the market environment changes or competitors react, the bird's-eye view created by the Brand Cockpit allows the brand manager to initiate actions to manage the brand in a timely manner.

Finally, in order for brand management to remain a top management priority, an appropriate *Brand Organization* is needed. The brand organization concept explores the range of alternative organizational structures that can develop effective and efficient processes to integrate all business units around the goals of brand management. These alternatives include, for instance, those that appoint a brand management board or that establish marketing and consumer intelligence departments that report directly to the CEO.

BrandMatics® is a holistic and consistent approach to brand management. That said, successful brand management is nearly always the result of strong partnerships. Often a key factor for success is the involvement of external service providers, that is, hiring a market research agency to conduct surveys or commissioning an advertising agency to design ways to communicate the brand proposition. The following chapters cover all these topics. They reflect the experience of McKinsey's Marketing Sales Practice regarding how senior management teams have used the tools and concepts of BrandMatics® to put brand decisions on a more objective footing, combining qualitative brand features with precise and reliable economic data, and thereby minimizing the risk of making serious investment errors.

What Brands Can
Do, and What
Makes Them
Strong

Interview with Pieter Nota:
»Brand Communication is a
Top Management Responsibility«

NIVEA is one of the world's leading personal care brands. The brand was launched in Germany in 1910/11 with a gentle skin cream in a characteristic blue tin that has long since become a packaging icon (see the illustration between chapters 2 and 3). NIVEA Creme remains the brand's trademark product to this day. Over the decades, NIVEA has expanded into neighboring categories such as body care (1963), men's care (1986), hair care (1991), deodorant (1991), and decorative cosmetics (1997), as well as into new territories such as China (1938), South America (1966), and the United States (1978). As of 2008, the brand is present in more than a dozen categories and some 160 countries. Pieter Nota is the Executive Board Member for Brands at NIVEA's parent company, Beiersdorf AG. A Dutch native, Pieter Nota started his career at Unilever in the Netherlands and held positions with the company in four different countries, most recently as Marketing Director for Germany. Jesko Perrey spoke to Pieter Nota about brand management at NIVEA.

Jesko Perrey: Let's start with a personal question. What is your daily beauty routine like?

Pieter Nota: It starts with a shower. My favorite shower product from NIVEA is the Lemongrass and Oil Shower Gel. Then I shave, using NIVEA Extreme Comfort, our newest shaving gel, and treat my skin with NIVEA for Men DNAge, with anti-wrinkle ingredients. DNAge was originally only for women, but this year we have extended it to men's care. It's really perfect for my age, early forties, to fight the first wrinkles.

Jesko Perrey: Yet you're a youngster compared to the NIVEA brand. NIVEA dates back to 1911; its hundredth anniversary is coming up in three years. What is the secret behind its success?

Pieter Nota: The company's first success was an excellent and honest product, NIVEA Creme. In marketing, everything starts with consumer needs. NIVEA Creme succeeded by meeting those needs. It's a very honest, nicely textured cream that can be used for many different needs. Over the years, consistent brand management has become another key success factor. I strongly believe that great brands are made by consistent and constant development. Zigzag courses are a danger for brands. Consistency matters most with tangible things like product or packaging design. If it's blue and white, people know it's NIVEA. The brand is very recognizable for consumers. But consistency is also important in other areas. There is very little fluctuation in Beiersdorf's top management. You can almost count the CEOs the company has had in its 100-year history on one hand. This has contributed to a very consistent approach to brand management. But I also think that Beiersdorf stays loyal to its roots: honest products of high quality. Despite a lot of internal discussions about our rigid standards, in general, we'd rather go for the higher quality and sacrifice a little profitability.

Jesko Perrey: What fascinates me is that you see NIVEA everywhere: it seems as if NIVEA is a brand for everybody. Yet experts tell you that a brand is only successful if it is positioned for a specific target group. How does NIVEA manage to focus on specific needs and appeal to so many different people at the same time?

Pieter Nota: NIVEA is clearly a mass brand. Indeed, it is for everybody. It's comparable to the Volkswagen Golf. It is almost classless. This is due to NIVEA's core values. They are centered around care, something that is really good for your skin, quality you can rely on. That's in everybody's interest. In conjunction with consistent brand development, this explains NIVEA's wide appeal. People probably are sometimes positively surprised by our product offerings, but NIVEA will never negatively surprise you by poor product quality or weird moves you wouldn't expect from the brand.

Jesko Perrey: In light of NIVEA's recent advertising campaigns, how have you managed to combine its emotional benefits with very concrete, functional benefits like »anti-aging« or »for shiny hair«?

Pieter Nota: Your question brings me to another success factor of NIVEA – innovation. NIVEA has always been innovative, both in expanding existing categories and in opening up new categories for the brand. In the care and cosmetics sector, we are very carefully opening up the brand right now. We are enhancing care, the traditional core of the brand, with beauty. Good care is a main contributor to beauty. This is something that will allow the brand to strengthen its footprint in exciting categories like hair care and decorative cosmetics. NIVEA will, of course, always stay true to its roots. If you look at the images we use and the way we show skin, it's always about care. You don't necessarily have to use the word »care« if you communicate it through the images.

Jesko Perrey: Consistency has always been one of the main strengths, if not the key competitive advantage of NIVEA. Isn't it a challenge to balance the kind of innovation you have just described with the need for consistency?

Pieter Nota: Yes, of course that's a big challenge, especially with regard to the future development of the brand. NIVEA, as of 2007, is the biggest skin and beauty care brand in the world, generating over EUR 6 billion in retail sales. Being so big and being so active in so many countries makes it a challenge to stay loyal to your roots. Take packaging design. The Lemon Grass shower gel I mentioned before is a borderline case because the bottle is a little too greenish, and maybe not quite »blue and white« enough. But when you look at the shelves, the NIVEA range is still predominantly »blue and white« – even though we have over 500 different products under the NIVEA brand alone. This is where the guidance of the top management is very important. Brand communication is a top management issue, so strong individual leaders who identify with the brand are a key success factor.

Jesko Perrey: Recently, there has been a lot of press coverage of Dove's »Campaign For Real Beauty,« highlighting its creativity. How important is creative advertising for NIVEA?

Pieter Nota: I think creativity is a means to an end, not an objective in its own right. Consumers always come first. What we offer our NIVEA customers are really honest skin and beauty care products with excellent product performance. This is what they appreciate about NIVEA. I think creativity has to be managed in a consistent way. It is always very tempting to go for a very creative short-term solution, like using humor in advertising. It's very tempting but it is rarely productive. Creativity comes into play when we talk about innovation. NIVEA has a very high innovation rate. In advertising, creativity is important for bringing out our new product concepts in a fresh and positive way, but it is not an objective in its own right.

Jesko Perrey: How do you manage your agencies to ensure these principles are reflected in NIVEA's advertising?

Pieter Nota: We work with a very systematic process. Concrete, detailed briefings are a key element. Of course, agencies sometimes have spontaneous ideas and, of course, we listen to them. But the normal process is that they work off the page of very strict briefings. Directional decisions

What Brands Can
Do, and What
Makes Them
Strong

about advertising are made at the executive board level of the company, basically by me. That doesn't mean that I decide on every advertising film or every single execution, but the concepts, the main ideas are decided by me and are not delegated.

Jesko Perrey: What is your perspective on keeping the evolving NIVEA brand alive and consistent across different touch points?

Pieter Nota: It is, in fact, getting increasingly difficult and complex to reach the consumer, especially because there are so many contact and interaction points.[72] What we have really been very adamant about is creating one look and feel for the brand: across all categories, across all the different touch points, across all countries. Take the example of NIVEA face care, e.g., the recent innovation NIVEA Visage DNAge. Across the globe you will find the same kind of images, the same kind of messages, whether you talk about television advertising, print, Internet, outdoor advertising, or point of sale – everything. And, of course, the touch points all reinforce each other. The same is true for different territories. Consider NIVEA's online presence. All our affiliates have the same platform for NIVEA. So if you were to go to the Dutch site, NIVEA.nl, or NIVEA.sa, the South African site, you would find NIVEA has the same look and feel. I think a lot of energy, a lot of efficiency in brand communication can be lost if the different departments don't talk to each other. But getting the mix of touch points right is an increasingly complex matter, depending on which target group we want to reach. This is a very sophisticated part of the business today. We work closely with our media agencies on this. The ultimate challenge is to get the mix of messages and touch points right across all categories and markets, and still maintain a consistent brand image. In terms of brand development, NIVEA will never see a revolution. The brand will always evolve step by step.

If you look at some of the great brands, they are big on consistency: Coca-Cola is red, NIVEA is blue, Marlboro is red. But it goes beyond colors in advertising and packaging. Marlboro is always about the freedom of the Wild West. That's a recipe for success, but it also requires very strong leadership. You need people who really put their foot down and decide where the brand is going. If you let it slip, it will drift.

Jesko Perrey: What is the role of the NIVEA House in NIVEA's touch point strategy? Is it a one-time effort, or do you plan to roll it out to other locations?

Pieter Nota: The NIVEA House is really an experiment in brand experience. We don't necessarily plan to start our own global retail effort. Of course nothing is impossible, but the objective is really to make people experience the brand just by touching and feeling it, getting facial treatments, getting hair and skin care advice. But there's no rush. We are taking our time to find out about the do's and don'ts at this unique touch point. We are about to take the most attractive elements of the NIVEA House and open smaller versions in Berlin and Dubai. If the concept works abroad, there may, in fact, be NIVEA Houses all over the world some day.

Jesko Perrey: From my perspective, marketing is as much a craft and a science as it is an art. Let us explore the science aspect. How do you use insights to develop the NIVEA brand?

Pieter Nota: We are pretty good at gathering consumer insights, but we are not as good as we want to be at gaining *shopper* insights. For the brand, however, our primary objective is to gain consumer insights. We have a new and innovative process in place to understand what consumers expect. It's called InTouch. It's something we've installed globally during the past three years. We have made it a point to empower our local affiliates to gather insights. Of course, we provide them with tools, but it's an illusion to think that, sitting here in Hamburg, we could know better than our Chinese colleagues about what makes the Chinese consumer tick. Once all the insights have been gathered, however, the responsibility for turning them into product concepts lies here in Hamburg with our brand leadership units. Many companies get this wrong: they confuse insights with product concepts and end up with mixed-up responsibilities.

Jesko Perrey: What would you say is Beiersdorf's competitive edge, from a brand management perspective?

Pieter Nota: I think it's the focus that comes from giving top management attention to brand development, and from balancing innovation with consistency, from developing the brand in an evolutionary, not a revolutionary manner, and in maintaining a consumer focus at all times. Of course, it helps that we concentrate on a few big brands, of which NIVEA is number one. As a company, Beiersdorf doesn't have to spread its attention over hundreds of brands. We basically have about 10 active brands and that, I think, gives us a real competitive edge.

Jesko Perrey: Thank you for your sharing the story behind NIVEA's continuing success. To wrap things up, what do you consider your biggest failure in brand management?

Pieter Nota: One significant learning comes to my mind: when I was with Unilever, I managed the »Lätta« margarine brand. I took over the brand from my predecessor, and we came up with a highly innovative product, »Lätta Hoch Zwei«. But in our enthusiasm, we forgot to communicate the benefits clearly. The advertising was pretty provocative and got a lot of attention at the time, but the message was all about emotions. In fact, »Lätta Hoch Zwei« is low in fat and high in natural ingredients that promote well-being. But we simply failed to bring out these tangible benefits. While it wasn't a major mistake for the company, it taught me that you have to balance emotional with rational benefits to create a successful brand. Having learnt this very significant lesson, I now consistently act accordingly. At NIVEA, we use the Brand Diamond to that end. The combination of balance, evolution, and top management attention will ensure NIVEA's success well beyond its centennial.

Notes

1 Kenning, Peter et al, »Die Entdeckung der kortikalen Entlastung,« *Neuroökonomische Forschungsberichte*, No. 1, 2002. University of Münster, Institute for Trade Management and Network Marketing, Prof. Dieter Ahlert. See also »Monetäre Markenbewertung: Die Marke als Kapitalanlage,« *Absatzwirtschaft 2*, 2004, pp. 26–41.

2 Kirchberger, Michael, »Zwei kleine Italiener,« *Frankfurter Allgemeine Sonntagszeitung*, No. 13, 30 Mar 2008.

3 Meffert, Heribert, and Christoph Burmann, »Markenbildung und Markenstrategien,« *Handbuch Produktmanagement*, ed. Sönke Albers and Andreas Herrmann, Wiesbaden: Gabler, 2000, pp. 167–187.

4 E. Leclerc, *press release*, Aug 2004.

5 »How to Resist the Private Label Threat in 2006,« *Datamonitor*, 26 Dec 2005.

6 »Auftritt der Woche,« *Horizont*, 10 Feb 2005.

7 »Der Markenartikel: Die Erreichbarkeit des Wünschenswerten,« *Austria Press Agentur*, 31 Jan 2008.

8 *Die Tabak Zeitung*, various years, 1997 to 2004.

9 »Better ROI From YouTube Video Than Super Bowl Spot,« *Advertising Age*, 29 Oct 2006.

10 Lippert, Barbara, »Pick-up Artistry,« *AdWeek*, 21 Jan 2008.

11 Bloom, Jonah, »Ogilvy, Dove miss chance to turn bad press into ›debate‹,« *Advertsing Age 42*, Vol. 79, No. 19, 12 May 2008, © Crain Communications; Collins, Lauren, »Pixel Perfect – Pascal Dangin's Virtual Reality,« *The New Yorker*, 12 May 2008.

12 Knudsen, Trond, »Confronting Proliferation in Mobile Communications,« *The McKinsey Quarterly* Web exclusive, May 2007, www.mckinseyquarterly.com.

13 Based on H&M (4 percent of sales volume), GAP (3 percent), C&A (4 percent). See also »Mode zum Anfassen,«

Manager Magazin 1, 2004, p. 74; »Gestreifte Schals wärmen die GAP-Aktie,« 28 Feb 2003, *www.faz.net*; »Zu modisch: C&A verlieren Kunden,« *Stuttgarter Nachrichten*, 7 Jun 2005, p. 10.

14 *Annual reports*, Inditex Group and H&M, various years.

15 The US distilled spirits market, Impact Databank, 2007.

16 Fischer, Marc, Fabian Hieronimus, and Marcel Kreuz, »Markenrelevanz in der Unternehmensführung: Messung, Erklärung und empirische Befunde für B2C-Märkte,« *Arbeitspapier Nr.* 1, ed. Klaus Backhaus, Heribert Meffert, Jürgen Meffert, Jesko Perrey, Jürgen Schröder, Düsseldorf: McKinsey & Company, Inc., 2002.

17 Knudsen, Trond, »Confronting proliferation in beer: An interview with Carlsberg's Alex Myers,« *The McKinsey Quarterly*, Web exclusive, May 2007, www.mckinseyquarterly.com.

18 Results from a search performed by ABI/Inform of international academic publications.

19 Brand loyalty barometer from the 2001 Consumer Analysis by Bauer Media KG and Axel Springer Verlag AG, www.bauermedia.com.

20 Martin, Andrew, »I'd Like to Sell the World a Coke,« *New York Times*, 27 May 2007.

21 Recent scientific research shows that the influence of rational vs. emotional brand aspects on the purchase decision varies across different industries and that it can be measured analytically. See, for example: Freundt, Tjark: »Emotionalisierung von Marken,« Wiesbaden: DuV, 2005.

22 *ADAC, AutomarxX,* various magazine issues. »Audi still leads Germany's ADAC AutoMarxX list: For the fourth time in a row, Audi has secured the top spot in the half-yearly AutoMarxX survey by Germany's motoring organisation ADAC,« *AutomarxX*, 13 Dec 2007, www.media.adac.de.

23 »Bekleidungskette C&A zeigt Expansionsgelüste,« *Frankfurter Allgemeine Zeitung*, 7 Jun 2005, p. 20; Weber, Stefan, »C&A trotzt der Krise im Textilhandel,« *Süddeutsche Zeitung*, 3 Jun 2003, p. 22; Werner, Markus, »Werbung und Wirkung,« *Textilwirtschaft*, 20 Feb 2003, p. 54.

24 *Annual reports*, BMW Group, various years; Ward's Automotive Yearbook, 2008; »BMW: We may need a green brand,« *Automotive News*, 21 Jan 2008; »Why BMW deep-sixed its people mover plan,« *Detroit News*, 22 Jan 2008.

25 Roosdorp, Alexander, »Coca-Cola: Leistungspflege durch agile Marktkommunikation,« *Best Practice in Marketing*, ed. Torsten Tomczak and Sven Reinecke, Vienna: Wirtschaftsverlag Carl Ueberreuter, 1998, pp. 241–251.

26 »Corporate Identity – nur anders,« *Wirtschaftswoche*, 25 Apr 1996, p. 134.

27 Dingler, Rolf, »Der Prototyp für erfolgreiches Markenmanagement,« *FVW International*, No. 22, 14 Oct 1997, p. 112.

28 *Die Tabak Zeitung*, various years.

29 *Brand Marketers Report*, Interbrand, 2007.

30 Ramge, Thomas, »Das Comeback der Wow-Wows,« *Brand Eins*, Mar 2005, pp. 44–50.

31 Hase, Michael, »Hippe Handys, träges Marketing,« *Werben & Verkaufen*, 13 Jan 2005, pp. 22–24.

32 www.samsung.com.

33 »Samsung's Goal: Be Like BMW,« *BusinessWeek*, 1 Aug 2005, www.businessweek.com.

34 »Samsung steigert Qualitätsgewinn,« *Frankfurter Allgemeine Zeitung*, 26 Apr 2008, p. 17.

35 www.effie.org.

36 »Die alten Marketing-Modelle funktionieren nicht mehr,« *Frankfurter Allgemeine Zeitung*, 21 Jun 2008, p. 16.

37 www.canneslionslive.com and www.gunnreport.com. For details on the ADC/McKinsey study, see »Der Code erfolgreicher Werbung,« *Werben & Verkaufen*, 4 Oct 2007; Perrey, Jesko, Nicola Wagener, and Carsten Wall-

mann, »Kreativität + Content Fit = Werbeerfolg,« 2007.

38 Pletter, Roman, »Kullmanns Moment,« *Brand Eins*, Feb 2008; Reuter, Heiko, »Weg mit der Kohle,« *Werben & Verkaufen,« 20 Sep 2007.

39 »Vergiss es, Baby,« *Der Spiegel*, 18 Feb 2002, p. 76.

40 Michael, Bernd M., »Wenn die Wertschöpfung weiter sinkt, stirbt die Marke,« *Zeitschrift für Betriebswirtschaftslehre 1*, suppl. vol., 2002, pp. 35–56.

41 »Klimaschutz-Tarif vom Billiganbieter,« *Energie & Management,* 15 Jan 2008; and Flauger, Jürgen, »Billigstrom – der zweite Anlauf,« *Handelsblatt*, 17 Apr 2008, www.handelsblatt.com; »Strompreise beflügeln E.ON-Geschäfte – E wie Einfach gut gestartet,« *dpa/verivox*, 15 Aug 2007, www.verivox.de; Bernotat, Wulf H., »Ausführungen zur Ordentlichen Hauptversammlung der E.ON AG,« 30 Apr 2008, www.eon.com; »FTD: Jeder vierte Stromwechsler bei ›E wie einfach‹,« 20 May 2008, www.clever-stromvergleich.de.

42 Ad spend per car according to »Wir wollen wieder auf Platz eins,« *Werben & Verkaufen*, 6 Mar 2008; »VW ist Werbekönig,« *Telebörse*, 28 Jan 2008, www.teleboerse.de.

43 *Stern MarkenProfile*, No. 10, Nov 2004.

44 *Annual reports*, Beiersdorf AG, various years.

45 Davidson, Andrew, »Puma's top cat Jochen Zeitz plays it cool,« *The Sunday Times*, 24 Feb 2008.

46 Fischer, Gabriele and Ralf Granel, »Porsche ist nicht mehr Porsche, wenn uns ein Großer übernimmt,« *Brand Eins*, Feb 2000.

47 »The Secrets behind McDonald's and Its Hamburgers,« *Business World*, 15 Sep 2000, p. 31.

48 Upton, David, »McDonald's Corporation (abridged),« *Harvard Business Online*, 3 Oct 2003, www.harvardbusiness.com.

49 Hickmann, Craig, and Christopher Raia, »Incubating Innovation: Companies Must Leverage the Full Spectrum of Innovation, from the Incremental to the Revolutionary,« *Journal of Business Strategy*, May 2002, p. 14.

50 Saal, Marco, »Krise bewältigt – Zauber verloren,« *Die Welt*, 28 Jan 2005, p. 15; Frühbrodt, Lutz, »Marktführer meldet sich zurück,« *Horizont*, 5 May 2005, p. 17.

51 Knudsen, Trond, »Confronting proliferation in mobile communications: An interview with Nokia's senior marketer,« *The McKinsey Quarterly*, Web exclusive, May 2007, www.mckinsey-quarterly.com.

52 Rücker, Martin, »Der gute Ton macht die Musik,« *Süddeutsche Zeitung*, 19 Nov 2003, p. 36; »Vivaldi unter der Motorhaube,« *Bonner Generalanzeiger*, 1 Mar 2003, p. 72.

53 Brandes, Dieter, *Die 11 Geheimnisse des Aldi-Erfolgs*, Frankfurt: Campus Verlag, 2003.

54 »Discounter Lidl wächst abermals schneller als Aldi,« *Die Welt*, 31 May 2005, p. 11; Schlitt, Petra, and Steffen Klusmann, »Angriff des Super-Krämers,« *Manager Magazin*, Sep 2003, p. 38; »Lidl bleibt dem Rivalen Aldi dicht auf den Fersen,« *Financial Times Deutschland*, 21 Oct 2003, p. 7.

55 Case studies, *The Times 100*, www.tt100.biz.

56 Yamada, Michele, »Japan's Vending Machines Want to Talk to You,« *The Industry Standard*, 4 Feb 2001, www.thestandard.com.

57 Wieking, Klaus, »Das Ende der Leidenschaft,« *Werben & Verkaufen*, 13 Jan 2005, p. 17.

58 »Howard Schultz's Starbucks memo,« *Financial Times*, 23 Feb 2007, www.ft.com; Gillespie, Elizabeth, »No more breakfast at Starbucks,« *The Providence Journal*, 1 Feb 2008.

59 Lindner, Roland, »Die neue Bescheidenheit von Starbucks,« *Frankfurter Allgemeine Zeitung*, 22 Mar 2008, No. 69, p. 20; interview with James Alling, President of Starbucks International, »Wir dachten, die Kunden kommen von

What Brands Can
Do, and What
Makes Them
Strong

selbst,« *Frankfurter Allgemeine Zeitung*, 21 Mar 2008, www.faz.net.

60 At the end of 2003, one year after the start of the campaign, Ikea drew up the balance sheet: the target of 7.5 percent more visitors to the stores had been exceeded by almost 100 percent, and customer figures had developed almost as strongly; sales growth had beaten the target of 7.5 percent within one year; and – particularly impressive in terms of efficiency – the advertising budget for 2003, with all the successes, was still EUR 1 million below that of the previous year. Janke, Klaus, »Effie 2004: Die Sieger. Die Werber meistern schwere Aufgaben,« *Horizont*, 14 Oct 2004, p. 22.

61 Wegner, Ralf, »Stil-Mix wird noch beliebter,« *Horizont*, 13 Nov 2003, p. 24.

62 Stevenson, Suzanne, »Ikea catalogue beats the Bible,«, *Evening Standard*, 27 Aug 2002, www.thisislondon.co.uk. For further details on Ikea, »Innovaro Innovation Briefing,« Nov 2005, www.innovaro.com; Furniture report on »fiffiga folket,« Mar 2008; Klingner, Susanne, »Der Spion, der aus der Kälte kam,« *Süddeutsche Zeitung Magazin*, No. 3, 2007; Meuli, Kaspar, »Blonde Möbel: Ikea ist überall gleich, einzig in Amerika macht man Konzessionen,« *NZZ Folio*, Oct 2001, www.nzzfolio.ch.

63 »EXTRA: Ikea ist Kult – Ein Mann vermöbelt die Welt,« 23 May 2003, www.stern.de.

64 Meuli, Kaspar, »Blonde Möbel: Ikea ist überall gleich, einzig in Amerika macht man Konzessionen,« *NZZ Folio*, Oct 2001, www.nzzfolio.ch.

65 »IKEA Facts & Figures 2007,« www.ikea-group.ikea.com.

66 Schmeh, Klaus, *Die 55 größten Flops der Wirtschaftsgeschichte: Krimis, Krisen, Kuriositäten*, Frankfurt: Redline Wirtschaft, 2002, p. 33.

67 Case study by Töpfer, Armin, »Rechenfehler im Pentium-Prozessor von Intel im Sommer 1994,« www.krisen-navigator.de.

68 *Annual Report*, Intel Corporation, 1998.

69 Clef, Ulrich, *Die Ausgezeichneten: Unternehmenskarrieren der 30 deutschen Marketing-Preisträger*, Munich: Clef Creative Communications, 2003.

70 Hirn, Wolfgang and Heide Neukirchen, »Fabrik-Verkauf,« *Manager Magazin*, Nov 2001, pp. 294–302.

71 *Annual reports*, Adidas, various years.

72 Throughout the remainder of the book, the term »touch points« is used to refer to all points at which brands communicate or interact with consumers, or consumers with brands. This is meant to include classic advertising, below-the-line communication such as PR, and also promotions and point-of-sale interaction as well as aftersales and service interactions. »Contact points« is used synonymously, if at all.

2.
Measuring Brands

2.1 The Brand Relevance Calculator: Assessing the Relative Importance of Brands

From financial services to telecommunications or electricity supply, there is hardly an industry today that does not hope to profit from the growing value of brands. And it is not just in established areas, such as consumer goods, where brands are important. Take retail banking, for instance. In a survey of 6,000 banking customers from 10 different European countries, respondents rated the brand as the second most important decision-making criterion (following their proximity to a branch) when choosing a bank. Furthermore, customers are willing to pay higher prices and fees for branded banking services. For a standard commodity, such as a current account, for example, some strong branded banks are able to charge more than twice as much as their lesser competitors. No wonder that Peter Wuffli, former CEO of UBS, said, »In the financial service industry, a strong brand is critical: it's one of the major factors that attracts clients. Strengthening and simplifying our brand identity and systematically capitalizing on it forms a key part of our organic growth drive.« The past success of the UBS brand appears to prove him right: UBS grew its brand value by more than EUR 3 billion from 2004 to 2007 (Interbrand).[1]

Though brands are increasingly important, they are not a universal panacea. A closer examination of the business-to-business (B2B) sector makes this point well. A study by Sattler and PricewaterhouseCoopers reveals that the B2B picture is much more complex than it appears at first sight. Whereas brands overall represent only 18 percent of company value in B2B markets, in the consumer goods segment this figure rises to an average of 53 percent for durable goods and 62 percent for non-durables.[2] In other words, brands are much more relevant to certain businesses than they are to others. A recent update of the survey revealed that the overall importance of brands continues to increase across all industries. While brand value accounted for 56 percent of company value in 1999, this rose to 67 percent in 2005.

Power Brands. H. Riesenbeck and J. Perrey
Copyright © 2009 WILEY-VCH Verlag GmbH & Co. KGaA, Weinheim
ISBN: 978-3-527-50390-2

Although the power of brands is certainly increasing, one shouldn't jump blindly onto the brand wagon. Fact-based brand management requires a good understanding of the role the brand plays in consumer decision making in a given industry. The mere assumption that »brands are always important« is misleading and can result in poor investment decisions. Like all marketing tools, brand investment must be assessed in terms of its potential economic impact and, specifically, in terms of its influence on consumer purchasing behavior. If a brand is unlikely to have a significant impact on consumer behavior, there is little point in making considerable investment in it. Nonetheless, this is a mistake that has been made time and again.

The German electricity sector is a particularly good example of how brand recognition does not necessarily translate into a positive impact on the bottom line. Mirroring the consumer goods industry, German electricity suppliers attempted to introduce a number of brands to the market (e.g., RWE's Avanza, PreussenElektra's ElektraDirekt, and EnBW's Yello, all launched in 1998). These brands were all relatively successful in securing name recognition at a level similar to that of leading consumer goods companies. However, of the three, only Yello is still around today (not counting eprimo, a local player taken over by RWE in 2007). Following its large initial investments in brand building, it has achieved almost 100 percent aided brand awareness. That the other two brands didn't survive shows that increased brand recognition doesn't necessarily translate into higher earnings as a matter of course. Yello's competitors had invested similar amounts and achieved levels of brand recognition similar to Yello's. Only in the niche market of »environmentally friendly« electricity supply has brand-name recognition had a consistent influence on purchasing behavior. This exception is significant because »green electricity« brands have translated successfully into greater financial returns for a number of electricity companies in the Netherlands as well as in the United Kingdom.

For private electricity consumers, there are other criteria that they consider more important than the brand in determining their choice of electricity provider. If brands have had any role in shaping the electricity market, it has only been at the local level. Surveys indicate that some 80 percent of consumers prefer their electricity to be supplied by their local public utilities company. This clearly shows that, prior to any brand investment, it is crucial to have a sound knowledge of the relevance of branding in shaping consumer purchasing in the specific sector in which the company is operating. Making generalizations or abstractions derived from other sectors that might well have little relevance to the sector concerned is likely to lead to poor investment decisions.

Determining brand relevance

The starting point of BrandMatics®, therefore, is to create transparency about the extent to which the brand shapes purchasing behavior in a given industry and market. The brand is only relevant and worthy of increased management attention if it can influence the behavior of consumers or intermediate companies, or a company's position in the war for talent.

In order to establish the relative importance of brands to various product segments, McKinsey conducted research into the German business-to-business (B2B) and business-to-consumer (B2C) markets in collaboration with a group of researchers from three well-respected German research institutions: the Marketing Centrum Münster at the University of Münster, the Institute for Innovation Research at the University of Kiel, and the Institute for Retail and Marketing at the University of Hamburg.[3] For the purpose of measuring brand relevance, a comprehensive scale was developed and validated according to scientific standards. The brand relevance measurement scale not only captures the overall relevance of brands as perceived by customers, but also breaks it down into the three functional components touched on in chapter 1:

- **Information efficiency as the time factor:** Brands make it easier for the consumer to gather and process information about a product.
- **Risk reduction as the trust factor:** Selecting a brand-name product reduces the consumer's (subjective) risk of making a purchase mistake. Brands create trust in the expected performance of the product and provide continuity in the predictability of the product benefit.
- **Image benefit as the expressive or »identity« factor:** Brands may offer the additional benefit of helping the customer foster a desired image. This benefit can be directed either outward or inward. It is directed outward when the customer uses the brand to cultivate a certain public image. The benefit is directed inward for purposes of self-expression or in identification with certain values and ideals.

The three brand functions cover the entire purchasing and consumption process. Information efficiency assists customers prior to the purchase decision, risk reduction influences the actual decision-making activity, and the image benefit emerges in the subsequent consumption phase.

The measurement instrument was applied in two large-scale national and international studies to a broad selection of B2B and B2C markets. The results provide interesting insights that are of high managerial relevance.

The importance of brands in consumer markets across the world

More than 12,000 consumers across the world took part in a representative online survey during the summer of 2006.[4] The survey covered 9 countries and 18 product categories. The countries covered were France, Germany, Japan, Poland, Russia, Spain, Sweden, the United Kingdom, and the United States. The product categories included fast-moving consumer goods, consumer durables, services, and retailers.

Across all countries and the 18 selected product categories, the three with the highest brand relevance are cars, beer, and mobile phones (Figure 2.1). In the mid-field rankings, the survey consistently identified mail order, express delivery services, and scheduled flights. Finally, and unsurprisingly, the product categories in which brands are least relevant across all countries are drugstores and paper tissues.

Which brand functions are important for which products?

The survey made it possible to determine the strengths of the selected brand functions in the individual product markets. The combination of these values with the relative importance of the individual brand functions produces the overall brand relevance shown in Figure 2.1. The analysis of consumer evaluations across the nine countries indicates that risk reduction is the most important brand function, followed by the image benefit and the information efficiency function. Analysis of the specific brand functions provides a number of further insights (Figure 2.2).

Information efficiency in the case of recurring purchase decisions

Information efficiency is the dominant brand function in the case of fast-moving consumer goods. The common factors in these markets are the consumer can select from many brands, the consumer must make a decision relatively quickly, and, of particular relevance, the consumer makes decisions on a regular basis. It should come as little surprise that information efficiency is particularly important in the case of beer and cigarettes: apart from obligatory health warnings, the packaging of these products is largely standardized, i.e., there is little variation in the shape and size of beer bottles and cigarette packs. What little space isn't taken up by health warnings consists almost entirely of brand-defining elements that reveal

Fig. 2.1: Overall relevance ranking in B2C: How important are brands to consumers in different product categories across the world?

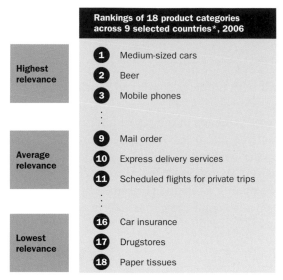

Rankings of 18 product categories across 9 selected countries*, 2006

Highest relevance
- 1 Medium-sized cars
- 2 Beer
- 3 Mobile phones

⋮

Average relevance
- 9 Mail order
- 10 Express delivery services
- 11 Scheduled flights for private trips

⋮

Lowest relevance
- 16 Car insurance
- 17 Drugstores
- 18 Paper tissues

* Countries in sample: France, Germany, Japan, Poland, Russia, Spain, Sweden, UK, USA
Source: MCM/McKinsey, 2006

little else about the product. Since in-store trial is not an option, consumers are entirely dependent on the brand to remind them of past associations or their previous experience with the product (if any) to guide them in their purchase.

Information efficiency loses importance when the consumer takes more time to make purchase decisions in order to collect information about various offers. This is the case, for instance, with durable consumer goods such as television sets and computers, but also in service sectors, such as car insurance.

Risk reduction for high-end consumer goods

The higher the purchase price and the lower the purchase frequency, the more important the brand becomes as an instrument of risk reduction. If a given purchase accounts for a large share of the consumer's budget and this item will not be replaced for a long period of time, the consequences of a poor decision are much greater than is the case, for example, in fast-moving consumer goods with a low purchase price. Unsurprisingly, medium-sized cars top the ranking for the role of brands in risk reduction,[5] followed by mobile phones and television sets. For drugstores or paper tissues, risk reduction plays only a secondary role. Even high-profile services such as banking are only located in the middle of the list.

Image benefit with publicly displayed products

Not only are cars at the top of the ranking for risk reduction, but they are also at the top of the global list for image benefit. They are followed by designer sunglasses and, more surprisingly, mobile network operators. Image benefit is also an important brand function across all countries with respect to mobile phones, beer, and cigarettes. By contrast, image benefit is of limited relevance in retail categories like drugstores and product types like paper tissues.

Fig. 2.2: Ranking of selected B2C product markets by brand function

Rankings of 18 product categories across 9 selected countries*, 2006			
	Information efficiency	Risk reduction	Image benefit
Highest relevance — 1	Beer	Medium-sized cars	Medium-sized cars
2	Cigarettes	Mobile phones	Designer sunglasses
3	Medium-sized cars	TV sets	Mobile network operators
⋮			
Average relevance — 9	TV sets	Scheduled flights for private trips	Express delivery services
10	Express delivery services	Designer sunglasses	Scheduled flights for private trips
11	Mail order	Bank accounts	TV sets
⋮			
Lowest relevance — 16	Drugstores	Car insurance	Detergents
17	Car insurance	Drugstores	Drugstores
18	Paper tissues	Paper tissues	Paper tissues

* Countries in sample: France, Germany, Japan, Poland, Russia, Spain, Sweden, UK, USA
Source: MCM/McKinsey, 2006

Image benefit is derived from influencing the perception of others as well as from one's own identification with the brand. The results of the study make sense intuitively. Sunglasses, for instance, are a prestige object visible to all. The same is true for cars and mobile phones. Even beer and cigarettes, although fast-moving consumer goods, are on display when consumed and possess very specific attributes, about which consumers care a great deal. Drinkers send very different messages about themselves by being seen with a pint of Guinness or a glass of Heineken, a half-liter bottle of Newcastle Brown Ale or a can of Bud Light. The same goes for cigarettes. As a legendary 2006 commercial for House of Prince, Denmark's only cigarette manufacturer, famously put it in the Prince Denmark brand claim: »It's not for everyone.«

The results clearly demonstrate that the relevance of brands and the importance of brand functions vary considerably across product markets. Although brands play an important role in consumer decision making in all countries covered in the survey, the question arises whether brands are equally important in every country. The answer to this is important in shaping a company's global marketing strategy.

Brand relevance across countries

Figure 2.3 provides a ranking of the overall brand relevance across the nine selected countries.[6] Russia, the United States, and Poland head the list. Brands possess the lowest overall relevance in Japan, Sweden, and Germany. Is this ranking useful? We believe it is. It is not surprising that brands have such a high importance in a country such as the United States where the ideas of economic freedom and individual choice have been paramount for a long time. After all, it was in the United States that the principles of modern marketing were born. In the highly competitive American market, brands play an important role in guiding consumer decisions and providing means of self-expression. By contrast, consumers in Poland and Russia are confronted with a high level of uncertainty due to the rapid transition of their economies from a fully regulated system to one of liberal markets. Individual accountability for the choices one makes as a consumer is a very recent development. The former communist markets have gone from hardly any choice at all to an almost infinite number of alternatives. This can lead to information overload for consumers. In this context, brands are an important instrument for reducing uncertainty and risk. Brands therefore serve as a compass to guide consumers through the jungle of products and services.

73

Fig. 2.3: Brand relevance ranking across countries: In which countries do consumers focus most on brands?

* Average ranking across all 9 countries and 18 product categories
Source: MCM/McKinsey, 2006

This helps explain why respondents in Poland and Russia consider information efficiency and risk reduction as highly important brand functions, ranking these higher than respondents in any other country (Figure 2.4). The United States heads the list when it comes to the image benefit of brands, followed by Russia and the United Kingdom. It makes perfect sense for the United States and the United Kingdom to score high on this dimension. The Hofstede system, which differentiates countries along several cultural dimensions, such as power distance, individualism, and uncertainty avoidance, assigns the highest degrees of individualism to the United States and the United Kingdom.[7] Brands are a perfect means of self-expression in today's individualistic societies, a trend Eastern European countries seem to be adopting very quickly.

One may be surprised to find Japan, Sweden, and Germany at the bottom of the ranking lists in Figures 2.3 and 2.4. First of all, it should be noted that although these lists rank countries relative to each other, they do not tell us anything about the absolute level of brand relevance. The analysis of individual product markets shows that brands are highly relevant to consumer decision making in all three countries, even though this relevance is

Fig. 2.4: Ranking of brand relevance by function across countries: Which brand function is most important?

Deviation from average*	Brand relevance by country and brand function, 2006		
	Information efficiency	Risk reduction	Image benefit
Deviation > +10%	1 Russia 2 Poland 3 USA	1 Russia 2 Poland 3 USA	1 USA 2 Russia
Deviation -10 to +10%	4 Spain 5 France	4 France 5 Spain 6 UK	3 UK 4 Poland 5 France 6 Japan 7 Spain
Deviation < -10%	6 Japan 7 UK 8 Germany 9 Sweden	7 Sweden 8 Germany 9 Japan	8 Sweden 9 Germany

* Average ranking across all 9 countries and 18 product categories
Source: MCM/McKinsey, 2006

higher in other countries. In Japan, Sweden, and Germany collective values, such as common welfare and a sense of duty, play an important role. In addition, Germans and Japanese are said to be very rational and to strive for perfection. It is probable that these values influence the decision making of consumers in these countries; this might explain why brands have a somewhat lesser importance compared to countries such as the United States or Russia. Furthermore, Germany has experienced a bargain craze in recent years, as exemplified by the increasing market share of discount retailers and private labels. No-frills players have consistently outgrown the market average since 2000. For example, budget carmakers Kia and Skoda have achieved growth rates of 14.5 percent and 9.3 percent respectively, at a time when the German car market has effectively stagnated at an annual growth rate of just 0.5 percent (2000 to 2006). Similarly, price-value players, such as the Spanish apparel manufacturer/retailer Zara, have outperformed their respective markets in Germany. In this context, the relatively low importance of the brand function »image benefit« in Germany is not much of a surprise.

Fig. 2.5: Variance of brand relevance across countries in selected product categories

Rank in overall brand relevance among 18 selected product categories			
Scheduled flights for private trips		**Medium-sized cars**	
France	1	France	2
Germany	8	Germany	2
Japan	4	Japan	1
Poland	9	Poland	2
Russia	14	Russia	3
Spain	15	Spain	3
Sweden	17	Sweden	1
UK	14	UK	1
USA	10	USA	1

Source: MCM/McKinsey, 2006

Brand relevance of product categories within countries

We saw that the product categories beer and medium-sized cars head the list of brand relevance worldwide (see again Figure 2.1). However, this ranking is not uniform across all countries in every product market. For example, the importance of airline brands for private trips varies substantially across countries (Figure 2.5). In France and Japan, airline travel belongs to the group of categories with the highest brand relevance, whereas it's in the group with the lowest brand relevance in the United Kingdom and Sweden. Again, a look at the Hofstede system of cultural characteristics might provide an explanation for this outcome. The French and Japanese both score high in terms of the »uncertainty avoidance« scale developed by Hofstede, while the United States and Sweden score lowest on this scale. Airline travel is perceived as risky by many people, and this can be a source of serious stress for some travelers. Brands are an important signal of quality and risk reduction, increasing the relative importance of brands in societies that are more focused on uncertainty avoidance. These intercultural differences regarding brand relevance are also reflected in the success of discount airlines with consumers in different countries. In the United Kingdom and Sweden, where the relevance of airline brands for private trips is relatively low, the market share of discount airlines is – not surprisingly – relatively high with around 34 percent in the United Kingdom and some 31 percent in Sweden.[8] In Japan, only one percent of international flights are made with low-cost airlines. This low market share reflects the relatively high importance of brands and perceived quality in this product category.

Although brands are equally important across all countries, their relative importance in specific categories varies significantly by country. It is therefore necessary to look at product markets country by country in order to identify any differences that might exist in brand relevance.

Brand relevance in Western European countries

The ranking of product categories within the three largest economies of the European Union reveals some significant differences. While cars belong to the highest brand relevance group in all three countries, scheduled flights for private trips and fast-food restaurants are part of this group in France, but not in Germany or the United Kingdom (Figure 2.6). We have already provided an explanation for the high rank of scheduled flights. The importance of brands in the fast-food business in France, the home of fine cooking, is somewhat unexpected. However, it mirrors the market situation fairly well. One would expect that in markets with high brand relevance for fast food there would be more room for the development of multiple brands, and this is indeed the case in France. Strong national chains, such as Quick Burger, have been established alongside the dominant American players such as McDonald's and Burger King.

At the same time, it comes as no surprise to see that brands are highly relevant to beer consumers in Germany and the United Kingdom, both home to notoriously passionate drinkers of barley-based beverages. At the bottom of the list, car insurance belongs to the group of categories with the lowest relevance. This is also true for paper tissues in all three countries. The low relevance of brands in car insurance accords with the fact that, at least in the German market, car insurance is a low-involvement category for most consumers and has, as a consequence, been driven almost purely by price competition over the last few years.

Fig. 2.6: Brand relevance by country: How important are brands to consumers across product categories in Western European countries?

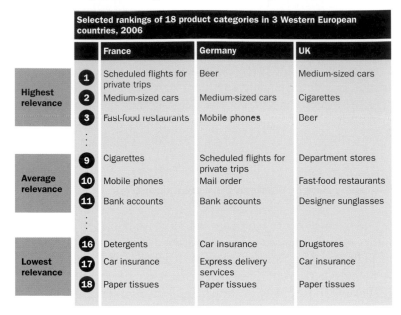

Selected rankings of 18 product categories in 3 Western European countries, 2006			
	France	**Germany**	**UK**
Highest relevance — 1	Scheduled flights for private trips	Beer	Medium-sized cars
2	Medium-sized cars	Medium-sized cars	Cigarettes
3	Fast-food restaurants	Mobile phones	Beer
⋮			
Average relevance — 9	Cigarettes	Scheduled flights for private trips	Department stores
10	Mobile phones	Mail order	Fast-food restaurants
11	Bank accounts	Bank accounts	Designer sunglasses
⋮			
Lowest relevance — 16	Detergents	Car insurance	Drugstores
17	Car insurance	Express delivery services	Car insurance
18	Paper tissues	Paper tissues	Paper tissues

Source: MCM/McKinsey, 2006

Brand relevance in the United States and Japan

Different categories head the list of brand relevance in the United States and Japan (Figure 2.7; note that the lists have been shortened; not all industries referred to in the text below appear in the exhibit). In the United States, the importance of brands is especially pronounced in service markets. Express delivery services is ranked number three and categories such as mobile network operators and fast-food restaurants are among the top ten categories. As in the United States, brands are highly relevant in Japanese service markets (in categories such as mobile network operators and scheduled flights for private trips), but we also find consumer durables, such as television sets and designer sunglasses, among the categories that have the highest relevance. Japan has strong brands in consumer electronics, and this might have contributed to the higher importance of these brands compared to other categories. Japanese customers are among the most valuable customers for luxury goods; the high-ranking position of sunglasses corroborates this observation.

Fig. 2.7: Brand relevance by country: How important are brands to consumers across product categories in the world's largest economies?

Selected rankings of 18 product categories in the USA and in Japan, 2006		
	USA	**Japan**
Highest relevance — 1	Medium-sized cars	Medium-sized cars
2	Beer	TV sets
3	Express delivery services	Mobile network operators
⋮		
Average relevance — 9	Mobile phones	Bank accounts
10	Scheduled flights for private trips	Beer
11	Designer sunglasses	Cigarettes
⋮		
Lowest relevance — 16	Department stores	Detergents
17	Bank accounts	Drugstores
18	Drugstores	Paper tissues

Source: MCM/McKinsey, 2006

Brand relevance in Eastern European countries

Although the Cold War ended nearly 20 years ago, Eastern Europe still feels the long-term effects of decades of centrally planned production. A closer look at Poland and Russia provides a number of interesting insights into this area. While cars and mobile phones lead in both countries, mail order is a category with high brand relevance in Poland but with significantly lower relevance in Russia (Figure 2.8). Although there are many parallels in the economic and political histories of these two countries, it is not correct to assume that there will be complete consistency in the consumption behavior of the two groups of consumers.

Fig. 2.8: Brand relevance by country: How important are brands to consumers across product categories in Eastern European countries?

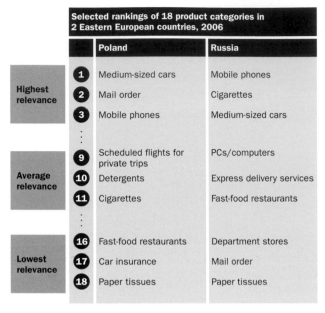

Selected rankings of 18 product categories in 2 Eastern European countries, 2006		
	Poland	**Russia**
Highest relevance 1	Medium-sized cars	Mobile phones
2	Mail order	Cigarettes
3	Mobile phones	Medium-sized cars
⋮		
Average relevance 9	Scheduled flights for private trips	PCs/computers
10	Detergents	Express delivery services
11	Cigarettes	Fast-food restaurants
⋮		
Lowest relevance 16	Fast-food restaurants	Department stores
17	Car insurance	Mail order
18	Paper tissues	Paper tissues

Source: MCM/McKinsey, 2006

Implications for brand managers

The survey provides a number of important insights into the functioning of consumer markets across the world. First, it should be noted that brands play an important role in many categories irrespective of the country. We identify a remarkable consistency in the high ratings for cars, beers, mobile phones, and cigarettes. International brand managers should continue to pay attention to the development of truly global brands in these categories, such as BMW, Nokia, or Marlboro. Second, brands apparently fulfill important functions in consumer decision making in emerging economies such as Russia and Poland. This observation suggests that despite the lower buying power of their populations, focusing on a low-price strategy might provide short-term success but is unlikely to be sustainable. Building the brand might well be equally successful in the short term and is likely to establish the roots for future growth. This is especially true given the dramatic rise of Eastern Europe as a market for luxury goods. The Polish luxury goods market, for example, has been growing at a compound annual growth rate of 27 percent over the past three years. Consumers appear to be skipping the value-for-money economy that focuses on brands as efficient carriers of information. After a short period in which brands are used to reduce risk, the most sophisticated brand function, image benefit, quickly becomes the most important one in these markets. As a result, the sales of luxury goods are booming. Other examples of this boom include Dom Perignon fine champagne (Czech sales grew by two thirds from 2004 to 2005, for example) and Daimler's prestigious Maybach luxury sedan. Although a niche brand, Maybach is said to have sold more cars in Moscow than in any other city in the world, totaling some 130 vehicles by mid-2007. Third, the results reveal considerable differences in brand relevance for categories across countries. Marketing managers can use these insights to identify the countries where brand relevance is highest in order to allocate scarce resources effectively. This will also help managers identify and evaluate the strategy options for the international market entry of new products.

Brand relevance in B2B markets

Recent analysis shows that the corporate brand can account for up to 20 percent of B2B companies' stock performance, especially in trust-based industries, such as medical supplies or mail services.[9] The significance of brands in the B2B sector has also been investigated comprehensively in market research in cooperation with Professor Backhaus from the Marketing Centrum Münster (MCM). A total of 769 businesses were surveyed in 2002 in an analysis of 18 German product markets. The study yielded results similar to those for the B2C sector, showing that the relevance of brands varies significantly between product markets.[10] Brand relevance is very strong in switchgear equipment, machine tools, and company cars (Figure 2.9). Brands have the lowest relevance for industrial chemicals; apparently they play a secondary role in such largely commoditized areas. One surprising result of this analysis is that, for some product markets, the relevance of brands in the B2B sector is rated as high as in B2C markets. This indicates that there is much untapped potential for B2B branding. In a separate, recent analysis of the industrial vehicles sector, for example, McKinsey found that soft, even emotional brand attributes, such as »good name,« »good design,« and »long tradition,« can be of the utmost importance, at least to certain groups of purchasing officers. In one case, »brand followers« turned out to be the second-largest segment of buyers at 28 percent of the total market, exceeded only by »value seekers« at 35 percent, but

Fig. 2.9: Relevance ranking in B2B: How important are brands to business customers?

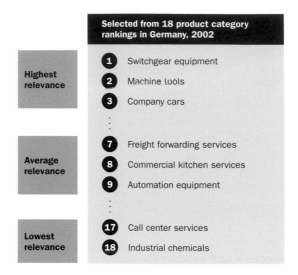

Selected from 18 product category rankings in Germany, 2002

Highest relevance
- 1 Switchgear equipment
- 2 Machine tools
- 3 Company cars

⋮

Average relevance
- 7 Freight forwarding services
- 8 Commercial kitchen services
- 9 Automation equipment

⋮

Lowest relevance
- 17 Call center services
- 18 Industrial chemicals

Source: MCM/McKinsey, 2006

easily outnumbering the »hard bargainers« you might think would dominate this type of category.

These observations should not create the impression, however, that it is sufficient for a business to determine brand relevance merely at the industry-specific level. It is much more important to understand the nature of the functions from which this brand relevance derives on a case-by-case basis. In order to make wise investment decisions, it is necessary to first understand the relative influence of each function and how it applies to certain brands. Not surprisingly, the three brand functions are also highly relevant to the B2B sector, because they reveal interesting aspects of sector-specific brand relevance. In B2B, brands carry information about a wide range of attributes of the respective product or service. Brands reduce the degree of complexity and facilitate communication between those involved in the purchase process: buyers, users, and managers.

Information efficiency is strongest for machines and equipment

The information efficiency function of the brand is at its most important for machines and equipment. Such purchases involve complex goods for which brands offer the customer an important orientation aid. For example, Siemens makes orientation easier for its customers by using the »Sie-« prefix for numerous product names (e.g., SieMatic); the origin and thus the quality of the product are quickly recognizable. In contrast, the situation is quite different for industrial chemicals or alarm systems, where information efficiency plays only a secondary role.

Risk reduction is strongest for large-investment products

»Nobody ever got fired for buying IBM,« or so they say.[11] Opinions differ about this oft-cited statement, but it does serve to highlight the fact that even in the B2B sector, brands can minimize the risk of making wrong investment decisions. Brands often represent a guarantee of consistent quality, and, especially in the area of complex systems, one of compatibility – a strong selling point of Microsoft programs, sometimes dubbed the »network effect.« In the B2B sector, brands thus on occasion appear to act as a sort of insurance, at least against senior management reproach.

Risk reduction is the most important brand feature for products such as switchgear equipment and machine tools. This hardly comes as a surprise, since such equipment is usually very expensive and acquired only infrequently, not unlike cars and television sets in the B2C arena. Moreover, this equipment plays a key role in the manufacturing process of the purchasing company, i.e., any equipment failure is likely to have very serious financial consequences. The acquisition of brand-name products is thus a guarantee for process reliability.

Industrial chemicals are commodity products and are purchased relatively frequently. Here the difference between individual brands is marginal. For this reason, the brand again plays only a secondary role in risk reduction, and brand relevance is correspondingly low in these sectors.

Image benefit is strongest for publicly visible goods

In the B2C sector, the image benefit of a product assists in cultivating the individual consumer's image or in fostering self-expression, as illustrated by the high relevance of brands in the designer sunglasses category. Somewhat less obvious is that image benefits are also an important function of brands in the B2B sector, especially in terms of the reputation of the company and its employees. This effect is strongest for publicly visible products and services, such as company cars, shipping companies, or accounting firms. B2B brands are often used as a way of adopting a partner's reputation as part of one's own. This phenomenon is often referred to as »component branding« or »ingredient branding« and can be observed among computer manufacturers who advertise with the »Intel inside« logo as well as among makers of textiles who highlight the use of GoreTex fabric or Scotch 3M functional elements. The value of a company's own products is enhanced by association with the image of the worldwide market leaders in these categories. There is also an upside for the component brand in this relationship. Following the introduction of Intel's co-branding campaign »Intel inside,« the joint market share of its competitors (AMD, Cyrix, Motorola, etc.) shrank from 44 percent (in 1989) to 17 percent (in 1998).

On the other hand, the public takes little notice of products such as chemicals or alarm systems, and so in these sectors the image function is not important. Such goods are found near the end of the image benefit ranking (Figure 2.10).

Fig. 2.10: Ranking of selected B2B product markets by brand function

Selected rankings of 18 product markets, Germany 2002			
	Information efficiency	**Risk reduction**	**Image benefit**
1	Switchgear equipment	Switchgear equipment	Auditing services
2	Refrigeration equipment	Machine tools	Freight forwarding
3	Machine tools	Company cars	Company cars
⋮			
7	Fire insurance	Freight forwarding	Production lines
8	Canteen services	Industrial automation	Call center services
9	Call center services	Canteen services	System software
⋮			
17	Alarm systems	Industrial chemicals	Alarm systems
18	Industrial chemicals	Call center services	Industrial chemicals

Source: MCM/McKinsey, 2006

As one might expect, the average general brand relevance in the B2B domain is somewhat lower than in the B2C sector. What might be more surprising is that the gap between the two is not overly large and that brands remain highly significant even for the B2B sector.

Determining brand relevance for non-surveyed markets

McKinsey, with the support of the Marketing Centrum Münster (MCM), developed the McKinsey Brand Relevance Calculator in order to predict brand relevance in all other B2B and B2C markets reliably, without resorting to time-consuming and expensive consumer surveys.

The Brand Relevance Calculator is based on the interrelationships ascertained in the study. As an input, the Brand Relevance Calculator requires information derived from a few simple questions, such as what kind of product is involved and how often the product is purchased. Using this information, the calculator predicts the brand relevance in the market in question on a scale from 0 to 5, including both the general brand relevance and the relative importance of each individual brand function.

Fig. 2.11: Luxury sports cars: The image benefit increases the brand's relevance significantly

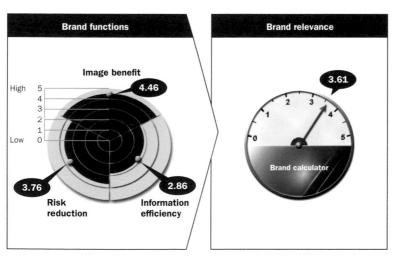

Source: MCM/McKinsey brand relevance survey, GfK

The Brand Relevance Calculator was used to analyze the market for luxury sports cars (Figure 2.11). Unsurprisingly, image benefit is the dominant brand function here. Luxury sports cars communicate prestige, promote self-expression, and help to cultivate a desired image. The second most important brand function is risk reduction, which is determined, among other factors, by the high average purchase price in this category: a major investment like a luxury car calls for a safe bet. Information efficiency, in contrast, is relatively unimportant. This also comes as no surprise, for in making such a purchase, the buyer is normally willing to take considerable time and effort before making a decision.

McKinsey's survey indicated that brand relevance is limited in the B2C domain of the German electricity market. The question arises whether this is also true for business users, or whether it might make more sense for electricity providers to invest in brand building in the corporate market. That this is indeed the case is supported by the fact that significantly stronger brand relevance was observed in the B2B sector (between corporate customers and public utility companies). Here electricity is ranked in the middle of the general brand relevance list. Its brand relevance derives primarily from the risk reduction function and has a value of approximately 2.5. The most plausible explanation for this is that corporate customers are concerned with minimizing any significant risk of power glitches or outages that might cause a stoppage in their production. The reliability promised by a well-respected brand is therefore a competitive advantage. This suggests that there are clear opportunities for brand building in the electricity market, as long as the focus is on the corporate customer rather than on the private consumer.

Implications for management

What lessons can be learned from these findings? The significance of brands for corporate success is indisputable, but this study on brand relevance shows that, because the leverage effect of brands varies from market to market, brand building is not likely to have the same impact in all cases. Companies first need to analyze what relevance brands possess in specific markets as well as the reasons for this pertinence. It is important to note that brands target several markets simultaneously (e.g., B2B, B2C, capital market, recruiting). It is therefore important to analyze the brand relevance in each individual segment as well as to prioritize target audiences and branding decisions accordingly.

Where there is market saturation in the end-consumer market, an analysis of brand relevance can help to avoid serious investment mistakes. In the B2B sector in particular, brand relevance analysis reveals that there are a number of significant market opportunities that companies have yet to capture.

2.2 From Insight to Impact: Customer Insights and Segmentation for Better Brand Management

As we have seen, any meaningful examination of brand relevance has to be differentiated by country and product category. But it doesn't stop there. Even within a single national product market, you have to go a lot deeper to capture the diversity of perceptions and desires. Successful brand managers go beyond the concept of »the consumer« and embrace the fact that several consumer profiles, or segments, coexist in the same market. Their value will increasingly be captured by companies that excel at understanding and serving their respective needs. There is no such thing as »the perfect product« or »superior service.« These days, it's almost always a question of »perfect for whom?« and »superior in which respect?« Take car insurance. While one policyholder favors a no-worries deal with extended personal advice and doesn't care too much about the rates, the next person may simply be looking for the best bargain, be it from his next-door agent or from an anonymous Web site. Needs, attitudes, values, consumption, or usage patterns as well as brand perception depend almost entirely on who you are dealing with (Figure 2.12).

As consumer needs, shopper behavior, and competitors' moves become more complex and changeable, the importance of market intelligence for brand management grows. An increasing number of touch points, brands, channels, and messages – as well as increasingly erratic consumer behavior – make it all the more critical to preempt what customers want. The challenge is to develop ever-more refined propositions without damaging profits through excessive customization. The value pool is deepest where marketing management and customer insights (CI) generation intersect, i.e., at the so-called »insight cells.« Increased proliferation leads to a higher number of cells, resulting in more opportunities to innovate in areas such as products, varieties, packaging, and channels. Pioneers in targeted marketing succeed by understanding and leveraging what happens at these cells.

In short, brand managers need to ramp up their game in customer insight management to stay competitive. It's a simple insight, but like all

Fig. 2.12: Patchwork consumers: They want it all

Patchwork consumers – They want it all

Consumers are erratic creatures. Their behavior is only partially rational. Take environmental friendliness. People will drive their Volkswagen Touareg or Mercedes M-Class SUV to an organic food store. They will buy a crate of "Bionade" [herbal lemonade], a pack of organic buffalo mozzarella cheese, and a pound of pesticide-free tomatoes. Then they store it all in a power-guzzling monster fridge equipped with "BioShield" antibacterial coating. Once the shopping is done, they will watch a documentary on endangered catfish on their 150" plasma screen if they feel like it. But the opposite is no less common: Other consumers ride their bicycles to a discount supermarket and "end up frying rotten meat on a designer stove," as Rainer Grießhammer of the Freiburg-based Öko-Institut puts it. He says we are dealing with "patchwork consumers" pursuing several lifestyles at the same time.

Sascha Lehnhartz, "Bionade im Monsterkühlschrank," Frankfurter Allgemeine Sonntagszeitung, 09.03.2008, No. 10, p. 59

Source: Provided with permission of the Frankfurter Allgemeine Archive.

insights of consequence, it isn't easy to generate and it's even harder to implement. This chapter outlines critical steps along the way towards insights-driven brand management, highlighting the most comprehensive customer insights application of all: segmentation.

Infusing your brand with the consumer's perspective

Customer-insights-driven brand development can take many shapes. It doesn't always have to take the form of a revolutionary product like Apple's iPod that quickly achieved market dominance in the MP3 player category, or Procter & Gamble's category-defining White Strip product that generated more than USD 500 million in new sales annually. Understanding what consumers value can also lead to innovations in the areas of individual product features or even packaging. After all, packaging is one of a brand's most important consumer-facing touch points, especially in the fast-moving consumer goods arena. Henkel's insights-driven product development helped it discover the need for well-designed air fresheners. A lot of potential customers simply considered existing products too ugly for their high-end bathrooms. Henkel introduced the FreshSurfer, an attractively packaged air freshener designed by Alessi, and managed to increase market share by five percentage points within a few months as well as to capture a three-figure price premium over its competitors. Similarly, Henkel pioneered the Theramed toothpaste dispenser as well as the 2-in-1 combination of toothpaste and mouthwash. Both innovations, recently combined in a Theramed 2-in-1 product, have contributed significantly to the sales of Henkel's oral care division and been copied by many competitors in the same and in neighboring categories. Theramed is Henkel's top oral care brand to this day and generated EUR 192 million in revenue in 2007.[12]

So is it all about thinking out of the box? When we take a closer look at how highly innovative companies differ from their competitors, we find that combining creativity with a systematic approach is the key to success. A highly original and very successful campaign like Dove's Campaign for Real Beauty doesn't happen by chance or coincidence; it is the result of careful planning that reflects deep consumer understanding (see below and section 1.2).

Successful innovations are often the result of active, open-minded, and diligent research well beyond the established frame of reference, combined with the will and skill to act swiftly and decisively on the insights generated. Says L'Oréal chairman Lindsay Owen-Jones: »If you wait until the consumer has told you everything, it's too late. The battle has already happened, somebody has taken the prize, and it's gone.«

So what does it take to stay ahead of the pack? Successful marketers generate customer insights that go well beyond the concept of the customer-centric company. They define consumer touch points much more comprehensively to include trial usage, aftersales experience, and word-of-mouth. They also dedicate a surprising amount of time and effort to the generation and analysis of details that often seem irrelevant at first. Many observations unfold their power only when seen from a bird's-eye perspective that combines the experience and expertise of multiple departments. By combining shopper data with sales feedback and branding information, cutting-edge marketers move from a wealth of information to actionable insights. In many cases, these insights can overturn long-established beliefs and necessitate leaving the trodden path. Let's take a quick look at some compelling cases of brand management informed by market research and, specifically, at insights-driven innovations that have led to substantial changes in the way companies do business and manage their brands:

Product feature innovation at Alcoa. Alcoa makes aluminum beverage cans for Coke. Traditionally, as the »owner« of the consumer relationship,

Coke would dictate the product specifications. Alcoa took a chance and looked at consumers' refrigerators. They found that the usual outer packaging of bundled cans didn't fit most fridges. Consumers had to take apart the bundle and refrigerate the cans individually. By developing a crate that fits the standard fridge and can be easily replaced as soon as it is empty, Alcoa boosted Coke's repurchase levels. This led to a 10 percent increase in US can sales within three months and helped strengthen Alcoa's reputation as a brand that listens not only to its customers, but to their customers' customers as well.[13]

Product brand innovation at Pepsi. Pepsi's parent company Stokely-Van Camp produces Gatorade. They understood there was significant demand for a low-calorie fitness drink in the US market, but assumed their product Gatorade Light was sufficient to meet this need. When they researched their target audience in more detail, however, they found it primarily consisted of health-conscious women who prefer water to soft drinks when they work out. But Gatorade Light was considered a soft drink by this audience. So Stokely developed Propel, a flavored-water brand, and discontinued Gatorade Light. Today, Propel contributes USD 155 million in annual sales (2005), making it the top-selling enhanced water in the United States. Effectively, this helped Pepsi to expand its brand portfolio from sweet fizzy drinks to lifestyle beverages.[14]

Brand communication innovation at Dove. In 2004, Unilever conducted a global study on the perceptions and attitudes of women with regard to their personal beauty and well-being. It turned out that a lot of women are actually repelled rather than attracted by the ubiquitous images of ultra-thin models and celebrities promoting beauty products. Only two percent said they felt beautiful, and two-thirds said this was chiefly due to the unrealistic ideal of beauty conveyed by advertising and media. As a result, Unilever launched their Campaign for Real Beauty for its leading personal care brand Dove. The campaign was multi-faceted and sought to challenge the stereotypes set by the beauty industry. The advertisements featured »regular« women who were beautiful in their own way without meeting the usual standards for models. The campaign was appreciated by many consumers. As one of the most daring repositioning efforts in recent branding history, it also generated plenty of buzz and wide media coverage for the Dove brand. Last but not least, it resulted in revenue growth. Since the debut of the campaign, Dove sales have increased significantly: 12.7 percent in 2005 and another 10.7 percent in 2006.[15] (Creativity in advertising is discussed in more detail in section 1.2.). Recently, the credibility of the

Dove campaign was challenged because the print and billboard advertisements showing supposedly natural women had been retouched to hide imperfections.[16]

Brand positioning at Yellow Tail. Originally an export cooperative of minor Australian winemakers started by the Casella family, Yellow Tail was established as a brand in 2001. The brand management team behind Yellow Tail, at W.J. Deutsch & Sons, understood that many American wine drinkers were confused or put off by complicated, old-school wine labels spelling out provenance and quality in a mix of jargon and foreign languages. They went for a clean-cut label featuring clean lettering and the prominent trademark image of a leaping yellow-tailed rock wallaby. Supported by a USD 24 million advertising campaign, one of the most aggressive ever for a wine brand, Yellow Tail leapt from 0 to 112,000 cases in its first year as a branded product. By 2003, the brand had overtaken Concho y Toro and became the number one imported wine in the United States. In 2005, it sold 7.5 million cases. In 2006, Yellow Tail surpassed Sutter Home and became the number one US supermarket brand. Yellow Tail enjoys similar success in the United Kingdom.[17]

None of these innovations would have happened without the generation and application of true customer insights across the entire value chain, from product development and channel management to brand communication. Taking insights seriously, generating them systematically, and applying them comprehensively are sure signs of a truly customer-centric, brand-driven company; these building blocks are described in Figure 2.13. Pioneers in this area move from insight to impact by infusing their brands with the consumer's perspective on an ongoing basis. Most of all, successful customer insights management is about the will to do things differently. Most successful cases of customer-insights-driven growth include the following key success factors:

Successful brand managers combine internal strengths and continuous innovation with **systematic gathering and processing of customer data**. Ensuring data quality and depth is the necessary first step. Leading companies collect data at all important touch points, ranging from checkouts and call centers to online chat rooms and proprietary research or observation. Tesco, for example, combines customer data derived from its loyalty program with market research to achieve new levels of store optimization and customized customer relationship management. Capital One, the credit card company, stores up to two megabytes of information per cardholder and uses it to tailor their terms and conditions. Establishing

Fig. 2.13: Building blocks of a customer-centric company

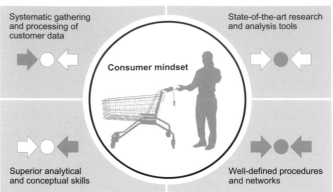

Systematic gathering and processing of customer data

State-of-the-art research and analysis tools

Consumer mindset

Superior analytical and conceptual skills

Well-defined procedures and networks

Source: McKinsey Customer Insights Group

exclusive access to third-party data is another powerful component of integrated customer insights management; some fast-moving consumer goods companies buy scanner data from gas stations and other such out-lets to monitor their front-line performance. Best-in-class players include Procter & Gamble, Henkel, and Beiersdorf in fast-moving consumer goods, and Philips in consumer durables.

State-of-the-art research and analysis tools should be a matter of course, but many companies underestimate the effort required to ensure their research captures actual customer behavior, rather than stated prefer-ences. It is a proven fact that customers are often wrong when asked to describe how they make their choices. Car buyers, for example, will say that safety or fuel economy matter most to them, when in fact design, performance, and value for money drive their choices (Figures 2.12 and 3.2). But even observational techniques don't get you to the holy grail of latent needs, i.e., dormant or inexplicit needs that consumers themselves are unaware of, or unable to realize because there are no products to match these needs. Because it is the very nature of these needs that consumers are not aware of them, they will not articulate them even in focus groups. The accompanying box on ethnography/netnography (on pp. 94/95) provides examples of the latest explorative techniques to help customer insights departments to go beyond the obvious. Bear in mind, however, that while successful players keep innovating on the tool front, the true power of customer insights comes from continuity. If you change your approach too often, you are likely to miss important trends. A recent McKinsey survey of 20 leading North American consumer goods companies revealed that high performers in the areas of insights management tend to have three things in common: standardized data collection processes and formats, frequent updates, and continuous trend observation. So executives at the intersection of insights and branding are well advised to think »motion picture, not snapshot.«

Since the finest tools are useless unless willingly applied, a **consumer mindset** is critical, as exemplified by best-in-class player Procter & Gamble. To counter the mid- to late-nineties downturn the company went through, CEO Alan G. Lafley decreed that the »consumer is boss« and started a major customer insights transformation program. He wanted Procter & Gamble to be the company that is »most in touch« with the consumer. As part of this program, brand managers are assigned to local sales teams temporarily to deepen their first-hand consumer expertise. Lafley himself spends two weeks every year in consumer households and at the point of sale. The »consumer is boss« initiative was rolled out to the entire organization and jumpstarted a new growth wave for the company. Within four years of its kickoff, Procter & Gamble's share price doubled and earnings rose by 9 percent annually.[13]

Having insights is not enough. Their power comes from being applied effectively all across the value chain. As a consequence, well-defined **procedures and networks** are a prerequisite of real insghts-driven impact.

Leading companies make sure insights are reflected throughout their business system from product development to distribution and aftersales management. Customer insights experts act as information brokers and are involved in all consumer-related strategic decision making. Consumer-centric companies move from a »make and sell« to a »sense and response« approach, as Hans-Willi Schroiff of Henkel's business intelligence unit is quoted in a 2005 press release by the company. Building networks includes being open to outside input from the best experts in their fields. At Procter & Gamble these days, up to 50 percent of all innovations are triggered by specialists outside the company. US electronics retailer Best Buy is focusing on the concept of cross-functional insights networks. By integrating shopper research, point-of-sale data, and demographic analysis, Best Buy identified underrepresented shopper segments in certain areas and adapted its store formats accordingly. Stores located near concentrations of affluent male professionals stocked up on high-end home theater equipment and introduced same-day delivery.

Stores closer to soccer moms started featuring softer colors, personal shopping assistance, and children-oriented technology sections. The company says that tests have showed a 7 percent sales uplift after the format change.[18]

It takes superior **analytical and conceptual skills** to process (and understand) the data. Leading companies invest heavily in this area, either by training in-house specialists or hiring external experts on an as-needed basis. Procter & Gamble has gone as far as hiring 60 insight specialists for a task force dubbed »The First Moment of Truth« and dealing exclusively with shopper insights. Because of the many trade-off decisions involved in insights management (tool innovation versus research continuity, depth of insight versus applicability of findings), customer insights excellence is ultimately about finding and developing the right kind of people. You'll be looking for candidates who combine the mindset of a manager with the skill set of an egghead. They're hard to find, so you'd better start looking today.[13]

A word of caution: just as airlines don't trust autopilots to fly their planes without the supervision of human professionals, even the most sophisticated research cannot and should not dictate your brand management actions. It is a combination of deep insights that go beyond the obvious and the kind of business judgment only entrepreneurial experience can bring that will separate the leaders from the followers in insights-driven brand management.

Qualitative Research helps identify Hidden Needs

Quantitative research and measurement are essential to fact-based brand management. But how do you know *what* exactly you should measure? Quantifying brand driver performance is all well and good, but *which* attributes should you even be looking at? One of the key challenges in brand-related insight generation is to go beyond the obvious, to move from diagnosis to prognosis. To stay competitive, understanding today's consumers is not enough. Your brand's future performance will depend on preempting, even shaping, tomorrow's trends and fashions. This is particularly important when it comes to determining the appropriate needs dimensions for a strategic segmentation. But how do you find out what even consumers themselves are not (yet) aware of? This is where qualitative research techniques come in.

While proven tools such as focus groups and in-store shopper observation are still widely used, new ways of generating insights outside the status quo are emerging. One of the most promising techniques is ethnographic research, including its online version known as »netnography.« To identify unfulfilled or hidden needs, you have to develop a deep understanding of consumers in broadly defined purchasing and consumption situations that reflect consumers' general living conditions. There are two advantages to this approach: it allows you to explore new ideas (rather than just test existing concepts), and it centers on the actual brand/consumer interaction experience. It's not meant to off-load the creative achievement to the consumer, but it gives brand managers and product developers much richer input than previously thought possible.

Perhaps the most prominent examples of ethnographic research are street sports events used by companies like Nike and Adidas to investigate brand image and product usage first hand. Procter & Gamble famously took market research from the studio to the bathroom, visiting consumers wherever and whenever shampoo or toothpaste is actually used. Says Procter & Gamble's former CMO Jim Stengel: »We've always tried to get our brand managers out of the building and to experience life like our consumers; I did it 15–18 years ago. But it was, I think, a little bit more programmed back then, a little more focus group-oriented or moderator-driven. What we're now trying to do is let people, without a filter, really be with our consumer and be in their lives. We think that's where a tremendous amount of innovation will come from.«[19]

Tesco recently took a similar approach to overhauling its US store formats in a major two-year customer insights effort. It hired a team of researchers to examine the shopping behavior, eating habits, and lifestyles of 60 American families on site, paying particular attention to the needs of Hispanic consumers. Says Tesco's US CEO Tim Mason: »We literally went into their kitchens and looked in their refrigerators.« One of the major findings was that consumers who have always visited a variety of different stores to buy their groceries are now demanding a one-stop shop for all their purchases. As a result, Tesco developed the »Fresh & Easy« format, aiming to provide shoppers with a one-store »neighborhood market« shopping experience offering about 3,000 products, focusing on fresh meat, vegetables, packaged goods, wine, and beer. Following extensive live tests at a prototype store set up in a Los Angeles warehouse, the first stores using the new format opened in late 2007.

Tesco is gathering online consumer feedback through its Web site www.freshandeasy.com to refine the format and support its national roll-out. While critics say Tesco is underestimating the challenges of the US grocery market, the firm says that it expects the venture to break even in two years.[20]

Ethnographic research is by no means limited to the B2C arena. Hilti, a maker and brand of premium power drills and other handheld tools, uses its own sales force to act as ethnographic researchers. By interviewing and observing construction workers on site, Hilti discovered that construction teams often include workers and engineers from multiple countries and backgrounds. As a result, there are often difficulties with written instructions, no matter what the language. To ensure that tools can be safely and easily operated nevertheless, Hilti introduced a color-coded tool design system: the company's trademark red for working parts, solid black for switches, and black trimming for handles and grips. The resulting color scheme doubles as a signature look reinforcing the brand identity. Hilti also developed a revolutionary self-sharpening power chisel when sales agents reported there is often no time for sharpening on construction sites, and that workers end up using dull chisels most of the time. Hilti CEO Marco Meyrat admits that direct sales is the most expensive distribution channel, but would not want to miss out on the instant, actionable feedback provided by his sales agents. Hilti has been rewarded with a 30- to 50-percent price premium over its competition.[21]

Netnography is the attempt to take this kind of first-hand exploration online, e.g., in the form of topical blogs, Web-based communities, and discussion groups (such as Epinions or Qype) that allow researchers to observe as well as to interact with current and future customers directly through text discourse. For example, manufacturers of hiking shoes and other sports gear have been known to refine and modify their products based on feedback from online outdoor communities. Electronic Arts (EA), the maker of entertainment software, uses consumer input from its moderated chat rooms to refine its products. Games that are released periodically incorporate feedback from consumers who have played earlier versions, for example, the football video game Madden NFL, a new version of which EA Sports releases every summer. An even more refined example of netnography is the kind of online store that allows consumers to create their own products, e.g., Puma's successful

Mongolian Shoe BBQ. By analyzing the kinds of shoes created, the company learns what trendsetting consumers want and applies these insights to future product development.

Fig. 2.14: Overview of qualitative research techniques

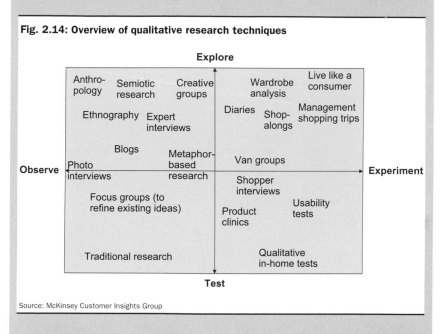

Source: McKinsey Customer Insights Group

Important and insightful as qualitative research techniques may be (Figure 2.14), their main function is to help enrich and complement the quantitative research approaches that are the backbone of brand measurement, such as the brand purchase funnel (discussed in more detail in sections 1.2 and 1.3; see 2.4 for details on this core brand measurement framework). Ideally, qualitative and quantitative research should work hand in hand. Typically, qualitative methods as described above would help *identify* relevant attributes that might be potential brand drivers. Subsequently, the actual relevance of these attributes will be *tested* in quantitative funnel research (section 2.4), *refined* in Brand Driver Analysis (3.1), and *used* to derive positioning options (3.2). Research is yet another area in which you need art (open-ended qualitative research) as well as science (dependable quantitative research), held together by craft (good judgment based on marketing and business expertise) to succeed.

* * *

Segmentation is the centerpiece of insights-driven brand management

In the age of IT-enabled one-to-one marketing, what would you need segmentation for? »As a map,« the former CEO of Esomar, Mario van Hamersfeld, said in an interview with McKinsey. The world of branding has become a jungle, and segmentation imposes order and provides orientation. Both are vital given the increasing pressure on the marketing function from ever-increasing numbers of brands, products, and channels, as well as the increasingly fierce fight over each and every customer. One indicator of the growing pressure is that, today, two out of every three customers are »brand switchers.« Take the example of fragrances in the German market. Back in the early 1990s, of every 100 new fragrances, 33 were still on the market two years later. Today that figure has shrunk to just three.[22] Decreasing loyalty and shortening life cycles make marketing more expensive than ever. Despite all the progress in information processing and logistics, one-to-one direct marketing is not the answer, particularly in the consumer goods industry, which depends on economies of scale to cover the fixed cost of product development and product launches. Even pioneers in »individualization,« such as Dell Computers, have recognized the limits of customization and tailoring and are now selling through traditional retail formats such as supermarkets or hypermarkets. In B2B sales, Dell has started segmenting its small and medium business customers to help them develop the most popular preconfigurations and limit the number of product models. Says Keith Pardy, Nokia's Senior Vice President of Strategic Marketing: »People are different, so why should we expect them all to want the same product? We recently completed a global segmentation study, with 77,000 consumers from all over the world, to really understand their needs, attitudes, beliefs, and lifestyles. It showed us that there are 12 different groups of consumers out there, all with very different needs. For some, fashion and stylish looks are the key factors in the mobile device they decide to buy; for others, it's about leading-edge technology and features. Or a device that helps you do your job on the move might be the must-have thing. If we are going to drive up our market share towards our goal of 40 percent, then we are going to need a product portfolio that's both broad and tightly targeted.«[23] Acknowledging the fact that finding the key that fits the lock of consumer needs is becoming more and more important, companies like Nokia make a point of developing a deep segment understanding to tailor their product offering and communication to specific target group needs. So how do you decide which horse to bet on? When marketing resources are scarce, which products and customer groups should you concentrate on?[24]

Segmentation may seem old-fashioned, but as products, brands, and channels proliferate, segmentation is precisely the antidote a company needs to ensure that marketing is profitable. Twenty years ago, the challenge was to promote customer-centric marketing and help it prevail over the notion that »Good products sell themselves.« In the future, however, customer segmentation will become crucial in the search for the most profitable position between customization and mass marketing. Most corporations can be expected to serve five segments in a tailored manner without going to rack and ruin, but fifty thousand or five million customers? Not likely. This is also why nine out of ten executives say their companies have a segmentation (B2C), used for both daily operations and long-term strategy development. In a recent survey, »segmentation« was one of the top three marketing concepts named by US executives.[25] Companies that know how to use a market segmentation achieve growth rates far higher than the market average. Done well, segmentation can unlock significant growth opportunities. For example, using a needs-based segmentation, PepsiCo has discovered a previously unserved segment: health-conscious young men who are reluctant to drink a »girl's drink,« such as Diet Pepsi. The product specifically developed for this segment, Pepsi Max, is the fastest-growing sugar-free soft drink (United Kingdom, 2006) and prompted the introduction of Coke Zero by Pepsi's long-standing rival.[26]

In short, proliferation in the market calls for granularity in brand management. But which cells, or segments, hold the biggest potential given the position of your brand and the benefits of your current product range? What should the value proposition for a promising, but currently unserved segment look like? The importance of this type of question for the profitability of targeted marketing makes segmentation the most comprehensive and perhaps the most important customer insights application of all.

Unlocking the power of segmentation with explicit objective setting

If segmentation is more important than ever, then why do so many marketing managers complain about expensive segmentation projects that just wind up gathering dust on the shelf? The complaints are well-known: the segmentations are hard to understand, difficult to communicate, and insufficiently actionable. Many segmentations are not total failures, but they fall short of executive expectations. It can't be lack of data; never before has so much data been available. Thanks to turnkey solutions such as the New Car Buyer Survey (NCBS) in the automotive industry, market researchers can get thousands of data sets in just a few clicks. Analytical weaknesses can be excluded, too. Few other types of data analysis have received so much attention in the past 20 years. Leading experts agree that the possibilities for further statistical refinement have been exhausted. In fact, the biggest issue is much closer to home. According to a recent McKinsey survey of marketing executives, the success of a segmentation depends primarily on the objectives set for it and on its implementation, and much less on market research and modeling.

The way forward is to treat segmentation as a structured process to create a foundation for strategic brand management, not as a piece of research or a tool. The process comprises (1) *objective setting*, perhaps the most important step in light of the issues described above; (2) the actual segmentation *research and analysis;* and (3) *implementation* of findings. This process is more than worthy of a senior management decision, especially in its critical early stages. In the past, the emphasis was on refining the second step, while the first step was often underestimated and, hence, neglected.

Phase I: Clarify segmentation objectives and frame of reference

Only a solution created with clear objectives in mind can serve as an effective guide to action. The wide variety of applications becomes tangible as soon as you think about the different stakeholders and what they are looking for:

- The **division head** wants to know which product categories have the highest growth potential; from their perspective, »type of product« should be the primary segmentation dimension.

- The **CMO** is struggling to position the brand globally and is looking for values and attitudes common to all markets the company operates in.

- The **product developer** has to decide what ingredients to use for a new product and suggests consumers' specific product needs as segment-building variables.

- The **media planner** at the agency needs to pick vehicles for the latest advertisements and wants segments profiled by media usage.

- The **sales department** is looking for an approach to help them prioritize existing customers according to their potential value.

It is clear even at first sight that a single segmentation solution cannot possibly satisfy all of these demands at the same time, let alone with equal depth and precision. So why have a single solution at all, and not as many as it takes to keep everybody happy? The reason is simple. If you want one brand with one position, speaking to the customer with one voice and offering a consistent value proposition, you need a common basis. Without a unified understanding of who customers are and what they want, different departments will wander off in different directions, creating conflicting messages and inefficient investment decisions. Given the wide variety of questions, any unified segmentation approach will always involve compromise. To make sure the interests of all relevant stakeholders are sufficiently balanced, the responsibility for setting segmentation parameters should reside as high up in the organization as practically possible.

To achieve this balance, phase I is all about setting clear objectives, defining the frame of reference, and managing stakeholder expectations. It may sound absurd at first, but if you ask two different executives in your company to describe the relevant market, you are likely to get three different answers (Figure 2.15). But in fact, this is a critical factor in pretty much every segmentation. For if you don't know who your (potential) customers are, you don't know whom you should segment, profile, and target. If you think growth is most likely to come from new markets, you will want to ensure a broad market definition that includes neighboring categories. Is a brand like Nivea, for example, necessarily limited to beauty products, or might it be extended to include day spas or even wellness resorts? Do coffee shops really deal in coffee, or should they aspire to become the much-touted »third place« beyond home and work? Howard Schultz of Starbucks is famously quoted as follows: »We're not in the coffee business, serving people. We're in the people business, serving coffee.«[27]

If you don't think fundamentally about your frame of reference, you're likely to miss out on major growth opportunities. Gatorade would never have attained its unique market position had its managers not expanded their frame of reference from »isotonic drinks« (US market volume of USD 7.5 billion) to »sports drinks« (US market volume of USD 23.6 billion) (Figure 2.16). The relevant market should, of course, also reflect brand heritage and in-house capabilities: Lamborghini is as unlikely to become a mass manufacturer as Kia is to go premium. In short, defining the frame of reference is a case-by-case decision that deserves senior management attention.

Any segmentation should have clear objectives, and its frame of reference should reflect your growth aspirations as well as your company's strengths and weaknesses. If the solution is intended to help design (rather than

101

Fig. 2.15: Clarifying the frame of reference is one of the most important steps in the segmentation process

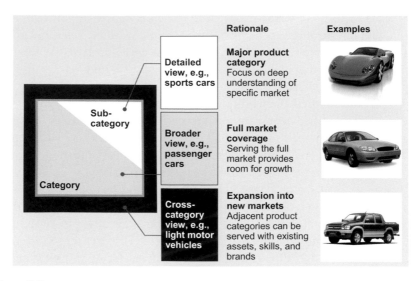

Source: McKinsey

Fig. 2.16: Relevant market definition determines revenue potential

Brand	Frame of reference	Competitive set	Innovation options	Market size USD billions
Gatorade	Narrow: sports drinks	Powerade, other sports drinks	Flavor extensions, package sizes	7.5
	Broad: physical activity	Bottled water, sports drinks, nutrition bars	Fitness water, performance bars	23.6
Uncle Ben's	Narrow: dried rice	Goya, Minute Rice	Flavor extensions	2.5
	Broad: ready meals	Hamburger Helper, Lipton, frozen meals, Progresso	One-bowl meals, multiple day-parts (e.g., breakfast)	18.2
Nivea	Narrow: skin care	Oil of Olay, Lubriderm	Fragrances, skin type formulations	7.8
	Broad: personal grooming	Gillette, P&G	Deodorant, sun protection, shampoo	26.2
Listerine	Narrow: mouthwash	Scope	Flavor extensions, efficacy improvements	0.9
	Broad: oral care	Wrigley's, Altoids, Crest	Pocket packs (breath freshening strips)	6.4

Source: Beverage Digest Handbook, 2007; Euromonitor

Measuring Brands

deliver) your value proposition, there should be only one of its kind. Additional, more tactical segmentations may be admissible to the extent they help you deliver your value proposition in distinctive ways. Holding-type companies operating in multiple industries will want to think about a segmentation architecture or hierarchy driven by the dynamics of their businesses and the portfolio of their brands, as discussed in the text box on »core beliefs« at the end of this section.

Phase II: Conducting research and deriving segmentation

Even once the relevant market (or frame of reference) has been defined as part of objective setting in phase I, it is not necessarily self-evident whom to segment. Should you be looking at consumers, shoppers, or intermediaries? To find out, it is essential to analyze the decision-making process in the relevant market you have defined, using qualitative market research if needed. Take the example of a US processed meat manufacturer. The company knew that roughly 80 percent of the products (by volume) were consumed by men, yet 80 percent of the purchases were made by women. The company felt that a segmentation of purchasers would be missing a key part of the equation, especially the needs of consumers. But a quick survey revealed that purchasers did in fact make the bulk of brand decisions. The company came within an inch of a misleading segmentation. Had it segmented consumers rather than purchasers (who also tend to be preparers), they would have looked at the needs of a group of people that has little say in the actual decision. Similarly, pharmaceutical companies typically look at prescribing physicians rather than patients, at least for prescription medication. But things are changing. For some types of drugs, such as sleeping pills or painkillers, physicians may continue to select the active agent, but consumers pick the actual brand they want. Nintendo recently shook the game console market by developing its Wii product with mothers' needs in mind: What would a console have to be for mothers to want to buy it for their kids? Says Beth Bulik, an industry expert: »Nintendo executives and designers conjured up a new target. And it began to look like, of all people, a mom. They settled on the household power purchaser – or at least the one with veto power.«[28] As a result, the Wii reflects one of the biggest concerns among most mothers when it comes to how their kids spend their free time: unlike competing products, the Wii gets kids on their feet – by combining entertainment with exercise. Entire workouts are built around the Wii, its motion-sensing »Wiimote« controller and, a recent addition, the

Wii balance board with its Wii Fit software. To top things off, the Wii comes in a small, light, and unobtrusive casing that differs significantly from its bulky black competitors and can be integrated with most interior decoration schemes much more easily. As a highly welcome side effect, this approach also got the mothers themselves interested; they came away thinking, »Maybe this isn't just something for my kids, maybe this could be something for me as well.« Julie Shumaker, former national sales director for gaming software giant Electronic Arts, sums it up as follows: »They brought people who don't consider themselves gamers into gaming. Data show people [...] still don't consider themselves gamers – and they own a Wii. Sheer marketing brilliance!«[28] Consumers across the globe have rewarded the »Wii way«; in the first quarter of 2008, the Nintendo Wii achieved almost twice the market share of the Microsoft Xbox in Germany. In the United States, the Wii has even outsold Sony's celebrated PlayStation 3.

Obviously, the cost of a short questionnaire or a few focus groups to determine the de facto decision maker in a given category far outweighs the aftereffects of a misguided segmentation, especially if it's meant for strategic applications such as brand positioning and future product development. Other than the segmentation sample, the fundamental parameter driving any segmentation solution is the variable, or set of variables, used to build the segments. Forty years after Russell Haley's groundbreaking 1968 article on »Benefit Segmentation,« benefits (or needs) are well established as the preferred segmentation dimension. At least that's true from the point of view of deep insight creation, simply because needs are the roots of consumer behavior: needs drive decision making, and understanding needs helps to develop relevant propositions. In this respect, needs are superior both to demographics and behavior (Figure 2.17).[29]

Having said that, it is important to acknowledge that there is almost always a conflict of interests when it comes to selecting the segmentation lens. Many users of segmentation solutions equate a good solution with a solution that enables them to identify segment members in the marketplace and to reach them easily through media or direct marketing. This is especially important for industries driven by personal relationships, or direct interactions, with their customers. An insurance company's sales agent may be able to grasp the key demographics and life stage of a potential policyholder quickly and adapt his pitch accordingly, but within the short time frame of a typical consultation, it is nearly impossible to assess the needs segment that same customer is in. The same goes for pharmaceutical sales agents (detailers) trying to guess what type of physician they are dealing with. To select the right kind of sales pitch, the detailer would, ideally, want to know whether the physician is an experimental, a conventional, or a flexible prescriber of drugs, since such attitudinal factors largely determine their choice of drug. But it is next to impossible to glean such information from how a physician looks, dresses, and responds to a few simple questions. Using demographics as a proxy of needs can be the more pragmatic choice in such situations; e.g., physicians who are in their late 50s now will typically have received their education and training around 1980 and, hence, often be averse to treatments devised later, or at least depend on the detailer to bridge the gap to drugs and treatments they are familiar with.

Useful as they may be in time-constrained situations, the downside of demographics and other such descriptors is that they rarely correlate with needs. Consider this example: think of two British subjects, both male, both born in 1948, both in their second marriage, both affluent and from well-known families. The first is Charles, Prince of Wales, and the other is Ozzy Osbourne, Prince of Darkness. You can tell by their outfits and hairstyles alone that their purchasing behavior is probably pretty different despite the demographic similarities. So while demographics can be a helpful needs proxy in one situation (compare the example of the physician), they may be misleading in another.

Ultimately, the choice of segmentation lens in a given situation should be driven by the primary purpose of the segmentation: the more it is about developing the value proposition, the more the success of the solution depends on a deep understanding of the needs. Only insights at the needs level – the «Why?» of consumer decision making – will enable marketers to develop a superior value proposition, set the right price, make their products available in the right channel, and create meaningful messages. If, however, the focus of the segmentation is to optimize the *delivery* of your value proposition, be it because of the nature of the industry or for other reasons, demographics, life stage, or, in B2B contexts, firmographics, such as number of employees or revenues, should feature prominently in your segmentation solution. At the very least, such external, easily observable factors should be used as profiling parameters to enable the sales team to derive insights into the needs of the person they are dealing with.[30]

To combine the advantages of insightful needs segmentation and more pragmatic demographic or behavioral approaches, there have been many attempts to create »dual objective« or »multi-lever« solutions. In some cases, this works surprisingly well, e.g., when demographic or behavioral attributes themselves reflect latent needs. Take the example of a leading global manufacturer of consumer electronics. This company took its

Fig. 2.17: Needs provide the deepest insight into consumer motivation
Bases for segmentation

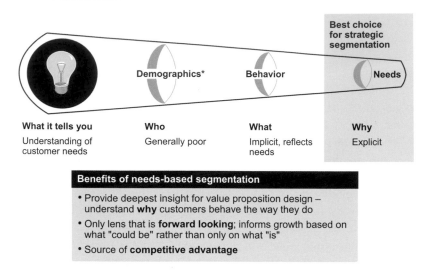

Best choice for strategic segmentation

	Demographics*	Behavior	Needs
What it tells you	**Who**	**What**	**Why**
Understanding of customer needs	Generally poor	Implicit, reflects needs	Explicit

Benefits of needs-based segmentation

• Provide deepest insight for value proposition design – understand **why** customers behave the way they do
• Only lens that is **forward looking**; informs growth based on what "could be" rather than only on what "is"
• Source of **competitive advantage**

*In some sectors or markets, demographics are correlated with needs (e.g., life stage in financial services); these demographics can be useful proxies for needs

Source: McKinsey

needs-based segmentation and added channel preference, primarily because that makes segment targeting much easier. Managers were astonished when they found that this step not only left the needs segments undamaged, but even improved their distinctiveness. It turned out that shoppers' choice of store actually reflected their latent needs: while bargain hunters would prefer Wal-Mart or Target, the more technically savvy buyers typically ended up at Best Buy or Circuit City. Despite such promising approaches, selecting the appropriate segmentation lens will have to remain a case-by-case decision reflecting the specific circumstances of the industry and the market environment a given brand is operating in.

Segmentation should reflect that needs vary with occasion

In many cases, ethnographic research and other deep-immersion techniques help researchers discover that needs are in fact highly dependent on the situation in which a product is purchased or used.[31] As a consequence, state-of-the-art segmentation solutions should differentiate needs by occasions/situations, or »states« for short. This is especially true as the proliferation of brands, products, and channels, and the fragmentation of demand continues. Needs do not only differ from country to country, category to category, and customer to customer. Until recently, conservative buyers may have bought conservative brands through a conservative channel. But today, even the same person will have different needs in different purchasing or consumption situations. The same traveler will buy discounted flight tickets from a no-frills carrier for most short-haul travel, but will buy fully priced, fully flexible tickets from leading airlines for intercontinental or business flights. Buyers of apparel or furniture gladly mix budget with luxury. Leading retailers such as H&M, Zara, or Ikea have recognized this development by complementing their portfolios with upmarket brands like Cos, Massimo Dutti, Habitat, and the Conran Shop respectively. To pick up on this kind of trend, state-of-the-art segmentations use *states* as a second dimension. Let's look at three cases in which differentiating needs by states led to far more practical insights:

Apparel. A US-based manufacturer of jeans found that needs in its category are predominantly driven by whether a pair of jeans is worn at work, after work or on weekends at home, to go out at night, or for outdoor activities. The usage situation determines what people are looking for in terms of style, cut, material, and price point. They found the situation to be so important that there are hardly any overarching needs other than »good value for money.« For example, while a dressy pair should be fashionable, form-fitting, and lightweight (and can be more expensive than others), a pair of jeans worn for gardening should be comfortably cut, durable, and comparatively low-price. That said, »fashionable« or »lowprice« can, of course, still mean different things to different segments. In fact, the company even used the segmentations to differentiate its brand portfolio in close cooperation with selected retail partners.

Bakery. An Italian manufacturer of wheat-based snacks found that consumer needs are primarily driven by consumers' eating habits: are they looking for a balanced diet, for quick calorie intake, or for lots of tasty treats? But even within these needs segments, preferences vary so widely that the company found it needed an additional dimension to inform its Brand Portfolio Management and product development (dependent factors range from salt, fat, and sugar content to package size and design). The relevant second dimension turned out to be purchasing occasion: Are consumers buying something to eat at work or on the go? Are they buying a snack or a main meal? Are they eating alone or with others?

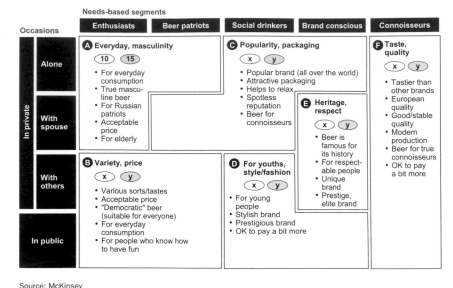

Fig. 2.18: Sample need-states segmentation for beer

x Population share (%)
y Volume share (%)

Needs-based segments

Occasions	Enthusiasts	Beer patriots	Social drinkers	Brand conscious	Connoisseurs

In private

Alone

Ⓐ Everyday, masculinity

(10) (15)

• For everyday consumption
• True masculine beer
• For Russian patriots
• Acceptable price
• For elderly

With spouse

Ⓒ Popularity, packaging

(x) (y)

• Popular brand (all over the world)
• Attractive packaging
• Helps to relax
• Spotless reputation
• Beer for connoisseurs

Ⓔ Heritage, respect

(x) (y)

• Beer is famous for its history
• For respectable people
• Unique brand
• Prestige, elite brand

Ⓕ Taste, quality

(x) (y)

• Tastier than other brands
• European quality
• Good/stable quality
• Modern production
• Beer for true connoisseurs
• OK to pay a bit more

With others

Ⓑ Variety, price

(x) (y)

• Various sorts/tastes
• Acceptable price
• "Democratic" beer (suitable for everyone)
• For everyday consumption
• For people who know how to have fun

Ⓓ For youths, style/fashion

(x) (y)

• For young people
• Stylish brand
• Prestigious brand
• OK to pay a bit more

In public

Source: McKinsey

Beer. An Eastern European brewery segmented beer drinkers by needs and attitudes and, predictably, came out with a range of segments based on varying mixtures of taste orientation, image benefit, and average beer intake. Unfortunately, the segments were blurry at best. Based on previous qualitative research, the brewery added contextual factors as a second dimension: Are consumers drinking at home or in the pub? Alone or with others? If with others, with their spouse or their friends? The second dimension made the solution much more informative, especially to derive concrete actions for the marketing mix, such as in-store promotions versus tastings and brand advertising in pubs (Figure 2.18).

Phase III: Defining actions and implementing findings

The implementation challenge is threefold: First, you have to select the most promising target groups for your brand or brands. Second, you have to derive and monitor action plans to serve these segments; actions may range from brand (re)positioning to proposition development and channel mix optimization. Third, you have to make sure segmentation findings are communicated broadly and absorbed by the organization.

Roughly speaking, target segment selection should recognize two types of criteria: segment attractiveness, comprising factors such as size or volume and (potential) value, on the one hand, and segment accessibility, recognizing elements such as brand image fit, need fit, or switching probability, on the other hand. While attractiveness should be the same for all players in a given category, accessibility is determined by the specific positioning of your brand (or brands), including its current position as well as any potential to stretch or reposition the brand.

Once the target segments have been selected and profiled, it is time for action. Successful action planning is all about using insights generated by the segmentation to do things differently. Because the range of actions taken based on a strategic segmentation is so wide, let's look at two companies that have started doing things differently after major segmentation efforts:

Convenience food. A maker of precooked meals and other convenience foods selected »time-pressed cooks« as its new key target segment based on a needs-driven segmentation. These people enjoy cooking as a creative activity, wish they had more time to cook, and want products to reduce preparation time without limiting their creativity. To cater to these needs, the company stopped producing ready-to-eat precooked meals, prepared salads, and savoury snacks. Instead, it started offering a wide range of semi-prepared ingredients to speed up the cooking process, like the prepared components many professional chefs use: sliced deli meats, washed and chopped vegetables, and ready-to-use marinades.

Mobile telecommunication. A mobile operator created a strategic segmentation of current and potential customers based on their needs (ranging from affordability focus to convenience focus) and their commitment level (prepaid versus flexible versus long-term contract). Having selected convenience-focused, heavy off-peak users as one of its key target groups, the company revamped its entire marketing mix based on the insights generated. Actions ranged from a tailor-made value proposition (e.g., attractive off-peak rates, 24/7 service promise, basic handset) to segment-based market share goal setting and monitoring to make sure the action plan was adhered to (Figure 2.19).

Using segmentation not only as a way of synthesizing insights and planning actions, but also as a tracking and controlling tool, makes it even more powerful as a strategic platform. Having a strategic goal, be it brand image or market share, revenue growth, or subscriber adds, set and monitored for individual segments, makes it much easier to derive targeted actions and track their effectiveness.

Fig. 2.19: Example of segmentation-based action planning for mobile phone operators

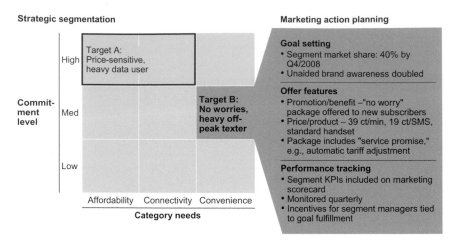

Source: McKinsey

The third and final step to making sure segmentation insight leads to tangible business impact is to make target segments come to life for an audience beyond the actual segmentation team. To unleash the full power of a segmentation and transform the way your organization thinks about its customers, all marketing and sales staff, as well as part of the product development staff, need to be aware of what the target segments are, what they are like, and what they are looking for.

There is a wide range of creative approaches to bring segments to life. Examples include segment handbooks, »quick identifier« segment typing tools (i.e., tools that allow employees to determine a customer's segment membership from a narrow set of questions), and true-to-life segment experiences conveyed in movies, rooms, and role playing (Figure 2.20). A leading food company has created an »exploration and training ground« for marketing employees by renting a warehouse, setting up fake living areas, and training actors to stand in as segment representatives. Marketing staff circle through the various rooms and interview the actors to investigate their needs, determine their segment membership, and understand their brand preferences. Similarly, BMW has created a »Mini-buyer living room« as well as a »BMW-buyer living room« for training purposes at the BMW brand academy.

Fig. 2.20: Overview of creative techniques to bring segments to life

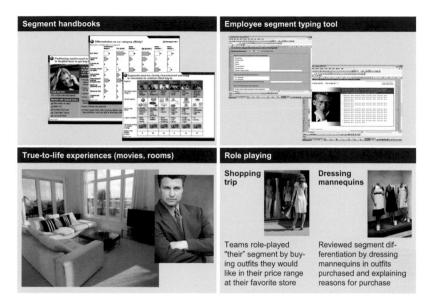

Source: McKinsey

Characteristics of a good segmentation

Segmentation is not an end in itself. It is a superior way to generate and integrate insight, and it provides a strategic platform for brand positioning and marketing action planning. Its ultimate purpose is to provide your brand with a more solid footing in the battle for customers. For a segmentation to be successful in its execution, it needs to be both robust and practical. Even the most sophisticated segmentation is of little use if the resulting target groups are not embedded in the company's structures and processes. A robust and practical segmentation has the following characteristics:

- The segments are distinct from one another in terms of brand and product preferences.
- The segmentation provides evidence of untapped customer needs.
- The segments are reachable through the channels or media that matter in your business.
- The segment names relate clearly to the market, are easy to comprehend, and are limited in number to remain manageable.

So, what changes after you complete a strategic segmentation project in line with these criteria? Most people notice three things. First, the target segments are no longer only profiled by income, gender, and level of education, but instead are *defined* based on customers' needs in various situations and *selected* based on customer value. Second, the brand management and product marketing are already working on attractive propositions for the growth segments of the future. Third, everyone in the company – from the department manager to the front line – and at the lead agency can name the current target segments in their sleep. The result: from insight to impact.

McKinsey's Core Beliefs about Segmentation

A one-size-fits-all segmentation solution is impossible given the differences between industries, markets, and company structures. Jointly working out the objectives and general conditions is at the heart of every segmentation project. Still, in our experience – since 2000, McKinsey has supported clients in all industries on some 500 segmentation engagements worldwide – there is clearly a handful of »golden rules« that executives can apply to get better results. They have proved their merit in many different situations and serve as guidelines for developing a tailored segmentation.

Focus. *Build one and only one strategic segmentation in each major product category to drive value proposition development.* The essential objectives of a strategic segmentation are the ability to manage the brand, product, and channel strategy. When there is more than one segmentation, the gaps and overlaps create confusion. Many companies have only one main product category and should consequently have only one strategic segmentation, whereas a conglomerate can easily have a dozen strategic segmentations.

Establish a clear hierarchy. *Consider additional go-to-market segmentations if needed, but ensure they are compatible with the strategic segmentation.* Customer relationship management and media planning depend on more details or higher granularity than the strategic segmentation can offer. Ideally, it should be possible to translate the operational segmentation into the strategic segmentation and vice versa.

Link choice of lens to segment objective. *Wherever possible, focus on customers' needs to understand why they make the choices they do.* The more a segmentation is meant to inform value proposition *development*, the more it should use needs to build segments. The more it is about *delivering* the value proposition, the more important observable factors such as demographics and behavior will be, at least as profiling parameters. Although lens selection is a case-by-case decision, using needs and demographics as the two dimensions of a segmentation matrix is often the best solution.

Embed results in the planning process. *Translate segmentation findings into action plans for each functional group, simplifying the communication as needed.* It is vital to anchor the results of the segmentation in the marketing planning and controlling processes. This is especially true for the prioritized target segments and for the activities and campaigns developed. Segment targets such as market share goals should be monitored and incorporated into the performance target agreements of the responsible employees. Try to simplify the solution as much as possible for communication purposes and make sure segments come to life in profiles and handbooks.

2.3 The Brand Diamond: Developing a Precise Understanding of Brand Image

As described in the first chapter, strong brands generate an unmistakable image in the minds of consumers. It is important for the company to understand the nature of this image in terms of how and why it influences the consumer. This knowledge provides the basis for assessing how management can develop the brand image further to trigger the decision to purchase. Success in influencing behavior in this manner will increase the value of the brand.[32]

In marketing science, both the foundations and the creation of brand image have been studied extensively.[33] Numerous approaches have been developed based on behavioral science and with the aid of brand equity research. These approaches seek to understand and structure brand associations.[34] Nearly all these concepts feature a hierarchical structure that differentiates between attributes, benefit perceptions formed from these attributes, and the resulting global attitudes or associations.[35]

Building on the work of others, McKinsey has developed its own empirically based structuring approach for analyzing brand image. With this method, the attribute and benefit associations of a brand image can be divided into four elements. These include the attributes that are inherent in

113

the brand, independent of its consumption, and the benefits it provides to the consumer. This yields the Brand Diamond, which represents all the associations linked to a brand and their relationship with one another (Figure 2.21). Note that in the text below, »attributes« is used both for statements on the right-hand side of the diamond (as opposed to »benefits« on the left-hand side), as well as the general term meant to include both attributes and benefits. The latter use is the more common outside the specific BrandMatics® context.

Tangible elements: The associations in this category are generally those that arise first in the perception of the consumer. This category includes all the characteristics that can be perceived by the senses, forming the basis for the strength of a brand's image in the minds of consumers. They can be physical or functional in nature, such as engine horsepower or product design, as well as those related to a brand's presentation, for instance, as communicated in advertising or promotional campaigns.

Intangible elements: The intangible elements comprise all the characteristics associated with a brand's origin, reputation, and personality that cannot be sensed directly but are nonetheless important to the consumer's understanding of the brand. These include associations such as »a brand with tradition« or »an innovative brand.« The intangible brand elements

Fig. 2.21: A holistic perspective on brands: The McKinsey brand diamond

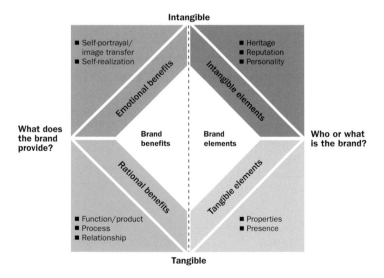

Source: McKinsey

Measuring Brands

typically build on tangible ones. The cowboy element in Marlboro's brand image, for instance, triggers associations of freedom and adventure. Today, these intangible elements are probably much more important for Marlboro's image than any tangible ones.

Rational benefits: All the measurable benefits the brand brings the consumer fall into this category. Rational benefits can be expressed in the product or its function (e.g., comfortable seats), the transaction process (convenient transaction handling), or in the relationship of the consumer to the brand or provider (good consultation from friendly staff). Rational benefits are directly related to tangible brand elements. A high-speed train, for instance, offers the rational benefit of reduced travel time.

Emotional benefits: Consumers associate an emotional benefit with a brand if it reinforces their personal self-image (image transfer) or self-expression. Brands can be used in this manner as status symbols that provide prestige, a Louis Vuitton handbag or a Porsche sports car being good examples.

The Brand Diamond can be used as the basis for an exhaustive analysis of the brand image in three steps. The first step is to determine all the relevant or potentially relevant brand associations in the pertinent market environment. The four dimensions of the Brand Diamond act as a structural aid that helps to ascertain accurately all the attributes influencing the brand image. These attributes are identified through a combination of management workshops, interviews, and preliminary quantitative market research. The old adage of »garbage in, garbage out« applies here, of course. If attributes that are important in influencing the brand image are not measured adequately or are neglected completely, the risk of an incorrect conclusion is high. This is particularly true in analyzing the emotional benefits of the brand (the upper-left corner of the Brand Diamond). In the B2B sector, for instance, many companies have reservations about addressing the emotional benefits of the brand (»We're talking about the forklift market, where the only thing that matters is what it can do and what it costs!«). Despite such misconceptions, a detailed analysis demonstrates how strongly the brand effect depends on the emotional benefit. These are revealed in such forms as »a brand you can trust,« »you can depend on it,« or »it fits my company.« These types of attributes are of vital importance in fulfilling a brand's fundamental risk-reducing function, even in B2B environments. In the forklift market, for example, there is a substantial segment of relationship-driven buyers. They make their brand choices based primarily on attributes such as »long tradition« and »good name« (see chapter 2.1 for further detail).

Typically, in the four Brand Diamond dimensions, a total of 20 to 50 specific aspects of the image are taken into consideration in a brand image analysis. Selecting the right number for the brand is a trade-off between cost and reliability (of the market research) on the one hand and actionable insight (gained through additional knowledge) on the other.

Once the image dimensions have been selected, the second step is to have these dimensions evaluated by (potential) customers in quantitative market research. A given brand's performance on these specific dimensions is typically measured with the help of rating scales.

The third and final step is to compare the image of the company's own brand with that of competing brands. In principle, it would be possible to make a comparison for each of the dimensions of brand image. However, in order to avoid excessive complexity (and cost), it is better to make a comparison of only those dimensions in which the brand possesses critical strengths or weaknesses.

It is helpful to look at how the Brand Diamond works in practice. In an outside-in independent market research study, McKinsey used the Brand Diamond to analyze the Mercedes C-Class in comparison with the Volkswagen Passat. From the results, it is evident that the Mercedes C-Class brand was clearly superior to that of the Passat in the emotional dimensions. Apparently, the Passat had not yet succeeded in completely shedding its image of being somewhat unexciting. Figure 2.22 provides an illustration of the use of the Brand Diamond in comparing the Volkswagen Passat and Mercedes C-Class on selected image dimensions.

As this example illustrates, a brand typically evokes several categories of association. The tangible brand elements, for instance, might include a superior product concept or a creative advertising presence, which might derive directly from the rational benefits of the brand. Though these are critical elements in a brand's success, an analysis of more than 100 Brand Diamonds in some 20 market environments confirms that the secret to the success of strong brands lies in the combination of rational and emotional benefits, as the leading brands demonstrate. Successful brand management needs to recognize this principle, regardless of whether the brand is in confectionery, detergent market, or the steel industry.

Once the Brand Diamond has been used to reveal all the associations linked to the brands being studied, the next task is to shape the image of your brand in the desired direction. For this purpose, it is important to gain a quantitative understanding of how a consumer's image of the brand influences his or her behavior.

Fig. 2.22: Brand diamond: Mercedes C-Class vs. VW Passat

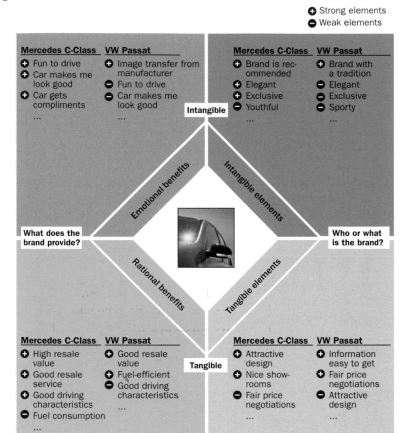

➕ Strong elements
➖ Weak elements

Mercedes C-Class | VW Passat
- ➕ Fun to drive
- ➕ Car makes me look good
- ➕ Car gets compliments
- ...

- ➕ Image transfer from manufacturer
- ➖ Fun to drive
- ➖ Car makes me look good
- ...

Intangible

Mercedes C-Class | VW Passat
- ➕ Brand is recommended
- ➕ Elegant
- ➕ Exclusive
- ➖ Youthful
- ...

- ➕ Brand with a tradition
- ➖ Elegant
- ➖ Exclusive
- ➖ Sporty
- ...

Emotional benefits

Intangible elements

What does the brand provide?

Who or what is the brand?

Rational benefits

Tangible elements

Mercedes C-Class | VW Passat
- ➕ High resale value
- ➕ Good resale service
- ➕ Good driving characteristics
- ➖ Fuel consumption
- ...

- ➕ Good resale value
- ➕ Fuel-efficient
- ➖ Good driving characteristics
- ...

Tangible

Mercedes C-Class | VW Passat
- ➕ Attractive design
- ➕ Nice showrooms
- ➖ Fair price negotiations
- ...

- ➕ Information easy to get
- ➕ Fair price negotiations
- ➖ Attractive design
- ...

Source: INRA consumer survey, Germany 2002, McKinsey

2.4 The Brand Purchase Funnel: Measuring and Quantifying Brand Performance

The crucial question that needs to be answered in quantifying the performance of the brand is how the brand image and consumer attitude influence purchase behavior. These aspects can be quantitatively measured and assessed; this is the core of BrandMatics®.

Establishing a correlation between the brand image and the attitudes and behavior of consumers is vital for the successful development and management of brands. But management often underestimates this aspect. In many cases, awareness of brands and global image value remain the exclusive indicators of brand success. These two criteria are even reflected in the business targets of the senior management of many top companies, despite the fact that neither brand awareness nor global image value says anything about the actual economic success of the brand (with the exception of Interbrand's brand value analysis that reflects both brand strength and financial performance). As an additional indicator of brand performance, advertising recall has been widely used for some time now. However, this is chiefly due to the fact that it can be easily measured and is being widely offered by tracking agencies. Yet recall is not directly tied to bottom-line impact either. Despite the proven effect of creative advertising (see section 1.2), a popular television commercial or an eye-catching billboard poster does not necessarily drive sales.

Measuring brand performance using the brand purchase funnel

A brand's impact on behavior can be measured using the brand purchase funnel (also referred to here as the brand funnel). The funnel structure is based on the AIDA model (Attention, Interest, Desire, Action) from the realm of behavioral science. It typically represents the purchase process in five idealized stages: What percentage of the target group 1) is aware of the brand? 2) is familiar with its products and services prior to deciding to buy? 3) will consider the brand for purchase? 4) has already purchased it once? and 5) would purchase it again, that is, are loyal customers? Strong brands tend to be successful at all stages: they achieve a high degree of awareness, are included in the consideration set, are purchased, and finally convert buyers into loyal customers. The last two stages of the brand funnel are crucial; this is where consumer behavior has a direct impact on the level of sales and earnings.

In order to measure the performance of a brand in the brand funnel, market research data on consumer behavior is collected at each stage. Using this data, it is possible to calculate the respective number of customers the brand retains from stage to stage. Figure 2.23 illustrates the schematic operation of the brand funnel in the automobile industry.

The brand funnel can, in principle, be applied to any B2B or B2C market, though it will need to be adapted to the industry segment under investigation. The number and structure of the stages will vary by industry. It is useful to look at a number of examples to see how this can be done. For fast-

Fig. 2.23: Applying the brand funnel to cars

	Aided awareness	Familiarity	Consideration	Purchase	Loyalty
Survey questions	Do you know this brand?	Are you familiar with the products/ models of this brand?	Did you consider this brand when you bought your last car?	Did you choose this brand when you last bought a car?	Will you choose this brand the next time you buy a car?

Source: McKinsey Brand Health Survey, MCM/McKinsey, 2002

moving consumer goods, such as cigarettes, shampoo, or mineral water, the »will consider« stage can be replaced or supplemented by »trial purchase.« In this way, occasional purchases of the products can be reflected accurately, as these are important to the brand. For financial investments, the stages of »ownership« and »main investment« (loyalty) would be integrated into the final stages of the purchase funnel. When applying the purchase funnel to the retail domain, the first stages would include »visiting the shop« or »visiting the store department.« The brand funnel can even be employed in non-business environments, for instance, in analyzing commitment to political parties. In this case, the final »purchase« and »repeat purchase« stages of the funnel would be replaced by »have voted for« and »will vote for again.«

Due to its broad foundation in behavioral science, purchase funnel analysis has been applied in marketing practice for a considerable time and is now a well-accepted tool for nearly all agencies and management consulting firms. It is important to note that despite fundamental similarities, the approaches often differ in the number of stages that are included in the funnel. This is an important distinction, because the number of stages determines the »effect hierarchy« that is under investigation. Even more important is that many users concentrate only on the absolute values in the process stages. But such an interpretation yields few meaningful results, since the absolute values of the process stages at the beginning of the purchase funnel – such as a high degree of awareness or familiarity – can be »purchased« through sufficiently extensive advertising campaigns. More important from a management point of view are the conversion rates,

119

which can be derived from the absolute values of the process stages. These indicate at which points in the purchase process a brand loses potential customers, thus revealing bottlenecks in the purchase process. By making management aware of weak points in the brand's performance, funnel analysis helps to focus investment on the most effective brand drivers (as discussed in the following pages).

This interrelationship is illustrated using the example of the Volkswagen Passat (Figure 2.24); the survey was conducted in Germany in 2002, when the model was in its eighth generation.[36] Nearly 100 percent of the group surveyed were aware of the Volkswagen Passat. As expected, at each successive stage of the purchase funnel the brand lost (potential) customers; at the end only 8 percent of those surveyed remained loyal Volkswagen Passat customers. At first sight, this appears to be a low level of customer loyalty.

It is hard to interpret these figures meaningfully, however, until they are compared with another car brand. A comparison with the Mercedes C-Class, then in its second generation, confirms that, as was first suspected, the loyalty rate for the Volkswagen Passat was indeed weak (Figure 2.25). Whereas the Passat succeeded in converting only 39 percent of purchasers to the »loyalty« stage, the Mercedes C-Class secured a much higher conversion rate of 63 percent. The Mercedes C-Class was also superior in

Fig. 2.24: The brand performance of the VW Passat in the purchase funnel
Percent

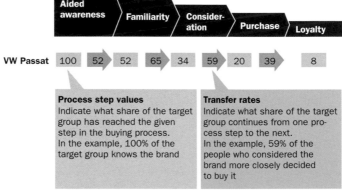

Source: MCM/McKinsey, 2002

Fig. 2.25: The funnel highlights the VW Passat's brand weaknesses in 2002
Percent

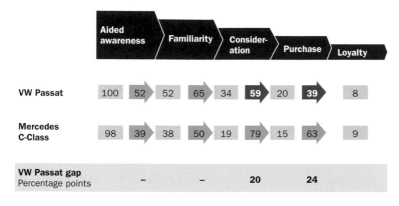

	Aided awareness	Familiarity	Consideration	Purchase	Loyalty
VW Passat	100 52 52	65 34	59 20	39	8
Mercedes C-Class	98 39 38	50 19	79 15	63	9
VW Passat gap Percentage points	–	–	20	24	

Source: McKinsey Brand Health Survey, MCM/McKinsey, 2002

converting customers from the »consideration« stage to »purchase,« with an edge of 20 percentage points over Volkswagen. From this it is clear that the Mercedes C-Class was significantly more successful than the Volkswagen Passat in turning potential customers into actual buyers or loyal repeat customers. In the light of Mercedes' strong performance in the final stages of the purchase funnel, the fact that it slightly trailed the Volkswagen Passat in the initial process stages hardly matters in the end.

Examples of the application of the brand purchase funnel

The power of the brand purchase funnel can be illustrated using various examples from a range of industries.

Mobile phones: The German mobile phone market provides a good example of how systematic, data-driven brand analysis can strongly support the assessment of a brand's performance and provide brand managers with valuable indicators for potential success or failure. Until quite recently, the German market for mobile phones was dominated for the most part by Nokia, followed by competing brands such as Motorola, Sony Ericsson, Samsung, and BenQ-Siemens. Although Siemens had been the second largest brand after Nokia in Germany for a long time, BenQ-Siemens exited the market about one year after BenQ took over Siemens' mobile phone business. The German division filed for bankruptcy in 2006. By contrast, the Korean Samsung brand has managed to increase its German market share continually over the past five years, reaching around 10 percent in 2006, making it the most successful recent entrant – despite fierce competition from market leaders Nokia and Sony Ericsson.

The results of outside-in market research conducted in mid-2006 show that the two brands Samsung and Nokia enter the purchase process with the same degree of brand awareness; both are at 98 percent. But already in the conversion to the »familiarity« stage, Nokia takes a clear lead, the gap between the two brands at this stage being 16 percentage points. This means that (potential) customers are apparently more familiar with Nokia-brand mobile phones than with those from Samsung. This is probably due in part to Nokia's twin advantages as incumbent market leader and single-category player. Whereas consumers associate Nokia almost exclusively with high-performance mobile telephones, the Samsung brand name is linked with numerous other products and services as well, including television sets and washing machines. Beyond the stage of brand familiarity, Nokia succeeds in converting 56 percent of those who consider buying a Nokia mobile phone into people who view Nokia as their favorite handset brand. At this transfer, Samsung achieves a conversion rate of just 23 percent, some 33 percentage points behind Nokia – resulting in the biggest gap along the funnel (Figure 2.26).

Fig. 2.26: Brand funnel analysis in mobile phones
Percent

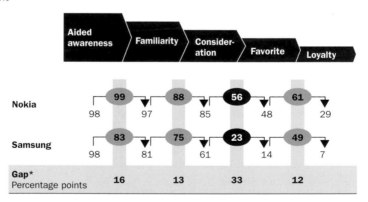

* Versus the benchmark
Source: McKinsey German consumer survey, 2006

Measuring Brands

Fig. 2.27: Brand funnel analysis in tobacco
Percent

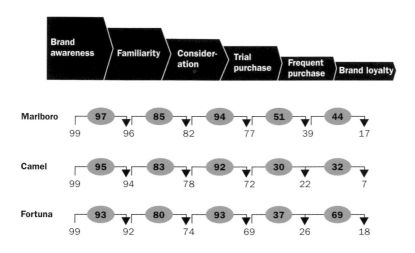

Source: McKinsey Spanish market research, April 2005 (n = 501)

Tobacco: An example from the Spanish cigarette market, based on McKinsey research carried out in 2005, illustrates how the brand funnel approach needs to be adapted depending on the industry or product market that is to be analyzed. Here, the »purchase« stage is divided into »trial purchase« and »frequent purchase« in order to integrate occasional buyers of the brand into the analysis (Figure 2.27). With an awareness of almost 100 percent, Camel and the domestic brand Fortuna are as well-known as the global market leader Marlboro. Furthermore, both Camel's and Fortuna's performance along the first four stages of the funnel, from brand awareness to familiarity, consideration, and trial purchase are also only a little behind that of Marlboro. It is the distinction between trial purchase and frequent purchase in the brand funnel that reveals the actions the cigarette brands need to take. Camel obviously fails to convert customers from trial purchase to frequent purchase. The same is true for Fortuna, which converts only slightly more customers (37 percent compared to Camel's 30 percent). Clearly, both brands therefore need to focus their marketing efforts on this bottleneck if they are to gain market share against Marlboro.

Tourism: A further example of the flexibility of the brand purchase funnel is demonstrated in its use in assessing competing tourist destinations (Figure 2.28). A market research study carried out in Germany in 2004

Measuring Brands

Fig. 2.28: The brand funnel is a highly versatile analytical tool: Tourism example
Percent

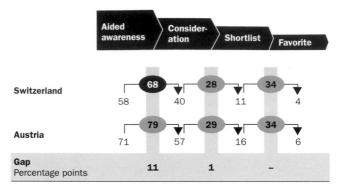

Source: McKinsey survey conducted in Germany, 2004

examined the various stages of the purchase funnel for holiday destinations in Austria and Switzerland. This analysis showed that, for German tourists, Austrian destinations were well ahead of Swiss ones. The major reason why is found in the front end of the purchasing funnel. In response to the question, »Do you know any Austrian tourist destinations?«, 71 percent of those surveyed answered »yes,« while only 58 percent said they knew Swiss ones. Similarly, the conversion rate from »familiarity« to »consideration« is 11 percentage points higher for Austria as a destination than for Switzerland. To counter this, Switzerland needs to invest in its tourism marketing in order to build familiarity with its destinations. One interesting aspect of the analysis is that it shows comparatively high loyalty rates for those who have already visited Swiss holiday destinations. In other words, once tourists get to Switzerland, they enjoy the experience and are likely to come back. So-called taster offers to drive »sampling« of Switzerland as a holiday destination might therefore help the country to secure a bigger slice of the tourism pie.

Once the brand funnel has been used to identify the gaps in a brand's performance relative to its relevant competitors, a natural next step is to invest in fixing those gaps. McKinsey has developed its brand potential method in cooperation with the Marketing Centrum Münster (MCM) in order to invest effectively in building and expanding a brand. The brand potential method can be used to quantify the potential sales improvement derived from improved conversion rates.

In calculating a brand's sales potential, it is important to realize that at any stage of the purchase funnel, consumer behavior is not only the result of brand impact, but also the interplay of all elements of the marketing mix. For instance, the Volkswagen Passat's high conversion rate from the awareness stage to the familiarity stage when compared with the Mercedes C-Class (52 percent versus 39 percent as shown in Figure 2.25) is more likely to originate from the significant price difference between the two automobiles (and the higher presence of the Passat on the road) than from the brand alone. In other words, in order to determine the brand potential, it is first necessary to separate the impact derived purely from the brand from that arising from other elements in the marketing mix. Only when the impact of the brand has been isolated in this way is it possible to determine what contribution the brand can make towards closing gaps in the funnel.

The McKinsey brand potential method makes such calculations possible using a multivariate analysis technique. Figure 2.29 illustrates the results of this approach using a simplified version and the example of the Volkswagen Passat/Mercedes C-Class comparison. In moving consumers from consideration to purchase, the Volkswagen Passat achieved a conversion rate of only 59 percent. The Mercedes C-Class, in contrast, achieved a rate of 79 percent, some 20 percentage points higher. With the help of the brand potential method, it is possible to calculate the contribution of the Mercedes C-Class brand to this higher conversion rate. This calculation shows that if the Volkswagen Passat were able to match its brand strength to that of the Mercedes C-Class, it would increase its conversion rate at the purchase stage to just 65 percent. In other words, 6 percentage points of the total 20-percentage-point gap can potentially be closed through branding. The remaining 14 percentage points of the gap are attributable to other elements of the marketing mix.

The analysis reveals a similar situation at the loyalty stage. Here the Volkswagen Passat trailed its Mercedes C-Class competitor by an even greater amount, showing a gap of 24 percentage points. However, investing in the brand's development alone can close only 3 percentage points of this gap. Obviously, other factors such as resale value, and the perceived price-performance ratio dominate at this stage.

The brand purchase funnel reveals how many customers can potentially be retained from stage to stage through improved brand management – but it does not reveal how this will translate into a concrete impact on sales. To establish this, the brand-potential calculation method developed by the Marketing Centrum Münster (MCM) and McKinsey uses a special assessment

Fig. 2.29: The funnel can reveal a brand's potential revenue value
Percent

	Aided awareness	Familiarity	Consider-ation	Purchase	Loyalty
VW Passat	52	65	59	39	
Mercedes C-Class	39	50	79	63	
Gap Percentage points	–	–	20	24	
Can be closed by the brand Percentage points	–	–	6	3	
Brand potential (revenue value) EUR millions	–	–	466	115	

Source: McKinsey Brand Health Survey, MCM/McKinsey, 2002

model. In this model, the total acquisition value of the additional customers that can be acquired is a combination of the purchase stage in the brand funnel and the additional value at the loyalty stage. In the Volkswagen Passat example, the model theoretically has a brand potential of EUR 466 million at the customer acquisition (purchase) stage, with an additional EUR 115 million at the customer retention (loyalty) stage. This calculation is based on the total size of the relevant market and the expected value of the market share increase generated by improved purchase and loyalty rates.

Purchase funnel analysis, in combination with the brand potential method, is thus an effective technique for deriving concrete, strategic brand targets, as well as for quantifying and prioritizing these targets. This enables brand management to become more efficient by focusing on those aspects of brand development that promise the highest return. Of course, the final decision about where to act first in the purchase funnel will still depend on management's assessment of the organizational capabilities of the company (we will discuss this further in chapter 4). When making such decisions, it is also important to take into account the potential responses of competitors to the intended brand-building activity. Finally, the selection of the appropriate benchmark is also critical to deriving the right conclusions. What the correct benchmark is will depend on the specific market situation as well as on the brand's strategic aspirations. Selecting the appropriate competitive set is as important for funnel benchmarking as frame-of-reference setting is for meaningful segmentation (see section 2.2).

To be actionable, the purchase funnel should be compiled and analyzed at a segment level (rather than based on an entire market) wherever possible. Given the considerable differences in needs outlined in section 2.2, it is not surprising that brand perception is also highly sensitive to which segment you are looking at. If we go back to the mobile phone example described above (Figure 2.26), we find that there are, in fact, substantial differences in brand driver performance between segments (compare figure 2.30). While an attribute such as »easy to use« is one of the top two attributes driving consumers from »consideration« to »favorite« in all segments, only members of the conservative segment care about a »broad range of products.« Similarly, only the »fancy fashionistas« want a »trendy brand you are happy to be seen using.« For »penny-pinching pragmatists,« »good quality« matters most, while this attribute is noticeably absent from the top drivers for the other two segments. If nothing else, this highlights the necessity to think about target segment selection very carefully. It is unlikely that the same (model) brand will be successful with segments as different as the »fashionistas« and the »pragmatists.«

Fig. 2.30: Brand drivers by segments: Mobile phones example

Conservative big spenders (22%)	Fancy fashionistas (45%)	Penny-pinching pragmatists (33%)
Behavioral relevance rank	Behavioral relevance rank	Behavioral relevance rank
1. **Offers a broad range of products**	1. Easy to use	1. **Good quality**
2. Easy to use	2. **A brand you are happy to be seen using**	2. Easy to use
3. A brand you can trust	3. Appealing design	3. A brand you can trust
4. Appealing design	4. A brand you see everywhere	4. Good customer service
5. Always receives high marks in consumer tests	5. Offers good business phones	5. Always receives high marks in consumer tests
	6. **Trendy**	6. A leader in practical features such as battery life

Source: McKinsey Germany, 2006

Measuring Brands

It needs to be noted, however, that this type of analysis is time and context specific. Because funnel transfer rates are not immune to competitor moves and other changes in market dynamics, the time frame in which the potential gains can be captured is limited, depending on the size of the potential and the initial situation specific to the industry and the individual brand; the opportunity is likely to range from two to five years at most.

Inside the Funnel: A Fresh Take on Consumer Decision Making [37]

The brand purchase funnel is a proven tool to capture and analyze consumer attitudes towards a set of brands in a specific category and market. In the form of its later stages – purchase, repurchase, loyalty, and the like – it even includes consumer behavior. It works as an attitudinal and behavioral snapshot cutting across all respondents in the research sample at a given point in time. It helps to detect bottlenecks in a brand's performance as well as the attributes that influence the average consumer's transfer from one stage to the next. In order to improve a brand's performance, brand managers focus on changing their target group's perception of the relevant attributes or »brand drivers.«

But in order to determine the most effective ways of achieving such changes in perception, it is important to understand that consumers have different ways of arriving at their purchase decisions. Specifically, individuals may »enter the funnel« at different stages, repeat parts of the process, even skip some stages, and, perhaps most importantly, use different touch points to gather the information and experience they need to move from one stage to the next. Understanding the diversity of consumer behavior at this more granular level can be an important source of competitive advantage. It can be thought of as a way of increasing the resolution of the big picture provided by the purchase funnel. This is why McKinsey has engaged in large-scale consumer research to deepen the understanding of different decision-making styles, and the specific roles individual touch points play at critical stages in the process. The research design comprised qualitative as well as quantitative elements; it included in-person interviews, consumer diaries, shop-alongs, and online surveys. Let's take a look at the decision-making profiles of two very different car buyers to see how this plays out in practice:

Car Buyer A, a self-proclaimed American-car enthusiast, accompanied a friend to a Suzuki dealership. Although he was not really in the market for a new car himself, A fell in love with an SUV he saw at the dealer lot.

He was thrilled to find it came with remote-controlled keyless access, a feature he had been fascinated by for some time. A said the »smart« key made the Suzuki feel like a luxury car. He neither researched the technical specs of the Suzuki SUV in any detail nor did he really look at any other car models. Less than two weeks after the first encounter, he bought the car that had caught his eye by chance on that fateful day.

Car Buyer B has never owned a car before, although she has quite a long commute to work. She had been thinking about getting a car for some time, but her decision to start looking systematically was triggered by a substantial inheritance from her grandmother. B always assumed she would eventually buy a Ford, since all her friends and relatives drove Fords, and she hardly noticed any other cars in the street. Even when she was ready to make the purchase, she didn't really look at other brands. Then B went on vacation, got a Seat Leon as a rental car, and really enjoyed driving it. When she got back from the trip, she felt paralyzed since she liked both the Ford and the Seat. She felt she had no way of deciding and postponed the purchase.

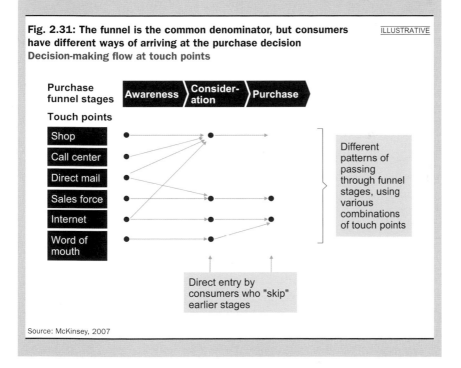

Fig. 2.31: The funnel is the common denominator, but consumers have different ways of arriving at the purchase decision
Decision-making flow at touch points

Source: McKinsey, 2007

Lessons learned from these examples, and others like them, include: **While the funnel is an ideal instrument for measuring the status quo of a brand's performance in the purchase process, not all consumers go through the stages in a linear fashion when making their decisions** (see Figure 2.31 for more details). The complications become particularly apparent when we look at trigger events, i.e., at the events that incite us to even start thinking about a purchase in a specific category. While some car buyers wait until their car breaks down, others buy a new car every two or three years to offset their expense with the resale value of the old car. Some people, like Car Buyer A, even make their decision on the spur of the moment and, effectively, jump straight to purchase without passing through any of the earlier stages. Others, like Car Buyer B, are pushed into the decision-making process by an unrelated event, such as inheriting a substantial sum of money. While some buyers go about their decision making in a highly fact-based way and start with a narrow consideration set for detailed comparisons, others absorb the full variety of what they see on the road or dealer lot and don't make up their mind until the very last minute.

Both the number of options considered and the number of touch points used by an individual are surprisingly small. Because of this, making it into the consideration set is often the biggest hurdle for a brand. The key to the consideration set is *word-of-mouth*. It is the most important touch point across all categories surveyed, especially for »opt-in,« i.e, as a reason to even consider a given product: if my friends say they like it, I might like it, too. While this is true even for a fairly simple item, such as many fast-moving consumer goods, word-of-mouth is even more important for complex and expensive purchases such as cars or mortgages. Although word-of-mouth is outside the realm of the brand manager's direct control, its importance should spur managers to keep looking for alternative ways of shaping consumer perception, e.g., by influencing the influencers.

Some touch points are better suited to conveying specific image attributes; there are even »winning combinations.« While a car's »reliability« is assessed almost exclusively based on consumers' previous experience and word-of-mouth, it's very different for an attribute like »good design«: Consumers' perceptions of a car's design primarily changed when they had *seen* the model in question, either »on the road« or in »advertising.« To determine whether a given model is »a car for someone like me,« a lot of consumers would specifically observe other drivers of the brand or model in question. For details, see section 3.2, on putting the brand promise into operation. It examines some of the latest findings on how concrete and quantifiable marketing actions at key touch points can improve brand driver performance, which, in turn, helps to close any gaps in a brand's funnel performance.

Addressing such differences in the insight generation phase, as well as in the more executional phase of actual brand management and communication planning, will become increasingly important. In recognition of the diversity of real-life decision making, market researchers will have to adapt their research designs. Agencies will have to make sure interviewers are equipped with the appropriate skills and methods. Brand managers will have to recognize that their promises need to appeal to very different types of decision makers. Last but not least, channel managers and communication planners will have to rethink the role of trigger events and »killer« touch points. Understanding when, where, and how consumers form perceptions and judgments of a brand is critical to succeed at influencing their behavior. It is also a key element of increasing marketing spend effectiveness: the more targeted a brand's influencing techniques are in terms of both brand drivers and touch points, the higher its return on marketing investments (see sections 3.3 and 4.1 for details).

Interview with Are Thu:
»Nokia is Moving to Value-Based Branding«

Developing from a riverside paper mill in southwestern Finland to a global telecommunications leader, Nokia is the world's number one manufacturer of mobile devices, with approximately 40 percent share of the world market for mobile telephones in 2007. It is also recognized as one of the most valued brands in the world.

Are Thu is Vice President Brand Strategy at Nokia. After a successful and prominent career in marketing at the Coca-Cola Company, Are Thu joined Nokia in 2005 as Director of Organizational Capability Development to focus on developing a marketing capability plan. His objective was to facilitate Nokia's transition from a product-driven organization to one centered around consumers and brands. In February 2006, Are Thu became Vice President to head a team of brand experts shaping Nokia's strategy for its brand and sub-brands. McKinsey Branding Experts Christoph Erbenich and Thomas Meyer talked to Are Thu about what drives Nokia's brand management.

McKinsey: How would you describe Nokia's current brand position and brand promise?

Are Thu: Nokia's brand promise is of »very human technology helping people feel close.« The heart of it is actually the word »help.« What Nokia does is give you technology that actually helps you feel close to what and, more importantly, who matters most to you. The way we summarize it in one line is »connecting people in new and better ways,« which is a powerful filter for us to put against the technology. We constantly ask: »Is this helping people connect in new and better ways?« If the answer is yes, it's on. If not, we ask the designers and engineers to go back to the drawing board.

McKinsey: Do you have a standardized set of questions to make sure that all products meet Nokia's brand promise?

Are Thu: We do have a product creation process, a stage-gate process where the brand promise is injected into each milestone. Right now, we're still in the process of making the questions more natural, less prescriptive, so the engineers can really get their minds around the role of the brand. We've been playing with an idea we call the »look-feel test.« The idea is that if we put five devices a couple of meters from you, you should be able to spot the one from Nokia right away. Or if we put five devices in a black bag and you stick your hand in, you should be able to feel the Nokia one. If we could do both these things for the brand, it would be fantastic!

McKinsey: Nokia launches 50 different products a year and is present in just about every niche imaginable. How do you retain the Nokia brand promise while stretching it at the same time?

Are Thu: This is actually a big debate at Nokia. Let me try to answer by telling you a story first. In my family we stay in touch with weekend phone calls. Last week, I made a little test, took a picture of my five-year-old, sent it to my mom. Two hours later, she texted back: »Love the picture, how do I print it? Can I get a Nokia with a bigger screen?« What this illustrates is that we must look beyond the needs of an individual and take a close look at how our technology helps the relationships between people. Some people may want the lower-end solution, just the image-receiving phone and, of course, we will sell you all the benefits of the image-receiving phone. Then there's another person who needs the best-of-breed camera phone. So, the basic idea of helping people feel close and connected is not to market to individuals but to people's relationships. Whether that will be successful or not, I don't know, but that is what we are betting on, that we can keep it all together under the slogan of Nokia Connecting People.

McKinsey: How do you deal with the rapid pace of innovation and change in your industry without risking the core of the Nokia experience and brand promise?

Are Thu: My belief is that the way to do this is to move up to a more value-based branding approach. Nokia starts to represent certain values, and we are beginning to think about the brand in terms of »brand character« instead of in terms of features and benefits alone. This can go all the way to using brand archetypes the way Marlboro does. Yes, it's really just a cigarette, but what the Marlboro brand is all about is freedom and adventure, »Come to Marlboro country.« You notice they're not saying »Your cigarettes taste better.« That is totally irrelevant.

What's important for us as a brand is not to get dragged down into feature wars, but to stay at the value level. We want to enable people to connect in new and better ways. But Nokia is not the only brand that does that. We do this together with other brands – in an ecosystem, if you will. But for

133

certain key experiences Nokia is the brand that is taking responsibility for the end-to-end solution. And when I say end-to-end solution, I don't mean a technical end-to-end solution, but the stuff that lets consumers start doing what they want to do and actually accomplish all of it in the timeframe that they wish to do it in. For these kinds of experiences, Nokia needs to find out which other brands have the most power to support the ecosystem and then make sure that we are the ones that take the lead in making it happen.

McKinsey: What about changing consumer behavior?

Are Thu: My belief is it is only when you have deep insights into consumer behavior and a profound understanding of technological changes at the same time – and only then – that you have the chance to get true innovation into the marketplace. We've had many inventions inside Nokia, and we have had a couple of insights into consumer behavior, but the actual marriage of the two, of a consumer-centered marketing organization with a core technology organization, is challenging. It's a cliché, but when you do a brand presentation to an audience of technology people, you get to the fourth page and you can tell they think it's just a bunch of fluff. There is still a huge amount of discomfort with the whole brand value conversation. So, at Nokia, we have a specific effort under way to drive behavioral understanding into the innovation space, because behavior seems to be something that clicks for the engineering folks as well as the marketing folks.

Building on my previous story: I want the grandmas like my mom to upgrade to a camera phone. And the engineers go: »Got it. I can make one. How big does the screen need to be? Let's talk about how it fits in the bag.« And the marketing people to say: »Wow, this is what cross-generational bonding is all about, connecting people in new and better ways. It's not just technical against technical: this is about connecting grandmas with grandkids and parents thinking: »I'm a good daughter because I sent grandma a photo of her grandson.« It's a culture clash, but what has helped us bridge the gulf are some behavioral insights that engineering and marketing can both build on. We are really pushing the whole behavioral angle right now.

McKinsey: »Marketing return on investment« – this must be a topic for you, given the sheer size of the company and a 40 percent market share. How do you arrive at a smart way of spending the money for your brand?

Are Thu: For us, the most important thing at this stage is to do fewer campaigns. We come from a culture in which, when we were launching five or six products a year, we would launch every product with a full-fledged, 360-degree campaign. That's totally unrealistic now. Now we have to pick the stuff that really makes a difference. The other very interesting challenge is in the difference between 360 marketing and an asymmetric marketing mix. We have a culture in which you do the TV commercial first – and then you do all the other touch points. But one agency asked us, »Why don't you first design what you want the results of the online search to look like, and then design the brand from there?« And they gave us a link to a very inspirational story, a petrol station brand, that was number three in their market. Life is not good as number three, so in trying to figure out what to do, they realized that the two competitors are pretty male-skewed. But 50 percent of the people who drive cars are female, hence the idea: »Why don't we skew female?« Then they carried out an ethnographic study: »What is the most important thing for a woman in a gas station? – the rest room.« So they designed the restroom first and designed the entire brand experience from the rest room outwards. Brilliant! This is exactly the sort of approach we need. Not to start with a TV commercial and then design the brand, but to start with the thing that matters most to the consumer, whatever that is – the restroom, or what really happens on the Web – and then work back from there to the TV commercial that will support it.

McKinsey: Nokia started out more than a hundred years ago as a paper mill. What are you going to be doing in another hundred years from now?

Are Thu: In a hundred years from now? Wow! I wonder if we'll be in the transporter business – you know how in *Star Trek* you can beam people to where they want to be? I think we might be in that business. If you think »virtual presence,« and you agree that face-to-face communication is the best, there must be a way to get away from all the CO_2 problems and figure out how to make people's presence much stronger, where the value added is in »transporting people,« which might start with really rich hologram systems. That type of thinking could be an area that would be a natural fit for Nokia as a technology company. It would really support our promise of »connecting people in new and better ways.«

McKinsey: Is there any other brand right now next to Nokia that you are fascinated by?

Are Thu: The one that makes me scratch my head is Amazon. Not just because it is a fantastic brand, but because the business model is very strong. And we've seen in several pieces of consumer data that people are bonding with Amazon and starting to trust the brand to help them find what they're looking for in a time of boundless variety. So Amazon is a brand that is growing nicely and slowly by *doing* good, not necessarily

135

claiming to be good. It has developed into a trusted transactional brand, and just imagine if Amazon starts expanding its portfolio to financial or commercial services and gets a global footprint – fascinating.

Notes

1 *UBS to adopt a single brand*, UBS AG media release, Zurich/Basel, 12 Nov 2002.

2 Sattler, Henrik (ed.), *Praxis von Markenbewertung und Markenmanagement in deutschen Unternehmen*, PwC Deutsche Revision, 2nd edition, Frankfurt: Fachverlag Moderne Wirtschaft, 2001, and Dr. Jutta Menninger, Annette Marschlich, Henrik Sattler, Siegfried Högl, Oliver Hupp et al., *Praxis von Markenbewertung und Markenmanagement in deutschen Unternehmen 2005*, Jan 2006.

3 Extensive primary market studies for both the B2C and the B2B sectors were carried out in conjunction with the market research institute, Marketing Centrum Münster (MCM) at the University of Münster, Germany. The research was directed by Professors Backhaus and Meffert.

4 Representativeness refers to the distribution of age and gender in the population.

5 Premium or luxury cars were not part of the survey.

6 To allow a meaningful comparison, the ratings were transferred into a standardized scale so that differences between countries become more obvious.

7 Hofstede, Geert, *Culture's Consequences: Comparing Values, Behaviors, Institutions, and Organizations Across Nations*, 2nd edition, Thousand Oaks, CA: Sage Publications, 2003.

8 Seat capacity share for international flights in 2007 according to Official Airline Guide (OAG).

9 Gregory, James R. and Donald E. Sexton, »Hidden Wealth in B2B,« *Harvard Business Review*, Mar 2007 (data for 2006).

10 Caspar, Mirko, Achim Hecker, and Tatjana Sabel, »Markenrelevanz in der Unternehmensführung: Messung, Erklärung und empirische Befunde für B2B-Märkte,« *Arbeitspapier Nr. 4*, ed. Klaus Backhaus et al., Düsseldorf, 2002. A total of 48 product markets were surveyed, 45 of which fulfilled the necessary requirements for validity.

11 Compare de Chernatony, Leslie and Malcolm McDonald, *Creating Powerful Brands in Consumer Services and Industrial Markets*, Oxford: Butterworth-Heinemann, 1998.

12 White Strip sales according to Felix Oberholzer-Gee and Dennis Yao, »Brighter Smiles for the Masses – Colgate vs. P&G,« Harvard Business School, 21 Mar 2007. Henkel sales according to Bear Sterns Report »The Drag of Invested Capital,« 10 Sep 2007.

13 Hölscher, Ansgar, »Customer Insights«, in Hajo Riesenbeck/Jesko Perrey (eds.): *Marketing nach Maß*, Heidelberg, 2007.

14 Deardorff, Julie, »Bottled elixirs vs. tap. Enhanced water is making the beverage industry healthier« *Chicago Tribune* Web edition, 23 Sep 2007; Deardorff, Julie, »Americans flocking to fortified water,« *Chicago Tribune* features blog, 25 Sep 2007; Associated Press, and John Sicher/*Beverage Digest*, 27 Sep 2007.

15 Brodbeck, Melinda, »Dove Campaign for Real Beauty Case Study«, Pennsylvania State University, 5 Mar 2007.

16 Bloom, Jonah, »Ogilvy, Dove miss chance to turn bad press into ›debate‹,« *Advertsing Age 42*, Vol. 79, No. 19, 12 May 2008, © Crain Communications; Lauren Collins, »Pixel Perfect – Pascal Dangin's Virtual Reality«, *The New Yorker*, 12 May 2008.

17 Wolfe Bieler, Kirsten, »Behind the Yellow Tail,« *Beverage Media*, Mar 2006.

18 H.W. Schroiff quote according to 28 Jul 2005 Henkel press release (»Reconnaissance«). Best Buy details based on Matthew Boyle »Best Buy's Giant Gamble«, CNN, 29 Mar 2006.

19 www.magnostic.wordpress.com.

20 »See inside the new Tesco US stores« on http://www.utalkmarketing.com.

21 Ramge, Thomas, »Ratatazong! Die Hilti ist der Rolls-Royce auf dem Bau. Nur innovativer. Wie machen die das? Vier Fragen zum Erfolgsmodell. Und deutlich mehr Antworten,« *Brand Eins*, Dec 2007.

22 Horizont/TNS Emnid, »Verbraucher werden Markenprodukten untreu,« 26 Mar 2003.

23 Knudsen, Trond, »Confronting Proliferation in Mobile Communications«, *The McKinsey Quarterly* Web exclusive, May 2007, www.mckinseyquarterly.com.

24 This is neither a debate about the merits and disadvantages of market segmentation nor a scientific discussion of the methods and techniques of determining target groups. The current marketing science literature provides comprehensive answers to nearly all these questions (e.g., Bonoma, Thomas V. and Benson P. Shapiro »Evaluating Market Segmentation Approaches,« *Industrial Marketing Managment* 13, 1984; Meffert, Heribert, and Christoph Burmann, »Markenbildung und Marketingstrategien,« *Handbuch Produktmanagement*, ed. Sönke Albers and Andreas Herrmann, Wiesbaden: Gabler 2000).

25 Marketing Executives Networking Group, 2007.

26 Schellekens, Maarten, »Segmentierung«, in Hajo Riesenbeck/Jesko Perrey (eds.): *Marketing nach Maß*, Heidelberg, 2007; PepsiMax performance according to PepsiCo Trade Marketing Manager Nicky Seal.

27 Sellers, Patricia, »Starbucks: The Next Generation,« *Fortune*, 4 Apr 2005.

28 Snyder Bulik, Beth, »Marketer of the year – Winner: Nintendo,« www.innerjoejoe.wordpress.com, 13 Oct 2007.

29 Haley, R. I., »Benefit Segmentation: A decision oriented tool,« *Journal of Marketing*, Jul 1968, pp. 30–35.

30 Perrey, Jesko and Ansgar Hölscher, »Nutzenorientierte Kundensegmentierung: Eine Zwischenbilanz nach 35 Jahren,« *Thexis* 20, No. 4, 2004, pp. 8–11; Bonoma, Thomas V. and Benson P. Shapiro, »Evaluating Market Segmentation Approaches,« *Industrial Marketing Management* 13, 1984, pp. 257–268; Perrey, Jesko, *Nutzenorientierte Marktsegmentierung: Ein integrativer Ansatz zum Zielgruppenmarketing im Verkehrsdienstleistungsbereich*, Wiesbaden: Gabler, 1999, p. 129.

31 Voeth, Markus, *Nutzenmessung in der Kaufverhaltensforschung: Die Hierarchisch Individualisierte Limit Conjoint-Analyse (HILCA)*, Wiesbaden: Deutscher Universitätsverlag, 2000.

32 Caspar, Mirko and Patrick Metzler, »Entscheidungsorientierte Markenführung: Aufbau und Führung starker Marken,« *Arbeitspapier Nr. 3*, ed: Klaus Backhaus et al., Düsseldorf, 2002.

33 For instance, the consumer behavior research group of the late Professor Kroeber-Riel; see also: Esch, Franz-Rudolf, *Ein verhaltenswissenschaflicher Ansatz für die Werbung*, Wiesbaden: Gabler, 1996.

34 See, for example, Low, George S. and Charles W. Lamb Jr., »The measurement and dimensionality of brand associations,« *Journal of Product & Brand Management*, 8, No. 6, 2000, pp. 350–368; Meffert, Heribert and Christoph Burmann, »Identitätsorientierte Markenführung: Grundlagen für das Management von Markenportfolios,« *Arbeitspapier Nr. 100*, Münster: Wissenschaftliche Gesellschaft für Marketing und Unternehmensführung e.V., 1996.

35 See, for instance, both the conceptualization of Keller, Kevin L., »Conceptualizing, Measuring, and Managing Customer-Based Brand Equity,« *Journal of Marketing* 57, Jan 1993, pp. 1–22, and Aaker, David A., *Building Strong Brands*, New York: The Free Press, 1996.

36 This example from the automobile industry as well as those described subsequently in this book are based on an outside-in analysis that McKinsey carried out as part of an international benchmark initiative in more than twenty product markets. The examples do not use any confidential data gathered within the framework of client relationships.

37 Based on qualitative research, comprising shopper interviews and shop-alongs, conducted by McKinsey & Company in multiple categories in the US and Germany in 2007.

3.
Making Brands

Brands are mostly made, not born. They do not arise accidentally; their growth and development can be measured and predicted. This is the main message of this book.

The success of a brand is measurable at every stage along its path: tools and methods exist that can measure the status of a brand in the competitive environment. We have already introduced four such tools and methods in chapter 2:

- **The Brand Relevance Calculator**: determines how relevant brands are in influencing purchasing decisions in a particular market.
- **Customer Insights and Market Segmentation**: identify, evaluate, and define a brand's target customer groups.
- **The Brand Diamond**: analyzes the various components of the brand image, i.e., tangible and intangible elements and rational and emotional benefits.
- **The Brand Purchase Funnel**: segments and compares customer recognition, affinity, and commitment to a brand at the various stages that lead to (and follow) purchase.

Brand managers need to be familiar with these analytical tools and methods and know how to apply them. They reveal the facts of the matter, but they do not tell you what to do to strengthen the brand. Therefore, for the brand manager, many questions have yet to be answered. What can be done to restore a luxury brand to its former glory? How can strong brands be protected from the competition and made even stronger? Can the existing brand and its promise be adjusted, or is it necessary to develop a completely new promise? What impact will it have on the organization if we follow advertising agency recommendations and make the brand more emotional? This chapter will begin to answer these important questions. In it, we describe four methods that are central to the »making« of power brands: Brand Driver Analysis, the resulting Matrix of Options, Brand Portfolio Management, and the Brand Personality Gameboard.

Power Brands. H. Riesenbeck and J. Perrey
Copyright © 2009 WILEY-VCH Verlag GmbH & Co. KGaA, Weinheim
ISBN: 978-3-527-50390-2

3.1 Brand Driver Analysis: Deriving Strategic Brand Direction and Initiatives for Growth

The brand purchase funnel measures the performance of the brand at the various stages leading to purchase and loyalty. It reveals where there are gaps in comparison with relevant competitors, quantifies these gaps, and ranks them according to their significance. This analysis creates transparency about a brand's strengths and weaknesses, but it leaves brand management with a serious question: How can these gaps, if at all, be closed? To be more precise, how can the brand be repositioned relative to its competitors so that current and potential customers will better notice it, and how can it capture the untapped sales indicated by the brand potential analysis? Looking back at the examples discussed in earlier sections, brand managers need to understand what factors are responsible for shortcomings along the purchase funnel.

- What accounts for the dramatic gap between the Volkswagen Passat and the Mercedes C-Class in converting potential customers into buyers? (While these models may be perceived as belonging to different sub-categories in some markets, i.e., medium vs. premium class in the United States, they are perceived as competing mid-sized models by many German car buyers.) (Figure 2.25)
- Why does Samsung lag behind industry leader Nokia in becoming a consumer's favorite mobile phone manufacturer? (Figure 2.26)
- What is the reason for Camel's gap compared with Marlboro in converting one-time customers into frequent buyers of the brand? (Figure 2.27)
- Why are German tourists less likely to consider Switzerland than Austria as a potential holiday destination? (Figure 2.28)

What is really important for the consumer?

To be able to establish what is really important for the consumer, we first need to identify all the necessary elements of the brand image in order to lead consumers from one stage of the purchase funnel to the next. We refer to these critical brand attributes as *brand drivers*. Comparing your own brand's performance on key brand drivers with the performance of competitors yields a profile of strengths and weaknesses. Brand drivers and their respective strengths can then be combined to form a matrix. From this matrix, it is possible to derive what options management has for growing the brand and setting its strategic direction.

Therefore, after compiling all the brand elements, the next step is to ensure that the brand drivers are correctly identified. To ensure that this is done, all the potential drivers, as well as the current ones, must be taken into consideration. It is best practice to structure each individual driver using the Brand Diamond (as described in section 2.2). Figure 3.1 shows a template of the potential drivers of brand image used as the starting point for a broad analysis of brand drivers in the retail trade.

Fig. 3.1: Brand diamond analysis of a retail chain

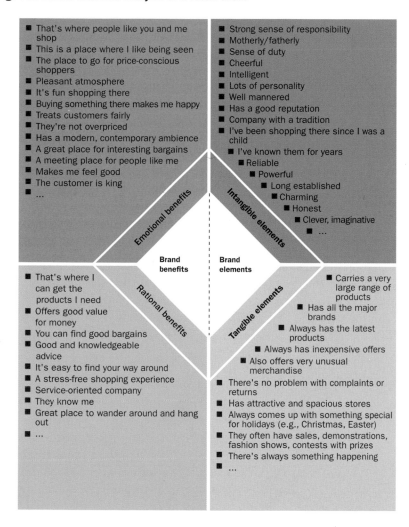

Source: McKinsey

The associations shown in Figure 3.1 are based on surveys of consumer focus groups and discussions with market experts. Qualitative research techniques such as these are especially insightful at this early stage of the positioning (refinement) process. They help to capture the richness of consumers' brand perceptions, including critical items possibly considered irrelevant by the marketing department, e.g., »a meeting place for people like me,« »great place to wander around,« or »also offers very unusual merchandise.« Further details are provided in the insert on qualitative research in section 2.2. The brand associations elicited from tangible elements essentially describe operational levers, such as the quality of product assortment (»always has the newest products«), the layout of the sales floor (»has attractive and spacious stores«), or distribution (»has a good location«). The other fields of the Brand Diamond comprise associations that reflect the perceived customer benefit or intangible brand elements (see section 2.3 for details).

This analysis produces a complete map of brand elements, analogous to Figure 3.1. This is the starting point for Brand Driver Analysis. The next step is to establish which associations are responsible for the consumer behavior in the purchase process (the brand *drivers*) and to determine how strongly the individual elements of the Brand Diamond are linked to a given brand (the brand *image*). The results indicate which brand elements best account for customer conversion at each stage in the purchase funnel, and how a given brand is performing on these conversion drivers.

Numerous methods of market research are available to analyze the behavioral relevance of the brand elements. A simple method frequently used is the direct customer survey of the most important attributes. It is important, however, to note that the results of such surveys can be misleading. The fact that all consumers would like the best possible performance for the least possible money actually tells you very little. Market researchers refer to this as *expectation inflation*.

A better method is to determine consumers' actual priorities indirectly using analytical methods. Although a range of multivariate techniques can be used to achieve this, the most common technique is to compare the average values. The average values of all brand elements are compared at two sequential stages of the purchase funnel. Those brand elements that show the greatest improvement in the average values from one stage to the next are the main brand drivers. In contrast, brand elements whose average values do not change in the transition from one stage to the next are not significant for that step in the purchase funnel. A good example of what this means in practice is the attribute of airline safety. The mean values of

Fig. 3.2: What customers say they want when they buy a car, and what they really value

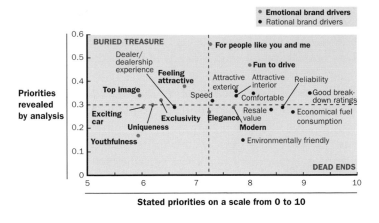

Stated priorities on a scale from 0 to 10

Key insights
■ Direct questions often lead to wrong results
■ Emotional brand drivers usually dominate

Source: MCM/McKinsey, 2002

this attribute will not differ at the purchase and loyalty stages. This is because the safety of major airlines is likely to be considered equally important by both one-time users and loyal customers. The situation might be very different, however, for an attribute such as punctuality. The punctuality (or lack thereof) of an airline might well be of great significance in encouraging (or discouraging) the transition from being a one-time customer to that of becoming a loyal customer.

As shown in Figure 3.2, using the example of a Brand Driver Analysis carried out by McKinsey in the automobile market, the priorities that consumers cite directly often differ considerably from those derived analytically, reinforcing the point that brand managers need to be cautious when using direct measurement methods. The reality is that people do not always do what they say they will. This discrepancy becomes particularly obvious when looking at environmental issues, for example. In direct surveys in the mid-sized automobile market, many consumers claim to place great value on environmental protection. This is not that surprising; who would say openly that they choose to be environmentally destructive after all? But when this statement is tested, environmental considerations do not turn

145

out to be truly relevant as a brand driver in purchasing a car. Consequently, it is not surprising that Europe's new generation of revolutionary, ultra-fuel-efficient cars have not been as successful as was expected. Despite what people might claim in surveys, fuel-guzzling SUVs continue to hog the roads. Chances are recent increases in sales of fuel-efficient vehicles are driven by rising fuel prices at least as much as by heightened environmental conciousness.[1]

An analysis of consumer priorities needs to be performed for each stage of the purchase funnel. Once complete, this analysis will paint a clear picture of the consumer's path through each subsequent stage of the purchase funnel. Figure 3.3 shows the results of this type of analysis using the automobile example. This illustration shows that the Volkswagen Passat had a high potential for capturing sales relative to its competitor, the Mercedes C-Class, especially in the transition from consideration to purchase. The analysis shows that the brand driver »fun to drive« had the strongest influence on consumer behavior. The next four brand elements are all of similar relevance in influencing the purchase decision, but are much less important than »fun to drive.«

The relative importance of the brand drivers is determined by the behavioral relevance index. According to this ranking, the element »vitality« is a brand liability. It has a negative influence on purchasing behavior and prevents a better conversion rate to the purchase stage. Just as positive brand drivers improve brand performance in the purchase process, negative ones adversely influence the mind of consumers. Although it might not be intui-

Fig. 3.3: When buying a car, customers value emotional benefits

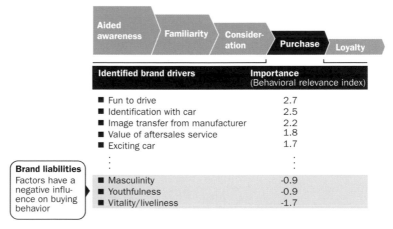

Source: MCM/McKinsey, 2002

Making Brands

Fig. 3.4: VW Passat and Mercedes C-Class: Comparison of strengths and weaknesses

(Difference in percent)

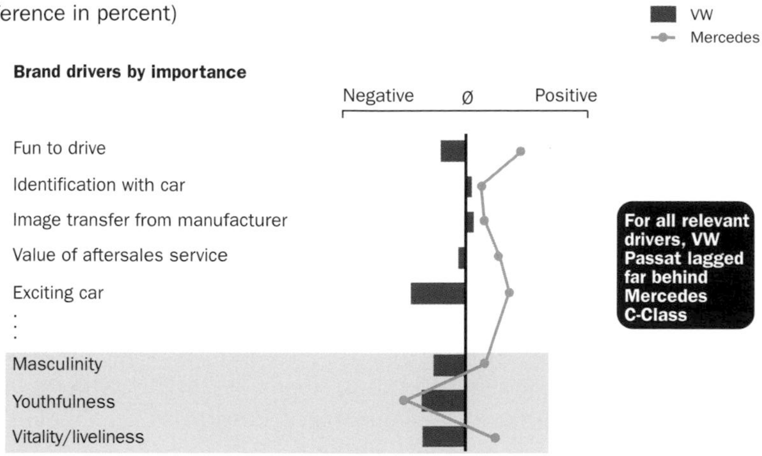

■ VW
●─ Mercedes

Brand drivers by importance

	Negative	Ø	Positive

Fun to drive

Identification with car

Image transfer from manufacturer

Value of aftersales service

Exciting car

⋮

Masculinity

Youthfulness

Vitality/liveliness

> **For all relevant drivers, VW Passat lagged far behind Mercedes C-Class**

Source: MCM/McKinsey, 2002

tively obvious, the analysis shows that an overly »vital« or »lively« image for the Volkswagen Passat would have had a negative impact on sales in its vehicle class.

Once the brand drivers have been determined, the next step is to carry out an analysis of the strengths and weaknesses of the brand. Quite simply, in this analysis, the benefits and elements of a company's brand are compared to those of the market average and the most important competitors, taking into consideration all the brand drivers prioritized for each stage of the brand funnel. This comparison reveals where a company's brand has been able to establish a strong, differentiated position, and in which brand drivers it lags behind the competition. Figure 3.4 illustrates the strengths and weaknesses analysis in the automotive market. The excerpt shown in Figure 3.4 clearly demonstrates that the Volkswagen Passat in 2002 not only performed worse than its competitor in the two relevant brand elements »fun to drive« and »exciting car,« but it also lagged behind the market average.

Defining the options for action

In order to define the options available to management for influencing the brand, the analyses of brand drivers and strengths and weaknesses are combined to produce a Matrix of Options for Action. This matrix will highlight key issues for management:

- If a company's brand shows weaknesses in key brand elements, these are potential starting points for improving the brand image. Strongly negative brand elements need to be addressed immediately; they must be eliminated or at least minimized in order to improve the brand's performance in the purchase process.
- Conversely, if the brand demonstrates strengths in important elements, these should be maintained or expanded. Less important brand attributes on which the brand performs particularly well may also help to differentiate the brand; however, it needs to be remembered that they have only an indirect impact on purchasing behavior.

Figure 3.5 shows an example of this type of actionable Matrix of Options for the Volkswagen Passat. While »fun to drive« is a highly relevant brand driver in the purchase process, the Volkswagen Passat was perceived as less »fun to drive« than its competitors. »Fun to drive« thus represents a potential starting point for brand image optimization. The matrix answers the question of why the Volkswagen Passat lagged so far behind the Mercedes C-Class when it came to converting potential customers into buyers: in the relevant emotional brand drivers, the Volkswagen Passat appeared to be

Fig. 3.5: The VW Passat needed to build emotional brand drivers in order to improve its performance in the purchase funnel

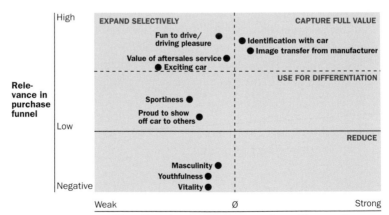

Strengths and weaknesses in comparison with competitors

Source: MCM/McKinsey, 2002

more weakly perceived than the competition. This is the point where management needed to intervene. (For further insights on which touch points to use for improvements on a given image statement, see the insert on consumer decision making at the end of section 2.4 as well as the discussion of customer-driven redesign at the end of section 3.2.)

We will now revisit the case studies mentioned earlier to examine the options for optimizing the brand image.

Mobile phones: Outside-in analysis of the purchase funnel in the summer of 2006 indicated that Samsung still lagged behind its competitor Nokia in becoming a consumer's favorite choice (Figure 2.26). The Brand Driver Analysis shows that key drivers to increase conversion rates in this case are »easy to use,« »a brand you can trust,« »good quality,« and »a brand you are happy to be seen using« (Figure 3.6). Despite its relative weaknesses, Samsung made significant progress in both perception and performance in the recent past. In 2006, the company was the global number three in the handset market at a market share of some 12 percent; Nokia and Motorola achieve a combined market share of some 50 percent.[2]

Fig. 3.6: Samsung and Nokia: Brand driver analysis shows differences in perceptions

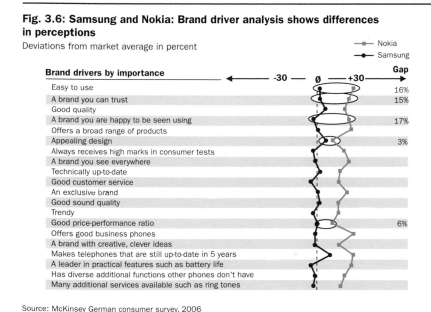

Source: McKinsey German consumer survey, 2006

The strengths and weaknesses profiles of Nokia and Samsung show that Nokia outperforms Samsung in consumers' perception overall. The profile also reveals that the Samsung brand achieves very similar ratings to Nokia's on attributes like »appealing design« and »good price-performance ratio.« However, these are not the main drivers that determined consumers' choice of their favorite mobile phone brand according to the purchase funnel and Brand Driver Analysis.

When this information is transferred to a Matrix of Options for Action, it is clear that Samsung had its work cut out for it at the time the analysis was conducted (Figure 3.7). To close the gap to Nokia, it will be insufficient to emphasize Samsung's strengths of modernity, quality, and design, as these brand elements are of medium to low importance to consumers. To increase funnel performance, Samsung must improve on the convenience aspect (»easy to use«) as well as on the emotional benefits of trust and reputation (»happy to be seen with«).

Samsung management began by increasing its emphasis on emotional brand features with the launch of its new »Imagine« campaign to replace the ubiquitous »DigitAll Everyone's invited« in 2005. Specifically, the company was hard at work to improve performance on critical attributes such as »happy to be seen with.« Recent efforts include the »Your music is

Fig. 3.7: "Easy to use" was the most important improvement point for Samsung in 2006

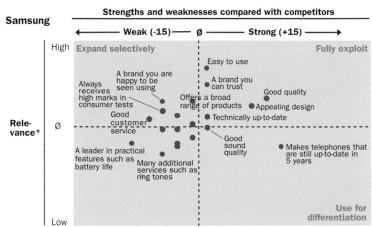

* Brand driver values are derived from the Consideration to Favorite stages of the funnel
Source: McKinsey German consumer survey, 2006

Making Brands

calling« campaign for selected music phones. Samsung hopes to stand out from the crowd by offering exclusive content such as only-from-Samsung DJ remixes of mainstream hits (e.g., Nelly Furtado's *Do it*), as well as matching sweepstakes and party events. Norbert Strixner of Samsung Mobile says: »Music is becoming increasingly important for us. It helps us reach young, fashion-conscious trendsetters focused on spare-time activities and entertainment. This is a target group we hope to expand in the future.«[3]

Tobacco: As the Matrix of Options for Action in Figure 3.8 shows, Camel is perceived as weaker than Marlboro in nearly all relevant drivers in the Spanish cigarette market. To build the brand, Camel needs to develop further key drivers in addition to its few existing functional strengths (its smooth taste and good value for money). Emotional benefits are highly relevant in this market, including, for instance, »makes me feel good,« »brand you trust,« and »for people like you and me.« Developing these brand drivers would help Camel to improve its position in the Spanish cigarette market.

Tourism: In the analysis comparing Switzerland and Austria as tourist destinations, Switzerland trailed Austria as a possible destination at the brand funnel stage »consideration.« A segment-specific evaluation shows that Switzerland's brand image (and the concomitant brand drivers) differs considerably across segments, depending on the age group of the potential tourists. For those under the age of 40, the most important criteria when it comes to considering a vacation destination are a »trendy destination« and »charming.« For the segment over the age of 40, the most important drivers are »good value for money« and »high quality« (Figure 3.9). The segment-specific analysis also shows that Switzerland's image is far more negative among younger people. To appeal to the younger age group, Switzerland will need to rejuvenate its image. Co-hosting the 2008 European soccer championship (UEFA Euro 2008) is a key event authorities hope will help to improve Switzerland's perceived trendiness. Roughly 85 percent of Swiss citizens expect the championship to improve Switzerland's image abroad, and experts at the University of Bern say it will attract up to 1.4 million additional foreign visitors.[4] For the older target group, Switzerland should emphasize the perception that it offers value for money. This example of the use of Brand Driver Analysis in tourism clearly demonstrates that the brand purchase funnel is most effective when the various purchasing stages are segmented and considered target group by target group.

Fig. 3.8: Matrix of Options for Action for Camel relative to Marlboro

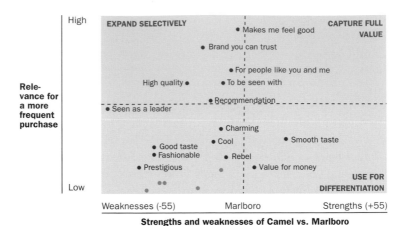

Strengths and weaknesses of Camel vs. Marlboro

Source: McKinsey Spanish market research, April 2005 (n = 501)

Fig. 3.9: Switzerland's image problem in tourism: "High-priced" and "old-fashioned"
Percent

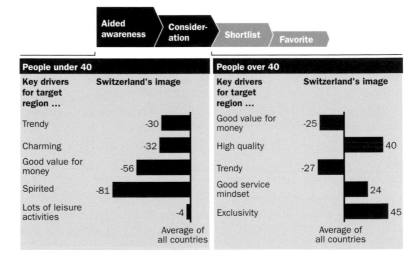

Source: McKinsey survey, conducted in Germany, 2004

Selecting benchmarks

In order to apply Brand Driver Analysis effectively, it is necessary to assess each stage of the purchase funnel separately and to select appropriate benchmarks for each stage.

Take into account the stage of the purchase funnel: The individual brand drivers do not possess the same relevance at all stages of the purchase funnel. Price, for instance, is very important at the transition from consideration to purchase. In establishing customer loyalty, however, price plays only a secondary role in many industries; dimensions of emotional benefit are much more important at this stage, as demonstrated in the mobile phone example. Similarly, a product's perceived price does not always correlate with actual price points. To improve a brand's performance on »value for money,« you don't necessarily have to lower prices (see section 4.3 on brand delivery for details).

A Matrix of Options for Action can, of course, be generated for each stage of the purchase funnel, but the matrix that addresses the stage with the highest potential for improvement is always of special interest for a brand. If no single stage stands out in the purchase funnel analysis, it makes sense to generate an aggregate Matrix of Options for Action. This ensures that all the main drivers of all the stages in the purchase funnel can be examined together.

Choosing the right benchmarks: In the Matrix of Options for Action, the strengths and weaknesses of a brand are always assessed in relation to those of a benchmark. This benchmark is usually either a single competitor brand or an industry average. Benchmark selection should reflect the given brand's history, current position, and aspiration. For a relatively new brand, for instance, selecting the market leader as the sole benchmark is unlikely to identify anything other than significant weaknesses in the Matrix of Options for Action. This wouldn't be very helpful, as it would make it almost impossible to choose a meaningful strategic option for building the brand. Instead, by considering a more conservative benchmark, in this case, for instance, the market average or another new entrant, more useful results can be developed.

Changing direction

Brand Driver Analysis allows management to determine the strategic direction of the brand using the Matrix of Options for Action. Orienting the brand strategy towards selected brand drivers will lead to improved brand performance at the respective stages of the purchase funnel. The unanswered question here is whether or not the competitors' brand strategy should also be taken into account.

It is a fundamental principle of brand management that a brand must not only be better than those of its competitors, but also distinctive from them. Often, it can even be sufficient to achieve only average performance on table-stake type attributes such as safety or affordability if the brand is sufficiently and prominently differentiated on a narrow set of highly relevant attributes. For example, a French fashion house may care very little about being perceived as the leader in »durability« as long as a sufficient number of A-list celebrities is seen (and photographed) with its handbags which, by association, become highly desirable »it« bags. If all brands in a given category relied on the same brand drivers (simply because they are relevant), they would be interchangeable from the consumer's perspective. In other words, market differentiation would disappear, commoditizing the category and the brands that play in it. To avoid this, it is important to examine whether a selected strategic direction potentially leads to:

• The brand assuming a position already held by another competing brand (in single-brand decisions); or
• The brand being oriented in such a way that it will conflict with another of the company's own brands (in multiple-brand decisions).

Of course, in certain cases, it may be in management's interest to attack the position of a competitor by repositioning a brand. Most of the time, however, sustainable brand building will aim towards differentiation from the competition.

This often proves to be especially challenging in multiple-brand strategies. Management of brand portfolios attempts, typically, to optimize positioning in the overall market through the selective positioning of single brands.[5] In a group of companies with several brands, however, single brands will often be repositioned without considering the consequences for the overall portfolio. In such circumstances, making the right decisions about prioritization while also balancing all the cost and profit effects presents a major challenge. Section 3.3 specifically covers this problem and describes how the BrandMatics® approach can help deal with it in a systematic manner.

Brand Management in the Kion Group of Companies

by Hubertus Krossa, CEO of Kion Group until April 2008, and Jens Menneke, Head of Strategic Marketing, Kion Group

The Linde MH brand – A »Leading« proposition[6]

While the Linde Group, comprising multiple brands in the material handling industry, became the Kion Group in September 2006 (referred to as »Kion Group« in the text below), Linde MH (MH for »material handling«) remains the group's forklift product brand despite the new structure and ownership.

In 1879, scientist Carl von Linde founded the »Gesellschaft für Lindes Eismaschinen AG« in Wiesbaden, laying the foundation for this international group of high-tech companies. The group aspires to expand its leading international position in the business divisions of Gas and Engineering continuously, and Material Handling through commitment to innovation and comprehensive expertise. The company focuses especially on providing complete solutions in order to understand and fulfill customers' individual needs more comprehensively.

The company's leading position is based on the values of quality, expertise, and innovation. »Made by Linde« has long been the anchor of its communication, both internally and externally. Quality, expertise, and innovation are the company's three overarching brand values that have enabled it to establish itself as the market leader in material handling. The Group, and Linde MH specifically, seek to fulfill the promise of its brand value not only for all its customers, but also for its employees.

The Kion Group has built itself into one of the world's largest manufacturers of industrial trucks, manufacturing three brands, Linde MH, Still, and OM. The Kion Group is one of the few suppliers to offer a complete range of products: engine-powered forklift trucks, electric trucks, and warehouse trucks. With more than 150,000 forklifts and warehouse trucks sold yearly, the Kion Group is the number one supplier in Europe today.

Linde MH represents a premium brand in the European market for industrial trucks. A European-wide study recently carried out on brand strength and customer satisfaction showed that in the overall market, Linde MH leads by a large margin in fulfilling the most demanding customer requirements. Alongside the high standard of quality and innovativeness of this long-standing brand, Linde MH's success is attributable

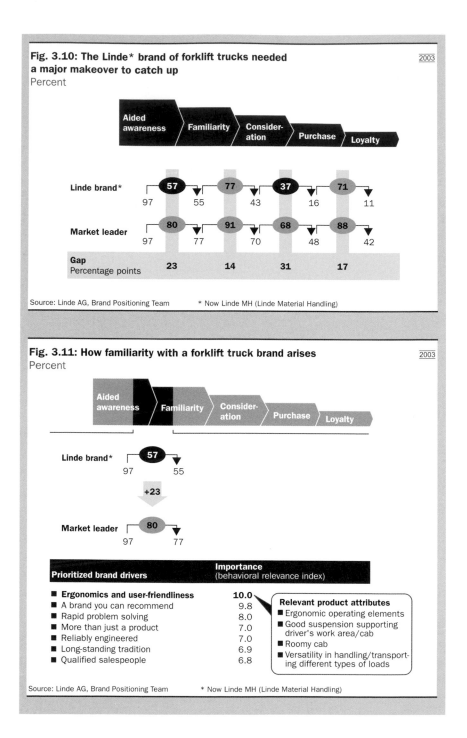

Fig. 3.10: The Linde* brand of forklift trucks needed a major makeover to catch up
Percent

2003

Aided awareness | Familiarity | Consideration | Purchase | Loyalty

Linde brand*
97 — 57 — 55 — 77 — 43 — 37 — 16 — 71 — 11

Market leader
97 — 80 — 77 — 91 — 70 — 68 — 48 — 88 — 42

Gap
Percentage points: 23 — 14 — 31 — 17

Source: Linde AG, Brand Positioning Team   * Now Linde MH (Linde Material Handling)

Fig. 3.11: How familiarity with a forklift truck brand arises
Percent

2003

Aided awareness | Familiarity | Consideration | Purchase | Loyalty

Linde brand*
97 — 57 — 55

+23

Market leader
97 — 80 — 77

Prioritized brand drivers	Importance (behavioral relevance index)
■ Ergonomics and user-friendliness	10.0
■ A brand you can recommend	9.8
■ Rapid problem solving	8.0
■ More than just a product	7.0
■ Reliably engineered	7.0
■ Long-standing tradition	6.9
■ Qualified salespeople	6.8

Relevant product attributes
■ Ergonomic operating elements
■ Good suspension supporting driver's work area/cab
■ Roomy cab
■ Versatility in handling/transporting different types of loads

Source: Linde AG, Brand Positioning Team   * Now Linde MH (Linde Material Handling)

to its professional, well-coordinated dealer structure in all markets. In France and England, the two leading brands Fenwick and Lansing have been successfully integrated into the Linde MH brand organization.

Still has been a part of Kion's brand portfolio in material handling since 1973. Historically strong in the domain of electric counterbalance forklift trucks, today Still covers the entire product portfolio of industrial trucks in Europe. Its distribution and service structure comprises company-owned branch offices that focus on the complete range of service packages for in-plant logistics, going well beyond the production, delivery, and maintenance of industrial trucks. The assortment of Still products and services ranges from complete, industry-specific solutions to computer-aided logistics programs for effective warehouse management.

OM (Officine Meccanice), an Italian brand with a long tradition, was integrated into the Kion Group (still called Linde Group at the time) in 1992. With its slogan »Designed to work,« this brand stands for reliable forklifts and warehouse trucks that give customers outstanding value for money. OM has long been the market leader in Italy using this positioning, but OM also maintains offices in other European markets. With its value-for-money strategy, the brand nicely rounds out the product assortment in the brand portfolio of Kion's material handling business.

Kion's strong commitment to this multiple-brand strategy in the Material Handling division is based on the realization that, in order to maximize success in the overall market, one needs to appeal specifically to different customer needs through separate brands. It is crucial here that the Kion Group assumes a different positioning with each brand so that it can minimize cannibalization and at the same time secure the best possible differentiation with respect to the relevant competition. It is important to understand the precise nature of the brands in order to perform this brand balancing act and to direct it actively in every product segment and in the various local markets.

Kion takes a systematic approach to this task based on a European, country-specific segmentation and a precise analysis of the purchase decision-making process both for Kion's brands and the most important competitors. This analysis is carried out in each relevant product category in the most important international markets. Figure 3.10 shows the results of a purchase funnel analysis that was conducted in 2003. The sample Linde MH brand selected for the analysis shows a brand awareness of 97 percent, an outstanding figure in this product category.

During subsequent process stages, however, the brand successively loses ground in comparison with the best in class. The main weaknesses arise in the transition to the familiarity and purchase stages. At these points in the purchase funnel, the brand significantly lags behind the best in class, with a gap of 23 and 31 percentage points respectively. Overall, the brand is able to convert only 11 percent of those surveyed into loyal customers.

Starting with the purchase funnel analysis, the reasons for the existing weaknesses of brands in the Kion Group can now be analyzed. It is, of course, important to know what brand elements are responsible in particular for the transition from one stage of the purchase funnel to the next. Figure 3.11 shows the results of this type of analysis for the transition from the »awareness« stage to that of »familiarity.« In order to derive targeted actions, the respective brand elements can also be subdivided into more detailed and concrete product attributes. It turns out that ergonomic operating elements, good suspension of the operator's work area/cab, and a spacious operator's cab are responsible for the overall perception of ergonomics and user-friendliness.

From the results of the Brand Driver Analysis, together with a strengths and weaknesses analysis, Linde MH is then in a position to derive the range of actions for brand optimization and to represent these in a matrix (Figure 3.12). This representation makes it possible to derive a clear indication of how to improve current brand positioning. The example shows that in the product segment under consideration, the Linde MH brand analyzed has weaknesses in the important drivers of »ergonomics« and »a brand you can recommend.« Potential for improvement also exists in the attribute »rapid problem solving.« In contrast, the brand's good price positioning should be maintained due to its strong differentiation.

This brief example illuminates the systematic approach Kion implemented in the course of optimizing and improving its multi-brand strategy; similar analyses have been conducted for the other brands in the Kion Group's portfolio. In addition to deriving short-term measures to improve the presence of every individual brand, the analysis and data acquired are also used to improve strategic brand positioning. It is, after all, very important that marketing decisions flow directly into product development. Besides taking advantage of existing synergies, Kion plans to pool technical expertise as well as to increase the share of the group's components used in the products significantly, while at the same time

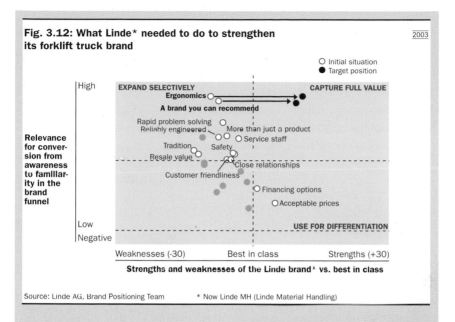

Fig. 3.12: What Linde* needed to do to strengthen its forklift truck brand

2003

○ Initial situation
● Target position

High

EXPAND SELECTIVELY

CAPTURE FULL VALUE

Ergonomics

A brand you can recommend

Rapid problem solving
Reliably engineered
More than just a product
Service staff

Tradition
Safety
Resale value
Close relationships
Customer friendliness

Financing options
Acceptable prices

Relevance for conversion from awareness to familiarity in the brand funnel

Low

USE FOR DIFFERENTIATION

Negative

Weaknesses (-30)   Best in class   Strengths (+30)

Strengths and weaknesses of the Linde brand* vs. best in class

Source: Linde AG, Brand Positioning Team   * Now Linde MH (Linde Material Handling)

being careful to ensure that the use of common parts never leads to products appearing the same from the customer's perspective.

For Kion, brand management is a top priority; decisions about brand portfolios are made at corporate headquarters. The independent implementation of these decisions in product development, distribution, and marketing strategies through the individual company brands is actively monitored and the results are reviewed on an ongoing basis. In this process, the corporate marketing department directs the development and implementation of strategies and marketing plans. The development of actions takes place in an ongoing dialogue between corporate headquarters, brand organization, and local subsidiaries. The corporate marketing department must mediate between the brand organizations in a neutral and objective manner. Although it is important to avoid internal cannibalization, internal competition can be useful in the search for better ideas. In this manner the Kion Group ensures that it achieves its aspiration of superior innovativeness, both now and in the future.

The company conducted an update of its 2003 brand diagnostic and expanded the scope to include Eastern Europe, one of the most important growth markets for the material handling business. In Germany, Linde MH successfully defends its top position with a strong performance throughout the purchase funnel. Specifically, the brand is now more successful at converting considerers (»purchase set«) into buyers (»purchase«) and has thus closed a key gap determined in the 2003 purchase funnel research (Figure 3.10). The market segments as identified in 2003 have proven stable. The most important next step for Linde MH in Germany is to strengthen the brand's target position. The updated brand diagnostic puts Linde MH in a position to tie its marketing actions to a deep understanding of what drives the brand's success.

For the first time, a similar study was conducted in Eastern Europe. In this region, the market segmentation is comparable to Western Europe with some differences in customer requirement profiles, e.g., »resale value of trucks« and »tradition of supplier« in the country. Overall, the group's brands have perceived positions similar to those in Western Europe. Again, Linde MH shows a strong performance along the whole purchase funnel, especially in the buying decision and the aftersales phases. In general, competing manufacturers are closer to one another in their positions than in Western Europe. This makes it even more important for brands to differentiate their positions.

3.2 Matrix of Options: Defining and Synthesizing the Brand Promise and Putting it into Operation

Brand Driver Analysis and the Matrix of Options for Action help companies to determine which brand elements drive the purchasing process, which are the best options in terms of positioning, and what effect these options will have on the competitive environment.

But brand building is more than merely specifying strategic direction. This direction must also be synthesized into an overall concept and then translated into operational terms, so that all employees are aware of exactly what individual contributions they can make in implementing the strategy so as to craft a strong brand. Due to their complexity, these tasks of making the brand strategy concrete and of putting it into operation frequently appear to be major stumbling blocks even for the best brand strategy.

- *Defining the brand promise:* The brand promise takes into account the analysis of the brand and the strategic considerations. It describes both the essence of the brand and its differentiation with respect to current and potential customers, as well as within the company's own portfolio.

Ideally, this promise culminates in a concise phrase, even if this conciseness comes somewhat at the cost of the various individual elements.

- *Putting the brand promise into operation:* Even the strongest brand promise will fall short if it is not embedded in the organization. The goal is to ensure that the brand promise is communicated to and understood by all the relevant employees and corporate units. It is only possible to implement a brand promise that is defined clearly so that it is connected to concrete actions, for instance, in terms of service and product design. The brand promise should always form the framework for all strategic and operational tasks of brand management, regardless of whether these involve developing a product concept, planning a product exhibition, optimizing a set of product components, or conducting a direct marketing campaign. Often, the brand promise is condensed into a short claim or statement used in external communication. This claim, sometimes referred to as the brand vision, serves as a point of reference both internally and externally.

Skoda automobiles can be used as an example to illustrate this process. Its brand promise at the time, developed jointly with Volkswagen Group Marketing in 1998, was: »Solid quality based on more than 100 years of tradition at reasonable prices.« This was put into operation by using a traditional and functional brand image that emphasizes rational benefits in its communication. Though Skoda's campaigns might not win prizes for their creativity, they nonetheless clearly appeal to its target group, as confirmed by Skoda's increased sales. In both 2006 and 2007, Skoda was the fastest-growing brand in the Volkswagen portfolio, delivering 16 percent year-to-year sales growth (2007: 15.7 percent). The Volkswagen brand itself gained 13 percent (2007: 8.3 percent). For comparison, Audi gained some 5 percent (2007: 1.3 percent), while Seat lost 3 percent (2007: +7.5 percent). Volkswagen reported that the first quarter in 2008 showed an upward trend for all brands including Seat.[7]

The brand promise does not appear like a bolt of lightning from the blue, however. It is derived through a step-by-step process.

Concentrating on the essentials

Summarizing the brand positioning in a brand promise is one of the most challenging tasks for management. Even if all the analyses described in section 3.1 are available, it is not easy to distill their essence. What makes it so challenging is that the brand promise needs to include, in a concise yet complete manner, all the factors that are essential to differentiating the brand.

The point from which to start is to ask what the brand represents from the consumer's point of view. In answering this question, agencies and consultants often create seemingly endless lists of visions, missions, values, emotional and rational attributes, core beliefs, supportive beliefs, personalities, identities, and so on, often not sufficiently backed up by facts.

A certain retailer, for instance, defined its brand promise using fifteen brand values, from »inspiration« to »ingenuity,« »fun,« »self-confidence,« and »trust« to »good value for money.« Nothing was left out. With this degree of fuzziness, the retailer could represent all conceivable formats, from Giorgio Armani to H&M or Gap. Additionally, the promise addressed nearly all conceivable dimensions of value. Who wouldn't want to shop there? When one of the authors of this book read aloud another colorful medley of positioning attributes, such as »friendly,« »honest,« and »helpful,« to his spouse, her guess as to the identity of the brand was, »It must be a church!« A reasonable guess under the circumstances.

Another example is a service provider that not only compiled a long list of general statements about its brand promise, but also went so far as to arrange them into a number of categories: from »value proposition« and »core values« to »inner-directed values,« »outer-directed values,« and »personality traits.« The brand promise seemed to be trying to answer questions that no one was asking. To top it off, the service provider took more than a hundred words to define who its target customers were. By contrast, a promise like Nokia's *Connecting People* is so simple and self-explanatory that it makes immediate sense even to non-native speakers of English and sticks almost as soon as you hear it. For further details, compare the interview with Are Thu, Vice President Brand Strategy at Nokia, and his comments on »connecting people in new and better ways« in the interview at the end of the previous chapter.

Establishing a successful brand promise is by no means child's play. It involves expert craftsmanship. Once complete it will define, for all those working with the brand, the brand's benefits for its customers, and will be encapsulated in a few short phrases as the basis for all marketing communication.

Once the Brand Driver Analysis has revealed the brand elements that support a company's own competitive position, the task is then to derive the optimal brand promise from this set of conceivable elements, identify its core areas of differentiation, review them on an ongoing basis, and update them as needed. Depending on the degree of aspiration involved, the brand promise may reflect current as well as future strengths of a given brand, but should not deviate too far from the brand's heritage. Unfortunately, there is no patented formula for which elements can be combined, and in what manner, to derive the brand promise. However, a checklist of guidelines does exist:

- *Distinctiveness:* Concentrate on unique and distinctive brand elements (derived from the Matrix of Options for Action).
- *Relevance:* Take into consideration the important brand elements in the customer's purchasing/selection decision (again, taken from the options for action).
- *Credibility:* Ensure that the brand promise is credible and reflects current strengths in brand perception as much as possible.
- *Consistency:* Maintain consistency with past brand image and brand heritage (see chapter 2 for examples of inconsistency in brand image).
- *Feasibility:* Secure internal performance capabilities. The company needs to possess the internal resources and capabilities necessary to ensure that the brand promise can be fulfilled consistently in all its contacts with customers. It is especially important to take into consideration the costs of implementing the brand promise.

Fig. 3.13: Checklist for deriving the brand promise

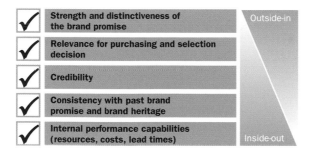

Source: McKinsey

Applying the Matrix of Options for Action

Which brand elements get priority; the most relevant or the strongest?

Brand managers frequently need to make fundamental decisions based on the assessment of the Matrix of Options for Action. Often this presents them with a dilemma: which of the two dimensions in the matrix – »strength« or »relevance« – (Figure 3.14) should be given preference? Should a company's own strengths, and thus its differentiation from competitors, be expanded first, even if the importance of these elements is relatively low? Or would it be better to eliminate existing weaknesses in important elements crucial to purchasing decisions?

Unfortunately, there is no universal answer to this question; a case-by-case approach is necessary. However, it is indisputable that any weaknesses in important »hygiene factors,« or table stakes, for the rational benefits of the brand need to be eliminated first. This means, for instance, that airlines must be safe, taxi services on time, and personal care products gentle on the skin. If a brand does not achieve at least an average performance on this kind of attribute, it loses the right to play. For example, Coke's British bottled water brand, Dasani, never recovered from a 2004 analysis revealing the water was contaminated with bromate, a cancer-causing chemical. The brand was discontinued in the United Kingdom and, against Coke's original plans, never introduced in Germany and France. If the next step involves further selection of brand-defining elements, a prioritization based on the checklist outlined in Figure 3.13 is necessary.

In making such decisions, the company always needs to weigh market requirements (the outside-in perspective or market-based view) against its own resources (the inside-out perspective or resource-based view). When taking an inside-out perspective, as well as considering financial resources and timing, brand managers need to consider staff and management capabilities and knowledge. The best theoretical brand promise is useless if it would take too long to deliver it effectively, or if the company lacks the capabilities and resources to carry it out.

Consequently, a compromise will often need to be made between a purely market-based approach and one that takes a more pragmatic line with the resources required to execute it. In other words, »strengthening your strengths« should take priority over »eliminating your weaknesses,« with the exception of weaknesses in table-stakes areas, such as safety.

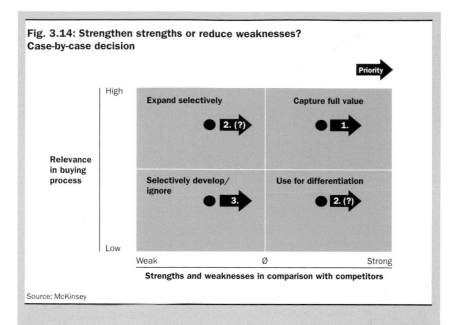

**Fig. 3.14: Strengthen strengths or reduce weaknesses?
Case-by-case decision**

Priority

High

Relevance
in buying
process

Expand selectively
● 2. (?)

Capture full value
● 1.

Selectively develop/
ignore
● 3.

Use for differentiation
● 2. (?)

Low

Weak   Ø   Strong

Strengths and weaknesses in comparison with competitors

Source: McKinsey

By proceeding in this manner, management can ensure that the brand remains unique and can retain its distinct profile in the competitive environment (Figure 3.14).[8]

Be careful, however. A brand's identity is worthless if the attributes that it conveys are perceived by customers to be of no interest, because they are not important for them today nor likely to be so in the future. Managing a brand along its identity, an approach outlined in numerous textbooks, does not free the brand manager from the responsibility for analyzing and improving the company's brand image in terms of the outside-in customer perspective. Regardless of how meticulous and cautious one is in developing brand identity, a brand's best assets, whether tangible or intangible, are of no use if they don't generate relevant associations among (potential) customers. A long-established retailer, for instance, might rely on its tradition all it wants, but if this image is outdated in many respects, or simply irrelevant to consumer decision making, it will fail. In other words, following a purely inside-out approach by focusing mainly on the brand's heritage and key strengths is not a foolproof recipe for success either.

Focusing exclusively on overcoming a brand's weaknesses is also a poor approach in most cases because it is likely to lead to »me too«

decisions. In the worst case, the company never gets off the treadmill of trying to catch up. Focusing too much on weak points can lead a company to invest in brand elements or positions that are already better covered by competitors' strong brands. Since these competitors will likely be striving to improve their strengths, this is very shaky ground on which to build. For example, a premium car brand might never catch up with the market average on »value for money,« but may well lose its luxury appeal, or even its profitability, in the process.

To sum up, in order to define the »right« brand promise, brand management needs to analyze and evaluate the market perspective, including the brand's current strengths and weaknesses, as well as the company's internal perspective with respect to its resources and capabilities. Bear in mind that the time horizon is of critical importance in this context. While a brand may aspire to develop a promise that differs from its current position and perception, it would be commercial suicide to communicate such an aspirational promise before the organization can live up to it. In other words, don't brag about what you wish you could do before you can actually do it. HVB, a German retail bank created after the merger of two regional banks, famously advertised a universal, no-worries service promise in 1998. They invested heavily in above-the-line advertising to push their message »You just live. We take care of the details.« Brand awareness soared, but when customers flocked to the bank's branches, they found out the hard way that HVB had neither the staff nor the processes to keep its promise. HVB lost 20 percent of its customers over the course of the next five years. While factors other than the broken brand promise are likely to have been involved in this decline, it is safe to say that HVB had not given sufficient attention to the credibility of its promise.[9]

The criteria included in the checklist shown in Figure 3.13 will form the basis for assessing and prioritizing the brand elements. For this purpose, the criteria are transformed into a simple scoring model. As with all scoring models, the key question is how to weight the criteria. Their weighting in the checklist should be oriented first and foremost towards the initial situation of the brand and the associated strategy. In a stable environment (e.g., in the case of market leaders such as BMW, Henkel's leading German detergent brand Persil, or Beiersdorf's Nivea), the most important criteria are certainly consistency and internal feasibility. In such cases, this exercise

Fig. 3.15: New profile for BMW

"The essence of the brand: joy"

BMW, Mini, Rolls-Royce – the three makes couldn't be more different. Thanks to an ingeniously designed and executed brand strategy, they each have personality traits that distinguish them for customers and against competitors.

The saying has been around for 25 years. It graces every advertisement and can be heard in every radio and TV spot. "BMW – Freude am Fahren." Or in English: "BMW – the ultimate driving machine." For Executive Board chairman Helmut Panke, that's what BMW stands for in the eyes of customers: "joy" as the brand essence, "dynamic" as the key brand value. Why does it matter? "The core is the heart or the essence of a brand, the ultimate customer value," says a BMW company report. "The values and their distinctive facets are the personality traits that collectively and uniquely stand for a brand."

In the past, BMW sought to associate its brand exclusively with "dynamic" and appeal primarily to career-minded go-getters on their way up. Now, because "one-dimensional positioning" jeopardizes the brand's success in the long term, the board has augmented it with the new elements "challenging" and "cultivated." As the Group's brand manifesto confidently announces: "To enable BMW to appeal to new target groups, we will position ourselves using all three brands." The Mini stands for "enthusiasm," its values are "chic, integrative, and extroverted."

As a result, the brand is said to have "a strong emotional appeal without being polarizing." It does not want to be a traditional automotive status symbol. Instead, its appeal is inclusiveness, "linking classes, peoples, countries, the young and the old."
Rolls-Royce is the "ultimate luxury brand." The car of choice for the super-rich conveys "presence," its values are "grace, endurance, and ambition." It is "admired and respected, it radiates majesty, charisma, and style and makes a clear statement – for itself and its owner."

Source: "Freude als Markenkern"; *Capital*, 19 September 2002, p. 45 (translation)

would typically not produce an entirely new brand promise but, would lead the company to update and improve the existing one (Figure 3.15).

Figure 3.16 demonstrates the concept of summarizing the brand promise in a short claim, using the example of the Skoda brand promise statement from 1998.

The Skoda brand promise was developed as part of a comprehensive process by which the Volkswagen Group has developed a multiple-brand strategy. After acquiring Seat in 1986 and Skoda in 1990, the Volkswagen Group was faced with a difficult task. On the one hand, the individual brands in the brand portfolio (including Volkswagen and Audi) needed to be positioned as leaders in as many attractive automobile segments as possible, but without competing with one another. On the other hand, it was important that the Group capture the cost synergies resulting from its integrated platform strategy. In this context, it was very important that the platform cost synergies should have no impact on the brand differentiation. These two aspects are therefore managed separately by the Group, so that customers remain unaware of the Group's platform synergies. Ford's Premier Group paid a hefty price when its newly introduced Jaguar X-type sedan was perceived, by some car buyers, as a »Mondeo in a party frock«

Fig. 3.16: The Skoda 1998 brand promise

Source: Volkswagen AG, 1998

(as one reviewer put it on www.ciao.co.uk in a February 2004 post) or even a »Jaguar Mondeo« (a blogger's joking reference to the X-type on www.edmunds.com) because it shared the Ford Mondeo's platform as well as many of its components. Jaguar never reached its sales target of 100,000 units annually. In its best year, 2003, the X-type sold 50,000 units. It seems unlikely that Indian automotive giant Tata Motors Ltd. will pursue a similar strategy after its takeover of Jaguar in March 2008. Says Group Chairman Ratan Tata: »We have enormous respect for the two brands [Jaguar and Land Rover] and will endeavor to preserve and build on their heritage and competitiveness, keeping their identities intact.«[10]

The new brand promises for the entire Volkswagen Group's corporate brands were created in 1998 in a joint development process headed by the corporate marketing department. Whereas Volkswagen is the universal brand of the »strong middle« (the mid-priced market that resides between economy cars and luxury models), Audi is the premium brand with a sporty, emotional orientation. In the more price-sensitive automobile segments, the Skoda brand is designed to appeal to the more functionally oriented buyers, whereas Seat is designed to have more of an emotional appeal.

The fundamental principles of Skoda's 1998 brand promise statement are still valid today; it has nevertheless been refined continuously over the years. As mentioned, »Solid quality based on more than 100 years of tradition at reasonable prices« was selected as the core (or the essence) of the brand. This brand essence was promoted through four differentiators or brand values: »reliable with innovative functionality,« »customer oriented,« »attractive purchase price and running costs,« and »future from tradition.« Considering Skoda's brand presence at the time, this brand promise certainly underlined the visionary aspiration of the Volkswagen Group and of Skoda in seeking to position the Eastern European brand in the functionality-oriented lower-price segment. In 2005, Skoda was able to increase the number of cars it sold by more than 10 percent compared with 2004. Though Volkswagen AG has faced a number of other problems in recent years, Skoda's success has confirmed the overall soundness of Volkswagen's multiple-brand strategy. The brand sold more than 600,000 units in 2006 alone. Skoda is the group's cash cow; it managed to increase its after-tax profits to EUR 577 million in 2007, up 40 percent from 2006.[11] To this day, Skoda has resisted the temptation of introducing a convertible or a sports car because these body types would not fit the no-nonsense brand promise. Although Skoda currently uses »Simply clever« as its claim, the company's most recent annual report still quotes reliability and value for money as core elements of the brand promise.

Note that Skoda's brand promise of solid quality at an attractive price is by no means inevitable. It was chosen as one of several possible strategic options, developed based on the brand's differentiating elements (Figure 3.16). There is nothing automatic about this process, and it is often far from trivial to condense a brand's identity into a single sentence or phrase. But McKinsey's work with clients has shown the value and the power of the concept of a short brand promise statement. It forces brand managers to clarify the brand essence. Successful companies don't necessarily use it as a client-facing claim, but more often as an internal touchstone for all major brand management decisions. Some brands, however, are explicitly meant to speak for themselves externally, especially in the luxury goods sector. Even if they have a claim or brand essence statement for internal purposes, they don't communicate it externally.

Dutch consumer electronics giant Philips is among the most determined companies when it comes to implementing the brand promise in its in-house decision making. Says Andrea Ragnetti, CEO of the Consumer Lifestyle division: »No matter how complex and advanced a product or solution is, it should make sense and be comfortable to use.« To make sure the brand conveys »Sense and Simplicity« at all touch points, Philips temporarily established a »Simplicity Advisory Board« to check key new product propositions and communication concepts for compliance. The board consisted of the CMO and five high-profile outside experts. CMO Geert van Kuyck, formerly Senior Vice President for Global Marketing, says about the work of the Advisory Board: »Philips has given the board members free rein to kick the tires. When the consumer electronics unit was ready to launch its Wireless Audio Center, a system for listening to different tunes in multiple rooms around the house, [John] Maeda gave it a whirl. His verdict: Too much computer jargon such as ›booting up, please wait.‹ His suggestions were mind-opening. He made us ask questions we hadn't asked before.«[12] After the introduction of the new brand promise and the board in 2004, Philips' brand value has grown consistently, from USD 5.9 billion in 2005 to 6.7 in 2006 and 7.7 in 2007 according to Interbrand,[13] although the brand, of course, was only one of multiple factors driving this development. In a recent interview, CMO Andrea Ragnetti said the Simplicity Advisory Board was instrumental in the ramp-up phase of »Sense and Simplicity« at Philips, but had been dissolved after two years of fruitful service. According to Ragnetti, the thinking the board was set up to promote »is now firmly ingrained in the organization.«[14] More details on the role of the board are provided in section 4.3.

Figure 3.17 shows two examples from the cosmetics and rental car industries. Nivea is often cited as a model of successful brand management, prevailing despite competitive pressure and price erosion. Nivea's brand success is clearly expressed in the promise of its brand. It consistently conveys »personal care,« »gentle care,« and »products for sensitive skin.« Even in its expansion into new product sectors, its products and other elements of the marketing mix remain devoted to the brand promise; see also the interview with Beiersdorf's Executive Board Member for Brands, Pieter Nota, at the end of chapter 1.

Sixt, the rental car company, has developed an innovative image as a car rental service that provides exceptionally good value. In less than two decades, Sixt has grown from being a regional player in the German market into a global car rental company offering services in 75 countries (and the market leader in Germany). In 1987, Sixt's share of the German car rental market was just 5 percent; by 2007, its market share had grown to 29 percent. From 1995 to 2005, Sixt's total revenue nearly doubled.[15] At the heart of this success is the brand promise »a lot of car for a little money.« This slogan is always the focus in Sixt's conspicuous advertising campaigns, most recently in the 2007 campaign featuring Matthias Reim, a minor German celebrity on the »oompah-pah« circuit. The singer was pictured renting a fancy Mercedes convertible although he is up to his ears in debt. The tagline was »If he can afford it, anyone can.« Subsequent to the

Fig. 3.17: Nivea and Sixt: Precise brand promises pay off

When I use	Nivea	When I go to	Sixt
Instead of	products made by another cosmetics company	**Instead of**	another car rental company
Then I get	gentle skin and beauty care	**Then I get**	a lot of car for a little money
Because	Nivea attaches great value to gentle ingredients and has decades of experience in preparing them	**Because**	only Sixt offers the most attractive cars at the best price

Source: McKinsey

introduction of Sixti, Sixt's no-frills brand, in 2003, the positioning of the Sixt brand itself has shifted from mere affordability to value for money, featuring attractive car models to support the promise of »a lot of car for a little money.« This latest twist to the brand promise was put into action as part of a campaign for Sixt's subbrand »Sixt Leasing.« The campaign's key television commercial features small-time German hip-hop star Manuellsen going from shame to fame thanks to flashy cars supplied by Sixt Leasing.

Ryanair has used a similar strategy to establish itself as a leading budget airline. Ryanair consistently offers the lowest fares and clearly positions itself as a »lean« alternative to existing premium airlines, most of which are former government-owned national carriers. Rynair is famous for the consistent implementation of its brand promise. Offering the cheapest airline tickets means doing without all the extras. Ryanair has no advance seat reservations, no sales through travel agencies, no free meals or beverages on board, no frequent flyer programs, no lounges, and tight restrictions on carry-on luggage. But passengers don't care, as long as Ryanair keeps the tickets cheap. Ryanair's consistent implementation of the brand promise is a model of brand management across all touch points. Despite Ryanair's notoriously cheap-looking advertising and Web site (90 percent of all tickets are sold online), Ryanair is the world's biggest international carrier according to IATA (International Air Transport Association), at least if you look at number of passengers carried by a single airline, as opposed to groups or alliances of multiple airlines (2007).[16] Most recently, Ryanair has been going from »low cost« to »no cost« by giving away a significant proportion of its seats for free, partly as a marketing device to attract traffic to their

Web site, partly to make money by selling travelers food and beverages, or by exposing them to in-flight advertising on tray tables and seatbacks. Ryanair's CEO Michael O'Leary promises that eventually »more than half of our passengers will fly free.«[17] Of course, free airfare doesn't prevent airlines and airports from charging a wide range of fees for credit card payments, checked luggage, or security. If you factor in value added and other taxes, a »free« ticket can, in fact, end up being quite expensive.

Nevertheless, there is no doubt that the brand promise represents an important, if not the decisive, component of a successful brand. But the brand promise is only a true guarantee of success if it is embedded in all business units and implemented in a consistent manner at every touch point.

From »all talk« to strategic brand management

It might at first sight seem obvious that brands can only be successful if clear, appropriate operational guidelines exist for all business units to ensure everybody is pursuing the same goal. Practical experience, however, shows that all too often reality falls well short of this ideal.

How often have you heard something like the following dialogue? The director of the marketing department is presenting the findings of the most recent market research together with a new creative brand claim. He tells his audience: »We must design our products so that the brand perception corresponds to customers' needs for security.« A murmur goes around the room, and he is immediately bombarded with questions: »And what does that mean, concretely, for our product design?« asks the director of research and development. »How can we implement this in our network of dealers?« the sales manager inquires. »It seems that it really has nothing to do with employee training then,« the head of personnel comments.

This exchange highlights the dilemma of art (the creative world) versus craft (the world of pragmatic implementation). The gulf between art and craft is not irreconcilable, however. As already mentioned in chapter 1, science, i.e., analytical tools, can bring these two worlds together. This, of course, also applies to the implementational phase of brand building. Through the consistent application of analytical tools and methods, the brand promise and thus the brand's strategic direction can be translated into operational guidelines for all business units.

The complex demands of comprehensive brand management are evident in the example of the Skoda brand promise. Some of the differentiators (i.e., differentiating brand elements from the Brand Diamond) defined by Skoda can be intuitively translated into operational measures, such as »attractive purchase price and running costs.« The devil is in the details, however. A good price or inexpensive optional equipment undoubtedly contributes to the fact that customers perceive Skoda as a brand with attractive prices. But what makes more sense in the end: a lower starting price, low prices for popular optional equipment, or both? Or would it be even better to optimize the prices of the higher-performance models instead of the starting price? And how does one define high performance: 90, 100, or 150 horsepower?

This problem is aggravated when the differentiator is more emotional than functional in nature. Unfortunately, it is often the intangible brand elements, that is, emotional benefits along with associations of origin and reputation, that emerge as especially relevant brand drivers in the purchase funnel.

Disaggregate brand drivers to translate them into practical action

To ensure sustainable success for a brand, it is crucial to tie its operations to the brand promise and to brand attributes that drive its performance in the purchase funnel. Perception may be, in many ways, reality, but broken promises are bound to come back and haunt the brand manager sooner or later (as was the case with HVB's shaky no-worries service promise discussed earlier in the insert »Applying the Matrix of Options for Action« above). To stay successful beyond the short term, brand operations need to match the brand's benefits as proclaimed by the brand promise and as communicated in advertising. Let's quickly recapitulate the tools and methods outlined so far to bring out the role a brand's operations play to drive its performance in the purchase funnel:
- Brand relevance measurement, customer insights, and segmentation are used to select and profile attractive target groups for a brand in a given category (sections 2.1 and 2.2).
- In these segments, quantified purchase funnel research is conducted to assess how the target group's awareness, familiarity, and purchase of the brand compares with that of competitors, thereby identifying gaps in funnel transfer rates for targeted improvement (section 2.4).
- The Brand Diamond and Brand Driver Analysis help to identify the image attributes that are critical to move consumers from stage to stage in the purchase funnel, especially those drivers that will help to close any transfer gaps (sections 2.3 and 3.1).

- These critical brand drivers are, finally, further broken down into operational actions at relevant touch points to improve the brand's performance on these attributes, ultimately to close the transfer gaps in the purchase funnel for which these attributes act as drivers (see below; also compare the insert at the end of section 2.4).

So there is a direct link from day-to-day operations to a brand's image and funnel performance that, by way of the »purchase« stage, translates into market share. Selecting both the appropriate touch points and the most relevant messages or actions is essential to make sure the brand promise is kept at the front line in interaction with customers. Let's assume a given brand lags behind the competition in transfering its target customers from »purchase« to »loyalty.« Let's also assume that the image attribute »good service« is a key driver of this transfer. In order to close its gap in creating loyalty, the brand in question needs to improve its perceived performance as a provider of »good service.« One obvious step the company can take is to convey a service promise in its above-the-line communication. But provident brand managers will also want to know how »good service« can effectively and efficiently be activated at other touch points. How can they put »good service« into practice at the point of sale, in customer call centers, and in aftersales relationship management?

The challenge is to disaggregate the components of the brand promise, such as »good service,« into concrete recommendations management can act on. Is the consumer's perception of »good service« driven by friendly staff, fast responses, or the look and feel of stores or branches? A range of multivariate analysis techniques is available to answer these questions, including *pathways analysis, causal analysis,* and *partial least square algorithms.* The common idea is to help to translate abstract brand elements into concrete actions in product design, service, and advertising. The causal relationships and interdependencies of brand elements are examined in such approaches, and brand attributes are disaggregated into their operational components to facilitate action planning. This section complements the discussion of customer decision making at the end of section 2.4; both decision process analysis and driver disaggregation are tools to identify critical touch points and relevant messages or actions to improve the performance on key brand drivers and corresponding transfers in the purchase process.

How driver disaggregation works can be demonstrated using the simplified example of an apparel mail-order firm (Figure 3.18). The individual brand elements are depicted in the boxes. The arrows represent the causal relationships between these elements. The brand promise consists of the

Fig. 3.18: In mail-order sales, pathways analyses help to identify the right operational definitions and targets to fulfill the brand promise

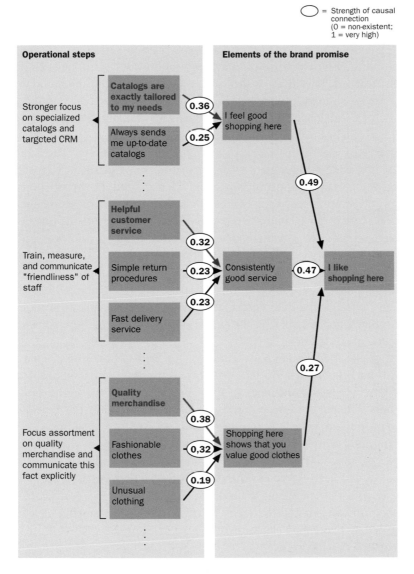

= Strength of causal connection
(0 = non-existent;
1 = very high)

Operational steps

Elements of the brand promise

Stronger focus on specialized catalogs and targeted CRM

Catalogs are exactly tailored to my needs — 0.36

Always sends me up-to-date catalogs — 0.25

I feel good shopping here

0.49

Train, measure, and communicate "friendliness" of staff

Helpful customer service — 0.32

Simple return procedures — 0.23

Fast delivery service — 0.23

Consistently good service — 0.47 — I like shopping here

0.27

Focus assortment on quality merchandise and communicate this fact explicitly

Quality merchandise — 0.38

Fashionable clothes — 0.32

Unusual clothing — 0.19

Shopping here shows that you value good clothes

Source: McKinsey

brand essence »I like shopping here« and the differentiators »I feel good shopping here,« »consistently good service,« and »shopping here shows that you value good clothes.« The strength of the causal relationship between the attributes is represented by the path coefficient. These coefficients are similar to correlations. Thus, the attribute »I feel good shopping here« has the strongest impact on the brand promise.

The causal interrelationships can now be subdivided until the operational level is reached. This analysis shows that the perception of the brand driver »I feel good shopping here« can be promoted, in particular, through custom-tailored catalogs. This realization leads to concrete measures for the mail-order firm, such as greater concentration on segment-specific catalogs, or a targeted customer relationship management program. The analysis also yields concrete guidelines for personnel management. The service image of the mail-order firm is apparently determined less by efficient processes and much more by the company's perceived willingness to help during contact with the customer. In other words, to strengthen its image as a service-oriented company, management should focus on improvements in customer interaction rather than back-office operations. Finally, in its product assortment, the mail-order firm should pay particular attention to maintaining consistent standards of quality: unusual seasonal goods or high-fashion clothing apparently contribute less than reliable, quality products to an improved performance on the brand driver »shopping here shows that you value good clothes.«

The causal model shown for a mail-order firm is based on simple outside-in market research. To this extent, it represents only a subsection of the complete problem context. In daily business, both the brand promise and how it is put into operation along all dimensions of the Brand Diamond need to be spelled out in more detail.

Using the example of the aforementioned retailer, Figure 3.19 provides a simplified, conceptual example of the chain of cause and effect that brand managers will need to keep in mind when translating purchase funnel targets into concrete marketing actions: Funnel transfers, e.g., from consideration to purchase, are influenced by brand drivers like »shopping pleasure.« These drivers depend on elements of the marketing mix, such as »(product) assortment« or »service.«

Optimizing the assortment can, for example, take the shape of stocking »better-known brands,« or offering a »larger selection« in general. This way, marketing actions will help to improve the brand's performance in the funnel.

Fig. 3.19: The right steps to strengthen the brand can be systematically derived

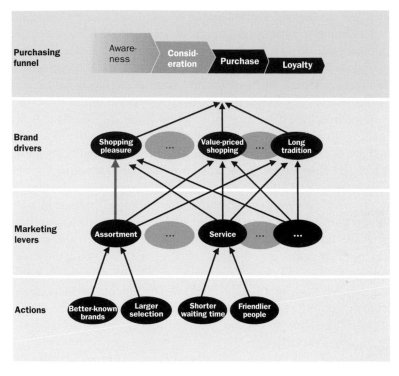

Source: McKinsey

In short, it is vital that management is familiar with the causal relationships between funnel performance and concrete marketing actions, including the intermediate levels of brand drivers and marketing levers. Only with this knowledge is it possible to translate the brand image and funnel objectives into targeted programs of action employing all tools of the marketing mix.

Let's take a look at the example of an apparel retailer to see how causal analysis of brand image attributes can be combined with the purchase funnel framework to derive operational measures. The apparel retailer in question is struggling with insufficient brand loyalty compared with its competitors. Its market share remains high, but this is primarily driven by the broad presence of its outlets at premium downtown locations, i.e., by distribution power rather than true brand assets.

First, the brand drivers are identified through a factor analysis of 30 individual statements. Figure 3.20 shows the causal relationships between the brand drivers and loyalty. The brand driver »shopping pleasure,« for instance, has the highest significance in establishing loyalty. The next step involves examining what marketing activities especially influence »shopping pleasure.« It turns out that the product assortment is of highest significance, followed at some distance by service and decor (i.e., ambience and merchandise presentation). The remaining marketing levers have no significant influence on this brand driver. As expected, the brand driver »value for money« is related first and foremost to price. In addition, however, advertising also promotes the image of value for money. Overall, the model shows that the product assortment is of overwhelming significance for customer loyalty. Price, service, decor, and advertising trail at some distance. In contrast, »events« and »distribution« are of little importance in strengthening loyalty. This does not mean that they are completely irrelevant. »Distribution,« in particular, is of relatively high importance in the early steps of the purchase funnel; »events« and »special sales« are of medium importance in the conversion from the stage of familiarity to visiting the store.

Driver disaggregation not only provides the insight that, for this leading clothing retailer, assortment is the most effective means of increasing customer loyalty, but it can also identify the subcomponents of individual marketing levers (see bottom of Figure 3.20). In this example, the main indicators influencing »assortment« are availability of major brands, products of good quality, and a large range of products. This level of granularity enables the retailer to derive a specific program for brand building. Potential initiatives can be assessed and prioritized in terms of their contribution to brand attributes that drive loyalty.

These examples illustrate that the pathways approach is a sophisticated, yet highly practical analysis tool that can be used to translate the abstract brand promise into operational guidelines for all business units.

Recent advances in multivariate analysis methods allow you to get even one step closer to concrete marketing action planning – provided the market research used is sufficiently detailed and marketing levers can be broken down to different performance levels. Imagine an insurance company that has identified »processes my requests quickly« as one of the top differentiators in its brand promise. One of the most important service levers, determining whether the brand is perceived to be performing well on this driver, is »speed of mail correspondence.« But just how speedy does the claims department have to be in order to satisfy consumer expectations? From the policyholder's perspective, it may not make much difference

Fig. 3.20: Brick-and-mortar clothing retail: Assortment still more important than price and service

Standardized pathway coefficients*

Brand drivers**	Effect on loyalty	Marketing levers						
		Assortment	Service	Decor	Price	Advertising	Events	Distribution
Shopping pleasure	**0.55**	0.55	0.27	0.25				
Value-priced shopping	**0.35**				0.64	0.32		
Individual shopping world	**0.10**	0.10	0.17	0.09		0.17	0.31	
Customer orientation	**0.12**		0.37	0.11		0.25		0.17
Familiarity	**0.11**							0.29
Total effect on loyalty*		**0.31**	**0.21**	**0.16**	**0.22**	**0.16**	**0.03**	**0.05**

Individual assortment indicators   **Importance**
- Has all the major brands   High
- Carries many products of good quality   High
- Carries a very large range of products   High
- Always has the latest products in stock   Medium
- Also offers very unusual merchandise   Medium
- ...   ...

* Other relationships not significant
** Result of the factor analysis of 30 individual statements
*** Factor weightings multiplied by total contribution to the effect of the factor
Source: McKinsey consumer survey, GfK market research 2001

whether it takes a day or a week for a request to be processed, as long as it is less than a month. But from a resource and cost perspective, the difference between these service levels is, of course, tremendous. The concept of customer-driven redesign helps to address this issue by reflecting consumers' elasticity of perception. In other words, any optimization should be based on an assessment of the expected gain in consumer satisfaction, addressing questions such as: How big a difference does an improvement from five to three days' lead time really make? This knowledge enables brand and marketing management to decide whether it's worth going the extra mile for all key drivers identified, and where to focus their investments. Figure 3.21 shows a sample output for »better performance than others« and »processes my requests quickly,« which are the key drivers of purchase in segment A (»needs-driven youngsters«). Similar insights can be derived for most rational benefits and tangible brand elements. Prominent examples include call center performance, service component selection, or performance level achieved in tests. For example, achieving a top rank may be very costly, yet not really necessary. Being ranked above average by a consumer or expert panel may be fully sufficient to be perceived as a brand that »performs better than others.« The impact of achieving specific performance levels is captured by the »gain in satisfaction« score. Depending on the research design, this kind of score can even be operationalized as »willingness to pay (more).«[18]

It is exactly this type of fact-based operational definition of business actions that will help branding shed its reputation as a »soft« discipline. Linking specific actions to key components of the brand promise enables executives both in the marketing function and elsewhere in the organization to improve a brand's performance in a targeted and cost-efficient way.

Fig. 3.21: Driver disaggregation helps to ensure efficient improvement of key purchase drivers

SIMPLIFIED INSURANCE EXAMPLE

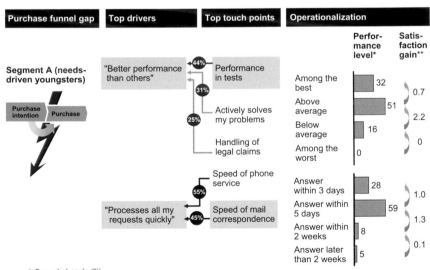

* On verbal scale (%)
** Gain in satisfaction on a scale of 1 to 7 (1 = very satisfied; 7 = very dissatisfied)
Source: McKinsey, 2007

Making Brands

3.3 Brand Portfolio Management: Coordinating Multiple-Brand Strategies Systematically

As we have seen in the last section, virtually no brand is an island these days. Many manufacturers of branded goods have reacted to the increasing fragmentation of their markets with larger and larger brand portfolios. This fragmentation is a consequence of the consumer trend towards individualization and self-expression. Theoreticians refer to »hybrid,« »multioptional,« and even »paradox« consumers who exhibit less and less brand loyalty. The building or acquisition of new brands was intended to appeal to the various individual market segments; those consumers switching brands were to be given the opportunity to select a different brand within the portfolio and thus remain as a customer of the company. At the same time, management hoped to capture synergies along the entire chain of value creation.

The portfolios of global players, such as Unilever, Henkel, and Procter & Gamble, typically comprise close to a thousand brands and sub-brands; Nestlé has even more. But brand portfolios are no longer a phenomenon limited to the consumer goods industry. In many industries, proliferation of consumer segments and consolidation of manufacturers has led to the coexistence of multiple brands under the same roof; such as Skoda, Seat, Audi, and Volkswagen, to name but the biggest brands in the Volkswagen portfolio. While some automobile manufacturers have successfully expanded their brand portfolios, others are revising their multiple brand strategies. For example, Ford has recently sold Jaguar and Land Rover to Tata Motors (Figure 3.22). Global automobile manufacturers compete around the world with various umbrella brands and numerous product brands, derivatives, and models.

The primary objective of Brand Portfolio Management can be summarized as: profitably capturing as much market potential as possible in the relevant market segments by positioning your own brands in such a way as to ensure that they do not cause cannibalization. In practice this is a highly complex task. Both multiple-brand and single-brand strategies carry specific advantages and disadvantages that call for careful trade-off decisions. Figure 3.23 provides a direct comparison of the extreme cases of a widely diversified portfolio and a single-brand strategy to bring out the upside and the downside of either approach.

Fig. 3.22: Multiple-brand strategies in the automotive industry

Volkswagen AG		Ford*		Porsche**
Audi	Seat	Ford	Volvo	Porsche
Bentley	Skoda	Lincoln	Mazda (30%)	
Bugatti	VW	Mercury		
Lamborghini				

BMW	Daimler	Chrysler	Honda	PSA
BMW	Maybach	Chrysler	Acura	Peugeot
Mini	Mercedes-Benz	Dodge	Honda	Citroen
Rolls-Royce	Smart	Jeep		

Fiat	GM			Toyota	Renault Nissan
Alfa Romeo	Buick	GMC	Pontiac	Daihatsu	Dacia
Fiat	Cadillac	Holden	Saab	Lexus	Infiniti
Ferrari	Chevrolet	Hummer	Saturn	Scion	Nissan
Lancia	Daewoo	Opel	Vauxhall	Toyota	Renault
Maserati					Lada (25%)

* Jaguar and Land Rover were sold to Tata in 2008   **Single-brand strategy

Source: Company Web sites, Global Insight 2006, McKinsey

Fig. 3.23: Advantages and disadvantages of different portfolio strategies

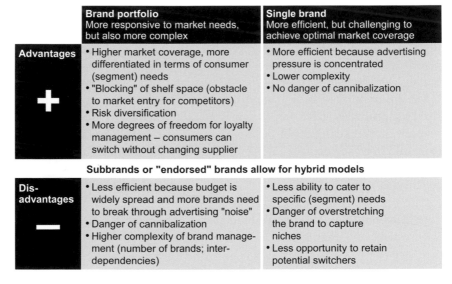

	Brand portfolio More responsive to market needs, but also more complex	Single brand More efficient, but challenging to achieve optimal market coverage
Advantages +	• Higher market coverage, more differentiated in terms of consumer (segment) needs • "Blocking" of shelf space (obstacle to market entry for competitors) • Risk diversification • More degrees of freedom for loyalty management – consumers can switch without changing supplier	• More efficient because advertising pressure is concentrated • Lower complexity • No danger of cannibalization

Subbrands or "endorsed" brands allow for hybrid models

Dis-advantages —	• Less efficient because budget is widely spread and more brands need to break through advertising "noise" • Danger of cannibalization • Higher complexity of brand management (number of brands; inter-dependencies)	• Less ability to cater to specific (segment) needs • Danger of overstretching the brand to capture niches • Less opportunity to retain potential switchers

Source: McKinsey

A fine example of how a brand portfolio can be leveraged to improve customer retention is provided by Condé Nast. The publisher's fashion magazine portfolio comprises, among other titles, *Teen Vogue* as well as *Vogue* itself; readers of *Teen Vogue* grow up to be *Vogue* readers. This type of brand hierarchy allows Condé Nast to capture the value of brand loyalty even in the face of changing needs. The success factor at work in this case is structuring the brand portfolio in a way that enables customers who wish to switch brands simply to select a different brand within the same portfolio, instead of migrating to the competition. Similarly, Toyota has introduced the Scion brand as their US entry-level brand for younger car buyers; at 39, the median age of Scion buyers is almost 20 years below that of Toyota drivers.[19] The fact that Scion and Toyota are distributed by the same dealers makes switching easier as drivers mature and their requirements for roominess and performance (as well as their buying power) grow.

In these cases, the success of brand portfolios was based on needs differentiation. But multiple brands also help achieve competitive advantages associated with scale. A larger portfolio, for example, can strengthen your position when negotiating with suppliers. Larger portfolios can, in effect, also create obstacles to market entry for competitors while distributing market risk across many brands. In the retail trade, for example, expanding shelf area can improve a company's competitive position. Unilever, for instance, largely dominates shelves of most German food retailers in the margarine segment with its brands Rama, Sanella, Becel, Lätta, Du darfst, and Bertolli. The dilemma for management, however, is that an ever-increasing number of brands will tend to reduce each individual brand's market share. At the same time, brand management costs will increase, because additional resources will be required in research and development, marketing, procurement, distribution, and sales and channel management – as well as in ensuring that resources are well coordinated and effectively and efficiently deployed!

Unilever also found that brand proliferation comes at a price; any advantages in market coverage and economies of scale need to be carefully balanced with the complexities that arise from portfolio management. Consolidation and brand expansion, repositioning and elimination, acquisition, launch, and restructuring are the key words in the strategy jungle. It comes as no surprise that the former enthusiasm for portfolios among the major market participants has long since given way to something resembling disillusionment. In 2000, Unilever initiated a restructuring program it called »Path to Growth,« the objectives of which were to decrease complexity, reduce costs, and increase efficiency by concentrating on the 400 core brands that accounted for 75 percent of its revenues in 1999 (Figure 3.24). The resources freed up by this program were to be used for researching and communicating successful brands. By the end of 2003, Unilever had reduced its portfolio from 1,600 brands to some 600; by 2004, it had whittled down the portfolio to 400. The target for the remaining 400 core brands was to achieve an annual growth rate of 5 to 6 percent and an operating margin of 16 percent.[20]

UBS has taken a similar path of portfolio consolidation after years of acquisitions. In 2002, they started out with a brand portfolio comprising half a dozen stand-alone brands, e.g., PaineWebber, Warburg Dillon Read, and philips & drew. In 2002, some of these were repositioned as UBS sub-brands, e.g., UBS Warburg, as part of an umbrella strategy. Since 2003, all businesses carry the UBS brand only, expressing the company's strategy to deliver a unified value proposition through an integrated global business model. This consolidation process has brought about a growth in total brand value, as measured by Interbrand, for UBS until 2007. The brand equity losses from discontinued (sub)brands have been more than made up for by gains by the UBS brand (Figure 3.25). While this past achievement is widely recognized as a best-practice example of Brand Portfolio Management[21], there is no doubt that the UBS brand has suffered from the 2007 subprime mortgage crisis. The company said in June 2008 that it »will need years to restore the brand image [...], which was hurt by massive sub-prime-related losses at the investment banking unit.«[22] The good news is that strong brands have successfully survived similarly testing times. Coke overcame the failed experiment of New Coke in the mid-1980s, Intel survived the outrage caused by a calculation error of its Pentium processor in the mid-1990s, and Mercedes Benz emerged largely unharmed from the fact that their A-Class model initially did not pass the maneuver avoidance test (commonly referred to as the »elk test« or »moose test«) in 1997; see »Strong brands can survive occasional mistakes« in section 1.2 of this book for details. It remains to be seen whether UBS is like these brands, whether past merits of brand management have sufficiently strengthened the brand to help it through its current crisis.

But which is the right strategy for your company? What brands should you abandon and which should you strengthen? In answering this, we come back to the three questions that need to be answered in the context of single-brand optimization: What are the true needs of potential customers? How attractive, economically as well as strategically, are the respective segments? How successful are your brands in reaching these segments?

Fig. 3.24: Unilever: In 5 years, 75% fewer brands
Number of Brands

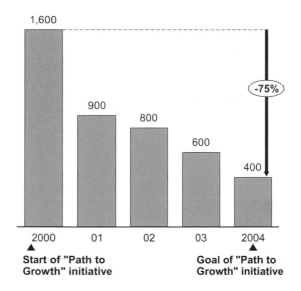

1,600

900

800

600

400

-75%

2000 ▲   01   02   03   2004 ▲

Start of "Path to Growth" initiative

Goal of "Path to Growth" initiative

Source: Unilever company data, press clippings

Fig. 3.25: Single-brand strategy triggered growth at UBS

Consolidation of brand portfolio ...

... leads to increase in brand value
Brand value, USD millions

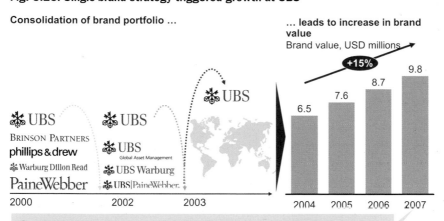

❄ UBS
BRINSON PARTNERS
phillips & drew
❄ Warburg Dillon Read
PaineWebber

❄ UBS
❄ UBS
Global Asset Management
❄ UBS Warburg
❄ UBS|PaineWebber.

❄ UBS

2000   2002   2003

+15%

6.5   7.6   8.7   9.8

2004   2005   2006   2007

- **Strong brand.** Portfolio consolidation led to an increase in brand value until 2007
- **Recent challenges.** However, UBS says it "will need years to restore the brand image [...], which was hurt by massive subprime-related losses" (June 2008)
- **Proof of principle pending.** The jury is still out on whether the UBS brand is strong enough to emerge without serious long-term damage from its current crisis

Source: Interbrand, CNBC/Thomson Financial, McKinsey analysis

1. Defining and segmenting the relevant market: Start with the customer

As with the process of single-brand optimization (see section 3.2), the optimization of a brand portfolio begins with defining and segmenting the relevant market and the relevant categories in a manner that the customer can understand. PepsiCo, for instance, has discovered over the course of the past decade that its customers in the US market select their soft drinks from among all alcohol-free beverages, not just from carbonated ones. This insight shaped PepsiCo's decision to acquire additional brands (Tropicana in 1999, Gatorade in 2001), to develop new products (Aquafina, for example), and to enter into joint ventures (bottled Frappuccino in cooperation with Starbucks). These portfolio expansions increased the global operating

Fig. 3.26: The benefit-based segmentation of an international brewery

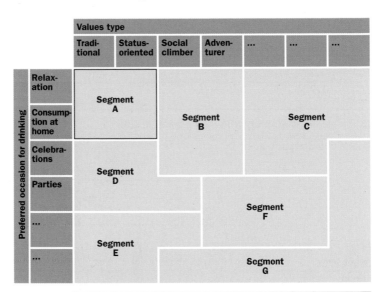

Source: McKinsey

profits of its beverage division from USD 1.03 billion in 1999 to USD 1.84 billion in 2002. By 2006, Pepsi had secured US market leadership in sports drinks (Gatorade), PET water (Aquafina), chilled juices and juice drinks (Dole and Tropicana), enhanced water (Propel), ready-to-drink coffee (bottled Frappuccino in cooperation with Starbucks), and ready-to-drink tea (Lipton). Non-carbonated drinks accounted for 69 percent of Pepsi's total 2006 sales in North America.

2. Analyzing the brand portfolio: Assess the attractiveness of segments and brands

Once the relevant market has been segmented distinctly, the next task is to assess the economic potential of the corresponding segments, similar to the procedure described in section 2.2. This kind of economic assessment is anything but trivial, since the segments are very seldom identical with classic product or market definitions.

Evaluating the size and profitability of these segments often requires the use of a sophisticated combination of existing data on segment shares, growth rates, and the channel mix. Trends in consumer behavior, categories, and products can give insight into the potential development of the market and its future profitability. This is one end of the analysis. The other end involves assessing the company's brands. How well does their value contribution and future potential match the segments under consideration? It makes sense to assign the existing brands to the segments that have been identified. Analytical methods such as factor analysis or multidimensional scaling can be used to place the brands of a portfolio together with relevant competitors in a »segmentation map« (Figure 3.27).

Comparing the identified target segments on the basis of their economic and strategic potential with the reality of the company's own brand portfolio provides the initial indications of the potential options for optimization. This makes clear where the company has »white spaces« (where relevant segments are not targeted by a brand currently) and brand overlaps. It is important not to jump to premature conclusions, however: an approach using »one brand per segment« may be incorrect! Sometimes, in fact, it makes sense to offer several brands to target customers in a single segment. For example, some breweries offer different brands for different consumption occasions; while the consumer prefers one brand »on tap« with friends at a bar, the same person may turn to a different brand when buying bottled beer for in-home consumption. Similarly, brand preference within a single

Fig. 3.27: Portfolio optimization of a financial services provider: Distinct differentiation between brand promises

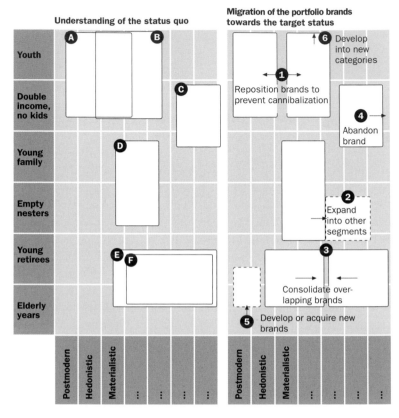

Source: McKinsey

segment has been found to differ in a category such as baked goods. While brand A is preferred for on-the-go snacks, the same consumer will turn to brand B when shopping for groceries.

A detailed understanding of the optimization options requires an economic analysis of portfolio performance (please refer to the insert on BrandMatics Advanced at the end of this section for details). The basic data required for this includes market shares, profitability, and growth rates of the individual brands in their target segments. Additionally, the analysis tools discussed in chapter 2, in particular the purchase funnel, should be applied to each individual brand. Including special portfolio figures in the analysis makes it easier to understand exactly what the relationships are between the individual brands of a portfolio. One method involves migration analysis: when formerly loyal customers migrate away from (or towards) another brand in the portfolio, this is referred to as positive or negative participation. These figures provide detailed information about brand competitiveness. The rates of purchase consideration in the brand funnel (second-choice data) can also be used to assess competition within the portfolio. These rates indicate what brand a consumer would have preferred if the brand actually purchased had not been available. In this manner, it is possible to differentiate between actual cannibalization and portfolio loyalty. In order to achieve an integrated overview of these economic interactions between individual brands, the key figures can be summarized in a »portfolio balance,« or net economic impact assessment. The insert at the end of this section, on the brand portfolio map, provides an example of how the simulation of net effects can inform the assessment of different positioning options for multiple brands in a single category.

These analyses often reveal that certain individual brands are relatively weak and are therefore candidates for elimination. Apparent brand overlap can be corrected by consolidation or repositioning, but only after the reasons for this overlap have been explored in detail. A segment-specific analysis of brand performance in the brand purchase funnel, combined with an analysis of the brand drivers as discussed in section 3.1, can be very helpful here.

3. Managing the brand portfolio: Decide on the right strategy, implement it, and refine it continually

The comprehensive analysis of the market segments, in combination with the current standing of your own brands, forms the basis for deciding upon the right strategy. In addition, in prioritizing the strategic options, the potential reactions of competitors must also be taken into account as well as the capabilities of your own organization. For instance, if the repositioning of several brands makes sense fundamentally, the next question is whether the company has access to the necessary resources (financial means, employee capabilities, etc.) to carry this out effectively and efficiently. Independent of this strategy selection, articulations of the distinct brand promise for each brand need to be formulated for all the brands remaining in the portfolio (analogous to the procedure described in section 3.2). These brand promises need to be made tangible at all relevant customer touch points.

Developing a mathematically sophisticated, multicausal optimization approach for deriving the perfect portfolio constellation usually only makes sense if the company can apply the approach in the long run. In most cases, it is more practical to develop and evaluate an easily manageable number of plausible scenarios.

Developing the strategy is the relatively easy bit. Now great courage and perseverance are required: courage to make difficult decisions and to see them through, and perseverance because the implementation of a portfolio strategy is anything but a short-term project.

However difficult dropping a cherished brand might be, retaining it can prove worse. When weak brands are maintained, these resources cannot be deployed elsewhere, thus weakening the performance of the entire portfolio. But dropping a brand is just the start. For many companies, full implementation is a long-term project. At Unilever, the »Path to Growth« project mentioned above started in 2000 and took about five years.

In short, deriving and implementing a viable portfolio strategy is a complex, dynamic task. Implementing a brand portfolio strategy requires even more endurance than single-brand optimization as often the target positions can only be reached through a carefully staged migration plan.

Brand Leverage: Five Observations about Brand Transfer [23]

Fragrant perfume and smoldering cigars: it's hard to imagine two products more diametrically opposed. It may initially seem inconceivable to sell the two under the same name. But with the worldwide success of its Cool Water fragrance, the Davidoff cigar brand has proved otherwise. Sir Richard Branson's successful extension of the Virgin brand from entertainment (Virgin Records, Virgin Megastores) to travel (Virgin Atlantic, Virgin America, Virgin Blue) and communication (Virgin Mobile) is another classic example.[24]

More and more companies are taking advantage of this type of brand transfer, referred to as *brand leverage*. This applies not only to consumer goods but to services, automobiles, and industrial goods as well. The big question is why some of these projects are hugely successful while others fail miserably.

McKinsey research has looked at the conditions that make successful brand transfer possible. In cooperation with the German Brands Association (Markenverband e.V.), a survey of some 40 companies in Germany was conducted in December 2004 and January 2005 to understand the specific objectives companies pursue in brand transfer. Of those surveyed, the vast majority (82 percent) considered these activities to be successful. One in five companies surveyed now develops more than 40 percent of its total revenue through new products derived from the parent brand.

The following five statements summarize the most important survey findings.

1. The true potential of brand leverage can only be achieved by looking beyond the immediate financial impact

Some 95 percent of the companies surveyed were interested primarily in additional profit or sales, while 84 percent hoped to gain easier market access as a result of using an established brand name. In contrast, only 65 percent wanted to expand brand image in a targeted manner and even fewer, just 57 percent, hoped to increase awareness of the brand.

It appears from this survey that many companies underestimate the impact of brand transfer on the parent brand, be it positive or negative. This is surprising, for other companies have found that brand leverage can, in addition to brand capitalization, serve as an outstanding opportunity to:

- Develop, change, or rejuvenate the image of the parent brand.
- Increase awareness of the brand outside the group of regular users.
- In some cases, help increase sales of the brand in the parent category.

Perhaps the best examples of how this can be done are found in the luxury goods market. For instance, Jil Sander did not develop into the successful fashion brand it is today until the company had first entered the fragrance market. Many other fashion brands that started out as couture houses generate a significant proportion of their current sales in adjacent categories such as leather goods, footwear, accessories, cosmetics, and fragrances as well. Conversely, nearly all best-selling fragrances bear fashion-house labels; Chanel and Calvin Klein are among the most prominent examples.

2. A close connection between the transfer product and the parent brand is a prerequisite for success

Brand leverage works especially well when consumers can recognize a logical, relevant, and credible brand fit between the parent brand and the transfer product. The companies surveyed use a range of approaches to establish such a connection: 82 percent emphasize a common basis of expertise in manufacturing the parent product and the transfer product;

a similar number also focuses on the products' common lifestyle and brand environments (Figure 3.28). As long as consumers perceive logical commonalities – in that the transfer product and the brand concept relate well with one another in terms of the brand – there are few other limits to the nature of the transfer. Caterpillar, for instance, using its well-defined brand attributes of »enduring,« »highest quality,« and »down-to-earth,« has seen impressive results from the transfer of its parent brand in construction machinery to its licensed merchandise lines of rugged work shoes and hiking boots. Similarly, Apple has successfully enhanced and rejuvenated its traditional computer business by launching the iPod and the iPhone, venturing into categories that are sufficiently close to personal computers to make Apple a credible player, yet novel enough to attract new business.

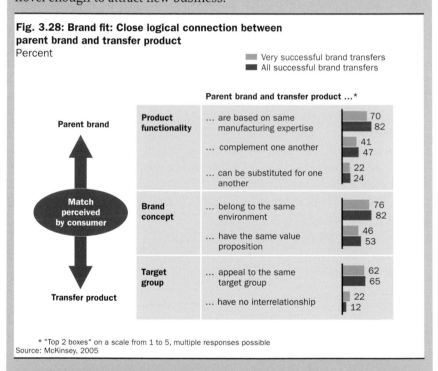

Fig. 3.28: Brand fit: Close logical connection between parent brand and transfer product
Percent

■ Very successful brand transfers
■ All successful brand transfers

Parent brand and transfer product ...*

			Very successful	All successful
Parent brand	Product functionality	... are based on same manufacturing expertise	70	82
		... complement one another	41	47
		... can be substituted for one another	22	24
Match perceived by consumer	Brand concept	... belong to the same environment	76	82
		... have the same value proposition	46	53
Transfer product	Target group	... appeal to the same target group	62	65
		... have no interrelationship	22	12

* "Top 2 boxes" on a scale from 1 to 5, multiple responses possible
Source: McKinsey, 2005

3. Transfer products require their own marketing

Of those surveyed, 95 percent use a similar price positioning for the transfer product as for the parent product. A number of significant differences were observed, however, in distribution and communication.

Some 38 percent of the companies use alternative distribution channels for the transfer product. The advantage of a different channel is that it opens up new groups of customers for the brand, while increasing the loyalty of existing customers by exposing them to products from the parent business in new environments. McDonald's, for instance, sells its ketchup at grocery stores in Germany, Bosch offers toy versions of its equipment at toy stores across Europe, and Harley Davidson markets its leather clothing at fashion retailers worldwide. More recent examples include Starbucks' bottled Frappuccino (with PepsiCo) and ground coffee products sold at supermarkets, or Mars Inc., Nestlé, or Cadbury candy products sold as ingredients of or toppings for desserts served at McDonald's restaurants.

Just over half of the companies (54 percent) surveyed design independent communication strategies for the transfer product. Successful companies have learned that the key to brand leverage is competitive marketing of the transfer product in its target category. Masterfoods, now Mars Inc., demonstrated its understanding of this success factor when first entering the ice cream category in 1989 in the United Kingdom. With Mars Ice Cream, the company effectively created ice cream bars as a new subcategory next to sticks, cones, and scoops. Mars further differentiated the product by using real chocolate and real milk, as opposed to flavors and powders used by competitors. To work around the fact that most in-store ice cream freezers holding portion packs for immediate consumption were owned and exclusively stocked by incumbent ice cream manufacturers, Mars launched its ice cream bar through the grocery sector. That is, it offered Mars Ice Cream in bulk packs for in-home rather than impulse consumption, worked its way into the fiercely competitive impulse sector with the aid of consumer pull, and eventually installed its own freezers. Within months, Mars accounted for a large part of the ice cream segment of the impulse market. Following the successful launch of Mars itself, a number of other popular confectionery lines including Bounty, Snickers, Galaxy Dove, and Opal Fruits have appeared as wrapped impulse ice cream products. Ten years later, Mars continued to outsell Nestlé in the wrapped singles sector. The market share captured by Mars Ice Cream was based on a combination of three factors: Firstly, leverage of existing strengths acquired in the impulse candy category, i.e., branded bar-shaped premium snack products with high-quality ingredients. Secondly, careful selection or, more accurately, creation of a neighboring category in which these strengths mattered, i.e., wrapped, bar-shaped ice cream (Mars never bothered with cones, sticks, or scoops). Thirdly, a deep understanding of the broader target category (wrapped impulse ice cream), especially of the unique dynamics of its distribution resulting from the forward integration of incumbent manufacturers.[25]

This differentiated approach was specific to Masterfoods' marketing approach in the United Kingdom; in the United States, the company chose to take on the incumbents more directly.

Similarly, when Bacardi entered the premixed beverage market with their Bacardi Rigo subbrand, they adapted both positioning and price points to the specific needs of the target category. The price per liter was some 60 percent lower than for Barcardi proper. Bacardi Rigo was positioned as an endorsed subbrand, adding differentiating attributes like urbanity, speed, and excitement, but is still connected to the core brand values (e.g., Caribbean flair). Rigo was packaged as a »ready-to-drink« product to address the needs of out-of-home drinkers. Due to the positioning as a premium product in the new segment, the cheaper product didn't damage the Bacardi brand. Not only was Bacardi Rigo a successful launch at 75 million bottles sold in its second year in Germany alone; it also helped increase the sales of the parent brand.

4. Good preparation increases the chances of success

One remarkable finding is that few companies hire managers familiar with the target market or consult professional external advisors or licensing agencies prior to the launch of the transferred brands (Figure 3.29). Although two-thirds (68 percent) do use quantitative market research, the vast majority (89 percent of those surveyed) rely primarily on their own internal experts. This is astounding, considering the high failure rates of new product launches and brand transfers.

A company that wants to increase its chances of success should, under no circumstances, do without expertise in the target market and professional market research. Companies with little or no experience in classic consumer marketing should seek external advice well in advance or, better yet, develop this expertise internally. The need for expertise in the new market is all the more critical because failure in brand transfer can dilute or even permanently damage the parent brand. A company that overextends its brand or chooses the wrong licensing and distribution partners can likewise dilute the brand. The once-exclusive designer brand Pierre Cardin, for instance, was overextended in the 1980s and has since lost much of its cachet. Fine foods manufacturer Mövenpick of Switzerland recently withdrew its license for premium chocolate from Katjes Fassin, saying its brand was »not a top priority« for Katjes. Mövenpick selected Halloren Schokoladenfabrik, a maker of premium chocolates dating back to the early 1800s, as the new license holder.[26]

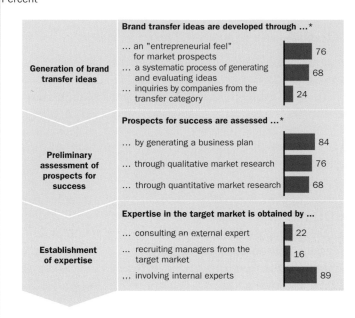

Fig. 3.29: Preparing brand transfer ideas
Percent

Generation of brand transfer ideas

Brand transfer ideas are developed through ...*

... an "entrepreneurial feel" for market prospects — 76
... a systematic process of generating and evaluating ideas — 68
... inquiries by companies from the transfer category — 24

Preliminary assessment of prospects for success

Prospects for success are assessed ...*

... by generating a business plan — 84
... through qualitative market research — 76
... through quantitative market research — 68

Establishment of expertise

Expertise in the target market is obtained by ...

... consulting an external expert — 22
... recruiting managers from the target market — 16
... involving internal experts — 89

* "Top 2 boxes" on a scale from 1 to 5, multiple responses possible
Source: McKinsey, 2005

5. There are many models for successful brand leverage

The survey shows that a variety of business models are very successful in leveraging the parent brand. Regardless of the business model selected, the crucial issue is to strike the right balance between adapting the new product to the target market and ensuring identity with the parent brand. This requires close monitoring and adequate control mechanisms, especially in the areas of product development, communication, and quality control.

The company that owns the parent brand has a good deal of freedom in deciding how to manage the actual production and distribution of the transfer product. Some 76 percent of the companies surveyed carry out brand transfer within their own company or in its subsidiaries, while 19 percent choose to use licensing. The success of licensing depends on the close cooperation of the brand owner with its business partner. There is obviously a degree of risk involved here, so a good foundation for this partnership is a common understanding of the brand and a match of business cultures.

Summary of prerequisites for successful brand transfer

Many companies have been successful in using brand leverage to launch new products, open up new customer groups, and even develop new business models. Entrepreneurial instinct and intuition in operational implementation have often played a key role. The numerous brand transfer failures prove, however, that an established brand and a certain amount of instinct by no means guarantee successful brand transfer. The chances of success can be significantly increased by following these few simple rules:

- Ensure the independent, competitive marketing of the transfer product in the target market.
- Establish a relevant and credible connection to the parent brand.
- Ensure professional preparation of the transfer.

Those who follow these rules are capable of selling smoldering cigars, fragrant perfume, and even premium cognac under a single brand.

BrandMatics Advanced

Background: Managing interdependencies of brands in the same category

Brand Portfolio Management is all about managing interdependencies. To decide whether offering multiple brands in the same category makes sense, the advantages of differentiation and market coverage have to be weighed carefully against the risks of management complexity and cannibalization as illustrated in Figure 3.23 above. This trade-off is the staff of life at consumer goods giants like Unilever or Procter & Gamble, both of which manage several hundred brands in a wide range of categories. But the fundamental questions remain the same no matter whether you manage 20 or just two brands. In fact, clear and fact-based relative positioning of neighboring brands is even more critical with a small number of brands, simply because the individual brands tend to have higher relative value for the company, and the potential downside of cannibalization is disproportionately large. The more brands you have, the more leeway there is for experiments like test launches and repeated repositioning. With only a few brands, you have to get it right the first time. This insert looks at recent advances in positioning and portfolio management methodology that help to take a holistic, multiple-brand perspective when assessing the risks and benefits of brand launches and brand positioning efforts within the same category combined with the proven tools described in previous sections, the approach outlined below forms the kernel of »BrandMatics Advanced.«

The positioning dilemma of Alphabet Inc.

Think of a company, Alphabet Inc., that offers brands A and B in the same category. A and B are complementary in several respects: while A is traditional, reliable, and medium-priced, B is a high-profile premium brand offering unique tangible as well as intangible benefits. Where A is »charming« and »trusted,« B is both »indestructible« and »glamourous.« Because of high entrance barriers, there are only a few competitors, including Numerical Inc.'s brands 1 and 2. To expand its market coverage in the category, Alphabet Inc. is thinking about relaunching its third brand, C. To date, C has a very limited share in most markets, a comparatively low profile, and no clear-cut position (Figure 3.30).

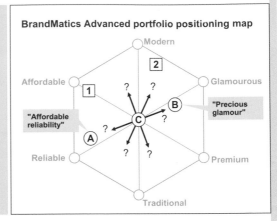

Fig. 3.30: Step 1: Map brand positions

Alphabet Inc. brands

Numerical Inc. brands

(Re)positioning options

- Establish brand positioning map on the basis of driver performance and importance from BrandMatics®
- Analyze absolute and relative strengths and weaknesses of each brand

BrandMatics Advanced portfolio positioning map

Modern

Affordable

Glamourous

"Affordable reliability"

"Precious glamour"

Reliable

Premium

Traditional

Source: McKinsey

Because of advances in technology and manufacturing, Alphabet Inc. has been able to improve and refine the intrinsics of brand C. C now shares many of B's premium characteristics, but can be offered at a price that is much closer to A, the company's mid-price bread-and-butter brand. The question is whether the potential upside of pushing C as a major third brand outweighs its potential cannibalization of A and B. Specifically, Alphabet Inc. wants to know how to position C in order to minimize that cannibalization and, hence, maximize C's net benefit. Ideally, C would gain market share mostly at the expense of Numerical Inc.'s brands 1 and 2, with minimal damage to the sales and market share of Alphabet's A and B. Any changes to C's positioning affect its performance in the purchase funnel (for a description of how brand attribute perception drives the purchase funnel, see sections 2.4 and 3.1). In the category in question, brand attributes such as »affordable« and »glamourous« act as drivers between the funnel stages »familiarity« and »consideration,« and »consideration« and »purchase.« Let's assume »glamourous« is a key driver that has a high impact on the transfer of consumers from »consideration« to »purchase.« This implies that, if Alphabet Inc. succeeds in repositioning and establishing C as a more »glamourous« brand, this move would help to increase C's performance on »purchase« and hence its market share. But it doesn't stop there.

Repositioning C also would have an effect on its neighboring brands A and B. Since B is also positioned as »glamourous,« part of C's gains would eat into B's market share. At the same time, promoting C as »value priced« could cannibalize the sales of A, which is also positioned as an affordable brand.

How BrandMatics Advanced helps to assess positioning alternatives

McKinsey has developed the BrandMatics Advanced portfolio positioning map, to assess and optimize the net effect of such (re)positioning efforts. To identify potential positions for C, the first step is to create a brand positioning map based on quantitative brand driver research not just for C, but for the entire category. This first step creates transparency about the current positions of existing brands in the category as shown in Figure 3.30. If two given positions, e.g., »affordable reliability« and »precious glamour« are already occupied, C could either attack one of these head on (which would make sense only if the incumbent is a competitor brand) or assume an intermediate position, e.g., »affordable glamour.« The map helps to identify such positioning alternatives; the arrows in the chart indicate potential repositioning directions for C. In the next step, the analytics behind the BrandMatics Advanced positioning map simulate the net portfolio impact of the various possible positioning alternatives for C. This is accomplished by using the brand potential approach outlined in section 2.4 and illustrated in Figure 2.29. Effectively, the tool estimates the repositioning impact on the funnel by way of quantified changes in brand attributes that act as funnel drivers; the illustrative results are shown in Figure 3.31. The simulation then subtracts the value of any market share captured from A and B; it is even set up to recognize indirect effects such as usage of C as an ingredient brand in either A or B. The result is a clear and fact-based ranking of positioning alternatives according to their net portfolio effect as shown in Figure 3.32. As the length of the »net gain« bars in the figure indicates, »Modern glamour« is the most attractive position from a portfolio perspective. Accordingly, Alphabet Inc. decided to relaunch C as a more modern, more natural, and slightly more affordable alternative to B, the premium brand. This position combines the advantage of appealing to a younger, more open-minded audience than A with the benefits of attracting a more price-conscious target group than B, effectively damaging neither in-house brand in any substantial way, but growing mostly at the expense of Numerical Inc.'s competitor brands.

Fig. 3.31: Step 2: Estimate future funnel performance

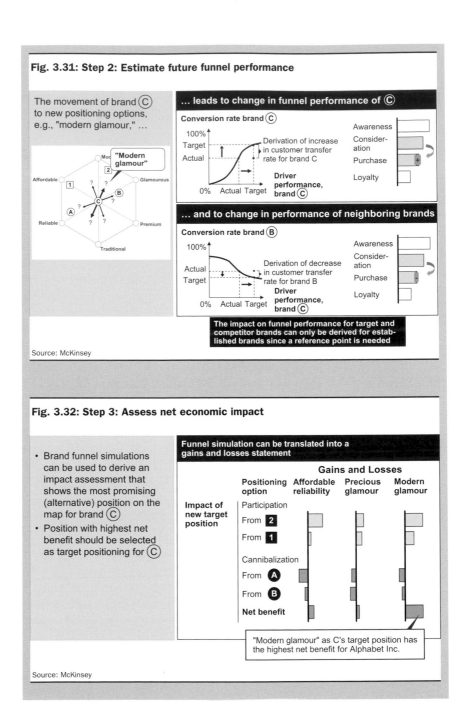

The movement of brand (C) to new positioning options, e.g., "modern glamour," ...

"Modern glamour"

Affordable | Glamourous | Reliable | Premium | Traditional | Mod

... leads to change in funnel performance of (C)

Conversion rate brand (C)

100%
Target
Actual
0%   Actual Target

Derivation of increase in customer transfer rate for brand C

Driver performance, brand (C)

Awareness
Consider-ation
Purchase
Loyalty

... and to change in performance of neighboring brands

Conversion rate brand (B)

100%
Actual
Target
0%   Actual Target

Derivation of decrease in customer transfer rate for brand B

Driver performance, brand (C)

Awareness
Consider-ation
Purchase
Loyalty

The impact on funnel performance for target and competitor brands can only be derived for established brands since a reference point is needed

Source: McKinsey

Fig. 3.32: Step 3: Assess net economic impact

- Brand funnel simulations can be used to derive an impact assessment that shows the most promising (alternative) position on the map for brand (C)
- Position with highest net benefit should be selected as target positioning for (C)

Funnel simulation can be translated into a gains and losses statement

Gains and Losses

	Positioning option	Affordable reliability	Precious glamour	Modern glamour
Impact of new target position	Participation			
	From **2**			
	From **1**			
	Cannibalization			
	From **A**			
	From **B**			
	Net benefit			

"Modern glamour" as C's target position has the highest net benefit for Alphabet Inc.

Source: McKinsey

Potential applications

The new portfolio positioning method is applicable both to companies that find themselves with multiple similar brands in the same category in a postmerger situation and to incumbents contemplating the discontinuation, repositioning, or (re)launch of individual brands in the same category. Its main limitation is that the simulation module works with *alternative* positions and compares their net benefit to any given *existing* position. This means the methodology may be applied to launches from scratch only if the company in question already operates at least one similar brand in the target category. In other words, it works for most in-category portfolio management challenges, but not for new category entry. Because it estimates the impact of positioning changes based on past purchase funnel performance, the BrandMatics Advanced portfolio positioning map is ideally suited to the requirements of repositioning efforts. The good news is that the starting point of the impact estimate can be a brand already owned by the company in question as well as a competitor brand operating in the target category or market.

Potential applications include, among others:

- Automotive companies managing multiple brands in the same category, e.g., premium passenger vehicles.
- Makers of branded components that act as alternative ingredients in third-party products in the same category, such as functional fabrics used in apparel or computer hardware components.
- Pharmaceutical and healthcare companies that manage multiple branded drugs or products for the same indication or application, such as sleeping medication or anti-aging skincare products.
- Fast-moving consumer goods manufacturers that want to optimize their brand portfolio within a given category, e.g., breakfast snacks or kitchen tissues.

No matter what the exact application, BrandMatics Advanced will help to make portfolio management decisions more fact based and more reliable by linking the estimation of their net impact to quantified market research and the proven methodology of potential brand value calculation based on the purchase funnel. In this respect, the portfolio positioning map complements the Brand Personality Gameboard, which is described in the next section and focuses on a brand's »softer« side, its emotional appeal.[27]

3.4 The Brand Personality Gameboard: Matching Celebrity Endorsements to Brand Personality Profiles

Most consumer brands are coming under increasing pressure as price competition intensifies and the homogenization of products and services continues. Because of this homogenization, rational benefits are becoming less and less relevant as brand differentiators. Only a few brands still possess objective performance advantages that are relevant in the perception of consumers. Most products consistently provide the basic benefits consumers expect; in product tests, more than 80 percent are ranked as »good.«[28] Furthermore, these products swim in a flood of advertising noise.[29] Each year consumers are subjected to nearly half a million commercial messages[30] as tens of thousands of newly registered brands compete for their attention.[31]

This onslaught is dulling the receptiveness of the consumer and reducing the potential impact of each individual advertisement. This makes it increasingly difficult to get brands noticed by consumers. Brand managers have long been aware that what they need is a distinct, consistent, well-implemented brand promise that can help differentiate their brand from its competitors on all the relevant performance dimensions. But even when all the fundamentals are in place and the brand's proposition is compelling and competitive, how do you ensure the brand stands out from the crowd and gets noticed by its target audience?

Achieving distinctiveness through the emotions of brand personality

As was evident in the analysis of the Brand Diamond, the ultimate key to the success of strong brands is their emotional benefit. Buyers are searching, whether they know it or not, for a personal, emotional advantage in consumption, one that goes well beyond the immediate and obvious promise of performance. »Value added« no longer means primarily what the brand provides, but increasingly what it stands for symbolically: the brand personality. The brand personality emerges from the consumer's interaction with the brand at all direct and indirect touch points. Typically, each contact involves a range of associations related to product category, brand name, advertising presence, and price. But the indirect reports, observations, and opinions of other users of a brand can also play an important part. This combination of one's own and others' experience ensures that many brands assume increasingly human-like features in the minds of consumers.

So if brands, in many ways, are like people in the consumer's mind, why not use real people to bring the brand personality to life emotionally? Ideally, these brand ambassadors would be well-known and evoke positive associations among the members of the brand's target group. Hence it is in no way surprising that celebrity endorsements are one of the most popular and most widespread marketing instruments to promote a brand's emotional appeal, especially in industries that are built on »selling dreams,« such as fashion, personal care, luxury goods, or entertainment. But more often than not, celebrities are selected purely based on their popularity. As a result, their individual profile rarely fits the brand personality. At the very least, it is often unclear which aspects of a brand's personality a given celebrity is hired to promote. This is all the more true if the same person acts as a spokesperson for multiple brands, let alone competing brands in the same category. Perhaps the most prominent example is Franz Beckenbauer, one of the world's foremost soccer personalities and also the first German athlete to appear in advertising, starting in the mid-1970s. At the peak of his testimonial career, Beckenbauer appeared on TV and in print ads to promote convenience food, financial services, pay TV channels, and two competing mobile phone operators almost in parallel. When spread so thinly, a celebrity endorsement can hardly help sharpen a brand's perceived personality. In fact, it may not even contribute much to the attention the brand receives because of sheer overload and misattribution.

The fact of the matter is that celebrity endorsements can do more than just grab attention, and in light of the astronomic fees captured by top celebrities they, indeed, *must* do more to ensure sufficient payback. If well selected, celebrities are ideally suited to bring out a brand's current or future target personality traits. So which brand *should* be hiring Beckenbauer as a spokesperson from a strategic brand management perspective? Respectively, can über-model Heidi Klum really be the ideal spokesperson for brands as diverse as McDonald's, Victoria's Secret, Henkel's hair-styling brand Taft, soft candy manufacturer Katjes, and beauty retailer Douglas? What qualifies a flashy guy like David Bowie to endorse a clean-cut brand like Vittel? Does Gwyneth Paltrow really embody the Estée Lauder brand personality? How does Madonna contribute to Versace's profile, or David Beckham to Gillette's? Is Harrison Ford the right man to vouch for both Lancia cars and Kirin beer?

Clearly, a systematic approach to determining brand personality and selecting appropriate testimonials is called for. To measure a brand's personality and identify potential celebrity sponsors that fit its profile, the BrandMatics® toolkit incorporates the Brand Personality Gameboard.[32]

Measuring brand personality using the Brand Personality Gameboard

The gameboard is based on the work of Jennifer L. Aaker, the internationally renowned Stanford University marketing professor who first succeeded in developing a reliable scale for measuring brand personality. The scale is based on personality traits that had previously been associated with the realm of psychology rather than that of marketing. Through a study of 37 representative brands, Aaker identified five core dimensions of brand personality, which can be further subdivided into facets (Figure 3.33).[33]

In order to make use of this approach in practical brand management, McKinsey carried out a multilevel study in cooperation with the German market research institute GfK. This study identified 13 elements that describe the personalities of brands in their entirety. Using methods of multidimensional scaling, it is possible to map these personality attributes and their interdependencies onto a positioning diagram, the Brand Personality Gameboard. The relative strengths of the 13 elements determine the

Fig. 3.33: The five dimensions of brand personality

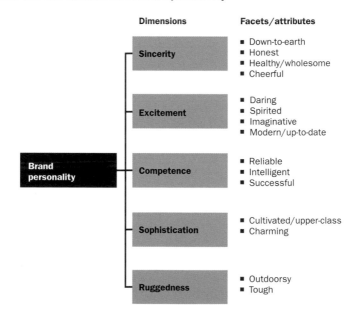

Source: Jennifer L. Aaker, Dimensions of Brand Personality, 1997

position of the brand personality profile on the board. The distance between the points reflects the degree of similarity of the perceived profiles, while the distance from the edge of the gameboard indicates the degree of uniqueness (the further outward, the more unique).

Figure 3.34 shows the position of selected brands in the German market alongside the personalities of contemporary celebrities. The distance of the brands from the celebrity (or the personality trait) reflects their degree of similarity. The closer a brand is to a certain trait or person, the stronger the brand is perceived in terms of this characteristic relative to its competitors. For instance, with its slogan »Sail away,« the Beck's beer brand expresses its pronounced freedom-loving personality. The core personality of Bruce Willis, for instance, corresponds especially well to this brand. L'Oréal, in contrast, represents charm, thus corresponding well to the positioning of Julia Roberts.

Fig. 3.34: The Brand Personality Gameboard maps celebrities and brand profiles to highlight affinities

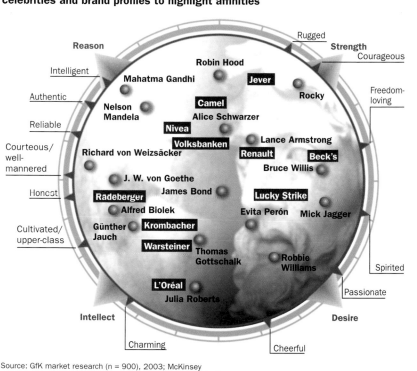

Source: GfK market research (n = 900), 2003; McKinsey

A brand's personality plays an important role in ensuring that it achieves a high degree of brand loyalty. To back up this claim, McKinsey investigated how closely brand strength and brand personality strength are related. In 900 interviews conducted in Germany, participants were asked to evaluate the personality profiles of 40 brands. It turned out that there is a very strong connection between brand strength and personality strength (Figure 3.35). For each attribute, the strength of the association and the uniqueness of positioning were weighted with the market-specific purchase relevance. This yielded an overall personality index. The results were then compared with the brand potential index, BPI, from the GfK market research institute. The BPI is a measure of brand attractiveness; it is an index number generated from a total of 10 different consumer attitudes.[34] This comparison of brand personality and brand potential revealed that brand strength is highly correlated with consumers' perception of a brand's personality. This link confirms that brand personality traits are particularly well suited to producing the emotional »added value« of a brand. However, not all of the various brand attributes that make up the Brand Personality Gameboard will be relevant to every industry; brand communication needs to focus on those that are relevant for the brand.

Fig. 3.35: Brand strength is highly correlated with personality perception

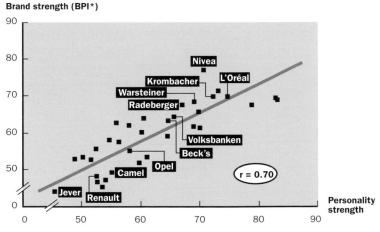

* Brand Potential Index
Source: GfK market research (n = 900), 2003; McKinsey

From brand mapping to implementation of the target personality

Determining the brand personality and mapping it onto the McKinsey Brand Personality Gameboard is only the first step. The next step is to decide whether to cultivate the current personality and enforce it with a fitting testimonial, or shift the brand towards a new personality and use a celebrity that embodies the target personality instead. The results from the brand segmentation (see section 2.2) play an important role in answering this question, since segmentation identifies the most promising consumer target groups for the brand. In addition, the market environment must be analyzed to determine which personality traits are most important for that sector. For instance, it goes without saying that for positioning in the financial services sector, personality traits like »reliable« and »honest« are likely to be more important than »passionate« or »cheerful.« The target personality should also recognize the competitive landscape. Mapping competitor brands onto the gameboard is an important step in ensuring commercial success, for even the most attractive target position should be avoided if it is already dominated by a competitor. Subsequent to the target personality definition, the gameboard can be used to select the most promising endorsement candidates.

Finally, the resulting positioning alternatives need to be reconciled with the capabilities, strengths, and weaknesses of your company. The personality positioning targeted in the gameboard must not only be credible, but also achievable for the brand in question. It should be able to embody the associated promise and be able to deliver on it in its daily business. If, for instance, the target positioning embodies reliability, good manners, and honesty as its core traits, this must also be reflected in the appearance and behavior of the sales team. If the sales team instead consists of a »wild bunch« of spirited, passionate, cagey fellows, the positioning will not be credible and the brand will be significantly weakened, as illustrated by the HVB service promise discussed in section 3.2.

A good example of how the use of a testimonial can successfully revitalize a brand image and sustain it over a long period of time is the above-the-line advertising of the German brewery Krombacher, featuring the well-known German television personality Günther Jauch, the popular host of *Who Wants to be a Millionaire* for many years. The profiles of the two personalities show the reason for this success (Figure 3.36). The perception of the celebrity's characteristics – »charming,« »intelligent,« and »cheerful« – match the profile of the advertised product and, thus, strengthen Krombacher's differentiation from its competition. Günther Jauch's endorsement of

**Fig. 3.36: Example of a good personality match:
Krombacher beer and television personality Günther Jauch**
Variance from product category average (percent)

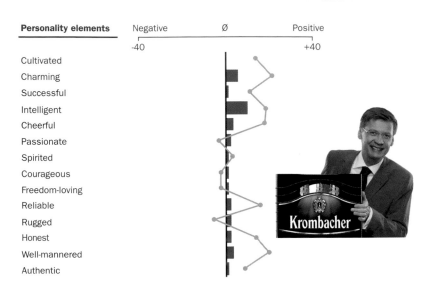

Personality elements	Krombacher
■ Krombacher	
● Günther Jauch	

Source: GfK market research (n = 900), 2003; McKinsey

the brand has helped Krombacher to improve its brand awareness and capture market share from key competitors such as Bitburger and Warsteiner. Since the start of the campaign, Krombacher's sales have increased 8 percent, despite a highly competitive market in which overall sales are stagnating. Several years and some disputes around the campaign's claims to charitable donations later, the collaboration between Jauch and Krombacher is still active. There were follow-up waves in 2006 (around the soccer World Cup) and 2008 (on air at the time of writing), making it one of the longest-standing and most consistent celebrity endorsements in recent German marketing history.

The Brand Personality Gameboard: A flexible tool

The gameboard can also be used to advantage as part of the fact base for co-branding efforts. Studies show that the combination of two brands in an advertising campaign increases the potential impact of a campaign. Not only does an advertising alliance help capture media-spending synergies, well-matched brand personalities may also strengthen each other's image in the consumer's mind. There are many potential partnerships in which such mutual reinforcement is likely to yield both direct and indirect benefits. As can be seen from Figure 3.34, Beck's beer and Lucky Strike cigarettes, for instance, might form a promising partnership according to the research the gameboard is based on. An advertising alliance holds the promise of mutually strengthening their current personalities, both of which are characterized by attributes such as »freedom-loving,« »spirited,« and »passionate.«

But the McKinsey Brand Personality Gameboard is by no means limited to applications related directly to brand management. Even tasks well beyond direct brand issues can benefit from personality analysis. Consider, for instance, the case of company takeovers or mergers. The respective brand portfolios represent significant values; ideally, they complement one another. But this ideal situation is rare. On the other hand, decisions about brand continuation, merging, or consolidation are often necessary early on in the mergers and acquisitions process. These decisions must be analytically well-founded, since they play a large part in determining the success of the new company. The Brand Personality Gameboard helps to distinguish critical from less important personality traits and allocate investments accordingly.

The gameboard is also a useful tool in the areas of brand architecture and umbrella brand management. For these applications, the Brand Personality Gameboard holds a particular advantage over many other brand measurement and management tools: whereas many brand positioning elements are market-specific in nature, the dimensions of brand personality are market-independent. They are thus ideally suited to positioning an umbrella brand that is intended to develop an equally high degree of relevance in all its categories and markets.

Interview with Prof. Dr.-Ing. Wolfgang Reitzle
»Consistency Takes Absolute Priority«

Prof. Dr.-Ing. Wolfgang Reitzle managed the BMW brand for many years and then spent three years in charge of the premium brands of the Ford Motor Company before becoming CEO at Linde. An engineer, he is familiar with the laws of brand management and urges consistency in all brand disciplines.

Since January 2003, Professor Reitzle has been molding the traditionally oriented Linde Group into a more profitable company with improved prospects for the future. The term »LeadIng» is a striking indication of the new positioning in the field of global competition – as a company with a claim to leadership in all its technology sectors. Dr. Jesko Perrey spoke with the successful manager about his most important experiences in brand management. Professor Reitzle's credo brings us full circle: mastery of the craft and continuity are the essentials of brand management – and should be dealt with at the CEO level.

Jesko Perrey: Professor Reitzle, you have long been known as someone who »eats, sleeps, and breathes cars« in recognition of your firm grasp of brand management. People who have worked closely with you emphasize your exceptionally systematic approach to your everyday work. What does brand management depend on?

Wolfgang Reitzle: I do indeed have a fondness for facts. I try to integrate, as much as possible, a systematic approach in brand management in order to reduce the possibility of error and to establish a reliable basis. On the other hand, I have never hesitated too long at crucial times. If the decision-making factors were pointing in a specific direction, I was able to see exactly what the brand in question really represented. Brand management ultimately means implementing a clearly defined idea consistently and in the finest detail. It is the consistency in particular that brings about success in brand management.

Jesko Perrey: What was your greatest success at BMW as part of this process?

Wolfgang Reitzle: The fact that throughout the years we were able to close the gap on our most important competitor by really »charging up« the brand essence. I was always sure that we should never compromise.

Jesko Perrey: How did the Mini, your last »BMW baby,« fit into this scheme of things?

Wolfgang Reitzle: I brought this car into the world with a lot of passion, together with the designer Frank Stephenson. In a narrower sense, however, the Mini was not a real BMW baby, and it was least of all a compromise. The Mini was always meant to be managed as a self-contained subbrand so as not to overstretch the branding of BMW. Young people – a new segment with a promising future for the company – elevated the Mini to an object with cult status.

Jesko Perrey: After achieving success, everything always seems so self-evident. Is there a reason for hitting the target in brand positioning that depends on the person?

Wolfgang Reitzle: The most important thing is a strong personal identification with the brand. That happens when someone is very intensely involved with the brand and develops the proper »nervous system« with regard to brand management. In order to make the right decisions, a brand manager must be completely immersed in the world of the product. The identification and the heated discussions among managers – especially with regard to the multi-faceted world of adventure that is a brand – must go further than in other areas of management. This makes great demands on people, because in this field the traditional man of action can reach the limits of what is possible just as easily as the sensitive and creative people. Regardless of the brand people work for, they must come to terms with its history in detail; they have to know how the products originated and how they changed as well as being aware of product successes and failures. You have to analyze market conditions, competitors and their strategies, their flops and tops, and all the other relevant matters involved.

Jesko Perrey: How do you measure failure?

Wolfgang Reitzle: It is precisely by carrying out an analytic review that it becomes obvious that certain products that seemed to have the appeal of an icon were, in reality, flops on the market. Brand management – I have never had a doubt about this – only works when the product is managed in such a way that it makes money. During the course of my career I haven't had a flop, and I have not undertaken anything that was economically inefficient.

Of course, I could have marketed some unusual products, but in the long run a lot of money would have been lost. In brand management it is particularly tempting to lose track of this guiding idea through pure enthusiasm for a magnificent product or for the attention received. A good brand manager always keeps track of the brand essence regardless of the decisions he has to make.

Jesko Perrey: What is the brand essence of Linde, and where are you leading the company?

Wolfgang Reitzle: Today it is in the engineering field that Linde is best established and has the most charisma – and an international reputation. Anyone needing something special in the field of plant construction comes to Linde. Our systems are protected by hundreds of patents. This is a tribute to the still-legendary German art of engineering. And it is in this environment that the whole company is also able to position itself without its functions ending up held together with a meaningless slogan. In cooperation with our agency, we have captured this commitment in what I believe is a catchy term, »Lead**Ing**.« We thus express our statement in one word; that is, the desire to play a leading role in the engineering field. Our logo as well, which was more suited to a food brand, was overhauled. The modified company logo symbolizes more powerfully the precision and high-tech claims of a progressive engineering brand. Just in the area of corporate identity alone, a lot has been done at Linde. The company ideally has a cohesive appearance, starting with products and services and going on to buildings and through to brochures, business reports, business cards, etc. Money invested here will be multiplied even if the return on the investment cannot be calculated exactly. For this purpose, however, everything must add up, from the top products to the right furniture in the offices. Our visitors must also get the impression that they are dealing with a leading engineering company.

Jesko Perrey: The common denominator is consistency, starting with the total identification of managers with their company and continued in the complete process chain of brand management and in the corporate identity strategy. Are there any further examples that serve to document the importance of consistency in brand management?

Wolfgang Reitzle: Yes, everything revolves around consistency. This is not only one of many crucial factors but the key word, the *sine qua non*. Consistency takes absolute priority. No matter what is done to the brand, it has to be consistent. There are first-class brands that can endure an enormous amount of stretching, brands that therefore can serve a very large market segment. Brands that do not forfeit their premium claim are very valuable economically.

Jesko Perrey: What do you think is the most valuable brand worldwide?

Wolfgang Reitzle: If I were to define »valuable« based on the sales that I can generate with a brand, then Mercedes-Benz is still a good example. There are other dream brands that have a comparatively limited potential. Fashion or watch brands, for example, can generate sales in the range of several hundred million euros, but never in the billions.

Jesko Perrey: What brand has the greatest unutilized potential?

Wolfgang Reitzle: Ferrari is the most emotional brand in the world. Visit a Formula I race: there you can see the truck driver with the Ferrari cap on his head and holding the expensive tickets that he has saved up for, although he will never be able to buy a Ferrari. Ferrari is a brand giant but an economic dwarf. The brand is virtually unused with the couple of thousand automobiles that are produced annually.

Jesko Perrey: There is often a fine line between top and flop. Decisions must therefore be carefully thought out. For example, because of the risk of overextending a brand, a lot of knowledge, experience, and sensitivity must be brought to bear. How has this dynamic played out in the car industry?

Wolfgang Reitzle: The watchwords here are timing and a profound appreciation of the power of one's own brand. Very powerful brands can lead the way as trendsetters and can create awareness for new products within your portfolio; for example, by rounding off the range of products of a premium brand with an addition in the lower mid-range segment. Smaller brands with the same objective can often fall by the wayside because market acceptance failed to materialize.

Jesko Perrey: Looking beyond the automobile industry and also beyond success, how do things look? Where have there been failures, and what can we learn from them?

Wolfgang Reitzle: A well-known fashion brand based in southern Germany was seriously overstretched. The company used to stand for high-quality belts and bags made of leather and was an »in« brand. Encouraged by their success, the company management extended their branding skills to include leather goods in general. So first they tried making shoes and then went on to produce numerous accessories, always using the familiar

213

trademark. The crash was unavoidable, because they had departed from the path of consistency and the company had been managed »into a void.« There are also examples of crises with even better-known brands. Levi's, which was once to jeans what Uhu in Germany is to glue, simply allowed themselves to be outstripped. English luxury brands, with their proud tradition, have become prisoners of old-brand positioning and in the end were simply bought up. Burberry also failed to plan for the future: people no longer wanted to be seen walking around with an outmoded trench coat – until Rosemary Bravo turned it into a cult brand again. Now even poodles are scurrying along wearing mini-suits with a Burberry pattern. You may find this foolish, but an English brand can take this kind of joke. The traditionalist Burberry has succeeded in presenting its brand as progressive and is again up there with the best of the field in a highly competitive business.

Jesko Perrey: And, again, what can we learn from these examples?

Wolfgang Reitzle: Well-managed brands must never be allowed to stick rigidly to tradition and have to undergo continuous further development, but not in an unmotivated or fitful way. Many companies and some branding experts find this hard to do, as it requires extensive knowledge, a solid mastery of execution, and ultimately the right »nose.« Consistency is the supporting pillar of brand management, while the second most important success factor is continuity.

Jesko Perrey: Where have these requirements been ideally met?

Wolfgang Reitzle: At Marlboro. For me, this is a brand that has completely internalized these principles. I had a real »aha!« experience many years ago on the way from JFK Airport to Manhattan, driving towards the enormous advertising sign with the cowboy in the canyon: the word Marlboro didn't appear anywhere; you could only see the evocative image. But there wasn't a shadow of a doubt about the brand involved. Anyone who has managed to get so far, continuously and consistently, can hardly be knocked out of the saddle. Marlboro could cut the poster into small pieces so that you only see the cowboy boots, and you would still instantly recognize the brand and the message. Marlboro has managed to do this because it has consistently used the same branding for decades, always with the same pattern.

Jesko Perrey: Aren't enormous sums of money being thrown out the window, especially in the advertising industry?

Wolfgang Reitzle: In the flush of creativity, for which many companies pay dearly, many a brand message was lost and failed to reach the customers. If we flicked through any magazine we picked up at random, I could show you examples. Many agencies are primarily out to cause a stir, even in their own sector, and to appear original and witty. But this is just a flash in the pan. At best they perk up short-term sales but they do not in any way enhance the continuous development of the brand.

Jesko Perrey: Isn't it often true that companies mishandle the agency briefing, in that they delegate it exclusively to the company's own advertising department?

Wolfgang Reitzle: This is surely one reason why many companies are really dependent on their agency. It is no longer possible to terminate the agreement, because all the knowledge about the brand and the company is stored up at the agency – without, however, the advertiser being able to fully implement this knowledge.

Jesko Perrey: How can this circle be broken?

Wolfgang Reitzle: This question about the right organization brings us to the subject of teamwork. With questions of design and in brand management, teamwork frequently results in mediocrity shaped by compromises. What can a CFO, for example, really contribute when asked to comment on a design because he happens to be on the relevant committee? As an important person, if he doesn't like the product design, he will make the designer back down. This is exactly the same with questions about the brand and decisions regarding advertising. You need only very few people who really know something about the subject. And these people should have the power of decision.

Jesko Perrey: Why are these people so rare?

Wolfgang Reitzle: A good question. Marketing often engages in brand management without having taken the measure of the specific abilities or without having asked who has really internalized the brand and has the knowledge or a real knack for dealing with it effectively. Or the task is often assigned to someone from sales. Decisions made in a completely different part of the company often have an impact on marketing. This can be the ruin of even the most attractive concept. There are many reasons for the organizational inadequacies. It is obvious that you need a handful of adept people in key positions; if possible, at the very top. You won't find many people who combine equal measures of intuition and drive or the ability to assert themselves. The fact is that many companies are not in good shape with regard to the organization of brand management, despite the fact that effective brand management is becoming increasingly important.

Jesko Perrey: And looking at the crisis in the German brand industry?

Wolfgang Reitzle: The greatest external danger to reasonable brand management is surely the discount battle. If customers no longer buy the products but the discounts, then there is the risk of permanent erosion in the consumer goods segment. The proclamation of penny-pinching as a fun factor is a great campaign for the discounter, but it is a sword of Damocles for the premium brands that play a significant part in economic progress. The belief in the value of a product is being lost. Companies that are unable to withstand these trends and participate in discount initiatives will be quickly damaged and will be sucked into a maelstrom that will pull them in deeper and deeper. If everything is being sold at a loss and the price is no longer an indication of exclusiveness, the system will lose its coordinates.

Jesko Perrey: Is there a way out?

Wolfgang Reitzle: In the short term, this is almost impossible. If the downward spiral has set in, you have to try to retain your share of the market. In the medium term, however, here as everywhere else, only innovation and differentiation will lead to success. I am still deeply convinced that you can set yourself apart from your competitors with services or products and innovation. This includes a very individualized branding environment, which has to be appropriately communicated. The more exclusive a brand is, the more scope I have with the price. If my product is reduced to a run-of-the-mill commodity, I will be caught in the discount quagmire and – to put it somewhat emotionally – doomed to destruction.

Jesko Perrey: One last question, Professor Reitzle. As a private consumer, what brand name do you start the day with?

Wolfgang Reitzle: The television stations ARD and ZDF, because the first thing I do is watch the morning news program Morgenmagazin.

Notes

1 VDA, the association of German car makers, reports that sales of »environmentally friendly« passenger cars had grown by 57 percent in 2007; these are defined as consuming less than 5 liters per 100 km and emitting less than 130 g of carbon dioxide per km, *Frankfurter Allgemeine Zeitung*, 7 Feb 2008.

2 Eiberger, Markus, »Basiszahlen Telekommunikation,« *Motor Presse Stuttgart*, May 2007; press clippings/company information.

3 *Samsung press release*, Dec 2007; »Samsung's Goal: Be like BMW,« *Business Week*, 1 Aug 2005, www.businessweek.com.

4 »Effekte der Euro 2008 auf die Nachhaltige Entwicklung«, Detailkonzept, Bern: University of Bern, 2005/2007.

5 Meffert, Heribert and Jesko Perrey, »Mehrmarkenstrategien,« *Markenmanagement*, ed. Heribert Meffert, Christoph Burmann, and Martin Koers, Wiesbaden: Gabler, 2002, p. 201 ff.

6 LeadIng is a half-English, half-German abbreviation for »leading engineering.« Discussed in the interview at the end of this chapter.

7 Units sold; growth from Jan 2006 to Jan 2007/2008. *Frankfurter Allgemeine Zeitung*, 23 Feb 2008; »Volkswagen verzeichnet einen Rekordabsatz,« *Neue Zürcher Zeitung*, 15 Apr 2008, No. 87, p. 25; *Volkswagen press release*, 30 Apr 2008. At the time of writing, Skoda did not use the brand promise statement as quoted any longer. Claims featured on corporate Web sites include »Simply clever.« (Germany and other countries, e.g., www.skoda.de) and »The manufacturers of happy drivers.« (United Kingdom, www.skoda.co.uk).

8 Meffert, Heribert and Christoph Burmann, »Identitätsorientierte Markenführung: Grundlagen für das Management von Markenportfolios,« *Arbeitspapier Nr. 100*, Münster: Wissenschaftliche Gesellschaft für Marketing und Unternehmensführung e.V., 1996.

9 Saalbach, Peter, »Gestern ein König«, *manager magazin*, Jun 2004

10 »Ford Motor Company announces agreement to sell Jaguar Land Rover to Tata Motors,« *Ford press release*, 26 Mar 2008.

11 Kirchgessner, Kilian, »Reinhard Jung: Herr der Zahlen,« *Financial Times Deutschland*, 18 Jan 2008.

12 Capell, Kerry, »Thinking Simple at Philips; A panel of outside experts is helping the electronics giant reinvent itself,« *BusinessWeek*, 11 Dec 2006. John Maeda is a leading expert on simplicity in information technology. He is an associate director at MIT's Media Lab and president of the Rhode Island School of Design. His 2006 book »The Laws of Simplicity« is one of the best-selling books on industrial design.

13 »Best Global Brands,« Interbrand, 2006 and 2007.

14 Saal, Marco, »Riesige Fokusgruppe; Philips-Marketingchef Andrea Ragnetti über eine ungewöhnliche Form der Ideenfindung,« *Horizont*, 12 Jul 2007.

15 Sixt annual reports; Köhn, Rüdiger, »Hertz lassen die Billigstrategien der Konkurrenten kalt,« *Frankfurter Allgemeine Zeitung*, 2 Feb 2004, p. 16; Diekhof, Rolf, »Grün sticht,« *Werben & Verkaufen*, 12 Sep 2003, p. 40.

16 Kroder, Titus, »Der Geizhals muss investieren,« *Financial Times Deutschland*, 15 Feb 2008; IATA (International Air Transport Association) and company information.

17 »Free Love,« Mar 2008, www.trendwatching.com.

18 Fanderl, Harald and Fabian Hieronimus, »Consumer Driven Redesign – Capturing New Potential Through Customer Insight,« *Recall No. 1*, Düsseldorf: McKinsey & Company, 2008.

19 Ohnsman, Alan and Jeff Bennett, »Toyota Puts Hipness Ahead of Sales

for New Scion Cars,« Update 4, 8 Feb 2007, www.bloomberg.com.

20 Unilever company information, »Path to Growth Summary and Implementation, Third Quarter 2003,« www.unilever.com.

21 Simonian, Haig, »Three letters gain a personality – UBS, Europe's biggest bank, has collapsed its multiple brands to focus on a single global name,« *Financial Times*, 18 Apr 2005.

22 Burger, Ludwig, »UBS will need ›years‹ to restore brand image in wealth management,« *CNBC/Thomson Financial*, 13 Jun 2008; Schreiber, Meike, »Der unter dem Ruf leidet,« *Financial Times Deutschland*, 6 Jun 2008.

23 Based on an article by Baumüller, Nicole and Christoph Erbenich, »Wege zum Erfolg: Fünf Thesen zum Markentransfer,« *Markenartikel*, Jun 2005.

24 Most recently, the company has started conquering not only new categories, but entirely new territories with the Virgin Brand as well: Africa, namely Nigeria, and India.

25 »The Market for Impulse Ice Cream,« A report on the supply in the UK of ice cream for immediate consumption, London: British Competition Commission, 1994 and 2000.

26 Janotta, Anja, »Mövenpick gibt Katjes den Laufpass,« *Werben & Verkaufen*, 28 Jan 2008, www.wuv.de.

27 Fanderl, Harald, Lars Köster, Jesko Perrey, and Dennis Spillecke, »Hohe Kunst: Wie Markenartikler ihr Portfolio optimieren,« *akzente* 2, Düsseldorf: McKinsey & Company, Inc., 2008.

28 *Test Jahrbuch*, Stiftung Warentest, 2004. 87 percent of tested products were awarded a grade of A or B, typically on an A to F grade scale.

29 Nöcker, Ralf, »Werber zwischen Hoffen und Bangen,« *Frankfurter Allgemeine Zeitung*, 11 Nov 2003, p. 13.

30 »Werbung in Deutschland 2003,« ZAW (central association of the German advertising trade), p. 297.

31 On average, the number of brands in Germany increased by 56,000 annually between 1992 and 2002; *Annual reports*, German Patent and Trade Mark Office, 2002 and 2006.

32 Fanderl, Harald, Ansgar Hölscher and Oliver Hupp, »Der Charakter der Marke – Die Messung der Markenpersönlichkeit: Das Brand Personality Gameboard,« Part 1, *Markenartikel*, Mar 2003, pp. 28–33; and Hölscher, Ansgar, Achim Hecker and Oliver Hupp, »Der Charakter der Marke – Die Messung der Markenpersönlichkeit: Das Brand Personality Gameboard,« Part 2, *Markenartikel*, Apr 2003, pp. 36–43.

33 Aaker, Jennifer L., »Dimensions of Brand Personality,« *Journal of Marketing Research 34*, Aug 1997, pp. 347–356.

34 The 10 attitudinal components of the BPI are allegiance, acceptance of premium pricing, quality, awareness, uniqueness, empathy, trust, identification, willingness to recommend, and buying intention. See Hupp, Oliver, Sven Mussler, Ken Powaga, »Evaluation of the Financial Value of Brands,« GfK/PWC (German society for consumer research/PricewaterhouseCoopers), Mar 2004.

4.
Managing Brands

Even the best brand strategy will come to nothing without effective and effi-cient investment. This investment needs not only to be channeled to the right brands in the portfolio but also directed to the brand levers that will ensure conversion and purchase. Of course, with limitless investment every brand would receive all the resources it needs to develop to the fullest extent. In the real world, however, trade-offs are necessary to ensure an effi-cient return on investment. We will now look at the tools brand manage-ment requires to ensure the right decisions are made about the brand.

Section 4.1 introduces the concept of brand delivery, while section 4.2 dis-cusses return on marketing investment in general; as part of this discus-sion, the section provides a comprehensive overview of levers that can be used to improve the return on marketing and branding investments. Selected brand management levers, namely controlling, organization, and steering of service providers, are discussed in more detail in sections 4.3 through 4.5.

4.1 Brand Delivery: How to Bring the Brand Promise to Life across All Customer Touch Points

Needless to say, strong brands are not created solely through creative advertising. A positive brand image is created through the individual's experiences of the brand on a daily basis. This image will only become anchored in customers' minds if it is consistent over a long period. In ser-vice industries like banking, insurance, telecommunications, retail, travel, or logistics, it is especially important to manage the delivery of the brand promise across all customer touch points. A well-defined brand promise often fails because it is not delivered consistently across the organization. As a past Allianz insurance television spot insisted, »a promise is a prom-ise.« Nothing harms a brand more than weak delivery.

Power Brands. H. Riesenbeck and J. Perrey
Copyright © 2009 WILEY-VCH Verlag GmbH & Co. KGaA, Weinheim
ISBN: 978-3-527-50390-2

Recognizing the importance of customer touch points

Customer touch points can take many shapes and forms. Communication in the form of advertising (above- and below-the-line) or public relations is, of course, very important. But in every industry there are many other touch points that are also of great importance, some even more so than communication. Think about the airline industry, where the customer's experience at touch points, such as reservations, check-in, boarding, or baggage claim, can have a much more significant impact on the brand image than any advertising campaign. But it does not stop there. Nowadays, there is a multitude of interaction points in this industry (Figure 4.1). They all need to be managed carefully to ensure the customer experience at these touch points reflects the brand's value proposition and desired brand image.

In retail banking, the important touch points include, among others, account statements, ATMs, branches, call centers, e-mail communication, Web sites, and sales agents. Consistent delivery of the brand promise will have a major impact on the required level and kind of service at each of

Fig. 4.1: Customer touch points in the airline industry

Source: McKinsey

these touch points. A bank that is known for its lean processes and cost efficiency, such as US Bancorp or Fifth Third, would obviously keep its branch service functions at a minimum, placing the emphasis on the use of direct sales channels instead of hiring and training a large branch-based

Managing Brands

sales force. However, power retailers (e.g., Wells Fargo Bank) or advisory banks (e.g., Dresdner Bank) require a high level of sales or service functions, respectively. Even regarding branch design, this emphasis on touch points means that every feature, from floor plan to carpeting, should be consistent with the overall brand strategy. If a bank targets an established, older customer base, promising to take care of all their financial matters, perhaps a conservative facade and a layout accommodating interview booths to be used for providing financial planning and customized sales would be in line with this promise. If, on the other hand, the bank is targeting a customer base skewed towards customers in their thirties, priding itself as a leader in technological sophistication and time efficiency, then probably a more modern design with an emphasis on self-service facilities for time-pressed customers would be more appropriate.

These examples show how and why an organization's brand promise requires careful thought about all its current customer interactions, whether they are providing the kind of service the brand promises, and whether the brand is delivering on its promises.

Achieving superior brand delivery along three stages

In order to align the organization and marketing instruments for handling these difficult tasks, companies need to master challenges on three fronts: first, a brand mindset must be created among all employees; second, companies need to determine whether they deliver the brand consistently across all customer touch points; and, third, the brand needs to be institutionalized for the long term (Figure 4.2).

Creation of a brand mindset

For many industries, branding in its holistic sense of art, science, and craft is still a fairly new concept. Often, many people within an organization understand the concept of branding only in an advertising or logo context.

Therefore, successful brand delivery entails a long transformational process to create the right mindset and make sure that every employee under-

Fig. 4.2: Three-stage approach to brand delivery

Creation of a
brand mindset

Brand delivery
across customer
touch points

Long-term
institutionalization

Familiarize major
stakeholders in the
organization with and
convince them of brand
promise (emotionally and
rationally)

Translate brand promise
into concrete actions;
assign ownership for
implementation in
respective work areas

Institutionalize brand
promise within the
organization

Source: McKinsey

stands his or her role and responsibility in creating a consistent brand experience for customers. This is especially critical in service industries, where many employees directly manage customer touch points.

There are two aspects that need to be managed in this process:

1. **Employees need to understand the concept of »brand delivery along all customer touch points.«** This makes every one of them an ambassador of the brand. They must understand that every action that is directed towards customers, implicitly or explicitly, influences their perceptions. In order to motivate members of the organization to act as responsible brand ambassadors, strong top management backing and involvement is a prerequisite. Recognizing this, Helmut Maucher, long-time CEO of Nestlé, said: »If you consider [your brand] to be the most important asset, brand management responsibility has to be a C-level issue.«[1] While organizations may understand theoretically that frontline employees are accountable for the full customer experience, they often fail to empower them or show them the kind of respect they deserve. As one frustrated call center manager at a leading telecommunications company reported: »As long as we are treated as second-class citizens in charge of protecting management from ›pesky customers,‹ our company will fail to keep its promises.«[2] Workshops, training sessions, manuals, and other reinforcing mechanisms will help the organization to stress the importance of each customer interaction and help the staff to adopt a *brand mindset* gradually.

2. **Identification with the brand promise.** The brand will be »lived« only if employees truly believe in what they are asked to deliver or, even better, are proud of what they do every day to satisfy their customers. An effective tool in this context can be *a brand book,* a document that is shared widely across the organization, defines the core brand identity, and provides a common language for consistent brand execution. Organizations with strong brands like IBM, Nivea, or DHL have created such a brand book and use it together with additional internal communication vehicles (like »brand days,« awards for behavior that conforms to the brand promise, or sweepstakes) to deepen their employees' identification with the brand promise (see the insert »DHL: Becoming the World's First Choice in Logistics through Systematic Brand Management« below).

In the day and age of 360-degree brand communication, brand managers need to think ever more holistically about delivering the promise of their brands. To come full circle, brand delivery planning needs to recognize the fact that brand positioning is not only an outbound game. Brands must be built consistently at all touch points. A lot of touch points involve direct interaction or communication with the customer, e.g., sales force, store design, or customer service. But there are also touch points at which customers are indirectly influenced by employees. Think, for example, of the image projected by the human resources department's employer branding efforts and recruiting events. Similarly, every marketing manager's idea of the brand influences the image conveyed in advertising materials. So when we say brands must be built at all touch points, that is meant to include a company's staff as well as their customers. Says Colin Mitchell of Ogilvy & Mather: »When you think of marketing, you more than likely think of marketing to your customers. But another ›market‹ is just as important: your employees; the very people who can make the brand come alive for your customers.«[3]

Often, executives assume that by defining a (new) brand positioning, their work is essentially done. They send out memos or even »brand books« to key players in their organizations and hope for the best. But a brand doesn't come to life in employees' hearts and minds on cue, nor does it happen automatically. According to a McKinsey survey, 60 percent of transformation efforts are considered failures, often because of a perceived lack of senior commitment, confusion among employees, and insufficient project management.[4] In fact, there is an entire subprocess behind the first stage described in Figure 4.2, »Creation of a brand mindset«; see Figure 4.3 for a more detailed breakdown of how to bring about such mindset changes internally. From numerous transformational programs at clients, a set

225

Fig. 4.3: Internal brand-building programs empower employees to live the brand

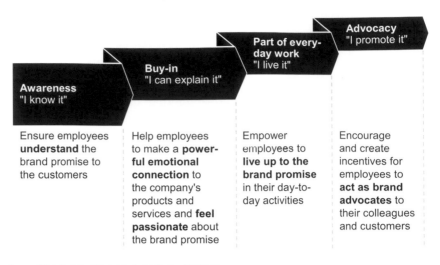

Awareness "I know it"	Buy-in "I can explain it"	Part of every-day work "I live it"	Advocacy "I promote it"
Ensure employees **understand** the brand promise to the customers	Help employees to make a **powerful emotional connection** to the company's products and services and **feel passionate** about the brand promise	Empower employees to **live up to the brand promise** in their day-to-day activities	Encourage and create incentives for employees to **act as brand advocates** to their colleagues and customers

Source: Mitchell, Colin, Harvard Business Review, McKinsey

of guiding principles has been identified for internal branding. To show how these success factors play out in practice, an example has been included for each factor:[5]

- **Ensure CEO sponsorship.** The best sponsor for internal brand building is the CEO. Although a purely top-down communication can lead to »not invented here« reactions, there is nothing like inspirational leadership when it comes to creating enthusiasm for the brand among your staff. At Virgin, CEO Richard Branson leads by example. He enters new categories and businesses simply because he feels passionately about them, manages his company in a hands-off fashion from his private yacht to give his executives greater autonomy, and puts people first: »Our first priority should be the people who work for the companies, then the customers, then the shareholders.«[6]
- **Choose the right moment.** Employees have to understand »why now.« Suitable triggers for major internal brand-building efforts can be the arrival of a new CEO as well as fundamental changes in company structure or business dynamics. British Petroleum (BP) used the occasion of its merger with Amoco and Arco to create a new, distinctive identity for employees of all premerger companies. Positioning itself as an energy company (»Beyond petroleum«), BP ventured to transform itself from an old-school corporation into an open, collaborative company. An internal

survey confirmed two-thirds of the staff are aware of and support the new brand values.

- **Apply holistic change management.** To shift mindsets and capabilities, simply announcing the (new) brand identity is not sufficient. Successful transformation takes clear instructions, role modeling, talent development, and formal reinforcement. When low-cost carrier JetBlue set out to »bring humanity back into the airline industry,« it made sure there were clear guidelines for key touch points (»BluePrint,« »BlueBook«), management got involved in passenger-facing operations at peak times, new employees were invited to a brand value training camp, and an annual brand value »speak up« survey was conducted to monitor the implementation of the new brand values.

- **Stick to it.** Internal brand building requires consistency; a one-shot effort is not enough. Leading players such as Ritz Carlton, Marriott's standalone luxury brand, have built continuous internal branding into their corporate DNA. Top management delivers inspirational speeches to the staff of every hotel several times a year, always building on the corporate credo »We are ladies and gentlemen serving ladies and gentlemen.« New hires go through two days of corporate philosophy training and are accompanied by a coach during their first four weeks. The first 15 minutes of every shift are set aside to discuss one of the 20 »brand basics.« Similarly, premium power tool maker Hilti (also see section 2.2) invests more than EUR 10 million to run »team camps« to promote its brand values of »outperformance« and »dependability.«

- **Link internal to external brand building.** Linking inbound to outbound brand communication gives employees a strong sense of direction and purpose. Sending one consistent message to internal and external audiences was IBM's top priority when it launched its e-business initiative. What was perceived as a normal marketing campaign externally, doubled as an internal effort to push the company to achieve goals previously thought out of reach. It helped change the way employees thought about processes, product development, product naming, and sales force organization, keeping in mind customers' perceptions and expectations of the brand as a provider of superior e-business solutions.

Examples such as these illustrate that internal brand building, let alone internal brand transformation, doesn't happen over night. It requires thorough preparation, a detailed roadmap, and rigorous implementation monitoring. In many ways, it isn't all that different from external brand building. This is all the more true in large and complex corporations. As a

227

Fig. 4.4: Internal target groups should play different roles

Target groups		Profiles	Recommended roles in internal branding
Top management		• Is powerful/influential • Is well-known in the organization • Has little time	• **Sender**/champion • **Multiplier/** role model
Managers of customer-facing departments*		• Frequently interact with customer-facing employees • Have relatively little time	• **Multipliers/** role models
Customer-facing units	**Marketing**	• Are usually in the office • Only indirectly influence customer touch points	• **Receivers –** influenced by role models and peers • **Informal multipliers –** act as role models for peers in everyday work environment, but not through formal channels
	Sales	• Have close customer contact, i.e., directly shape customer touch points • Are rarely in the office	
	Operations	• Have close customer contact, i.e., directly influence a lot of customer touch points	
Other managers and employees		• Are not exposed to brand-related topics regularly • Don't have direct customer contact	• **Receivers**

* All employees with personnel responsibilities in marketing, sales, and operations departments, excl. top management

Source: McKinsey

consequence, understanding, segmenting, and addressing different internal target groups is one of the key prerequisites of successful internal branding. Internal target groups, whether they have direct customer contact or not, have different profiles, should play different roles in brand transformation efforts, and must receive tailored communication (Figure 4.4). Says Nader Tavassoli of the London Business School: »One-size-fits-all programs simply will not work when trying to win over people. Segmenting people based on their various mindsets is critical to taking the organization to the next level.« A group brand manager at an international multi-category conglomerate agrees: »You need to segment your internal population just as you would your external audience and communicate appropriately.«[7]

Brand delivery across customer touch points

A motivated staff is the basis for delivering the brand promise to the customer. However, customers will »experience« the brand promise only if they constantly encounter a consistent brand message at every customer touch point.

As mentioned earlier in the book, a good example of this is Marlboro. For more than 50 years, Marlboro has been communicating its freedom-loving cowboy image and, consequently, has managed to build one of the most powerful brands in the world. What is more, strong brands do not stop at advertising but align behavior and processes at all customer touch points according to the brand promise. When UBS, for example, decided to consolidate all of its brands under a single global brand with a client-focused approach (see section 3.3), it not only reworked its entire marketing communication to support the »You & Us« message, it also changed its internal processes. These changes included using a consultative four-step approach to ensure that UBS was not only promising but also delivering »You & Us« to its clients.[8]

Accordingly, the brand promise should generally be translated along the entire business system, including territories well outside the traditional purview of the marketing department, such as research and development or production. For example, BMW's clearly defined value proposition of »The Ultimate Driving Machine« is being translated into tangible research and development objectives for the chassis frame so that it will support driving pleasure, using clearly defined guidelines for the product design. As CEO Dr. Helmut Panke put it: »The BMW brand stands for a promise of fascinating, individual automobiles, and we shall continue to keep our promise in this respect. A part of this promise is never to build a boring BMW [...]. We will only break into new segments if we remain true to the BMW image.«[9] Since the entire organization needs to be aligned with the brand promise, this process should be driven by the CEO, not by the chief marketing officer (CMO) or marketing director alone. BMW has taken the dual challenge of external and internal branding seriously. To make sure the entire organization knows and lives the brand values, BMW established the BMW Group Brand Academy in 2002. It is a training center that brings to life the three main brands – BMW, Mini, and Rolls-Royce – for managers from all departments. Upon »graduating« from the academy, they return to their teams and divisions as persuasive ambassadors of the brand.[10]

Less is more: Muji's end-to-end »no brand« brand delivery

Another inspiring example of end-to-end brand delivery is Muji, the Japanese company that manufactures and distributes stationery, household goods, clothing, and small items of furniture. Somewhat paradoxically, Muji has made »no brand« its brand philosophy. The company's promise of sleek minimalism has been implemented so rigidly that it is widely considered a role model for consistent brand delivery. Tadao Ando, the celebrated Japanese architect, sums up the company's philosophy as follows: »Muji's succinct design reveals a Japanese aesthetic that values sustaining simplicity by completely discarding all worthless decoration.«[11] The delivery of this promise starts with the products. Mostly made from natural materials, they are translucent white or entirely colorless, made from cardboard, untreated wood, matte aluminum, undyed natural fabrics, or transparent acrylic glass. What technical features they may have are simple to operate. The packaging is equally plain. A lot of products are not packaged or wrapped at all; they simply bear a tiny label giving the name and price, rendered in unadorned lettering, always in the company's trademark chestnut red on an ivory background. Shopping bags are made of plain, recycled paper with nothing but the company logo, also in chestnut red. The same design principles apply to Muji's catalogs, the company's chief form of communication with its growing customer base, as well as to the interior design of the 416 exclusive stores it currently operates (2008). Because of its unique appeal, the brand receives so much editorial attention that Muji hardly needs any advertising. What little advertising it does is, again, very simple, featuring line art and photographs in toned-down, natural colors. The brand itself is a tribute to stylish simplicity. Muji is an acronym denoting »**mu ji**rushi ryô hin,« meaning »unbranded quality products.« »Mu jirushi« can, in fact, also be translated as »no logo.« Registered in 1979 and launched in 1989, Muji pre-dates Naomi Klein's famous book of the same title by more than a decade.[12]

Muji's consistent delivery on the simplicity promise at all touch points has been richly rewarded by its customers. Both revenue and sales have been growing for years. Between 2003 and 2006 alone, the Group's revenue has grown at a compound annual rate of 9.4 percent. Recently, the company announced the imminent opening of its 41st European store in Berlin. To guarantee consistent delivery of the brand promise, all overseas stores are exclusively tied to the Muji brand, with the sole exception of the design store in New York's Metropolitan Museum of Art.[13]

Nestlé, with its premium coffee capsule brand Nespresso, has gone as far as establishing its own branded outlets to ensure a holistic brand experience, effectively adding an entirely new type of touch point to its consumer interaction platform. This step was based on the insight that people considered Nespresso to be inferior to coffee brewed and sold at coffee shops. Research indicated that more than 60 percent of the perceived coffee flavor is influenced by environmental factors, which is why the same coffee seems to taste better at a Starbucks coffee shop than at a gas station. Nespresso's

Fig. 4.5: Muji consistently delivers its brand promise of simplicity at all key touch points

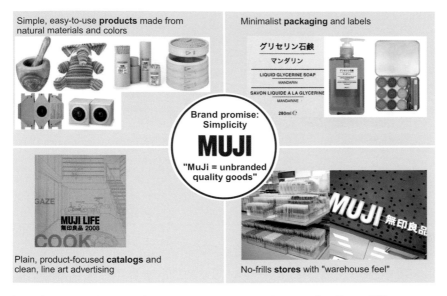

Simple, easy-to-use **products** made from natural materials and colors

Minimalist **packaging** and labels

グリセリン石鹸
マンダリン

LIQUID GLYCERINE SOAP
MANDARIN

SAVON LIQUIDE A LA GLYCERINE
MANDARINE

280ml ℮

Brand promise:
Simplicity

MUJI

"MuJi = unbranded
quality goods"

GAZE

MUJI LIFE
無印良品 2008

COOK

MUJI 無印良品

Plain, product-focused **catalogs** and clean, line art advertising

No-frills **stores** with "warehouse feel"

Source: Corporate Web sites (www.muji.co.uk, www.muji.com, www.muji.net), consumer blogs, Pictures: MUJI

high-class outlets in premium locations are specifically designed to promote the core brand value of a guaranteed premium, full-flavor experience. In parallel, Nespresso-branded coffee makers were reengineered to emit more aroma during the brewing process to replicate the coffee shop experience in consumers' homes.[14]

To develop and reinforce integrated end-to-end delivery of the brand promise as observed at BMW, Muji, and Nespresso, a useful format is the cross-functional workshop. Bringing together the expertise and experience from multiple functions, such workshops help to develop brand delivery programs that go well beyond classic communication. Typically, the workshops follow a three-step approach (Figure 4.6):

- *Generation of ideas:* Once the desired brand positioning and implicit value proposition have been defined and understood, new ideas for a targeted implementation are generated in workshops held within the various corporate functions.
- *Transformation of ideas into programs:* These ideas are then refined and aggregated into specific activities that influence customer interactions. Programs are developed to facilitate the implementation of these activities.

231

Fig. 4.6: Development of brand delivery activities

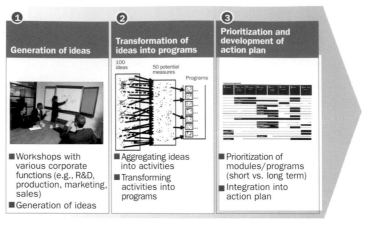

Source: McKinsey

- *Prioritization and development of action plans:* The various programs need to be prioritized according to their improvement potential (cost/benefit) and the resources required to turn them into action.

Long-term institutionalization

Once the plans for the brand's delivery are in place throughout the organization, the next step is to ensure the long-term institutionalization of the brand. Achieving this usually depends upon three key dimensions: people, processes, and tools. In the people dimension, it is critical to design a marketing organization that not only works effectively within itself but also connects well with the rest of the business system, such as product development. Good marketers have well-established processes in place that link marketing and customer insight to each relevant business process using objective milestones and defining clear responsibilities. This often means bringing qualified personnel into the organization and anchoring responsibility with the brand manager. Some successful marketers have even installed a board to monitor the progress of brand delivery and to support departments in putting the brand promise into action. Philips, for example, temporarily had a Simplicity Advisory Board to act as a think tank and sounding board to enhance the implementation of its brand promise of »sense and simplicity.« It brought together experts from the worlds of healthcare, lifestyle, and technology and provided the organization with an additional outside perspective on its efforts to deliver the simplicity promise.[15] In a recent interview, CMO Andrea Ragnetti said the Simplicity Advisory Board was instrumental in the ramp-up phase of »sense and simplicity« at Philips, but had been dissolved after two years of fruitful service. According to Ragnetti, the thinking the board was set up to promote »is now firmly ingrained in the organization.«[16] (See also the more detailed discussion of the role of the board in section 3.2.)

Orange Brand Launch in France – Inside=Outside: Brand Transformation

by Jean-Baptiste Coumau and Emmanuel Josserand.

Jean-Baptiste Coumau oversaw the launch of the Orange brand, by France Telecom, in 2001 as a partner at Izsak Grapin & Associés, a Paris-based management consulting firm, and member of the Blue Ocean Network. In 2007, he joined McKinsey & Company's Marketing & Sales Practice at the firm's Paris office. Emmanuel Josserand is a professor at the University of Geneva as well as an associate researcher at CREPA University of Paris Dauphine.[17]

The »inside=outside« brand transformation concept originates from the authors' experience during the launch of Orange in France in 2001. The brand, used to motivate 8,000 employees, was a key enabler for success. Several similar experiences followed in other European countries, reinforcing the authors' conviction about the strength of the inside=outside equation. In a truly »inside=outside« company, each employee, because he or she identifies with the company brand, will consistently make decisions that honor the brand and its promise.

Re-branding France Telecom Mobile as Orange was part of the plan when France Telecom purchased Orange in 2001; the objective was to refreshen the image and positioning of the company's mobile business. Initially, however, the re-branding faced several challenges. In the market, there was the challenge of not harming France Telecom Mobile's leading position (with Itineris at the high end of the market, Mobicarte in the prepaid segment, and Ola targeting women and families). Within the organization, there were the challenges of employee skepticism; a corporate culture dominated by networks, technologies, and engineers; and cultural differences between French and English management teams. At the time, marketing was seen as a cost position, and nobody thought that branding the entire company – and not just a product – could pay big dividends.

A year later, many indicators showed that the Orange re-branding had been a success, both externally and internally. Market share was up slightly from 47 percent (with three product brands combined) to 48 percent (with the single Orange brand). Brand preference rose to ten points above the level of Orange's major competitor SFR, »churn« fell to the lowest level in the French market, and »customer satisfaction« ranked the highest. Internally, 89 percent of the new Orange France employees believed in the company's future, and 78 percent thought that the Orange launch had had a positive effect.

Three years later, in 2005, the indicators continued to be positive. In the Interbrand France Best Brand study of the strongest brands in France, Orange was the only telecommunications brand (in eleventh place) and had the fastest growth.

This success didn't come just from changing a logo, nor just from launching new offers or tariffs and setting up a new style of communication. It was about changing the entire business ethos. You couldn't have a France Telecom culture delivering an Orange brand promise. It wouldn't work. One of the Orange brand management beliefs professes that »Orange is the same inside and outside.« A brand is mainly a promise to customers, combined with certain distinctive values. The only people who can deliver that promise are the people inside the company, both management and staff. How they perceive the brand inside can also be perceived outside.

In our experience, the following ingredients are critical in transforming a company through its brand:

Brand project setup – An ad-hoc organization across the company for breadth, but supported by a team of brand ambassadors for speed

The first prerequisite is speed. For a brand to transform an organization, you have to ensure that the pace of change is fast enough. This is true both for re-branding and for creating new momentum using an existing brand. If the change is perceived as hesitant or superficial, or if the actions and results do not happen fast enough, internal communication about the brand will be considered only another element of the official rhetoric, and the »inside=outside« mantra just another buzzword.

Adopting a project mode of operation is a good way to move fast. At Orange in 2001, the re-branding team set up a project organization linked directly to the CEO. The CEO's perspective and clout made it possible to change processes across departments, which was instrumental in re-branding quickly and successfully. Only six months elapsed between the go-ahead and the overnight brand change for the entire technical and commercial network.

The team of »brand ambassadors« that supported the project structure also played a critical role in this process. Organized as a network, dedicated part-time to the project, the ambassadors' role was to plan the brand deployment in their own units, organize the follow-up, stimulate local initiatives, and organize local events.

Brand induction – Combining total immersion with training processes and managerial tools to shape brand understanding and encourage new behavior

No »inside« branding is possible without explaining the brand to the employees. In order for them to discover what they need to change in their day-to-day work, they need to understand the company's vision, the brand values, and the brand promise as well as the company's ethos. The purpose of brand induction is to take this understanding one step further, enabling every single employee to contribute to the dynamic of change by living the brand themselves.

At Orange, all employees are »brand inducted« by their local or functional ambassador. During a four-hour session, each employee is exposed to the context, strategy, brand values, brand promise, and brand identity guidelines. Selected games and group exercises allow participants to put the brand elements into practice. Brand induction is not a magic wand, but its impact on specific populations, such as trade union leaders, is sometimes astonishing. This is essential to creating the cultural shock and momentum needed to transform the company.

Brand commitments – Improving brand delivery externally and internally with a simple, but strategic list

The brand commitment is a strategic list of brand management areas selected for improvement. It has the double role of guiding changes to the organization and its processes and proving that change has occurred. At Orange, we asked each business unit and function to identify areas of progress regarding brand values, where they are committed to change, and how they have followed up on their brand commitments both externally and internally. Most commitments imply collaboration across technical, marketing, and sales departments. Resource management and planning are critical to maximize impact. For example, at Orange, front-line employees were given negotiation and decision-making power to avoid confronting customers with multiple contacts. But to make it happen, Orange also had to develop and implement a new information system and training program.

In the brand commitment process, Orange repeatedly experienced the same problem: a big gap between employee and management perceptions about where the company stands. Managers, particularly top managers, are often much more optimistic than employees. Employees, particularly on the front line, are closer to customer perceptions. This point is critical: if management involvement is low at the beginning (because managers optimistically believe »everything is fine«), the opportunity for change at the end of the process is near zero. The brand commitments selected will be inappropriate and the implementation weak and fuzzy.

A bottom-up gap analysis with employee and customer panels at the beginning of the process can both create the right pressure and specify key areas for improvement. For the same reason, it is important to encourage employees to give their feedback when commitments are delivered (or not delivered). This comprehensive process, including the bottom-up gap analysis, the brand commitments, and the employee feedback, serves to bring »inside=outside« alive within the company. Thanks to the brand commitments, employees come to believe that what you do inside is reflected on the outside.

Leadership and empowerment – Providing role-model leadership to inspire people and enable power delegation

Leaders show the way. For a new brand, the organization's leaders need to ensure the consistency of the brand vision and promise. They must also reflect the values, be present in the field, and be role models for their employees.

One of the challenges in the selection of brand commitments is that it requires a strong commitment by the company's leaders, and the courage to select the right commitments.

Another critical factor in the successful launch of the »inside=outside« plan at Orange was to associate middle managers with the project, both in order to deliver against the large number of commitments that Orange wanted and also to integrate and involve people from various parts of the organization. The integration of middle management helped ensure that the organization was fully »inside=outside.«

External and internal sequencing – Timing the elements of change to build synergies

The fine-tuning of the rhythm of the project is an essential part of its management. At Orange, reasonable risks were taken in order to put the organization under pressure to change, so the external changes were launched first. Launching the changes in this manner had the advantage of breaking barriers and energizing the organization. This created a momentum within the organization by making change necessary and urgent. We still consider this an ambitious, but risky strategy. Another approach, safer but also more time consuming, consists of launching the internal changes first, so that the capacity to deliver the promise is built up before the external changes. Every company faces its own constraints, and there are many factors such as employee mindsets, competitor moves, and investor expectations that need to be taken into account when deciding between the two extremes.

Identification – Transforming employee mindset and consumer perception in parallel

How do you make the brand a driver for change? The answer in a word: identification. A brand is conceived for people (customers and employees) who identify with certain values and beliefs. The strength of the brand relies on several elements that can be explicit (a claim) or symbolic (a logo), rational (associated with the value of the product) or emotional (as in a beautiful advertisement). Each customer or employee will not only identify with the common ground, but will also project his or her own values and beliefs onto the brand. At Orange, we knew that change was taking place successfully when we heard the hotline staff saying, »What you just said, that's not really Orange.«

As the Orange France case shows, a truly »inside=outside« company is based on people that identify with the brand. Employees will seek to make the best decisions to show respect for the brand. This is the mobilizing power of the brand that allows it to be used as a driver or management tool for change. It is about each employee living the brand, being the brand. This identification makes it possible for a company to be coherent externally (strategy, products, and services) and internally (culture, organization, employees, and managers). The motivation and strategic alignment produced by successful »inside=outside« branding confers a clear competitive advantage.

DHL: Becoming the World's First Choice in Logistics through Systematic Brand Management

by Wolfgang Giehl, responsible for corporate advertising and brand management in the Deutsche Post World Net group.

DHL, the international logistics brand within the Deutsche Post World Net Group, is the global market leader for logistics services. In 2007, DHL was present at almost 5,000 locations in 220 countries and territories, employing some 250,000 people and generating more than EUR 38 billion in annual sales.

Strong brands create value for companies. They generate trust in a company's services and form the basis for a long-term relationship with customers. Increasingly, this applies not only to B2C markets, but to B2B categories such as express delivery services and freight forwarding services as well. As a consequence, we at Deutsche Post World Net have made systematic brand management for DHL one of our top priorities. The way we see it, brand management comprises brand *architecture, positioning* of individual brands, and *delivery* of a brand's promise in daily operations.

The origins of DHL date back to the pre-1995 era of Deutsche Bundespost (German federal post office), a public service provider owned and run by one of the federal government's ministries. After intermediate stages as a European and global portfolio of brands (including Danzas and EuroExpress), an integrated brand architecture for all global logistics services was put into place in 2003. The rebranding required coordinated implementation of all activities across the organization. The entire fleet of DHL trucks was painted yellow almost overnight. This was accompanied by an international advertising campaign, highlighting our new capabilities of global reach and integrated solutions. DHL has since become the successful global umbrella brand of Deutsche Post's global mail, express, freight, and logistics services. The last two years have seen the acquisition and integration of Exel, a leading contract logistics provider, that made DHL the global leader in its industry. Going forward, the DHL brand will co-exist with two German national brands for mail and financial services, Deutsche Post and Postbank. Deutsche Post World Net is the Group's corporate umbrella brand, targeted at investors and Group stakeholders rather than customers.

Having clarified the brand architecture for logistics services, our priority for the future is twofold: sharpening the DHL brand positioning, and ensuring its promise is delivered reliably and consistently in everyday customer interaction and experience. Recognizing that a global brand needs not only a consistent appearance but also a credible, relevant, and distinctive identity, the DHL brand management carried out extensive market research and intensive interviews both with customers and employees. The outcome of the positioning process is a very ambitious brand promise: DHL aspires to be the first choice for its customers worldwide. This promise rests on three pillars: the personal commitment of all employees, proactive solution development, and local strength, worldwide (Figure 4.7).

Fig. 4.7: DHL brand positioning is delivered both directly and indirectly

Source: Deutsche Post World Net

To ensure reliable and consistent delivery of the DHL positioning, we need to ensure that our three brand dimensions are fulfilled whenever and wherever our customers interact with the DHL brand. Our promise of personal commitment, proactive solutions, and local strength, worldwide must be kept in all markets, at all touch points, and by our entire staff.

To this end, we have introduced Brand Dynamics, an integrated system of brand steering tools, designed to measure brand performance and ensure consistency despite our considerable size and global reach. The foundation of Brand Dynamics is a diagnosis of brand funnel performance as well as brand perception in all key markets. Our analysis covers global basic attributes such as »reliability« and »speed,« but also includes local differentiators. For example, »likeability« is a key brand driver in Latin America, while Middle Eastern and Asian markets particularly value »ease of use.« All attributes and their impact on driving purchase decisions are being measured at segment level.

In parallel, brand delivery is being monitored at key customer touch points. For example, we check whether »speed,« a core brand driver in multiple markets, is kept not only in our product and service range (Do we offer the express services our customers require?), or as part of our pick-up service (Do our trucks arrive on time at the sender's lot?), but also during handling of enquiries (Are we sufficiently responsive when being called or e-mailed by customers?). Regional business unit managers are regularly provided with a standardized set of performance figures that cover the complete customer brand experience, from brand awareness to concrete interactions with (potential) customers. This makes it possible to derive clear goals for brand development, plan targeted measures, and monitor them systematically. Brand management thus becomes a closed cycle, from the initial brand positioning and value proposition through to the integrated implementation and ongoing control (Figure 4.8).

Fig. 4.8: DHL Brand Dynamics research

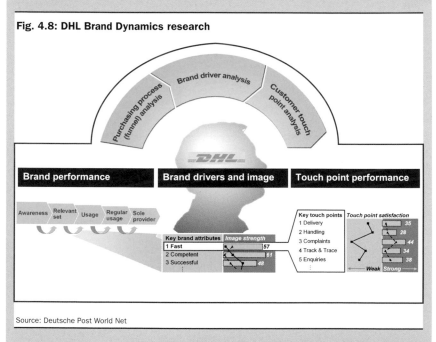

Source: Deutsche Post World Net

The fact base created by these diagnostic and monitoring elements of Brand Dynamics is used to guide our organizational development as well as the everyday management of the company's operations. We engage in extensive skill and mindset building to make sure the DHL promise comes to life in the hearts and minds of our staff. Standardized brand implementation guidelines to ensure a strong and consistent performance of the DHL brand around the globe have been defined. The results were synthesized into a Brand Book, structured around the three main chapters of Brand Context, Brand Identity, and Brand Performance (Figure 4.9). This document contains clear guidelines on all aspects of brand management and execution, including the development of commercial and creative initiatives. Supported by a comprehensive workshop series, the Brand Book offered employees a framework and common language for consistent brand execution. The Brand Book and other internal brand building materials are directly tied in with our external advertising and communication, such as our 2007/2008 brand campaign in multinational media, highlighting the unwavering commitment of our front-line staff to provide solutions around the globe proactively.

Fig. 4.9: The DHL Brand Book

Source: Deutsche Post World Net

As a comprehensive brand management toolkit, Brand Dynamics will help to make DHL the number one in logistics not only in terms of revenue, but throughout the purchase funnel and in the minds of our customers. This will build the basis for the long-term health and growth of the brand as well as the Group.

4.2 Marketing RoI: Quest for the Holy Grail

»Half of my advertising money is wasted. I wish I knew which half!«
This is an old quip, probably as old as the earliest branded goods, and one
that has many and various attributions. Whether it was Henry Ford or Lord
Leverhulme, the founder of Lever Brothers (later Unilever), who first said
this, it remains all too apt today. Many companies still waste a large percentage of their advertising and marketing spending. Though advertising is
often one of the largest items in company budgets, especially in the consumer goods sector, it seems to escape the rigorous review most other
expenditures are subject to.

At first sight, this is surprising, considering the scale of expenditure
involved. Procter & Gamble, for example, invested around USD 7.9 billion
in above-the-line advertising in 2007, equivalent to some 10.4 percent of
its revenue, while the Adidas Group's marketing working budget increased
to EUR 1.4 billion in 2007, equivalent to 13.4 percent of its revenue. Taking
into account marketing overheads of EUR 322 million as well, the marketing budget even accounts for 15.5 percent of the company's revenue.[18] On
the other hand, the general proliferation of media and distribution channels, declining trust in advertising, multitasking by consumers, and digital
technologies that give users more control over their media time all make it
more difficult than ever before for marketers to manage their marketing
investments effectively. It is therefore not surprising, that the search for
greater accountability in marketing expenditure has become the quest for
the Holy Grail in today's marketing world: According to a McKinsey global survey of more than 40 chief marketing officers, ensuring higher marketing
RoI has become their number one priority in this environment of proliferating marketing complexity.

Marketing spending: Too much of a good thing?

Marketing has always been expensive and is becoming more so as it
becomes ever more difficult to gain consumer attention due to trends that
are simultaneously fragmenting audiences and the channels needed to
reach them. After a slight drop in 2001 and 2002, spending on advertising
in Germany has started growing again (Figure 4.10). Total spending on traditional advertising expanded by 4.0 percent per year over the past five
years, reaching EUR 20.9 billion in 2007, with a corresponding increase in
individual firms' advertising budgets. The same is true for the

Fig. 4.10: Marketing spending remains high – example: Germany

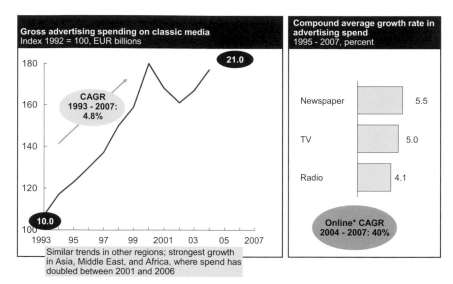

Gross advertising spending on classic media
Index 1992 = 100, EUR billions

Compound average growth rate in advertising spend
1995 - 2007, percent

CAGR 1993 - 2007: 4.8%

21.0

10.0

Newspaper 5.5

TV 5.0

Radio 4.1

Online* CAGR 2004 - 2007: 40%

Similar trends in other regions; strongest growth in Asia, Middle East, and Africa, where spend has doubled between 2001 and 2006

Source: AC Nielsen   *Classic online advertising like banners only

United Kingdom, where total expenditure on classic media has increased by some 38 percent over 10 years, from around GBP 13.3 billion in 1997 to GBP 18.4 billion in 2007. The biggest advertising market remains the United States, where approximately USD 149 billion was spent on advertising in 2007.[19]

Because of heavy discounts, real growth may not be quite as high, and things may even turn grim again soon, at least for classic media. In September 2007, the Financial Times reported that »the US economic downturn squeezes the advertising sector as a whole.« In August 2007, Clay Shirky, professor of new media at New York University, was quoted saying that sellers of (TV) advertising slots would not only have to worry about »the cyclical effects of an economic downturn on advertising revenues,« but should also watch out lest they repeat the mistakes of the music industry by assuming »that they own the means of production.«[20]

Media consumption is now changing at a rate that few could have predicted two decades ago. Between 2004 and 2006, the number of TV channels increased by 50 percent. In the United Kingdom, the area with the widest channel network, more than 650 TV channels were competing for consumers' attention by 2007. The number of TV channels in Germany has grown from 8 in 1988 to 469 in 2007, while the number of radio stations has increased from 84 to 340. In the last five years alone, the number of radio stations has increased by 50 percent.[21] Moreover, the Internet already accounts for almost an hour a day of consumers' media consumption in all Western European countries, and consumption is still increasing substantially in most countries. The 16-to-24-year-olds now spend 10 percent more time online than watching TV.[22] With increasing digitization, the media landscape will become more and more fragmented over time, and it will become increasingly difficult to grab potential customers' attention. Thirty years ago, the average consumer was subject to around 170 commercial stimuli each day. Today, the figure is more than 1,300. If you not only count traditional advertising stimuli, but also include logos on products or shopping windows as well, the figure can even surpass 6,000 stimuli per day, depending on the city.[23]

As the number of media channels proliferates, we are seeing a greater spread of marketing investment, resulting in a shift away from traditional types of advertising towards newer and less conventional forms. Companies are looking harder than ever for new ways of communicating that enable them to reach customers, engage them in dialog, and maximize the power of their marketing. The time is long over when advertising stuck to tried-and-tested media. Spending on new media, events, promotions, sponsorship, and direct marketing has increased significantly in recent years, and research shows that this is likely to continue. In Germany, for example, the total investment in sponsorship rose from EUR 0.6 billion in 1989 to a predicted total of EUR 4.6 billion in 2008, an average annual increase of 11.3 percent.[24]

According to a survey of 250 representatives from advertising companies and agencies carried out by the Pilot Group in 2007, sponsorship spending accounted for an average of 21 percent of the marketing budget in 2007 compared to 15 percent in 2000.[24] The soccer Euro 2008 Cup was financed largely by sponsorship. Eighteen major international sponsors, including Adidas, Carlsberg, and Coca-Cola, provided a total of more than EUR 250 million. For the 2010 and 2014 World Cup events, the six main sponsors, which include Adidas, Hyundai, and Sony, will supply between EUR 200 million and EUR 300 million each.[25] Direct marketing has developed almost as strongly in recent years. Revenues in Germany increased from EUR 21.2 billion to EUR 32.0 billion between 2002 and 2006, an annual growth rate of 8.6 percent.[26]

Product placement is also growing quickly. In 2006, the global market for product placements grew by 37.2 percent to USD 3.36 billion.[27] Over the next few years, the market is expected to keep growing substantially. In Europe, this growth is partly driven by the relaxation of rules regarding product placements in the revised Audio Visual Media Services Directive of the European Commission. The Volkswagen Group signed a deal with the US media group NBC Universal in 2005, which, for around EUR 40 million, promised to feature Volkswagen vehicles prominently in its movies, TV shows, premiere events, and theme parks.[28] Volkswagen's stated aim is to increase emotional ties with the brand. Its new focus on product placement could well be due in part to the success of its subsidiary Audi with the movie *I, Robot* featuring Will Smith. Company sources state that the use of the Audi RSQ (an Audi sports model of the future) led to a clear increase in the brand's rating with audiences for qualities such as attractiveness, uniqueness, and appeal. »That placement has reinforced the core values of the Audi brand,« says Audi's product placement representative Tim Miksche. Over 55 million people have seen the movie in cinemas alone, not even taking into account the millions of viewers of DVDs and TV broadcasts.[29] Audi hopes to replicate this success with the appearance of the Audi R8 in Marvel's new USD 186 million movie *Iron Man*, which opened globally in April/May 2008.

New advertising vehicles seem to be created almost weekly, and they are growing fast. Spending on word-of-mouth marketing was close to USD 1 billion in 2007, 35.9 percent higher than in 2006. The leading German word-of-mouth agency TRND already has more than 55,000 members. According to a survey among 300 advertising companies and agencies, conducted in 2008 in Germany, 80 percent confirmed that they are using ambient media. This comes as no surprise, given that another study on the media behavior of almost 2,000 participants discovered that ambient media accounts for 13 percent of all media contacts.[30] Recent McKinsey research confirms the paramount importance of word-of-mouth as a key consumer touch point (see section 2.4).

With immense sums being spent, top management is naturally turning its attention to the effectiveness of marketing and communications budgets. In many industry sectors, companies are looking with some skepticism at individual marketing activities and overall spending, especially given that in many cases they have had only limited effectiveness in stimulating customer demand in recent years. Though marketing managers are proud of having achieved high levels of brand awareness through large-scale campaigns, they will admit in private that sales and market shares have stagnated nonetheless. Sponsorship of league soccer, Formula 1 racing (Figure 4.11), and exhibitions and concerts all create a positive image, but is this really enough?

Fig. 4.11: Alain Dassas, President of Renault Formula 1, on sponsorship as an investment

Interview with Alain Dassas

"We are in charge "

Mr Dassas, as a former financial services executive, what is your verdict after one year as President of Renault F1: Is the Formula 1 a good investment for a car maker?
I think so. To begin with, it is a great show that draws an audience of millions of people. Only the soccer world championship has an even wider appeal. [...] And what's in it for Renault? Internally, it makes our employees proud to see our cars in top positions. [...] The Formula 1 stands for top performance and reliability, virtues we foster in our company. The Formula 1 is especially beneficial for our image. Brand awareness has grown significantly over the past two years – even in markets we have entered only recently, or not at all at this point.

How expensive were your team and driver victories?
I'm not going to tell you that. What I can tell you is that we have the smallest budget of all car manufacturers in this racing series. It is in the magnitude of EUR 200 to 300 million. And we are fully in charge at all times. Renault's President Carlos Ghosn has tied the continuation to conditions such as further victories, brand image improvements, and lower costs.

What feedback do you get on the brand image front?
There is a whole range of indicators that tell us our brand image has improved significantly since 2006. [...] But despite our victory in the 2006 world championship, sales decreased in Europe in 2006. Whether the championship helped us to sell more cars, I can't say at this point. The Formula 1 is a long-term investment; it will pay off only in the long run. It doesn't give you quick wins in sales.

Source: Wirtschaftswoche, March 17, 2007

From a commercial point of view, it is important to know whether potential customers are positive enough about the company's products or services to consider buying them. Effective advertising (and all marketing communication) needs to address all stages of the purchase funnel, so that would-be customers are not just familiar with the brand but also prompted to buy it – and buy it again. Converting awareness into purchases is the only way that companies can achieve an adequate return on investment, thereby justifying the large amounts of money spent on marketing.

There are a couple of rules of thumb when it comes to advertising and media planning. If you plot marketing effectiveness (as sales revenue) against communications expenditure, you'll get an S-curve; the marginal profit of marketing effectiveness first grows and levels off, then falls. This is because, the experts argue, a certain level of spending must be reached before the contact is intense enough for people to hear the message. Academics also point out that there is the factor of saturation: an individual consumer's readiness to make a purchase is limited practically and cannot exceed a certain level, however much is spent on communication.[31] Another well-known rule says that advertising works better if several different media are combined within a campaign. Several media studies discovered that campaign recall of cross-media campaigns is higher than for single-media campaigns; ideally, the media should even be integrated.[32] Furthermore, it is known that opportunities to see (OTS) have a diminishing marginal utility. This means that viewing an advertisement for the first time will generate a higher impact on awareness and recall than the tenth time seeing the same advertisement. While all these rules of thumb are often directionally correct and thus helpful, they are insufficient to answer the really important questions such as: Which media are most effective and efficient for my offering? Which marketing vehicles are best to emotionalize my brand? How should I allocate my marketing budget among countries, regions, business units, products, and marketing vehicles?

A scientific approach is practicable not only in traditional advertising but also in other areas of marketing. Though a great deal of money is spent on advertising price promotions as a way of stimulating sales in the short term, they have inherent problems. Price promotions tend to weaken the brand image. A brand with a clear value proposition and a specific price-value relationship for consumers may well see demand go up in the short term following a price promotion, but at a longer-term cost. Following the initial price promotion, the perception of the price-value relationship will change for consumers. In the medium term, consumers will tend to wait for the next special offer rather than buying at full price. This leads to price erosion, a weakening of the brand, and undermining of profitability. Such phenomena are increasingly common across Europe in the retail industry.

This brings us back to the Holy Grail of marketing: How can companies optimize their marketing expenditure so as to gain the maximum return on their marketing investment?

Marketing at Sony Ericsson Mobile Communications: Spending in the Right Place

by Dee Dutta, Global Head of Marketing for Sony Ericsson Mobile Communications

Sony Ericsson Mobile Communications is one of the world's leading global brands in the mobile multimedia device space. Established in October 2001 by telecommunications pioneer Ericsson and consumer electronics powerhouse Sony Corporation, the company launched its first joint products in March 2002. The beginnings were difficult. With

Ericsson's mobile business in trouble and Sony being new to the industry, the joint venture's task was nothing less than building a successful consumer brand – from scratch. By 2006 the joint venture employed around 6,000 people globally and had first-quarter sales of nearly EUR 2 billion. Today Sony Ericsson has grown into one of the most successful consumer electronics brands in the market, based on deep customer insights and a passion for marketing.

The fast-paced dynamics of the mobile phone market make marketing especially challenging. First, we spend a significant amount of the marketing budget jointly with our channel partners and have to find joint win-win campaigns for both parties. Second, with our rapid growth, we need to support a growing number of new phones every year, creating additional complexity for campaign planning. And finally, the fierce competition for market share among handset manufacturers is driving an upward spiral in marketing spending by all players year after year, which raises the question: »How much is efficient?«

This naturally puts the spotlight on the budget and on marketing spending efficiency. Where should we spend our limited resources? And how? To support the country marketing teams, we have developed a set of tools:

- To create full understanding of our marketing spending
- To understand completely where consumers stand in the purchasing process and when they make their purchase decision
- To choose a marketing instrument mix that generates the best possible trade-off between the various marketing instruments' reach, cost, and quality.

This set of tools has equipped us to increase our marketing effectiveness significantly and contributes to the success of the Sony Ericsson brand.

The starting point for boosting our effectiveness was creating a full understanding of our spending. Frankly, this was a challenge for us in the beginning. As in most companies, our spending is organized according to cost keys, but not always allocated to specific marketing instruments. We reclassified the budget by the areas of impact. We are now able to understand what the consumer sees of our brand, and this builds the base for marketing instrument mix adjustment.

Fully understanding the performance of our brand in the purchasing process by target segment using the funnel analysis is another essential ingredient. In one leading country, for example, our brand now enjoys strong ratings at the »consideration« stage across most consumer segments. We reinforce this by ensuring continuity in our marketing communication and by taking actions to strengthen customer loyalty. In other European countries, we face different challenges. For example, by taking a deeper look at several markets where we were not ranked among the leading mobile phones, we discovered that our position in the purchase funnel varies widely by target group. Although we do well overall in brand awareness and consideration, we have not always been able to translate this strength into adequate usage rates for some target groups. So, for these segments, we decided to change our marketing communication and adjust our spending accordingly.

First, we wanted to have a deep understanding of the consumer. To achieve this we built a state-of-the-art segmentation that looked at consumer attitudes towards technology combined with mobile phone usage. This model led to prospective target customers that provide the main driving force of our growth. For us, identifying the consumer was not based on age or sociodemographics, but on a clear understanding of life and mobile living.

Second, consumers also differ in terms of where they make their purchase decision, both across countries as well as across segments. Some consumers are already predisposed to buy a certain brand before they start thinking actively about buying a new mobile phone and enter a store. Other consumers can still be influenced at this stage. This difference in decision behavior is reflected in our marketing budget split. We address the first group with more passively absorbed marketing instruments (e.g., television, print media) to affect their preferred choice before their purchasing decision even starts. We target the second group with marketing communication closer to the point of sale (e.g., by topic-specific magazines or in-store information events).

Finally, to make sure that our marketing spending is in the right place, we fine-tuned our marketing communication mix based on the trade-offs between reach, cost, and quality. From our dedicated market research, we know in detail how the consumption of marketing instruments varies, broken down by instrument and target group. We also collected data on the cost per contact and investigated the differences in quality, or the impact on attitudes and behavior, of the different marketing instruments. With this knowledge, it is much easier for us to optimize the marketing communication mix for the best possible trade-off between the reach of the instruments in the target group, their different costs, and their varying quality. These analyses helped us to raise the contact pressure of our marketing communication by 10 to 30 percent depending on the market – without increasing our budget.

Because we regularly measure the effectiveness of our marketing activities, we are in a position to optimize our marketing communication mix on an ongoing basis, which is obviously a boon in our dynamic market. As many of the factors involved are in constant flux, we regularly monitor our purchasing process performance, our consumers' purchasing decisions, and the reach of each marketing instrument across our target segments. This enables us to adjust our activities practically as fast as new developments occur. And we can be confident that we are putting our spending in the right place.

Marketing return on investment (RoI): A three-step process

Among marketers, there's much frustration and little agreement about what to do in order to maximize the effectiveness of marketing expenditure. Some are using sophisticated econometric methods to tease out the effects of the mix of marketing media on business results. But the historical data that fuel such techniques may prove an unreliable guide to future returns, at least if used undiscerningly. In certain situations, such models might prove unreliable, as in the automotive industry (where the Internet is transforming decision-making processes) or with packaged goods (where indirect marketing approaches, such as product placement, are gaining importance for many brands). Not only are the forecasts likely to prove unreliable, but they raise another problem: right or wrong, the sophistication of the models inspires blind faith in their results. In our experience, ensuring that marketing expenditure brings greater returns must start with a holistic understanding of both the brand and the role marketing plays in the business.

To understand their fragmenting world, marketers need a more rigorous approach, one that treats marketing not merely as expenditure but as investment. In other words, it is necessary to focus on increasing marketing's RoI. By adhering to the same investment principles that other departments follow, a CMO can improve the alignment between marketing and the businesses' financial objectives, capitalize on a brand's most distinctive elements, target the customers more precisely (using communication vehicles that yield the greatest returns), manage risk more effectively, and track

Fig. 4.12: Three-step approach to marketing RoI excellence

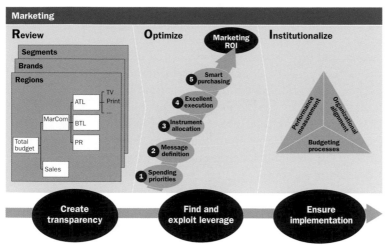

Source: McKinsey

returns more accurately. In short, CMOs hoping to master the proliferating marketing environment must, in a thoughtful and systematic manner, apply investment fundamentals to marketing planning and performance management. This requires establishing both full transparency of expenditure and clarity in the objectives of investments. These principles can help to achieve greater accuracy and accountability and to overcome inertia in spending patterns.

This involves three simple and intuitive, but effective, steps (Figure 4.12). The first job is to create transparency in targets, spending, and activities connected with brand communication at all points of customer contact or touch points. Next, the marketing budget must be optimized for effectiveness (with spending organized according to country, brand, customer segment, stages in the purchasing funnel, messages, and media) and efficiency (establishing the optimum level of spending by looking at the relationship between input and results). The final step is then to anchor these systems, instruments, and processes in the organization, so that the benefits can continue in the long term.

Step 1: Review – Make the marketing budget as transparent as possible

Achieving transparency in targets, spending, and activities connected with brand communication is a prerequisite for effective and efficient use of a marketing budget. At first sight, this appears to be a simple task. However, in our experience, it takes much more time and effort than companies expect. Time and again, we find that acquiring detailed information on targets, spending, and communication activities for the entire brand is a real challenge.

One area that proves particularly difficult is setting clear, quantitative targets for marketing that are broken down by brand, product, and country, as appropriate. Target fulfillment can be measured by looking at the strengths and weaknesses of a brand in the Brand Diamond and the brand's performance along the purchase funnel by target segment. This analysis will soon reveal where problems lie and indicate potential solutions. A poor performance in the area of brand awareness, for example, can be countered by a broad-based mass communication campaign using television, billboards, or perimeter advertising. A drop in the area »intention to buy,« on the other hand, can be countered by samples and price promotions or by strengthening the presentation of the brand's value proposition.

Ideally, spending on marketing activities should be broken down by medium or customer touch point as well as by stage of the purchase funnel. Difficulties often arise in achieving this ideal because budgets are split between different parts of the organization, each of which has its own controlling department and accounting system. For example, traditional marketing budgets are run by the marketing division or a special advertising unit, together with product management; the public relations budget is run by the PR department or the board itself; events and promotions come under the promotions division. Further touch points might create costs in several departments, for example, the cost of the corporate home page might be shared between IT, PR, marketing, and several other business units. In addition to this, there may be marketing spending on outdoor advertising, sports sponsorship, or co-branding that has been planned many years in advance. In many cases, this type of marketing is not arranged by the marketing department at all. As a result, partly for contractual and partly for historical or political reasons, these areas are out of bounds for the purpose of annual review and so the company ends up excluding them from the current marketing spending. These »forgotten investments« might include the sponsorship of a local horse race originally agreed because of a past CEO's daughter's passion for horses, or a long-running sponsorship contract which can't be cancelled, but does not play an active role in the communication strategy anymore. Yet all these activities either strengthen or weaken the brand and should thus be included in the drive towards achieving transparency.

The larger and more complex the company, the more difficult it is to get hold of full, transparent data, especially historical data. Many marketing managers and controllers appear unable to pin down how much was spent on advertising in the past or to say exactly how the budget was spent. Often this is due in part to the complexity of organization; things get really complicated where there are not just different departments but different organizational levels or countries involved. For example, in large corporations with eight-figure budgets, sometimes one level of the organization will carry out advertising for another level, or one part will pay another part to do its marketing. Thus a subsidiary might reap the benefits of a marketing campaign carried out by the parent company or another country, while at the same time being involved in sponsorship carried out together with another subsidiary. The same goes for spillover effects between multiple brands under the same roof; for example, Land Rover may benefit from Range Rover investments, and vice versa. From an efficiency perspective, killing two birds with one stone seems tempting. But in reality, such multipurpose marketing activities often represent a considerable challenge for international companies trying to produce a rational framework for how much they spend and where.

For traditional advertising, a useful tool for investigating overall spending and media mix is to compare the visible spending in the market (as tracked by NielsenMedia Research, for example) and the costs recorded internally by the company. In general, outside observers perceive companies as spending about one-and-a-half times what they actually do, because of media buying discounts. Any significant deviation from this ratio should sound alarms for the company and be investigated thoroughly in order to determine what is causing the discrepancy.

The quest for transparency needs to apply to all items in the budget. Cooperative marketing arrangements represent a further complication when studying budgets, especially in cases where a company both receives payments from suppliers to run joint marketing campaigns (incoming payments) and at the same time makes payments to sales partners for further joint campaigns (outgoing payments), as in the retail sector, or between mobile operators, mobile phone producers, and distributors. Financial controllers need to include these payments in the quest for transparency as they also have an impact on the market, in the presentation of goods, packaging, advertising by commercial partners, and so on. Some controllers face a rude awakening when they look into the effect of such cooperative payments. In retailing, for example, free advertising (i.e., that paid for by the campaign partner) is often tied to bundled goods. In the worst case, miscalculations can lead to the company suddenly finding itself in possession of large stocks of surplus merchandise. It cannot be assumed that the goals of both partners in a cooperative campaign are exactly the same. Often, the supplier subsidizing the marketing is thinking purely in terms of sales or revenue goals, with little regard to the impact on the brand. Caution is therefore required; just because such cooperative advertising is free does not mean that it makes sense strategically or economically. Companies must also take into account the consequential costs for write-offs.

Full budget transparency will only be achieved if investment in all the customer touch points is taken into account. Call centers, customer service, the corporate home page, and the sales force can be considered touch points, and improving service, offering rewards and discounts, or subsidized financing will all have an impact on sales and marketing. Because all customer touch points have an influence on customer behavior, they need to be considered part of marketing expenditure.

The goal in creating full budget transparency is to give as complete a picture as possible of the brand's direct and indirect customer touch points. These can then be summarized in an overall Brand Cockpit (the use of which we will examine in the next section). As figure 4.13 illustrates, achieving the preconditions for such transparency can be a difficult and lengthy process. In this example, 20 percent of marketing spending was completely opaque to begin with and did not feature at all in the marketing budget-planning process. A further 40 percent was spent on instruments whose

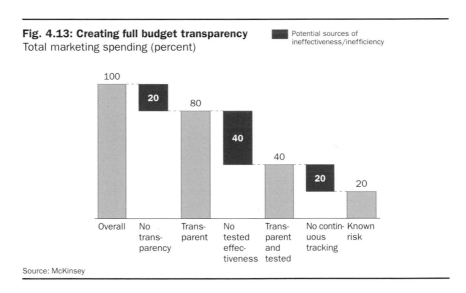

Fig. 4.13: Creating full budget transparency
Total marketing spending (percent)

■ Potential sources of ineffectiveness/inefficiency

Source: McKinsey

Managing Brands

use was transparent, but whose effectiveness had never been tested. Another 20 percent was spent on marketing, the impact of which had been tested in the past but was not regularly monitored or tracked. Only one-fifth of marketing spending could be backed up by data showing that there was a clear relationship between the amount of money spent and its influence on the target customers' perception of the brand.

Step 2: Optimize – Ensure the budget is used efficiently and effectively

Once companies have a detailed picture of their marketing spending and their brand profile, in terms of brand image and the purchase funnel, they can start to optimize the impact of their marketing by retargeting their advertising expenditure and adjusting the portfolio of marketing activities. This is a dual task. On the one hand, management needs to raise the effectiveness of marketing by prioritizing marketing investments by country, brand, target group, and stage of the purchase funnel using the right instruments (the correct medium or combination of media) to convey the message. On the other hand, management needs to optimize the relationship between cost and impact, that is, ensure the efficiency of marketing activities. These two activities will help managers derive the optimal size and shape for the marketing budget.

No one has yet come up with a fully comprehensive method of calculating the effects of individual marketing instruments, let alone one that is truly reliable. As a result, print advertising, for example, is measured in a different manner than television or radio advertising, making accurate comparison all but impossible. Marketing managers are therefore faced with a decision about what the right instruments and measures of impact are for their needs. The work of the AG.MA (working group for media analysis), which is monitoring the reach of media in Germany, is a good example. In the attempt to create a common currency for all media, AG.MA proudly announced in July 2007 it had defined a way to make television and print comparable, after 17 years of discussions. According to this rather scientific definition, the reach of one reader per advertising page in print equals seven seconds of consecutively viewed advertising on television within 30 minutes.[33] In the next step, outdoor and online will be included, but the numerous below-the-line media that fight for the attention of the marketers will probably never find their way into this intermedia comparison. Thus, making marketing accountable and fact-based remains a challenge, despite the undisputed urgency of the topic. In 2006, marketing accountability was rated as the most important topic on the minds of CMOs according to the Association of National Advertisers (ANA). While some 60 percent of senior-level marketers said that defining, measuring, and taking action on marketing RoI is important, only about 20 percent said they were satisfied with their ability to do so.[34] Jim Stengel, Procter & Gamble's former CMO and one of the world's most respected marketers, says: »Today's marketing model is broken. We're applying antiquated thinking and work systems to a new world of possibilities.«[35] The topic has also captured the attention of the academic world. Leading marketing scientists are hard at work to help resolve the issue of marketing resource allocation in a changing environment. Compare, for example, the recent Harvard Business School paper »Allocating Marketing Resources« by Sunil Gupta and Thomas J. Steenburgh.[36]

We are still a long way away from finding a common currency when it comes to measuring marketing effectiveness. In fact, input and output can only be measured accurately in very particular circumstances, for example, as in assessing the impact of marketing in retail, where it is possible to compare promotional activities with cash point data. Where quantifiable data like this is lacking, the only reliable way to measure marketing impact is to use »single source« market research, looking at customer touch points and brand attributes. This helps companies assess the relative impact of spending on different media and the effect of different brand attributes on the purchase funnel.

As should now be clear, the purpose of evaluating advertising impact is to establish the relationship between advertising spending at different customer touch points and various brand drivers. This evaluation should take into account the large number of interdependencies, qualitative factors such as the execution and consistency of marketing, and the overall limits of what is in fact measurable. It is hardly possible to express the relationship between advertising spending and market drivers in exact figures, let alone to transfer these figures one-to-one to future budget plans. Indeed, this is not what companies should aim for. Bearing in mind that marketing is art, science, and craft, companies will find their business sense and experience just as important as sound analysis in dealing with this interface. As Carlsberg's Alex Myers said in a McKinsey interview: »The marketing function is developing along two extremes: the advertising guru, on the one hand, and what one might term the fact-based businessman, on the other. The trick is to find the right balance.« [37]

For some time now, McKinsey, together with media companies, market research institutes, and advertisers, has been studying how marketing budgets around the world can be optimized. As a result, we have developed an understanding of marketing impact as well as practical approaches to

Fig. 4.14: Levers of marketing spending excellence

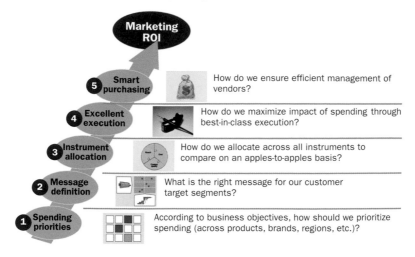

5 Smart purchasing	How do we ensure efficient management of vendors?
4 Excellent execution	How do we maximize impact of spending through best-in-class execution?
3 Instrument allocation	How do we allocate across all instruments to compare on an apples-to-apples basis?
2 Message definition	What is the right message for our customer target segments?
1 Spending priorities	According to business objectives, how should we prioritize spending (across products, brands, regions, etc.)?

Source: McKinsey

managing and measuring marketing RoI.[38] All of this has highlighted that there are five basic questions that a marketing manager must be in a position to answer when managing a budget (Figure 4.14).

1. Is the marketing spending allocated correctly according to business priorities and the stages of the purchase process?

Companies must first check that they are allocating their marketing expenditure (by countries, business areas, brands/products, customer segments, etc.) in line with their own strategic goals. Our experience is that companies in fact rarely follow a clear prioritization of different areas based on strategy (e.g., »grow« versus »maintain«), their financial significance for the company, or other factors that affect revenues (e.g., their place in the product life cycle). Moreover, companies need to allocate their marketing spending so as to achieve maximum impact for each customer segment. This assumes that they have first defined the various target segments (see section 2.2), calculated their potential, measured their brand image in each segment (see section 2.3), and derived their marketing priorities from this data. Companies need this overview if they are to address the growth segments in a targeted way. They must also adjust the allocation of marketing funds to take into account critical points in the purchase funnel. Our experience shows that companies all too often spend money on marketing that has no direct impact on the purchase funnel, for example, in long-forgotten sponsorships that no longer have any relevance to the target groups. On other occasions, they over-focus on the early stages in the purchase funnel, such as »awareness« and »consideration« (using above-the-line media only, for example) and neglect later stages such as »purchase« and »loyalty,« even though this is where their brand might be weakest.

A clear example of this phenomenon was revealed when we helped a large German retail chain to optimize its marketing budget. For one particular product category, the retailer performed much better than its main competitor in the first two stages of the funnel, »brand awareness« and »store visit.« However, in the latter two stages of the funnel (»customer acquisition« and »customer loyalty«), it trailed its competitor by 15 to 20 points. This was being exacerbated by the marketing department's focus on traditional advertising media, such as newspaper ads and leaflets. In response, a range of impact studies was commissioned to determine how strongly each of the individual media, as well as the overall media mix, affected each stage of the purchase funnel. The studies revealed that the media mix, with its concentration on newspaper ads and leaflets, increased both »store visit« and »customer acquisition« by one-third, but increased »loyalty« by just one-fifth. Clearly, the company had been doing too little in the area of customer loyalty, a critical point and the main bottleneck in the funnel. The company therefore made a shift in its marketing activity and funds towards reinforcing customer loyalty. A portion of the money previously spent on newspaper ads and leaflets was redirected to activities such as customer loyalty cards and in-store communications.

Experience has shown that while it is impossible for companies to allocate marketing funds on a completely scientific basis given the large number of decisions on priorities, companies that address these questions in a systematic way, applying some practical rules of thumb, can achieve major improvements in the level of impact of their marketing spending. When allocating marketing funds, a simple scoring model (Figure 4.15) that takes into account economic, strategic, and impact-oriented dimensions, weighing them against the overall objectives of the company, can help align the brand and the business unit managers.

The output, often in form of a *heat map*, highlights the marketing priorities by geography, segment, and/or business unit. This map produces a helpful fact base for a detailed discussion of the budgeting process.

Fig. 4.15: The budgeting process needs to be based on clearly defined criteria, in line with strategic priorities
Percent

⬛ Emphasized variables

		Economic		Strategic			Marketing oriented	
Weighting options	**Budgeting objectives**	**Net sales plan**	**Profit contribution**	**Product activity**	**Segment attractive-ness**	**Relative growth plan**	**Competitive intensity**	**Funnel performance**
Ⓐ Even distribution	Ensure balanced allocation	10 - 20	10 - 20	10 - 20	10 - 20	10 - 20	10 - 20	10 - 20
Ⓑ Maintenance orientation	Strengthe "sales stars"	**20 - 40**	**20 - 40**	5 - 15	5 - 15	5 - 15	5 - 15	5 - 15
Ⓒ Growth/portfolio orientation	Expand future growth areas	5 - 20	5 - 15	**10 - 20**	**10 - 20**	**20 - 30**	5 - 10	**10 - 20**
Ⓓ Competition orientation	Match competitive situation	5 - 15	5 - 15	5 - 15	5 - 15	5 - 15	**20 - 40**	**20 - 40**
Weightings suggested Resembles growth/ portfolio orientation		20	5	20	15	20	10	10

Variables in scoring model

Source: McKinsey

2. What are the most compelling messages?

When clients ask for help in planning or managing their marketing spending, often what they actually want is support in finding the right marketing instruments and media mix. Marketing and communications specialists know, however, that the marketing message itself forms the heart of any drive towards optimization, as we have tried to show in these pages. Studies of marketing effectiveness prove that the relevance of the marketing message has a much greater influence on the target group than the nature of the medium. For instance, think of the »Evolution« campaign by Dove, which showed cosmetic and airbrushing efforts to transform an average woman into a billboard model and thereby criticized its own industry for creating a distorted beauty standard. The message of the spot spread like a virus all over the world. This wasn't primarily due to paid advertising, but mostly resulted from the spot's availability on YouTube. Its unusual and provocative message generated widespread media and consumer attention. (Ironically, Dove made the headlines again when it came out that the images of its supposedly »natural« beauties had been airbrush retouched to remove skin imperfections and stray hairs during post production.)[39] Dove had a similar experience with a spot broadcasted only once during the Super Bowl. It generated 90 million direct impressions, but pre- and post-game publicity resulting from its provocative message generated an additional 400 million impressions[40]; Sixt's controversial advert featuring German politician Angela Merkel received the same kind of attention. The advertisement ran only once, but generated press coverage valued at more than EUR 3 million (see section 4.5). Companies can come up with compelling messages using the tools presented in the previous chapters, such as using brand driver analyses to select the content for the most relevant, credible, and differentiated messages. In addition, a range of approaches exists for evaluating the impact of marketing messages before they are launched on the public, such as those used by the market research institutes GfK (Ad*Vantage), Millward Brown (Link), and IMAS (Psychometer).

In general, such approaches investigate people's cognitive, emotional, and behavioral reactions to different advertising media and measure the strengths and weakness of particular messages along relevant dimensions. But it takes as much art as it takes science to achieve compelling messages; creativity is a key prerequisite of appropriate, relevant, and original communication (refer to the insert in section 1.2 for details).

3. What instruments or types of media usage have the greatest impact?

Once companies have developed and tested their advertising message, they need to find the right instruments for communicating it to target groups. Sometimes they can evaluate instruments by looking at visible effects, for example by using cash point data in retailing. However, this is very much the exception rather than the rule. More often, companies will need to use their own market research, or at least fact-based estimates, to quantify in a systematic way the impact of each marketing instrument at each of the various customer touch points.

As the heart of the RoI approach, McKinsey developed the »Reach-Cost-Quality« (RCQ) concept for allocating marketing funds more precisely. In several client engagements, the RCQ concept has been successfully applied in order to compare marketing instruments along the dimensions reach, cost, and quality (Figure 4.16).

Reach. What are the best ways to reach the target customer segments for each product at each of the stages prioritized in the purchase funnel? A brand in the private banking arena might best address customers by sponsoring exclusive events (e.g., polo matches or golf tournaments), while a youth-oriented bank might better reach its intended customers by creating Internet communities or conducting on-campus activities. In our experience, many banks do not understand in sufficient detail the reach of their instruments for their intended target group. Even the best marketers in the

Fig. 4.16: The "Reach-Cost-Quality" approach helps to target the choice of media

Understand which marketing instruments **provide the best access to your target group**

Reach

Cost

Know what cost is incurred for each instrument based on **actual coverage in target range**

Quality

Assess the **quality of an instrument** at each stage of the buying process

Source: McKinsey

world struggle with this point when it comes to below-the-line media. For example, a US personal care manufacturer thought that putting advertisements for one of its beauty products on supermarket freezer doors would be a great idea after it discovered in focus groups that buyers of its personal care products also like ice cream. After the fact, however, in-store research showed that fewer than 10 percent of the company's main target group actually go down the ice-cream aisle on a shopping trip.[41]

To calculate the actual reach, reported media contacts need to be adjusted by the tune-out factor, which accounts for the fact that many viewers do not really pay attention. The tune-out factor depends especially on the medium. While most consumers pay attention to cinema advertising (unavailable in the United States, but a popular niche touch point in many other countries) due to the overwhelming audio-video equipment and the setting, many go to the kitchen or bathroom during television commercials. Focusing on target customer segments and prioritizing purchase funnel steps will help determine the actual number of required viewers more accurately and provide marketers with greater precision in their results.

Cost. Once the media reach has been calculated for the given target group, its relative cost efficiency can be analyzed. All too often, only the reported media costs are used for comparison. However, agency costs, production costs, and infrastructure costs can easily account for a major share of the total costs and therefore these positions need to be incorporated into the equation. Combining cost and reach will lead to an actual CPM number (cost per 1,000 people reached by a marketing instrument).

Contact quality. Here, the metric is focused on results: how well does this approach support the defined marketing objective compared to all other options? For example, will a targeted direct mail campaign generate greater interest than a broadcast media campaign? Will invitation-only test drives on a test course be more effective than a brand-sponsored concert series? What might make a lot of sense for one industry might be meaningless for another. While a sponsored search result at Google can be very relevant for the sales stimulation of an airline, it will be less effective to emotionalize the brand, and is likely to be irrelevant for the sales stimulation of a soft drink. Multiple methods, ranging from simple rules of thumb to more sophisticated structural equation modeling, can be used to support this process. One way to define the quality of marketing vehicles is by applying behavioral science and evaluating the vehicles regarding their impact on consumer involvement and behavior, as well as on the ability to emotionalize and to communicate rational information. Another way is to evaluate the impact of the vehicles on specific marketing objectives directly, e.g., sales stimulation, increase of loyalty, or the creation of awareness for a new offering.

A global car manufacturer sought to use the RCQ model to strengthen its brand while boosting growth and profitability in what is an increasingly complex segment, channel, and media environment. The company focused initially on understanding bottlenecks in the brand funnel for each of its customer segments. Studies show that many consumers move through the purchase process predictably (from awareness to familiarity to consideration to the test-drive and, finally, to purchase) making new requirements on the brand at every stage of their selection process (but also see the insert on new insights into consumers' sometimes erratic decision making at the end of section 2.4). The brand funnel helped the company realize it was overspending at the purchase stage (at the dealerships) while under-spending on building awareness through mass advertising. However, this method was not precise enough as a basis to optimize marketing investments by segment, brand, and model at each stage in the funnel.

To accomplish this goal, the company developed a methodology for combining measures of reach (the number of unique, relevant customers who are actually exposed to the message), cost (the actual cost to reach 1,000 such customers), and quality (the relative quality of various marketing and trade activities). This allowed the company to understand the trade-offs between different investment choices. For one of its models, the carmaker wanted to invest in ways to move consumers along the brand funnel from familiarity to trial (test drive). By combining standard measures of reach and cost with quality factors such as the length, interactivity, credibility, and emotional strength of sixteen different media types, the company arrived at the real cost of engaging customers through each medium. Figure 4.17 shows the results of an analysis of the real cost per qualified contact, in this case conducted by a consumer goods company. Companies using such an approach sometimes find they are getting less bang for their buck through traditional media (such as television advertising) than with a targeted instrument (for example, appearances at car shows).

The car manufacturer still uses the brand funnel to determine where its message will have the biggest impact. It also still employs Brand Driver Analysis to determine the type of message that will resonate most with each customer segment. And the addition of the RCQ methodology has allowed it to allocate marketing funds more precisely. Early results suggest that the new approach, while still imperfect, is helping the company to make better apples-to-apples comparisons across a wide range of media choices, influence customers more effectively, and save money on marketing investment.

Once again, it is impossible to give an entirely scientific basis for this optimization. Consider, for example, the thirty or so advertising forms used in television alone – trailers, television specials, news specials, alternative split-screen formats, game shows, quizzes. There are endless creative possi-

Fig. 4.17: Real cost per qualified contact allows apples-to-apples comparison

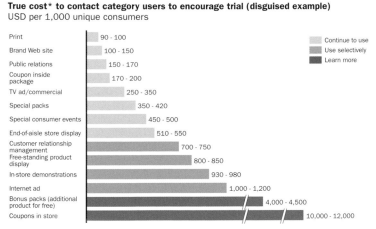

True cost* to contact category users to encourage trial (disguised example)
USD per 1,000 unique consumers

Print	90 - 100	Continue to use
Brand Web site	100 - 150	Use selectively
Public relations	150 - 170	Learn more
Coupon inside package	170 - 200	
TV ad/commercial	250 - 350	
Special packs	350 - 420	
Special consumer events	450 - 500	
End-of-aisle store display	510 - 550	
Customer relationship management	700 - 750	
Free-standing product display	800 - 850	
In-store demonstrations	930 - 980	
Internet ad	1,000 - 1,200	
Bonus packs (additional product for free)	4,000 - 4,500	
Coupons in store	10,000 - 12,000	

* Derived from combining standard measures of reach and cost with quality factors
   (e.g., length, interactivity, credibility, emotional strength) for each medium
Source: McKinsey USA, 2005

bilities for optimizing marketing instruments. This is the art part of the trinity of art, science, and craft. Yet science also plays its role, with both sophisticated analyses and simple rules of thumb providing a more solid fact base for choosing among marketing instruments. It is important that companies use these techniques to avoid serious mistakes.

When management has found and prioritized the most suitable media, they must then decide on the frequency and intensity with which to use them and integrate this information into a suitable plan for the media mix. They can do this with different techniques and efficiency analyses for different media campaigns, depending on data availability and desired level of sophistication. Perhaps the most common approach is the S-curve analysis mentioned earlier, which pinpoints the critical level (or margin) of marketing spending for traditional advertising. The efficiency of other marketing instruments can also be checked. For example, a car company can measure the impact of attending a motor show simply by looking at the customer contact rate, and television contacts can be fine-tuned by optimizing gross rating points (GRP), as is common practice with agencies.

As an example, let us take the case of a company selling upmarket consumer goods. The company enjoyed a high level of brand awareness but had a bottleneck in the purchase funnel when it came to converting »buyers« into »loyal customers.« Market research found that conversion was driven mainly by the attribute »is solid and durable« and could be influenced effectively by newspaper ads. The company, on the other hand, had been concentrating on radio commercials to support brand awareness, although, even here, spending was below the threshold level for effective advertising (according to research into the cost of raising brand awareness by one point). It was clear what had to be done: the company needed to cut back on radio commercials and redirect some of the money into newspaper ads that stressed the solidity and durability of its products, thereby promoting customer loyalty. The end effect was a reduction of the overall marketing budget and a better performance in the purchase funnel.

4. What does best-in-class execution look like?

As well as ensuring they are making use of the levers described above (spending priorities, message definition, and instrument allocation), best-in-class companies need to worry about optimizing their marketing efficiency if they are to achieve superior marketing RoI. Typical areas of inefficiency are:

- Too many messages,
- Inconsistencies of messages over time, countries, products or media,

- Unclear agency briefings,
- Poor agency management and control, and
- Inefficient execution in a medium.

Best-practice companies have established clear guidelines for campaign sequencing, advertising development, and creative agency briefings. By creating one standardized global process for advertising development from setting the objectives to airing the communication, they can decrease the cost of remaking campaigns significantly without neglecting the art of creating campaigns; bear in mind, however, that actual execution may still require significant local adaptation to work in markets as diverse as, say, Japan, Russia, and Brazil. By adding clearly defined quality gates in the process, best-practice players enable their marketing departments to build up knowledge over time, as both successful and unsuccessful campaigns can be compared over all decision gates. They also have quality and cost-control mechanisms in place and conduct periodic internal benchmarking in order to facilitate cross-departmental learning and efficient execution. To institutionalize cross-departmental learning and exchange of best practices, leading marketing companies have internal universities (e.g., the Unilever Marketing Academy) or central marketing departments that identify and share best practices across countries and business units. Best-in-class execution also extends to applying the 10 criteria for creativity and content fit for effective advertising, as described in the insert in section 1.2, as well as internal branding processes to turn employees into real brand advocates (see section 4.1).

5. What is the best way to ensure the efficient management of marketing vendors?
Another critical but often underleveraged element for ensuring efficiency in marketing expenditure is to optimize purchasing of media, creative services, and other branding-related third-party services. There are three problem areas that result in suboptimal performance in purchasing:
- Decision-making processes that are too decentralized, causing local marketing managers to rule their own kingdoms with little top-down direction setting;
- Heterogeneous agency selection by geography or business unit, with little coordination of contractual obligations and insufficient use of buying power; and
- Lack of transparency in purchasing costs, poor RoI knowledge, and little follow-up on campaigns, which results in a lack of central knowledge on how agencies perform and little sharing of best practice.

To overcome these problems, companies need to introduce greater coordination in purchasing, following principles agreed upon at the center. This can include consolidating the approved vendors between departments for all brands in all markets in all countries. Even if the result is a pool rather than a shortlist of vendors, this can form a good basis for comparison of cost efficiency. A second facet of this coordination is to optimize and standardize contract terms. Similarly, wherever possible, companies can pool purchasing to increase order volumes. This will help eliminate unnecessary purchases or duplicate orders. To make this agenda work, there needs to be a consistent purchasing process in place that standardizes and streamlines purchasing. Much of the process can be automated, from planning to purchasing requests and pricing comparisons. Finally, the company needs to revisit the overall structure of purchasing from the point of view of make-or-buy on a regular basis. If a given service or resource is to be retained within the company in its present form in the business unit or department, can it be integrated with other similar units? Or should it be centralized outside the present structure? This requires examining options for outsourcing and offshoring.

In our experience, the potential impact of a review of all marketing purchasing activities is huge. In some cases, the savings potential has been as high as 40 percent of total pre-optimization expenditure. For details on marketing service provider management, see section 4.5.

Step 3: Institutionalize – Anchor transparency in the organization, processes, and systems

Finally, companies should not treat their marketing review as a one-off event. A proper review of marketing expenditure and activities, which asks all the above questions, should be instituted as an ongoing process. This is why the final, and perhaps most important, step for companies is to anchor the new-found transparency and marketing optimization in their organizations, processes, and systems. Moreover, if companies wish to continue raising their marketing RoI, they will need something over and above their tried and tested instruments and established messages. They should also run tests to help develop innovative new instruments, refresh their messages, or adjust the intensity and frequency of using particular instruments.

One of the best ways to diagnose a marketing organization's RoI discipline is to assess the extent and quality of media and messaging tests in progress at any given time. Some tests will be simple, such as testing higher levels of expenditure or the use of new media for an established message, reducing the frequency of mailings to see if response rates change, and testing a new advertising message in a particular region. Other methods, such as the simultaneous testing of a new message and new media for a growing segment of profitable customers, are bigger departures from the routine. Marketers who skimp on experimentation may be overtaken by changing media patterns or be forced to assume large risks in unproven programs when markets suddenly shift. Upstart brands such as Red Bull have demonstrated the power of alternative approaches by successfully building consumer awareness through trade promotions, sponsorships, and word-of-mouth.

As fruitful as tests and new communication methods can be, shifting the bulk of an established marketing plan to them is too risky, because none of these approaches has achieved the scale needed to replace television, radio, direct mail, or other broad-reach media vehicles. So, even in today's fragmenting world, marketers should invest roughly 80 percent of their money in proven messages (such as advertising copy qualified in research) that are placed in proven media vehicles and supported by proven funding levels (at or just above the threshold levels needed to influence customers). The remaining 20 percent can be considered marketing R&D. The extremely successful launch of Sony's PlayStation 2 offers a good example. Sony used many nontraditional vehicles such as ambient, guerrilla, and viral marketing to communicate the brand personality and to bring the product into the »right hands« to create early and credible word-of-mouth. Nevertheless, mass-media was still necessary. The launch was »supported by more highly targeted customer communications, but at the top of it all was television, like a big hammer banging home the message,« says Phil Harrison, Executive Vice President of Development at Sony Computer Entertainment Europe.[42]

An important enabler of continuous transparency about the impact and results of such marketing actions is the setup of a Brand Cockpit (a process described in detail in the next section). Next, company staff should be given incentives that reward transparent, effective, and efficient use of resources. Companies need to develop performance management systems that link marketing investment to profitability and brand performance ratios, thereby supporting the efficient use of resources. Finally, they should set up clearly defined processes that support marketing budget planning.

The marketing budget planning process is what separates truly successful companies from run-of-the-mill performers. All too often, companies do this on a one-off basis rather than as part of an annual planning cycle. The result is that the scientific instruments and processes are soon forgotten, and allocation of resources reverts to the former status quo.

It needs to be acknowledged that taking a single brand and running it through the three steps of the marketing RoI program requires considerable effort. Things get more complicated still when the company has a whole portfolio of brands and operates in a number of different countries. And the complexity appears almost insuperable when a large company has operations in dozens of different countries across all continents, sometimes with a single brand, sometimes with subsidiary brands, and sometimes with completely new brands. The goal should be to reduce this complexity. Experience shows that fixing priorities and running pilot projects in selected areas is the right way to show the organization as a whole that an across-the-board optimization of marketing expenditure is worthwhile and creates a basis for extending the work to other parts of the organization, giving those responsible a handle on the overall complexity.

The path to major savings and new growth opportunities

Time and again, this systematic three-step marketing RoI approach has proved its merit. Companies have often been able to reduce their marketing spending by 5 to 15 percent in the short term, without adversely affecting marketing effectiveness or revenues. In the medium term, they have frequently realized revenue growth of 5 to 10 percent, depending on the sector, by redirecting expenditure to bottlenecks in the purchase funnel. These companies now also use a systematic approach to budgeting and controlling their overall marketing spending, enabling them to introduce continuous tracking.

To take one example, with the help of a marketing RoI program, a European beverage company determined that between 14 and 22 percent of its marketing expenditure had very little impact. The wasted expenditure included the expensive sponsorship of sports events that had no relevance for the target group. At the same time, the beverage company carried out a media effectiveness analysis that resulted in the decision to redirect a fifth of its budget to media that were more effective in fulfilling the company's marketing objectives.

In another example, a textile retailer was able to realize short-term efficiency gains of 10 to 15 percent while redirecting almost a third of its budget to areas that were more effective in achieving its new marketing strategy. Sometimes a simple comparison of how much is spent to raise brand awareness or familiarity by a single percentage point is enough to reveal the potential savings in switching from one medium to another. Though the targets remain the same, the money is used more effectively.

A leading consumer goods company that had multiyear sponsorship deals costing over USD 400 million was able to use the reach, contact, quality (RCQ) approach to compare the effectiveness of these to traditional media benchmarks. By developing additional lenses for measuring the ancillary benefits of sponsorship deals and creating a clear marketing assets strategy focused on priority channels, the company was able to divest non-strategic sponsorships and to renegotiate contracts of those for which effectiveness was less than that of traditional television. Savings amounted to more than EUR 40 million annually.

The marketing RoI approach represents a major revolution in brand management. As the old maxim has it: »If it can't be measured, it doesn't change.« Brand managers, agencies, and others responsible for brands have often been misled by their gut feelings. Now, companies have more precise tools at their disposal. This will inevitably lead to important changes in the size and structure of marketing spending.

4.3 The Brand Cockpit: Collecting and Using Data Systematically and Effectively

Marketing and financial control: are they at all compatible with one another? In modern, professionally managed companies, the financial controller supervises even the most remote links in the chain of value creation, including materials purchasing and processing/manufacturing all the way to sales and distribution. With the aid of division-specific indicators, the effectiveness and efficiency of decisions, activities, processes, and contracts are analyzed and controlled to maximize company success. On a regular basis (at the end of the month, or quarter at the latest), the management board requests controlling data on the profit contribution of its profit centers and the efficiency of its cost centers. It concludes its work at the end of the day, confident that the financial department will continue to closely monitor all business areas the following day. But does it really monitor all of them? Not quite. The marketing department remained largely untouched by controlling mechanisms until about a decade ago; for example, the standard reference, *Measuring Brand Communication RoI* by Don E. Schultz of Northwestern University, first came out in 1997.[43]

If the marketing department has not managed to avoid the grasp of financial control completely, it often happens that the only thing that gets checked is budget compliance. Until very recently, few chief financial officers demanded fact-based arguments regarding the order of magnitude of expenditure or its distribution between the various media and campaigns. The problem has been that it is unclear what financial indicators should be used. As a result, even »old hands« such as David Ogilvy complain about the lack of advertising effectiveness.

Even when the marketing department documents the effectiveness of its own activities and expenditures, for instance, through tracking advertising or surveys of brand awareness, there is almost never any kind of coordination with the controlling department. The result is a wide discrepancy between the two departments' views of the actual expenditure. In the German retail market, for example, certain retailers get by with a marketing budget equivalent to just 0.5 percent of revenue (for example, Aldi, the discount grocery chain), whereas others spend seven times that amount (for example, a leading clothing retailer spends 3.7 percent). In certain segments of consumer goods, such as consumer electronics, marketing expenditure is as high as 7 percent of revenue, and some consumer goods manufacturers even exceed 10 percent. Yet there is little apparent correlation between expenditure and effectiveness.[44] The fact that there is major variation in the ratio of advertising spend to sales (Figure 4.18) shows that there is a lot of leeway for efficiency improvements. Take the example of the car industry. In Germany, why does Toyota spend more than three times as much as Volkswagen on above-the-line advertising per newly registered vehicle?[45] Admittedly, this type of question is hard to answer in any meaningful detail; besides, the ad-to-sales ratio (or even share of voice versus share of market) is only a rough indicator of whether your spending is in the right neighborhood. But how do you even get to a state of affairs where you know exactly how much you are spending, and what for, and what the money is or isn't doing for you?

Obviously, transparency is key. In many companies, there is hardly any clarity in terms of goals, in the desired content of the marketing campaign and expenditures, or in success in marketing or brand communication. Despite heated discussions of content and implementation, how many companies have launched expensive advertising campaigns not based on any kind of clear measurement parameters?

Though this situation, in which advertising expenditure appears wildly variable in nature, is unsustainable in the longer term as CEOs come to demand the same control over marketing as over other areas of their business, it is nonetheless, to some extent, understandable. The measurement

Fig. 4.18: There is a wide variation of ad-to-sales ratios

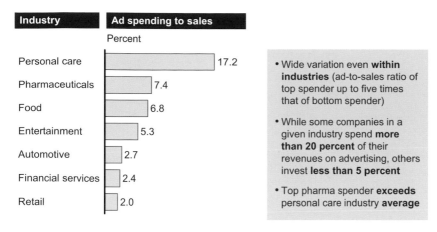

Industry	Ad spending to sales
	Percent
Personal care	17.2
Pharmaceuticals	7.4
Food	6.8
Entertainment	5.3
Automotive	2.7
Financial services	2.4
Retail	2.0

- Wide variation even **within industries** (ad-to-sales ratio of top spender up to five times that of bottom spender)
- While some companies in a given industry spend **more than 20 percent** of their revenues on advertising, others invest **less than 5 percent**
- Top pharma spender **exceeds** personal care industry **average**

Source: Advertising Age, TNS, company information, McKinsey

of marketing effectiveness and efficiency is more difficult than in other areas for at least two reasons.

First, marketing has an effect that, for many companies, is primarily indirect. Whereas pricing, product design, and sales structures can be linked directly to established measurement parameters such as number of units, revenues, or contract fulfillment, marketing typically has an indirect impact on success, through building the brand. This indirectness often results in an almost fatalistic attitude about assessing the impact of marketing: »But it's something you can't even measure!«

Second, the fast pace of marketing also makes measurement difficult. Run times for advertising campaigns and promotions are typically much shorter than most product cycles, contract periods, or customer relationships. The automotive industry is a good example of this.

The good news for management is that these challenges can be overcome through the use of financial indicators, key performance indicators, monitoring cycles, and control processes. Many large companies have already had positive experiences using such tools. The key to their success is a combination of three components:

- Systematic logging of input (investment) and output (effectiveness) data at regular intervals
- Actionable reporting showing causal relationships between investment and effect

Fig. 4.19: The brand cockpit gives a structure to the input and output variables of brand management

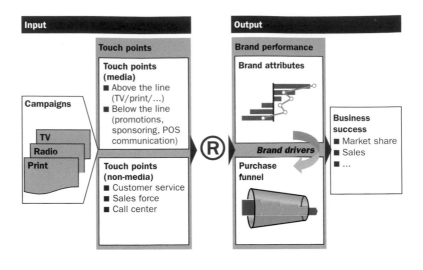

Source: McKinsey

- Targeted use of selected indicators of effectiveness and efficiency to inform decision making

McKinsey calls the combination of these components the *Brand Cockpit* (Figure 4.19).

A Brand Cockpit increases transparency dramatically by providing a regularly updated representation of brand communication or marketing activities according to expenditures and results. This information enables financial controlling and management to direct the effectiveness and efficiency of marketing. The concept of marketing RoI – as discussed in section 4.2 – provides the contextual framework for fact-based brand management. The Brand Cockpit should be understood as the next stage of brand development and as a universal brand management tool. Think of the Brand Cockpit as the hard-wired version of a marketing RoI effort: not as a single project, but as an ongoing process embedded in the company. The highest level of development is an integrated marketing cockpit detailing comprehensive data and interrelationships, including content and monetary input (campaigns, expenditures for communication, and other elements of the marketing mix) and their effects on brand image, drivers, purchase funnel performance, and company earnings.

This may be the point when the marketing manager, who works largely independently of financial control, slams the book shut and hopes that it never occurs to the management board or the controlling unit to consider implementing such »technocratic whims« seriously. This is why it is important to emphasize once again that successful brand management is dependent on the combination of art, science, and craft. Although the Brand Cockpit is referred to here as the pinnacle of quantitative brand management, this is not to say that creative work should be given up in favor of automated marketing management. Controlling of performance figures is a necessary, but not sufficient means. No one would conduct a brand campaign as if it were a form of production planning or product life cycle management. Automating brand management not only carries the danger of producing countless me-too campaigns (which will quickly become ineffective). It would also make brand management unattractive to young marketing executives. As no marketing department can survive without a constant influx of new creative managers, this alone is reason enough to stay away from a »science only« approach.

The Brand Cockpit provides transparency and control

Once correctly installed and maintained, the Brand Cockpit offers users fact-based insights into three problem areas: input transparency, output transparency, and performance assessment.

Input transparency: A Brand Cockpit needs to ensure that the objectives, content (messages and campaigns), spending, and customer touch points of brand communication or marketing are compiled and depicted systematically over time. This supports financial control by providing clarity about the when, what, and where of marketing spending. It shows what amount of expenditure is directed to which target group. Depending on the sector, this might include current and potential customers, dealers, and distribution partners. The core of the cockpit function is the categorization of expenditures according to clearly defined customer touch points (Figure 4.20). Which of the individual customer touch points are involved depends largely on the type of business (e.g., B2C versus B2B, contract-based versus case-by-case purchase decisions) as well as on market size, products, target groups, legal regulations, geographic features, and on the nature of the company itself.

Fig. 4.20: Checklist of possible customer touch points

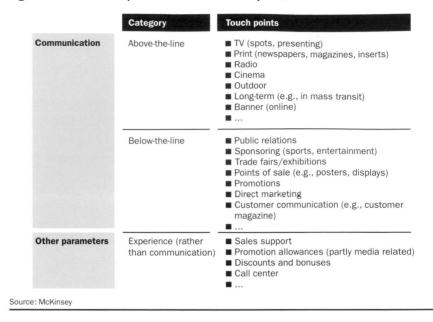

	Category	Touch points
Communication	Above-the-line	■ TV (spots, presenting) ■ Print (newspapers, magazines, inserts) ■ Radio ■ Cinema ■ Outdoor ■ Long-term (e.g., in mass transit) ■ Banner (online) ■ …
	Below-the-line	■ Public relations ■ Sponsoring (sports, entertainment) ■ Trade fairs/exhibitions ■ Points of sale (e.g., posters, displays) ■ Promotions ■ Direct marketing ■ Customer communication (e.g., customer magazine) ■ …
Other parameters	Experience (rather than communication)	■ Sales support ■ Promotion allowances (partly media related) ■ Discounts and bonuses ■ Call center ■ …

Source: McKinsey

To give some structure to the wide range of marketing and communication vehicles, the Brand Cockpit differentiates between above-the-line and below-the-line communication on the one hand and non-media touch points on the other hand. High precision is necessary initially in compiling campaign and spending data so as to maximize input transparency. It pays to think ahead about how to represent the defined touch points in effectiveness-oriented market research projects. What marketing manager would not like to know what the company's head of distribution support wants to do with EUR 3 million for »point-of-sale materials«? At the same time, it is impossible to examine the impact of every single flyer without spending a disproportionate amount of time and money on the analysis.

Output transparency. As with the objectives, content, spending, and customer touch points on the input side, companies need to compile and interpret data and information regarding developments directly or indirectly influenced by brand communication and marketing activities systematically in order to make interrelationships between input and output transparent. This data includes overall brand image performance, the most important brand drivers in the purchase funnel, and the performance of the brand in the purchase funnel itself. The second output category, not always directly coupled to brand performance, is the development of economic indicators such as revenue or market share by brand. Any interrelationships that have been ascertained through one-time or repeat market research can be integrated into the structure and the priorities of the cockpit. Such data might include, for instance, the touch points that influence specific brand attributes, the media that influence the various individual stages of the purchase funnel, the elements that drive customer transfer through the purchase funnel, and the financial indicators that are influenced (where possible, directly) by specific marketing activities.

Like the input factors, the output factors need to be differentiated according to company, brand, business model, product, and so on. The relevant brand drivers, structure of the purchase funnel, and economic indicators depend largely on the nature of the business involved, for instance, whether the company and its marketing are targeting private or business customers, or whether the business model revolves around relatively long-term contracts (e.g., pay TV, subscriptions, mobile communication services), occasional large acquisitions (e.g., cars, household appliances), or repeat single purchases (e.g., fast-moving consumer goods and retail).

Performance assessment: The function of a Brand Cockpit from the perspective of management and financial controlling is to check the effectiveness and efficiency of marketing spending. Depending on the stage of cockpit development and the availability of data, there are three principal options for integrating the cockpit into the company's overall performance management system. The first is to assess performance relative to targets (are the activities as effective and efficient as expected?); the second is to assess performance relative to earlier time periods (are they more effective/ efficient than last year?); the third is to assess performance relative to competitors (are they as effective/efficient as those of the strongest competitor?). The systematic monitoring of performance using what is perhaps the simplest reference parameter, the company's own targets, is often very enlightening – not least because such an approach forces the company to specify concrete targets for itself, its brands, and its products in advance.

The heart of the cockpit: Deriving key performance indicators

Let us now focus on the main task and the *raison d'être* of the Brand Cockpit: the sustainable assessment, control, and optimization of the effectiveness and efficiency of marketing spending. To support fact-based decisions about marketing expenditure, the cockpit must help create meaningful key performance indicators (KPIs). With the help of action-oriented scorecards, these will be used to answer questions about the performance of the marketing function.

Figures 4.21 and 4.22 provide typical examples of questions about marketing expenditures and corresponding KPIs categorized in terms of whether they relate to effectiveness or to efficiency.[46]

Effectiveness: Did our most recent campaign achieve the intended target awareness of 70 percent among 14-to-49-year-olds? Did we achieve an improvement in brand perception in the main loyalty driver »forward-looking«? The corresponding KPIs can be calculated, for instance, as the awareness growth ratio over the course of the campaign, or as the ratio of actual-to-desired score for the driver »forward-looking.«

Efficiency: What is the connection between brand or marketing spending and revenues or corporate earnings? How much did the increase in awareness cost? How much was spent on below-the-line efforts in the past quar-

Fig. 4.21: Success indicators for campaign tracking

<u>ILLUSTRATIVE</u>

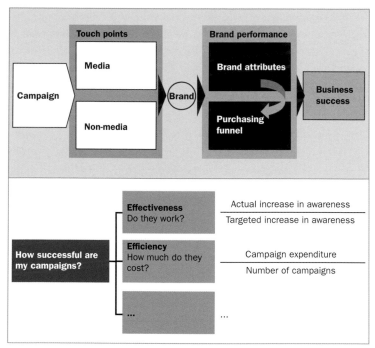

Source: McKinsey

Fig. 4.22: Success indicators for brand management

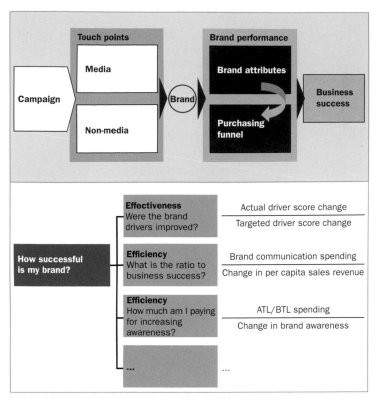

ILLUSTRATIVE

Source: McKinsey

ter per percentage point of additional buying propensity? Corresponding KPIs might include the ratio of brand or marketing spending to revenue or company earnings, the percentage increase in awareness relative to total advertising expenditures, or the ratio of below-the-line expenditures to the increase in »propensity to buy« in the brand funnel in terms of percentage points per quarter. Much more complex interrelationships can also be translated into performance indicators, such as the relationship between brand spending and the company's business results as indicated, for instance, by shareholder value.

A scorecard based on these KPIs, generated semiannually or annually for the director of marketing, the marketing controller, or, depending on the organizational design, even the CEO, might include, for instance, two sets of data on input and effect over a defined period of time. The input side would include marketing spending categorized by touch points and campaign; the output side would show change in brand awareness or achievement of brand awareness targets and the three most important brand drivers in the purchase funnel. Such an overview makes it easy to see whether marketing expenditures were successful in reaching their targets over the specified period of time, as indicated by objective performance criteria. If corrections are necessary, marketing managers can use the detailed KPIs to derive options for optimizing the amount and mix of expenditures. The higher up in the organization a given user of the Brand Cockpit resides, the more important aggregated indicators, such as total marketing spending over sales, or actual brand awareness over targeted brand awareness, will become. While full clarity regarding input and output is important for day-to-day marketing management, top management will be looking for composite performance indicators, relative to predefined targets, to other brands in the company's portfolio, or to competitors. Some executives find it easier to make sense of the KPIs when they are visualized in the form of a color-coded scale, e.g., a traffic light.

The cockpit in Figure 4.23 shows a real-life (though disguised) example from a consumer high-tech company. The cockpit is used by the corporate marketing function to control and monitor the accomplishment of prioritized objectives by region based on KPIs. Note that each KPI has been tied to a concrete marketing objective, so that they are not measured for their own sake.

The objectives include product-, brand-, customer-, and capabilities-oriented categories and therefore encompass more than a mere brand tracking tool. The corresponding KPIs need to be selected based on the following criteria:

- *Actionability*: Does the KPI enable decision making, such as budget allocation or activity prioritization?
- *Controllability*: Does it improve the influence of the respective stakeholder?
- *Educational effect*: Does tracking or monitoring the KPI improve the brand orientation of the organization?
- *Data availability*: Can the KPI data be easily acquired or generated, either internally or externally?
- *Comparability*: Does the KPI metric allow for consistent application and comparison across businesses, brands, and markets?

Fig. 4.23: Example of a brand cockpit

Manage · Monitor

Objective	KPI	Figures	Global Target	%	North America Target	%	Europe Target	%	Asia-Pacific Target	%	ROW Target	%
Budget												
Plan compliance	Compliance with budget plan	YTD										
Sales alignment	Total Spending over sales ratio	YTD										
	Spending over gross margin elasticity	YTD										
Product												
Product leadership	Focus product sales	YTD										
Brand												
Premium brand positioning	Premium brand attribute 1	Semiannual										
	Premium brand attribute 2	Semiannual										
	Average price premium	Semiannual										
Awareness	(Unaided) awareness	Semiannual										
Customer												
Prominent presence	Share of shelf	Semiannual										
Capabilities												
Empowered organization	Organizational footprint	Quarterly										
	Average capability score	Annual										
Return on investment	ROI	Quarterly										
Budget base	ROI	Quarterly										
Specific/temporary												
Tbd	...	...										

Source: McKinsey

No off-the-shelf cockpit solutions

A cockpit's degree of detail, structural complexity, data collection frequency, and graphic interface depend largely on the underlying economic and organizational conditions. A standardized Brand Cockpit does not and will never exist, as any turnkey solution will fall short of the specific marketing requirements of a company's brand or brands. The content, structure, update frequency, and organizational integration of a well-designed cockpit should reflect the company's specific strengths and challenges. The Brand Cockpit for the management board of a large international conglomerate with numerous single brands will obviously differ from the cockpit for a single-country consumer goods producer with one brand or the cockpit used by the marketing department for tracking the performance of a particular campaign. That said, solutions catering to these different types of demand can, of course, be integrated into a modular »master« cockpit. However, it is important to balance the costs of data collection with the required level of detail or timeliness of the data carefully. The finest, most detailed cockpit is useless if its upkeep requires an entire department and is thus prohibitively expensive.

279

Managing Brands

Overall responsibility for the cockpit should rest at senior level, above functional interests, and may be supported by internal or external auditing as necessary. Leading companies have established functional controlling as the default owner of the Brand Cockpit to ensure that both financial and functional expertise go into its design and maintenance. Functional controlling can either be part of the CFO's team or reside in the marketing function itself.

Regardless of the stage of cockpit development, it is always worthwhile to involve external partners, such as media and advertising agencies, early on in its design and execution. Especially with respect to the interaction of individual media, agencies are often good sources of conceptual and practical expertise whose potential should not go untapped. Agencies are also often helpful in reconciling different sources of data, such as gross versus net, spending versus placements, and so on. Cutting-edge companies even get their key providers to send them periodic hard-coded updates of market research or advertising tracking. By minimizing manual data entry, the Brand Cockpit becomes more cost efficient to maintain and less susceptible to reporting errors; see the insert on Astra Zeneca's Brand Equity Analyst Tool below.

The three stages of cockpit development

Three stages of complexity and sophistication can be observed in the development of the Brand Cockpit, each of which makes different demands in terms of structure, content, and organizational foundation (Figure 4.24).

The path of development from the early days of campaign tracking to a comprehensive Brand Cockpit, in other words, from the descriptive to the explanatory to the prescriptive, should always be understood as an iterative process. Refinement takes time; as the adage has it: »Learn to walk before you run.« In addition to the two basic cockpit modules, a more advanced and comprehensive marketing cockpit would reflect additional customer touch points, brand performance, and company success.

The first stage of development is that of tracking campaign success. This will indicate whether targets have been fulfilled over time, and whether the expenditure is warranted by the results. As part of this, it is also useful to use prelaunch tests to estimate the likely outcome of the campaign. Such prelaunch tests are often more effective in deriving causal relationships than extrapolating from the outcomes of previous campaigns. It is vital to track the campaign's success in terms of the effectiveness of the concept, its execution, and its compliance with the advertising schedule.

Fig. 4.24: Three development stages for the cockpit

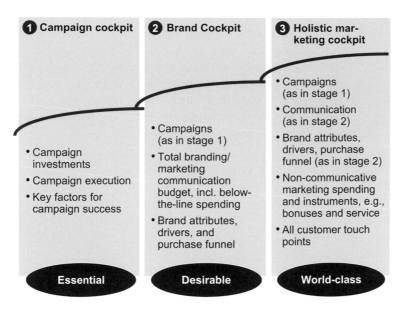

Source: McKinsey

The second stage in the development of the Brand Cockpit is to move to tracking all spending at media-based customer touch points. Tracking should cover performance metrics for selected brand drivers and the various stages of the purchase funnel. From the results, you can derive content-related, touch-point-based interrelationships and correlations. This is essential for companies in marketing-intensive sectors or competitive environments, as it ensures that the marketing budget is invested at the most effective points and in a sufficient but not uneconomic manner. This data will provide the basis for the ongoing optimization of brand investments in the context of a company-wide optimization of marketing RoI.

The third and final stage of refinement is a comprehensive Brand Cockpit that also includes non-media touch points and factors of influence. On the input side, this will include investments for distribution channels, call centers, customer service, products and prices, and all essential market performance indicators for all products, brands, and countries. This type of integrated marketing cockpit makes it possible to derive trade-offs between the individual cost and profit centers throughout the company. It is also suitable as a component in a Brand Portfolio Management system. Although this model is certainly

Managing Brands

ideal from a corporate point of view, it can only be the outcome of strategic customer management and might be beyond the skills and scope of most brand communication and marketing departments. This form of the Brand Cockpit is found today in only a few of the largest and most progressive marketing organizations.

Generally speaking, it is as tempting as it is dangerous to go over board with the level of detail and technical sophistication. Various departments are making demands on the scope of the cockpit. Marketing planners request features that enable them to slice and dice the data any way they want, enabling them to pull reports on a by brand, by product, by country, by type of advertising spending, by campaign, essentially: a *by anything* basis. If the IT department is involved, chances are they will get excited about the user interface and, more importantly, the technical back end of the cockpit. Before you know it, they will be implementing hotlinks to the company's data warehouse and automated uploads from the market research agency. But experience shows that it is usually the simple solutions that survive and help to change management thinking. Some of the most successful solutions take the tangible shape of a laminated, pocket-sized chart displaying the top indicators for the CMO and the team to carry around (Figure 4.25). In a recent study on the more general concept of the balanced scorecard, controlling guru Utz Schäffer came to a similar conclusion. He found that 15 years after Kaplan and Norton first introduced the concept, most efforts to introduce elaborate scorecard-based controlling systems are considered flawed or have been discontinued altogether. Today, only 24 percent of all publicly listed companies in Germany claim to use scorecards at all. Many have gone from complex, highly integrated systems back to just a handful of key performance indicators, with the emphasis on *key*. Schäffer found that the more complex the scorecard, the less likely it is to survive changes in management or strategy: »Pretty much all surviving scorecards are very hands-on.« Says one of the executives Schäffer interviewed: »It just seems easier to adapt the scorecard to the company than vice versa.« The lesson is to keep the cockpit simple, especially if your company or department is new to the idea of KPI-based management. Needless to say, this is all the more true for the marketing department, given that it is typically less number-driven than the rest of the organization in most companies.[47]

Fig. 4.25: Example of monthly scorecard

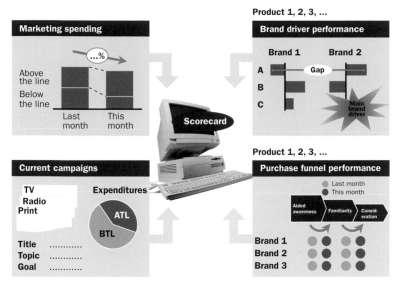

Source: McKinsey

Ongoing compilation of input and output data

For the Brand Cockpit to be successful, it is necessary to collect selected input and output data in a careful and meticulous manner and on a regular basis. The scope and frequency of this compilation depends, as already described, on the nature of the organization. The essential input factors for a typical Brand Cockpit include data on individual campaigns and their content, target groups, and objectives over defined time periods on the one hand, and spending on brand communication or overall marketing by touch points on the other. The most important output dimensions are brand performance, including brand drivers, stages, and conversion rates in the purchase funnel, and, depending on development stage, key indicators of company success such as revenues or market share.

It is not a simple task to ensure the quality and consistency of this data. It involves both vertical (cross-sector) and horizontal (temporal) comparability. If, for instance, spending information is recorded in one place as budgeted amounts, in another as actual expenditure, and in a third as actual expenditure to date plus an updated forecast, and if there have been changes to the organization during the chosen time period that are relevant to the touch points in question, then it is unlikely that the desired degree of transparency will be achieved. For example, if the responsibility and budgeting for point-of-sale materials moves from the marketing to the sales department, or vice versa, this change needs to be reflected in the data-gathering process. In any case, it is important that potential limitations to the accuracy and granularity of the data are themselves made transparent; otherwise, the cockpit will generate a false impression of reality. For example, if point-of-sale investments are shifted from the marketing to the sales function, lead generation at the point of sale may appear more efficient practically over night, while in fact the investments have not changed, but are simply accounted for elsewhere in the company.

Following a limited test phase within the organization, the process of data collection and evaluation should be automated, at least partially. Whether a well-developed Brand Cockpit can be updated and maintained regularly and conscientiously in the end depends on good coordination with the respective marketing or controlling unit's data warehouse. Of equal importance for its success is the dovetailing of the Brand Cockpit into the organization's processes for decision making and action. There is little point in investing in a Brand Cockpit if the insights are not considered in designing future marketing plans and campaigns.

Experience and training in applying this powerful tool are essential for its success. Even a theoretically outstanding tool is useless if it is not implemented with a good portion of common sense.

How the Dashboard became a Cashboard: Cisco Systems' Award-winning Marketing Cockpit

When James Richardson started out as CMO for Cisco Systems in 2001, all was not well at the IT hardware pioneer. Once celebrated as the backbone of the dot.com craze, the company had just posted its first loss since going public in 1990, and laid off about 8,500 employees, then the equivalent of over 20 percent of its workforce. Richardson found the company's marketing function was far from being »managed and rewarded based on the ability to meet goals.« Having had a favorable experience with KPI-based management as a line manager in the company's regional organization (Richardson was Cisco's president for Europe, the Middle East, and Asia and Vice President for North America before taking the CMO post), he made a pledge to make marketing more measurable at Cisco. He introduced a marketing cockpit to increase the effectiveness and efficiency of marketing investments. Despite its relative simplicity, the cockpit's scope was holistic in terms of touch points. Regardless of whether people just perceived Cisco as a brand, bought the products, or worked for the company, their perception was reflected in the cockpit. It included key indicators for brand image, employee retention, and customer satisfaction.

As part of the cockpit's implementation, Cisco developed automated systems to track the effectiveness of leads generated by global marketing campaigns, enabling it to link marketing spending with revenues more directly than ever before. Since Richardson took the CMO post, he used the marketing cockpit to drive marketing spending from 5 percent of annual sales to a mere 3.3 percent. Specifically, he cut back on Cisco's various sports sponsorships, which he found did not contribute sufficiently to the company's marketing goals. Richardson's KPI-based overhaul of the budget went down without apparent damage to the company's marketing success. On the contrary: some of Cisco's most effective campaigns were launched during his tenure, notably »Power of the Network.« The USD 160 million advertising campaign, focusing on network security, voice-over-IP, and wireless technology, helped boost Cisco's »top-of-mind« awareness with key audiences by over 25 percent in North America and generated hundreds of millions of dollars in sales leads. Denise Peck, Cisco's Vice President for marketing operations, highlights the integrative aspect of the central dashboard: »Cisco has always been a very data-rich company, but we needed to develop standard terminology for metrics, a process for collection, and internal education processes. Every organization has a lot of metrics associated with operational performance, customer insight, and marketing data,« Peck says. »We brought all the key pieces into one place to provide further insight into where we needed to put emphasis and make corrections. When people know what they're being measured on, it brings more clarity.«[48]

In 2005, Cisco was awarded IDC's CMO Best Practice Award for its marketing dashboard. Michael Gerard of IDC (International Data Corporation) comments that they »developed a culture of measurement within their organization. Each of the groups within marketing knew they needed to be accountable for whatever activities they implemented.« It is exactly this spirit of accountability that enabled Cisco to use the marketing dashboard to determine in which areas marketing investments make the biggest difference, and refine their allocation accordingly. Says Richardson: »I want to get to a point where I can say ›If you give me another USD 200 million, I can deliver another USD 1 billion [in revenue]‹.« After his five-year tenure as CMO, Richardson became Cisco's Senior Vice President for Commercial Business in early 2006, focusing on the company's fastest-growing customer segment, small and medium-sized businesses.[49]

AstraZeneca's Brand Equity Tool

by Tarja Stenvall, Director, Marketing Excellence, AstraZeneca ISMO

Context

AstraZeneca seeks constantly to enrich its brand management approach. To this end, over the last few years we have developed a number of distinctive frameworks and made significant investment in their delivery. The main focus of these efforts has been to gain greater understanding of how customers view AstraZeneca's brand in our various markets. This investment has provided the company with the facts and insights to keep on building our brands in a targeted and sustainable manner.

Due to the company's sheer size and complexity, we depend on quick access to reliable and easy to use brand performance data. One framework we have introduced to achieve this is brand equity, which has become one of the main building blocks in achieving marketing excellence. Brand equity is instrumental in helping us understand the current perceptions of key customers about our brands within the overall competitive landscape.

Challenge

A core objective of AstraZeneca's brand management has been to weave best-practice thinking on customer-driven marketing into the very fabric of the company, rather than letting it remain in isolated pockets of the organization. In the past, our approach to brand equity tracking comprised a multitude of stand-alone components: research agency reports, multiple spreadsheets, manual output analyses, and multimedia presentations. While this may have once been sufficient, the growing demands of global portfolio management and the increased relevance of brands in many of our categories called for a new approach. In addition, it was clear to us that the sheer tedium of manual tracking sometimes created a reluctance to monitor brand performance. Specifically, we identified three challenges in our brand-equity tracking processes we wished to put right:

1. Overly time-consuming processes: We found we were investing significant time each year in coordinating with outside agencies to collect and analyze the data required for the desired brand equity outputs. Further time was then invested so that the marketing and market research teams could interpret these findings, and in customizing and presenting the outputs. Overall, we found that while 70 percent

of our time was spent on handling these reports and spreadsheets, only 30 percent was given to reviewing and discussing their implications for brand management.

2. Insufficient accuracy of results: The traditional way of doing brand equity tracking required us to have dedicated, in-house analytic experts and in-market research teams spend significant time doing the analysis. Nevertheless, the sheer volume of work involved in handling the data sometimes led to inaccuracies in calculation. As a result, the quality of the analyses was sometimes uneven, and this could on occasion even lead to incorrect interpretation of the data. We were concerned that this was the early sign of an emerging quality issue that could slow down our entire process and might even make brand equity tracking unreliable.

3. Threat to sustainability: Despite the value that brand equity has brought us, the significant time investment it required and the danger of data inaccuracy led to the perception that it was a cumbersome process. We saw this was potentially a threat to its continued use in our local marketing companies. The inadequacies of the process were therefore in danger of getting in the way of how we wanted our product managers to think about managing brand image at AstraZeneca.

Solution

As part of a broader brand management transformation effort, we created a user-friendly brand equity tool to replace the previous manual process. This tool gives us easy access to brand-tracking data and quickly shows the brands' image data across all of AstraZeneca's markets.

The brand equity tool creates its output automatically and in real time, bypassing the time-consuming and somewhat cumbersome manual processes that were required previously. Before the introduction of the brand equity tool, significant time had to be invested whenever we received research reports from agencies and local insights groups. The new tool, in contrast, automatically pulls research data that has been entered remotely by agencies and does all the analyses needed to produce the output for AstraZeneca's standard brand image frameworks. The brand equity tool is also linked to AstraZeneca's brand management methodology user guide to ensure the output is fully in line with the company's marketing approach. Finally, being IT enabled, the tool prevents calculation errors that can result from manual intervention.

The new tool enables brand teams to compare the key factors that are critical to their customers' brand choice across time frames and locations. The tool is also much easier and more intuitive to use when comparing AstraZeneca brands' performance to that of its competitors. As a key feature, it enables »one-click« access to the data over predefined periods of time and for any location. This enables us to understand how the market landscape is evolving, and makes it very easy to compare the data for the different brands in their various markets.

Impact and reactions

The tool has now been rolled out in most of our key markets and has transformed the way AstraZeneca makes use of brand tracking. Having ready access to real-time brand image data feels like a whole new world to our marketing managers. Now that there is no longer any need to handle reports and analyses manually, they have much more time to spend on their core work.

Key success factors

We found that there were a number of elements that proved critical to the success of this program, but three stand out in particular:

1. Strong link to capability building and learning: As a result of the tool's easy-to-use interface, we were able to roll it out quickly to a large number of market researchers and brand leaders. The rollout included an in-depth training program that covered all the key global, regional, and country users, introducing them to the brand equity methodology and the usage of the tool. This not only built their capabilities, but ensured that we have their buy-in for the new approach. It has also helped our marketing staff see that we are not just talking about a piece of software, but about a new approach that is a critical element in building AstraZeneca's marketing skills in all its markets.

2. Close collaboration across functions: Working closely across functions helped us to balance the need to deliver on time with the necessary analytical rigor. AstraZeneca's central teams for marketing, country, IT, and legal affairs have therefore cooperated very closely throughout the brand equity tool's development.

3. Daring to take a new path: Initially, there was some concern that the tool would not be delivered on time within budget, and that its demands on our resources could have an unforeseen impact on the way we work. However, these fears proved unfounded, and we have

meanwhile developed a new way of working that has significantly strengthened our marketing capabilities. Going forward, because it will be easier to obtain an overview of the core issues our brands face in their markets, we will be more targeted and more meaningful in discussions about the real brand issues.

The brand equity tool will help AstraZeneca create transparency about how our brands operate in their various markets. This is in line with our aspiration to establish strong, fact-based brand management and to create a common language for brand management. This is very important for AstraZeneca, as the company manages multiple brands across multiple categories in many different markets and countries. We believe this investment is also testimony to how AstraZeneca continues to invest in building its core marketing capabilities. We now plan to explore how we can use similarly innovative techniques to make sure other elements of the »AstraZeneca way of marketing« become deeply ingrained within the organization.

Fig. 4.26: Sample output of AstraZeneca's Brand Equity Analyst Tool

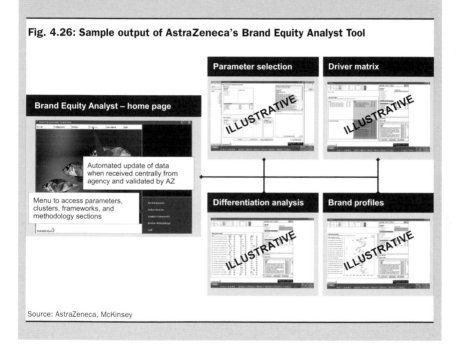

Source: AstraZeneca, McKinsey

4.4 The Brand Organization: Systems and Requirements

Successful brand management demands a powerful brand organization, including an appropriate structure, suitable management qualifications, and the right decision-making processes. Many companies appear to believe that installing the right structure alone will be decisive. It is as if they expect a new organization chart to be sufficient for ensuring marketing success.

That such a misconception should persist more than a quarter century after the publication of Tom Peters' and Robert Waterman's best seller *In Search of Excellence* is hard to believe.[50] Their research showed, among other things, that the »ideal« organizational structures do not guarantee success. The structure of a company not only has to fit its strategic goals, but also orient the processes and systems of the organization and the talents and skills of its people toward the same ends. In other words, the structure of the organization is only part of the solution; there is no point in employing talented and highly qualified brand managers if they do not have sufficient authority within the organization, be it formal or informal, to make a difference to the outcome. Often, this is not primarily a question of boxes, lines, decision rights, and job descriptions, but of the role and recognition of the executive in charge of a given brand. Since the power wielded by a brand manager ultimately depends on the qualifications of the individual in question, hiring and developing top brand management talent is a critical component of successful brand organization.

Only an executive of sufficient caliber and credibility will be able to ensure the brand is recognized as a valuable asset well beyond next year's EBIT, whether the brand is managed as a profit center in its own right or not. No matter what the short-term business targets may be, it is the brand manager's paramount goal to safeguard and develop the brand for the future. It's obvious that this role sometimes requires tough decisions; consider Skoda's much disputed, but ultimately successful strategy of staying away from high-margin, lifestyle vehicles to protect its no-nonsense brand image (see chapter 3). It takes an executive of considerable standing, and with strong support from the board, to deliver on this promise of the brand manager as the brand's caretaker and watchdog. In recognition of this challenge, many companies have created the role of chief marketing officer. IBM, Pepsi, and Procter & Gamble were among the pioneers to hire CMOs, thereby effectively moving brand management to executive or even supervisory board level. And with good reason. As the Skoda example shows, sustainable brand management is of the utmost importance from a shareholder perspective. This section provides an examination of how resolute brand management helps to create and sustain value, especially in today's changing market environments.

Best practice in the brand manager organization

But before we get into the ins and outs of successful brand organization, let's take a look at the origins of the brand manager organization. It can be traced back to 1919 at Libby, McNeill & Libby, which was the first company to place emphasis on managing individual brands (Figure 4.27).[51] It was Procter & Gamble, however, that introduced the classic brand manager organization in 1931, with one brand manager responsible for one product.[52] This was in accordance with the Procter & Gamble belief that a product must have distinct tangible and rational benefits, which were then communicated through the product's brand.

As manager of Procter & Gamble's marketing department, Neil McElroy recognized that his company's own brands were struggling unsuccessfully for market share against competing products. He developed a plan in which every Procter & Gamble brand would be managed by independent brand managers and brand assistants. The brand manager would be responsible for advertising and all other marketing activities of that single brand. By approving the plan, Procter & Gamble's president Richard Deupree established the world's first formal brand manager organization.

The previous forms of brand organization typical at that time had a coordination problem. Responsibility for a brand was distributed across several functional managers, resulting in poor coordination of activities. But Procter & Gamble found a solution. The brand manager alone was responsible for sales figures, market share, and brand profit (Figure 4.28). A secondary goal of this new form of organization was to foster stronger competition between multiple brands under the same corporate roof. McElroy believed that it was better to lose market share to his own Procter & Gamble products than to competitors.[53]

Soon Procter & Gamble's system was widely imitated by consumer goods companies. Even today the Procter & Gamble model characterizes the structures of marketing-oriented companies in many industries. In the years of strong growth following the Second World War, it was this brand management system that helped many companies to establish and maintain innovative products and new brands. But the model has its limitations. In a phase of market stagnation, or when the innovation potential of the products has been largely exhausted, the classic brand manager system tends

Fig. 4.27: Year of introduction of brand manager organization in selected companies

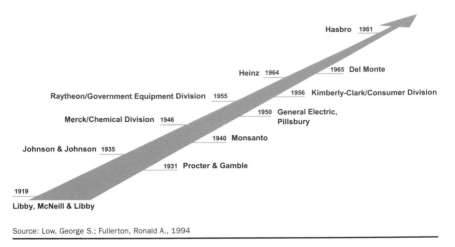

Hasbro 1981

Heinz 1964

1965 Del Monte

Raytheon/Government Equipment Division 1955

1956 Kimberly-Clark/Consumer Division

1950 General Electric, Pillsbury

Merck/Chemical Division 1946

1940 Monsanto

Johnson & Johnson 1935

1931 Procter & Gamble

1919

Libby, McNeill & Libby

Source: Low, George S.; Fullerton, Ronald A., 1994

to hinder growth. This is because the basic perspective is narrow: the individual brand manager is focused on only his or her brand. Taken as a whole, the structure tends to neglect the potential for growth associated with new business systems, customer groups, or sales channels.

Frozen food offers a good illustration of such growth opportunities in sales channels. Whereas the product management systems at the German competitors Langnese-Iglo (previously a Unilever brand), Dr. Oetker, and other established frozen food and ice cream suppliers prevent the development of a direct-to-home distribution system, newcomers such as Eismann (a Nestlé subsidiary from 2001 to 2004) and Bofrost have tapped this potential and become successful through direct-to-home distribution. These innovative new companies now even aspire to surpass the established players in size and profit. Bofrost and Eismann, the two dominant distributors of frozen food products in Germany, have achieved enormous growth through their home delivery services. Today, Bofrost is the global market leader in direct-to-home frozen foods. In Germany, it dominates the category with a market share of 70.5 percent; its share of all frozen foods and ice cream comes to 16.3 percent. In 2006 to 2007, Bofrost served more than 4 million customers and generated European revenues of approximately EUR 1.11 billion, up from EUR 500,000 in 1992. Eismann, the number two in Germany in the frozen foods direct-distribution industry, achieved revenues of some EUR 500 million in 2007, catering to 2.5 million customers.[54] Nestlé's

Fig. 4.28: Example of brand management organization

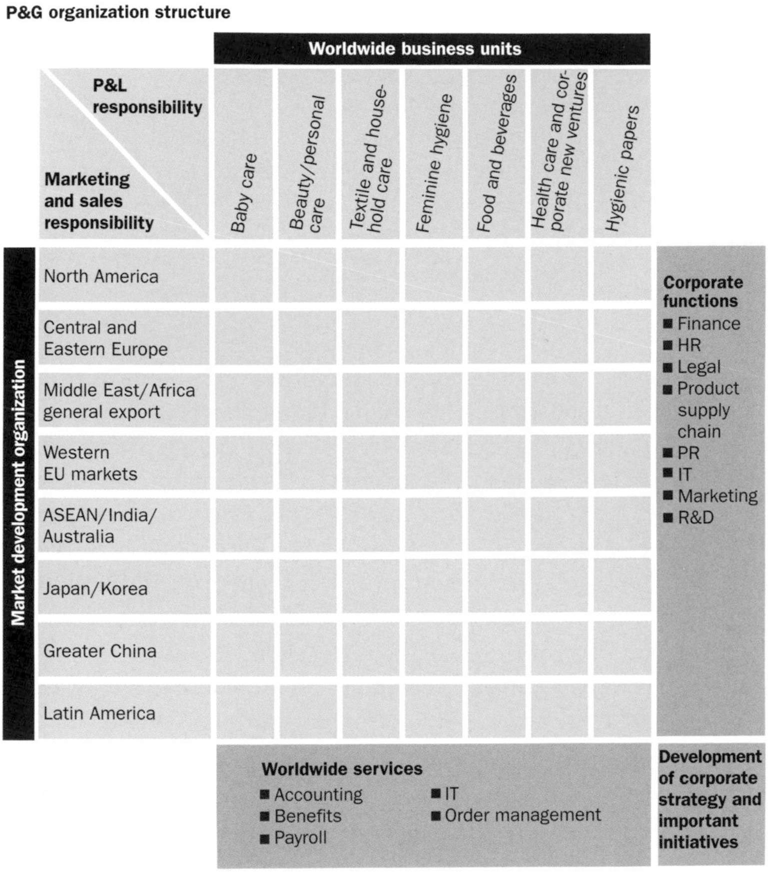

P&G organization structure

Market development organization	Worldwide business units							
P&L responsibility / Marketing and sales responsibility	Baby care	Beauty/personal care	Textile and household care	Feminine hygiene	Food and beverages	Health care and corporate new ventures	Hygienic papers	Corporate functions
North America								■ Finance
Central and Eastern Europe								■ HR
Middle East/Africa general export								■ Legal ■ Product supply chain
Western EU markets								■ PR
ASEAN/India/Australia								■ IT
Japan/Korea								■ Marketing
Greater China								■ R&D
Latin America								

Worldwide services
- Accounting
- Benefits
- Payroll
- IT
- Order management

Development of corporate strategy and important initiatives

Source: Press clippings

Nespresso brand, launched in its present form around 1990, follows a similar direct approach. Nespresso's coffee capsules are sold directly to consumers through the company's online store and a few branded premium outlets. At a market share of 11 percent, Nespresso is currently the number three in its industry, after Sara Lee and Lavazza.[55]

The increased competitive pressure from home delivery services led to a change in the frozen foods market that affected even the former market leaders in ice cream production. The established frozen-food subsidiary of the Anglo-Dutch Unilever Group, Langnese-Iglo, for instance, was unable to keep pace with the growth of its new competitors. Unilever sold the Iglo brand to Permira in 2006.[56]

In other sectors, organizational forms developed along the lines of customer groups/segments or sales channels also face similar hindrances to growth as soon as the potential of the respective customer group or sales channel has been exhausted. Financial service providers, for instance, frequently use a customer group organization; insurance companies are arranged according to industrial and private customers, who are each offered different brands and products. Commercial enterprises are organized according to sales channels; this again typically involves different brands that serve as distinguishing elements.

As described in chapter 3, Volkswagen AG has also developed a brand organization. The company's four volume brands VW, Audi, Seat, and Skoda are managed more or less independently in order to differentiate the brands as much as possible. The Group Marketing function of the corporation coordinates the brand portfolio and is in charge of capturing the synergies that do not influence the consumer's perception of independent brands in areas such as market research. Specifically, Group Marketing oversees customer segment management and positioning of brands relative to one another to help avoid in-house cannibalization. In addition, the corporate function also manages the »internal brand identity« of each brand organization.

A brand's potential can only be captured completely through a brand-oriented organization. This is demonstrated best by companies with a strong individual brand or umbrella brand, such as Adidas, Nike, Sony, or Virgin. In such an approach, not only are a wide range of products developed under the umbrella brand, but all the potential sales channels are also used. For example, Tchibo, the German coffee company, has channels that range from its own retail shops to direct distribution, mail-order catalogs, and online sales.

It is instructive to look at Adidas as an example of the path of evolution a brand takes in becoming an umbrella brand. In 1925, the founder of Adidas, Adi Dassler, developed the first running shoe. For many decades, Adidas meant just this one product. But in 1963, Adidas expanded its portfolio to include the production of soccer balls. Sports apparel was added four years later. In the 1990s, Adidas again expanded its array of products into sports niches such as streetball.[57] Its brand strategy has included cooperation with famous designers such as Stella McCartney and Yohji Yamamoto. This has helped Adidas to complete the transition from being a traditional sports shoe producer to becoming a modern lifestyle company positioned in numerous product segments. Today, Adidas products, such as shoes, clothing, and accessories, are seen not only on the sports field but in practically every walk of life.

Sony presents another example of this evolution. From its founding in 1946 onwards, Sony has been characterized by a high degree of innovation (Figure 4.29). In 1955, Sony built the first Japanese transistor radio. It developed the first portable stereo, the Walkman, in 1970 and created the world's first CD player in 1982. Parallel to these developments, Sony established a worldwide network of manufacturing sites. But Sony did not stop with conquering the worldwide market for consumer electronics. In 1988, Sony acquired CBS Records, Inc., and founded Sony Music Entertainment. In 1989, it purchased Columbia Pictures as the cornerstone for Sony Pictures Entertainment. This was followed by the debut of the first Sony PlayStation in 1995.[58]

Right from the start, Sony's founder, Akio Morita, advocated distributing all the company's products under a single brand name. This paved the way for the worldwide recognition of the Sony brand. Just as important was the fact that Sony knew how to redefine itself time and again. As a result, not only did Sony continue to be considered one of the world's leading suppliers of information and communication technologies, such as computers, mobile telephones, and microchips, but, in recent years, it has become just

---

Fig. 4.29: Sony: Innovation ensured its success

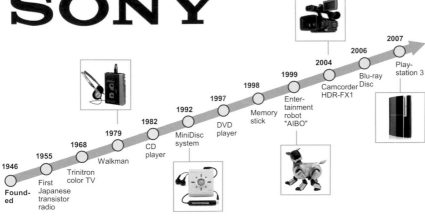

Source: Sony Europe

Managing Brands

as important in entertainment. Sony might have lost its place as the largest consumer electronics manufacturer in the world to Samsung, but its merger with and eventual takeover of BMG (2004 and 2008) made it one of the largest music companies. In the fiscal year 2004/05, Sony, with its some 900 subsidiaries, employed more than 150,000 people around the globe and achieved a revenue of EUR 51.9 billion. Nonetheless, Sony has faced significant challenges in the recent past. Some commentators think it has lost its innovative edge while facing increasing competition from emerging electronics giants, such as Samsung and LG in Korea, or more specialized single-category players such as Lenovo and Acer, both Taiwanese makers of laptop computers. Others have argued that the increasing proliferation of subbrands is unfocused and that vertical silos between divisions have led to the brand's decline in recent years. Howard Stringer, the CEO newly appointed in 2005 and the first non-Japanese to fill this role, has recognized the challenge. At the beginning of his term he stated: »We need to increase the visibility of the Sony brand [...]. We're trying to avoid the downside of fragmentation and create a uniform identity where the sum of the parts is greater than the whole.«[59] As part of its attempt to sharpen the profile of the Sony brand, the company adapted the positioning of the PlayStation brand, originally positioned as the »Sony PlayStation.« Stringer's turnaround program shows some early signs of success; *Business Week's* 2006 brand valuation survey recorded a net gain for Sony in brand value for the first time in five years.[60] In 2006 to 2007, Sony generated global revenues equivalent to EUR 55.4 billion, up 10 percent from the previous year.

Brand management leadership

Akio Morita and Howard Stringer at Sony exemplify the leadership required to build a brand. Brand management has to emanate right from the top. It requires great clarity of vision to develop a company from a single product brand into an umbrella brand with a complex group of companies or subsidiaries that have a diverse range of products, customer target segments, sales channels, and countries of distribution.

Whether the responsibility rests with the chair of the management board or an executive relatively high in the company hierarchy, those involved must have a deep understanding of the company's brand positioning as well as the potential and limits for expanding the brand into other products, sales channels, and countries. In addition to painstaking market research, which is, of course, necessary for systematic planning, interpretation is always required, along with the occasional executive decision on expansion alternatives.

Core marketing skills

Brand management requires a broad range of expertise: product and supply expertise, pricing expertise, promotion management, sales channel management, customer service management, market research skills, and insights that cannot be provided by one person alone. Instead they must be brought together in a marketing team under the supervision of the head of marketing. This person therefore plays a vital role as the coordinator, or perhaps we should say: the integrator of the brand process (Figure 4.30).

The brand integrator has a major task in ensuring that all aspects of brand management are given adequate attention and held in balance, always keeping the long-term health and value-creation potential of the brand in mind. Activities aimed at individual target groups and individual brands need to be orchestrated as part of the development of the umbrella brand. Similarly, product development and marketing need to share a common language about what they are trying to achieve as well as a set of complementary goals. All too often, pricing, sales, and marketing can be at loggerheads or can unwittingly undo whatever the other sets out to achieve. Promotions need to work towards the same ends as advertising. Similarly, the brand integrator needs to manage the external specialists brought in to develop the brand (such as marketing research and advertising experts) and ensure that they, too, are focused around this same set of common goals.

A crucial part of this task is to determine what special marketing expertise is required for the organization and whether this is available in-house or needs to be acquired externally. This requires the marketing leadership to keep up to date with the state of the art in marketing knowledge. It is important for this group to scrutinize the know-how of internal and external specialists, and to ensure that it is robust and applied well. If they fail to do so, marketing organizations face the risk of never moving beyond the conventional answers to important questions. It is all too easy for a successful company to become comfortable with the conventional and complacent about change. Coca-Cola, a well-managed brand, also fell in this trap by being slow to adapt to the general fitness and wellness trend and, in particular, to the growing popularity of mineral water as a branded lifestyle product, rather than a no-name commodity. »The emerging consumer trends in health and wellness were missed,« admitted CEO Isdell in 2004.[61]

Fig. 4.30: The brand manager

Career with logos and slogans
Career perspectives for brand managers by Karsten Kilian

Brands are often a company's most valuable asset for three main reasons: First, launching a new product is usually very expensive. Depending on the industry, a new product introduction can cost as much as EUR 100 million – and the rate of failure is as high as 75 percent. Second, without a strong brand, it is more and more difficult these days to earn above-average profits and avoid a disastrous price war, because most markets are saturated and competition is becoming more international. Current studies confirm that both the return to shareholders and the market capitalization of publicly listed brand-name companies grow faster than that of non-brand-name companies. Third, well-managed brands give the products and services offered a longer lease on life and thus lead to more sales and profits, thereby sustainably increasing corporate value, precisely because product life cycles are shrinking and spending on research and development is continually rising.

Multi-faceted tasks

Brands are becoming more and more important – and this trend is also increasing both the number of career opportunities for brand managers and the requirements that they need to fulfill. The range of tasks is as multi-faceted as the qualifications a typical brand manager brings to the job. There is no single profile for a "brand manager." In consumer goods, one finds MBAs who have specialized in marketing; in advertising and the entertainment industry, brand managers are more likely to have a background in commu-nications or design; and some have made a lateral career switch from a completely different field …

… The brand manager's specific tasks depend on the industry and the type of product and services offered. The work often overlaps with that of marketing and product managers and is therefore subsumed in these positions. The core task of a brand manager is to establish the optimal design of the identity of one or more brands and to improve it continually. The starting point for this is permanent monitoring of the twists, turns, and trends in the market. The brand manager's efforts are dedicated to establishing a clear and differentiated performance profile. The objective is to satisfy customers and gain their trust, keep the brand up-to-date and appealing, and build customer loyalty. The work of a brand manager at Kraft Foods, for example, includes finding answers to the following questions: "How is the brand presented? In what direction should it be developed? Which products are included in the current portfolio? How will we market them? Which target groups should be addressed now and in the future? How should we position a new product?"

In the past, brand management was mainly focused on products. But with the shift to a service and information economy, the range of roles has expanded. Brand managers today are increasingly employed by service companies and also by cities and regions. Even hospitals and universities are working on professionalizing their brand management.

SAP, the worldwide market leader in business administration software, is another example of a strong company initially missing out. SAP did not recognize the importance of the Internet revolution early enough. Assuming this invention was just a fad, it underestimated the importance of the innovation. Once it recognized this mistake, SAP adjusted its brand and charted a new course into the network era by developing the mySAP.com software. Within three years, it started once again to close the gap with its competitors and is currently the indisputable market leader.[62]

One of the most critical roles in marketing is that of the integrator. It is also one of the most difficult to fill, as only rarely can the necessary skills be acquired through training in special marketing departments or through job rotation between marketing, sales, and other departments. As a manager, the integrator needs to have the fundamental capability of being able to find the right balance between art, science, and craft and then to make decisions that are consistent in the longer term (while meeting shorter-term targets, or at least managing expectations around them). Ideal brand integrators do much more than just love the brand; they must be able to demonstrate it on a daily basis, both internally to the company's employees, and externally. This is the capability that Wendelin Wiedeking displays at Porsche, Lindsay Owen-Jones at L'Oréal, and Sir Richard Branson at Virgin.

The organization's leadership needs to be able to make effective use of marketing expertise in their decision-making processes. Conversely, this expertise shouldn't be allowed to hold the organization hostage. As the brand leader, the integrator on the one hand needs to be receptive to special knowledge, but on the other hand, he or she must make decisions independently in the end. Only when this balance is maintained can speed of action be ensured. In the fast-moving world of brands, letting things degenerate into consensus-seeking can spell disaster.

4.5 Involving External Service Providers: True Partnerships that Lead to Joint Success

Every brand will need to engage external assistance at many points along its journey to success. Any successful brand that hasn't done so is the exception that proves the rule.

Brand management must not only combine art, science, and craft, but do so while relying on external specialists in many fields. Regardless of how well-qualified the marketing department of a company might be, it is never likely to be in a position to manage all these tasks without external assistance. Communicating a good brand concept requires the outstanding *art* and creativity of an advertising agency as well as the network and ideas of a good PR consultant. The *craft* requires the technical proficiency of a market research institute in measuring consumer needs and in producing the right market segmentation as well as an experienced media agency's target group understanding and touch point expertise. The *science* requires thorough analysis by independent and objective specialists on issues of brand valuation, strategy, and portfolio management.

Such relationships often prove to be of a long-term nature, as a true partnership is developed around the brand. In advertising communications, there are many long-lasting relationships. TBWA has been working with Absolut Vodka since 1981 and is currently promoting the brand in 48 countries. Since the mid-1990s, it has also had a relationship with Apple, which it currently serves in 23 countries. Nestlé and McCann-Erickson have worked together for more than 25 years. BBDO and Pepsi have been partners since the early 1980s. McDonald's established its cooperation with Heye & Partner in 1971.[63] As part of the DDB network, Heye & Partner created the concept for McDonald's »I'm loving it« campaign that was rolled out globally.[64] Sports goods giant Nike's partnership with Wieden + Kennedy dates back to the early 1980s. The agency was started, at the suggestion of Nike's then-CEO Phil Knight, as a two-person boutique by Dan Wieden and David Kennedy. The agency has grown with its client; Wieden + Kennedy currently employs some 500 people and has offices in London, Amsterdam, Tokyo, and New York City.[65] Strong brands often have similar long-standing relationships with market research institutes, media agencies, and other external service providers.

Some brand managers even go so far as to concentrate on defining the concept, the positioning for the respective target group, and the corresponding brand value proposition, and leave everything else to external service providers. The Red Bull brand, for instance, now a company with annual sales of more than EUR 2.1 billion, was the brainchild of the brand manager (Red Bull's owner, Dietrich Mateschitz), who developed the concept from an initial idea. The agency Kastner & Partner in Frankfurt was responsible for the creative implementation of the concept, the fruit juice giant Rauch took over responsibility for production, and local associations are responsible for distribution.[66]

Both Adidas and Nike operate in a similar way, retaining their areas of core expertise in product development and design in-house, while relying almost exclusively on Asian suppliers for manufacturing. Certain luxury goods manufacturers monitor the design and manufacturing of their main product lines, but grant licenses for brand extensions. Such developments are evident even in the automotive industry. Porsche is responsible for the concept and distribution of its Boxster model; almost everything else is taken care of by external service providers.

In many cases, the success of a brand would not have happened if it had not been for the cooperation between the company's brand managers, the

Fig. 4.31: Sixt campaigns: Witty, provocative, and successful

Source: Sixt AG

creative agency, and other external service providers. The Sixt brand, for instance, reached today's level of success through such a partnership. In the mid-1980s, there was only average awareness of Erich Sixt's car rental company in Germany. Then Sixt hired the creative advertising expert Jean-Remy von Matt to generate a highly creative but inexpensive communication approach. The resulting campaigns were successful in ensuring a rapid increase in awareness among the target group of business travelers in Germany.

Through its humorous, at times provocative, and aggressive communication strategy, Sixt grew to become the industry leader in Germany in the 1990s and one of the largest car rental companies in Europe. By 2005, Sixt had achieved a market share of 26 percent in Germany and became number one, overtaking its competitor and European market leader Europcar. In 2007, Sixt's market share climbed to 29 percent.[67] It is indisputable that Sixt's advertising images possess a unique recognition value. Their approach is considered lively and attention-grabbing, featuring advertisements that now have near-cult status in their target group (Figure 4.31). Yet these campaigns were inexpensive. In 2001, it cost just EUR 100,000 to place the controversial E-Sixt advertisement making fun of conservative

German politician (now chancellor) Angela Merkel's hairstyle. The advertisement ran only once, but the total value of the resulting press coverage is estimated to have exceeded EUR 3 million.[68] In 2006, the campaign was modestly relaunched with updated imagery and design that did not significantly change the key message. Sixt has been more successful than most other companies in running excellent, creative, and consistent campaigns that contribute to its reputation and, even more importantly, increase its revenues.

Involving external service providers is not without its pitfalls

There are many problems that companies face when working with external service providers. These can be classified usefully into five categories: (1) identifying suitable potential service providers, (2) selecting the right external partners, (3) optimizing the use of external partners over the longer term, (4) assessing performance, and (5) setting financial compensation and incentives.

Identifying suitable service providers: In selecting suitable external service providers, companies are forced to rely largely on word-of-mouth and personal references. Even today, there's no systematic evaluation of the qualifications of external service providers. Although isolated rankings by university institutes may appear periodically in newspapers and magazines, they are rarely sufficiently detailed to be of use in decision making.

Successful partnerships are often the result of a degree of serendipity. For instance, in 1988 British American Tobacco (BAT) found in KNS (Knopf, Nägeli, Schnakenberg, now KNSK and a member of the BBDO/Omnicom network) the optimal partner for the Germany-wide launch of a filter version of its Lucky Strike cigarettes. At the time, KNS was still a small and unknown agency based in Hamburg. KNS had started working with Pall Mall, one of BAT's four global brands, in 1987. Its other major client was the brewery Lüneberger Pils. In facing the challenge of developing a modern, believable campaign for Lucky Strike, the agency rejected the then-current advertising images of the brand owner, American Brands, which used »cool« motorcycle riders in the style of *Easy Rider*. KNS believed that these images were too similar to the Marlboro cowboy. Instead, the creative team selected a minimalist approach, shifting the focus to the cigarette packet, with the addition of a witty headline, »Lucky Strike. Nothing else.« (Figure 4.32).

Whereas the concept initially focused on large cities and a target group of 18- to 29-year-old male smoker, the advertisements later ran throughout

Fig. 4.32: Lucky Strike campaigns: The product is the star

1988	1994	2008
Do you smoke ads or cigarettes? Lucky Strike. Nothing else.	Fewer than 5% of our smokers are horse owners. Lucky Strike. Nothing else.	iSmoke. Lucky Strike. Nothing else.

Source: British American Tobacco (Germany) GmbH

Germany and were expanded to appeal to female smokers and to the age group up to 39. Since the launch of the campaign, some 3,000 Lucky Strike print advertisements and numerous cinema advertisements have been released, all in accordance with the same underlying idea but always with a different angle and topic.[69]

Lucky Strike was the most successful cigarette launch in Germany in the past 15 years. As early as 1994, Lucky Strike ranked among the top ten German cigarette brands. BAT cautiously expanded the initial filter product line to include Lucky Strike Lights (1991), Lucky Strike Big Pack (1995), and Lucky Strike Ultra (1999). By 2002, it was number three in the market and the brand family had a market share of more than 5 percent. In May 2003 Lights and Ultra were removed from the market and replaced by the newly developed, more sophisticated Lucky Strike Silver.

Despite KNSK's past success, Lucky Strike decided, in February 2005, on a new creative partner in Germany and switched to G2 Hamburg, ending a 16-year partnership. BAT explained this change by emphasizing the increasing imponderability of tobacco advertising and the advantages of a global network. G2 Hamburg is part of the WPP network, which serves Lucky Strike as well as other BAT brands in all its other markets.

The pitch: selecting the right external service provider. Making a selection from several potential providers is always difficult. The traditional approach

303

used by advertising agencies is the *pitch,* in which the agency makes a presentation to the potential client in order to sell its campaign ideas. For the agencies, such competitive presentations are the typical method for acquiring new business. According to a 2002 survey of the 100 largest agencies in Germany by the online magazine *werben & verkaufen,* a German journal on advertising and media, 41 percent of new business arises through competitive presentations. Another 25 percent of new clients are acquired through recommendations.[70]

A large amount of money is invested in such presentations. On average, the cost of applying for an important contract lies between EUR 30,000 and EUR 50,000, but can run as high as EUR 100,000. Pitches are usually paid for in part by the client, but the payment typically covers only 30 percent of the costs. Volkswagen's competitive pitch for the launch of its high-end Phaeton model is an example of how this practice can lead to agencies spending a great deal of time and money on a pitch. Volkswagen's lead agency, DDB, spared no expense to win the contract. Its creative team worked almost exclusively on their presentation for six months, at times involving as many as 50 employees. Unfortunately, their hard work didn't pay off, as Grabarz & Partner from Hamburg won the competition, leaving DDB to make up for its out-of-pocket expenses elsewhere.[70] A similar situation occurred when the agencies MECH, DDB Berlin, and Leo Burnett (as well as Interone and Wundermann) competed in 2005 for Lufthansa's prestigious classic and dialog media budget. Lufthansa decided in favor of its old account holders MECH and Wundermann in June that year, after almost six months of unpaid competition.

The high cost isn't the only problem with competitive pitches; the procedure also rarely leads to the optimal result. Outstanding creative work depends on the agency having a thorough understanding of the brand. For this, it needs to have access to the detail and background of the brand, its strengths and weaknesses, its brand proposition, and other similar factors. It is rare for this information to be available in a competitive pitch, but even when it is, it is usually impossible for the agency to grasp it fully and process it properly in the brief application period. As a result, it is not uncommon for agencies to concentrate almost exclusively on the purely creative end of things. This leaves the management board in the position of having to make a selection based on their own judgment of the agencies' creativity. This situation is far from optimal. First of all, the board seldom belongs to the target group to which the product or brand is to be marketed, and so they lack an insider perspective. Second, with the exception of the marketing manager, most board members are typically not properly qualified to assess advertising campaigns and creative concepts. Third, the assessment often does not follow any transparent criteria or a predefined scoring system, but is simply based on gut feeling. That isn't playing to management strengths, so the management is forced to rely on the explanation and rationale the agencies present to them in making their choice among creative ideas. The same goes for media agencies. In an ideal world, media agency selection should be governed by a critical assessment of the agency's understanding of the target group, insight into consumers' media usage, and touch point expertise. But unfortunately, most campaign plans and activation roadmaps look the same to untrained eyes.

What can be done to improve this situation? A different approach might be to select a creative agency on the basis of one of its previous executions, choosing those that have produced similar campaigns in the past. The agencies would need to prove their comprehension of the issues and present a suitable advertising campaign from their repertoire, including solutions that could be transferred from previous campaigns. That makes it much easier for the company to assess the qualifications of the service providers. This, after all, is the decisive criterion, as each agency is dependent on the creative skills already inherent in its business. Such a process would reduce the total expenditures of time, effort, and money for all parties considerably. It could also be carried out much more quickly and lead to better results. Although this process may perhaps be seen to handicap new and innovative agencies that don't have a lot of history behind them, it should still be an important (although not exclusive) part of the decision criteria. The time has come to reconsider the conventional pitch process and incorporate new ways of thinking. To a certain extent, advertising awards can serve as a proxy of past campaign performance. The creative or conceptual merits of a campaign or agency alone may not be direct indicators of bottom-line impact. But recent research indicates that, other things being equal, creativity does indeed boost a campaign's economic impact (for details, see the insert on creative advertising in section 1.2). That said, brand managers still prefer awards that also reflect advertising impact directly, such as the Effies that were set up specifically to reward »ideas that work,« to awards that only look at creativity, such as the Cannes Lions.

Optimizing the use of external partners. As a partnership develops with an external service provider in the longer term, it is important to ensure that there is continuity of personnel on both sides of the relationship. Since experience and good judgment are critical, this continuity over the course of years is a key criterion for managing the relationship successfully. Yet the reality is that large, top-performing companies encourage a rapid turnover of brand managers in order to develop their employees' skills. In order to get around the problem of lack of continuity, they institutionalize their capabilities. This can be seen at both Unilever and Procter & Gamble, where the product or brand manager is changed every couple of years. What is important is consistency. Incessant relaunches and the associated changes in brand positioning, or frequent switching from one agency to another, can dilute the brand profile and thereby weaken the brand in the longer term.

In order to establish consistency across regions, companies are increasingly consolidating their accounts around a single agency that handles the entire budget over substantial periods of time, as the example of HSBC shows. Until 2004, HSBC spread its USD 600 million account across hundreds of agencies. After an extensive review, HSBC consolidated its business with the WPP Group, working directly with one single point of contact. Peter Stringham, Group General Manager of Marketing for HSBC, argues that »HSBC is keen to integrate its marketing more effectively, to apply brand and communications strategies consistently, and to maximize synergies and cost-effectiveness across the Group.«[71] But consistency isn't everything. To combine the benefits of global consistency with local relevance, Coca-Cola has pioneered a global advertising model that is based on a single creative idea to be developed centrally, in some cases even by non-traditional »rogue« agencies, and orchestrated by local agencies.[71]

This is not to say that all long-term or single-source relationships are healthy. They are also associated with a danger: the risk of insufficient adaptation to modern developments. An example of this is the Jägermeister brand, which tiresomely recycled its claim »I drink Jägermeister because ...« in more than 3,500 advertisements. Although the brand remained highly profitable, it did not grow. It was not until 1998, when Hasso Kaempfe took over leadership from Günter Mast and started to work with new agencies (first the Hamburg-based agency Economia and, from 2002 onwards, Philipp und Keuntje) that the brand was updated and internationalized, and its potential for growth was again realized.[72] Since then, average revenue has increased by approximately 5 percent annually, rising from DM 365 million in 1998 (EUR 187 million) to EUR 294 million in 2004. About 70 percent of all Jägermeister bottles were sold outside Germany in 2004, two-thirds of them to the United States. It was these foreign markets that drove the overall growth of the brand. With this approach, Jägermeister was able to achieve an overall return on sales before tax of more than 30 percent in 2004.[73] In its most recent and possibly most unusual feat, Philipp und Keuntje has the company promoting the brand's »wild« image by showing

Managing Brands

Fig. 4.33: Fresh thinking from new agencies – "Indirect brand building": Philipp und Keuntje campaign for Jägermeister

"This isn't Jägermeister. Pretty tame."

Bringing the brand to life by showing what it is not

Source: Philipp und Keuntje, Picture: Mast-Jägermeister AG

what Jägermeister is not, namely, »tame« (»Kein Jägermeister«; in English: »No Jägermeister«) (Figure 4.33).

But even when brand managers consciously decide against changing horses, they are well advised to probe whether what they expect is what they get from long-term agency relationships. Because of churn and frequent account team changes within many agencies, staying with the same agency for a long time does not necessarily protect companies from inconsistencies or brain drain. As a consequence, the benefits of the fresh thinking that often comes from challenger agencies can outweigh the assumed advantages of long-term agency loyalty. More and more companies are moving from the now classic model of a single roster agency to a small group or even a larger pool of agencies, either instead of or in addition to their lead agency. Ikea, for example, is among the companies working with multiple creative agency partners. The company has modularized its creative service requirements and selects agency partners depending on the media for which a creative concept is to be developed. Since 2004, Ikea has worked with a network of partners. While the company adheres to the concept of the lead agency, e.g., Grabarz & Partner for classical advertising and Grimm Gallun Holtappels for Internet marketing in Germany, Ikea also works with other agencies on a project basis, e.g., Nordpol. So far, the approach seems to be working for Ikea. Grabarz & Partner has developed a deep understanding of the company's evolving brand promise that combines affordability with the idea of a holistic experience (see section 1.2).

Other companies stick with a global roster agency, but invite external agencies to pitch for specific projects selected based on budget, strategic importance, special skill requirements, or type of communication objective. For example, the lead agency may be in charge of brand campaigns, while selected product launches may be handled by challenger agencies. Time will tell which agency cooperation models are successful. However, even with innovative strategies such as pools of challenger agencies, selective pitches, or modularized service procurement, companies cannot afford to neglect the overall success factor of consistency, especially regarding external partners.

The 2008 Art Directors Club of Europe awards show that both longstanding relationships and more flexible collaboration models can lead to success. Both Sixt's long-term partner Jung von Matt and Ikea's creative collaborator in Germany, Grabarz & Partner, walked away with awards (Figures 4.31 and 4.34).

Increasingly, optimal results depend on more than just managing individual service providers effectively. Successful brand communication is never the work of a soloist, but of an orchestra of highly specialized professionals. Not only do agencies have to develop a deep understanding of their clients'

Fig. 4.34: Award-winning visual for Ikea

Source: Inter IKEA Systems B.V.

brands and target groups to provide superior services, but they also need to connect with each other. As a consequence, the brand manager and his or her team need to go beyond requesting services from various types of agencies individually. The creative agency can hardly develop meaningful ideas without a sound understanding of brand objectives and relevant touch points. What good is a groundbreaking creative idea when it cannot be properly activated given the target group's media usage and decision-making patterns? Similarly, the media agency depends on a creative idea that is universal or at least applicable to the media and channels that are used by the target group. A great idea for a TV commercial may be useless for a younger, technology-savvy audience that gets its kicks online or by word of mouth. Further down the communication chain, production firms cannot unleash the full power of their skills unless well briefed by the creative team. A vague production briefing will almost inevitably lead to loops over loops of reshoots and other revisions that are as time-consuming as they are costly. In short, coordination is key. This is all the more true as agencies are expanding their service portfolios and integrating upward or downward in the communication planning process. Many creative agencies such as TBWA and McCann also offer touch point strategy planning or media buying to capture a bigger slice of the advertising budget. Similarly, media agencies such as OMD and Carat offer more strategic planning to justify higher fees. As a consequence, creative and media agencies increasingly see each other as competitors because of the forward integration of the former (i.e., creative agencies developing touch point strategy) and the backward integration of the latter (i.e., media agencies providing strategic communication planning and consulting). Says Jim Taylor, formerly of Ogilvy & Partners and founder of Nota Bene, South Africa's self-proclaimed »first media strategy agency«: »The communications industry is in a period of structural and cultural turmoil, based on the collapse of the full-service agency model.«[74]

In short, successful service provider steering is not simply about managing a single one-stop-shopping partner, or even multiple agency relationships individually. It is about coordinating a network of partners that will often include the client's own product development, marketing, and distribution departments. The overarching objective is to foster a smooth flow of information, joint problem solving, and, ultimately, integrated creative concepts and brand activation solutions. Nevertheless, some success factors still depend on the type of service provider:

- **Creative agencies:** Other things being equal, a good brief that clearly specifies brand or product objectives is the key to a successful creation and campaign. A communication planner in a luxury-goods company says:

»Creative teams work off the page of the brief.« The challenge is to find the right mix between effective performance incentives (tell the agency exactly what you want to achieve and tie the objective to compensation) and the freedom the agency team needs to unfold its creativity. For details, refer to section 1.2.

- **Media agencies:** What matters most is that the media planner is sufficiently qualified and has all the information required to develop a deep understanding of the brand's target groups, including their media and channel usage patterns as well as their decision-making styles. Furthermore, it is key to facilitate the media agency's interaction with the creative agency to ensure creative ideas are well orchestrated and consistently delivered at critical touch points.

- **Production service providers:** Depending on the lead agency's service portfolio, it can be beneficial to put all production steering and quality management in the hands of the creative agency to ensure consistent communication quality. Leading marketers such as Procter & Gamble have their creative agency coordinate all production at no extra cost.

- **Market research agencies:** While ad hoc concept testing or pre-entry investigations of new markets and categories may be provided by specialized or local agencies, consistency is key in the relationship with the lead research agency. Sustainable brand management is impossible without reliable tracking of brand image as well as consumer needs and attitudes over extended periods of time. For details, refer to section 2.2.

As far as actual media buying is concerned, companies should be wary of overstepping the limits of optimization. Too much pressure to reduce fees or commissions for media planning and buying can lead to so much margin pressure that agencies may be tempted to resort to dangerous practices that may come back to haunt their clients. Recently, covert alliances between sellers of advertising space (e.g., publishers or television networks), media agencies, supposedly independent third-party auditors, and clients' procurement departments have led to arrangements bordering on the illegal, or even crossing the line drawn by antitrust legislation, anticorruption laws, and competition protection acts. It is widely known that sellers of advertising space often grant massive rebates to major advertisers, sometimes as high as 50 percent of the listed price (see the discussion of nominal versus real cost of contacts in section 4.3). These kickbacks act as an incentive for agencies and clients to pool advertising volume; some intermediary players are known to live off nothing but kickbacks, which they don't (fully) disclose to their clients. Some executives have even found themselves subject to criminal investigations.[75]

Assessment of performance: Advertising campaigns, market research methods, and other external services need to be reviewed periodically. This process should encompass a formal assessment of the performance of external service providers. In section 4.3 we addressed the topic of the Brand Cockpit. As much as is practicable, the performance of external service providers should be included in the Brand Cockpit metrics. Leading companies are in the process of forming mixed teams that comprise experts from their brand management, procurement, functional controlling, and market research departments to ensure consistent and sustainable monitoring of agency performance.

Each external provider will require a different method of assessment. Ideally, this should involve a handful of tailored key performance indicators. A market research institute, for example, can be assessed in terms of its precision and the quality of its forecasts based on its own market research. An advertising agency can be evaluated against the targets it achieves in the rates of awareness, recall, and recognition, as well as in the comprehension of its advertising messages. Including such metrics in a Brand Cockpit, and using the cockpit for agency performance monitoring, is a way of tying management to measurement. It also helps to align the steering of service providers with the wider BrandMatics® approach. Core BrandMatics® frameworks such as the consumer purchase funnel (see section 2.4) are well established these days, even in the agency world. As a consequence, changes in funnel-related attitudinal metrics, such as brand awareness, familiarity, or purchase intention, are well suited to monitoring the performance of agencies that provide client-facing services such as advertising campaigns, media planning, point-of-sale materials, or loyalty programs.

The process of evaluation need not become overly burdensome. It is sufficient to calculate a few performance indicators for each external service provider. This is not to underestimate the importance of the evaluation, however. Indeed, the corporate center's role in evaluating the performance of the marketing organization needs to be directed largely towards the performance of external service providers. As is the case in all other business functions, performance indicators are often only taken seriously if they are compiled by a neutral third party.

Setting financial compensation and incentives: The classic agency compensation model, a commission fee on total advertising spending (typically 5 to 10 percent for creative agencies and 2 to 6 percent for media agencies), has many obvious disadvantages. Not only does it incite agencies to favor »expensive« classic media over potentially more efficient or innovative below-the-line touch points. It also gives companies an incentive to cut back

311

on upfront planning and keep requesting reworks from their agencies, simply because they come at no additional cost. Therefore it's no surprise that a 2007 survey among German advertisers (GWA) shows that the traditional commission is going out of style; its use has decreased by 60 percent over the past three years. At the same time, performance-based compensation is spreading. According to industry estimates, as early as 2003 a total of 80 to 90 percent of *new* contracts signed with agencies included performance-based components.[76] In a survey conducted by the Association of National Advertisers (ANA) in the United States in 2006, 47 percent of all respondents said they used performance incentives as part of their agency compensation systems, for creative and media agencies as well as for direct marketing agencies. Nearly 70 percent say this helps to maintain (11 percent) or improve (58 percent) agency performance, and an overwhelming majority of advertisers surveyed say they will continue to use performance incentives (82 percent). As the basis for such incentives, most players (53 percent) use a combination of client and agency performance. Popular indicators include agency performance review scores (82 percent) and client sales or client brand/advertising awareness (more than 50 percent). Only a minority uses market share or profit targets (24 percent).[76]

In typical performance-based models, a share (often 20 percent) of the payment depends on achieving objectives defined as part of the contract. As indicated by the ANA survey results, these objectives are most commonly quantitative targets, but qualitative criteria are also widely used. Common quantitative targets include achieving planned sales figures, acquiring new customers or leads, or changes in market share. Communication-related quantitative targets include indicators of awareness building, recall values, customer attitudes towards the product, and brand loyalty. The qualitative criteria include assessments of how well the partnership is functioning, the quality of the services provided, and the overall impression of the agency's creative work.[76] Many of these performance models already seem to be standard, or at least this is what most companies would argue. At any rate, advertisers say they increasingly use performance incentives as part of their agency compensation (Figure 4.35). Overusing targets can cause problems, however. Reaching agreement on targets and evaluation parameters can prove difficult. All too easily, a company can develop a highly complex compensation package that succeeds only in producing time-consuming debate. Moreover, the underlying conditions that first led to the specification of the targets might well change during the course of the evaluation period. Also, not all indicators are under the agency's full control. A campaign's success is typically driven by the level of activation spending as much as by

Fig. 4.35: Agency payment practices

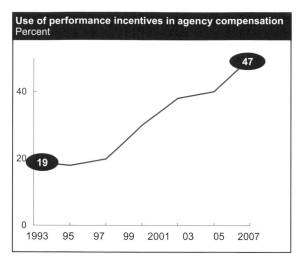

Use of performance incentives in agency compensation
Percent

"The use of performance incentives continues to grow, and is generally gaining popularity across the board, regardless of advertiser type or size, or type of agency service."

– Association of National Advertisers (ANA), "Trends in Agency Compensation 2007"

Source: Association of National Advertisers (ANA)

its creative quality, and the media budget is under the client's, not the agency's, control. Even competitor moves have an influence on communication impact. The same campaign, with the same activation spending, may be successful in a »quiet« quarter, but ineffective in a period of high competitive advertising noise, or when challenged head-on by a strong competitor campaign. Measuring performance is even more difficult when a company has engaged several agencies simultaneously.

The goal of all remuneration systems should be to compensate high-quality work fairly, to maintain the objectivity of the external service provider, and to secure its interest in the success of the brand. It is also clear that concentrating on price components may lead to unsatisfactory or unprofessional work by the service provider. This problem is independent of whether the remuneration model is input-oriented or output-oriented; the outcome ultimately depends on the level and quality of effort invested in the service performed. The recent increase in criticism of and dissatisfaction with the creative work of agencies is not surprising in light of the increasingly price-driven selection processes, including unpaid pitches. Good services require good money. This rule applies as much to the war for talent as it does to the selection and compensation of external service providers. The art, craft, and science that go into building successful brands are very different from raw materials or energy. While it may make sense to bargain for supplies that can be easily replaced, it can be just as rational to pay above-average fees for superior creative and professional services. Brilliant ideas are anything but a commodity. Creative agencies, in particular, tend to do their best work as their clients' performance partners. Trying to pinch a few pennies in agency fees has, on occassion, proved a risky strategy. Few companies would want to suffer the drain in expertise and experience that comes from their creative agency dropping the account in favor of a larger, more exciting, or more generous competitor. In other areas, such as media buying and advertising production, cost cutting and hard bargaining are less risky. Bundled buying, requests for quotes, and resolute auditing can yield substantial savings without any perceptible changes to the services provided. As has already been stressed, strong brands require strong partnerships with external providers. One implication of this is that short-term hiring and firing of service providers needs to be avoided. Too much change, with the hectic coming-and-going of external partners, can weaken the brand. The basics of any relationship between the brand management and external service providers are those of strong motivation, long-term dedication, and trust-based cooperation.

Agencies themselves can play an active role in improving relationships. New incentives, such as licensing, could be deployed as part of the agency's remuneration package to reduce the risk of agency hopping. With this approach, in exchange for their highly creative work, agencies would receive a corresponding license fee during the time their work is used by the company. Hence, if the company plans to switch agencies, then its use of the agency's work would either cease or, alternatively, the rights to the work would be purchased by the subsequent agency. Of course, a single agency alone, regardless of its quality, cannot achieve such a revolution in payment practices. The umbrella organizations of the advertising industry, such as the World Federation of Advertisers (WFA) or its local counterparts such as the OWM in Germany (Organisation Werbetreibende im Markenverband), need to pave the way for such changes.

A company's decision to change agencies can produce explosive and unpredictable results. For example, the debate about the Sixt contract between Jung von Matt and BBDO, which flared up in early 2004, eventually engulfed practically the entire German advertising industry and much of the media.[77] In the end, Jung von Matt retained the contract, which was most likely the right decision, as it was in the interest of consistent brand management.

Interview with Chris Burggraeve:
»New Models and Measurements to Stay
the Number One Global Brand in the Digital Age«

Coca-Cola as a brand truly needs no introduction. In 2006, Interbrand ranked it number one in the world in terms of brand value, estimating its value at USD 67 billion. Chris Burggraeve, as the Group Marketing Director of Coca-Cola's European Union Group, is responsible for marketing and branding this giant across Europe. After a career start in consulting and with Procter & Gamble, he has worked in a variety of marketing positions and in general management in European markets since joining Coke in 1995. Jesko Perrey, co-author of this book, spoke to Chris Burggraeve about brand management at Coca-Cola. – In November 2007, Chris Burggraeve joined InBev, the Belgium-based international brewery, as Chief Marketing Officer.

Jesko Perrey: Marketing is facing huge challenges in the proliferation of markets, customer segments, media, and so on. How are you tackling these changes at Coke?

Chris Burggraeve: On the one hand, these trends are challenging, but at Coke we see proliferation as an opportunity. Consumers require more choices today, and that gives us the chance to deliver against those different preferences. We have more opportunities for customer segmentation and for different offerings by segment. That means that we, as a company, have more chances to differentiate ourselves and to capture the premium in each segment.

Jesko Perrey: Coke is telling one of the most impressive brand stories in history. How have you managed to be so strong for such a long time?

Chris Burggraeve: Well, yes, Coke has been pretty successful over the last 120 years. But I would like to emphasize that we don't feel like we're 120. As we see it, we're just getting started. We're on a journey with our consumers.

In the nineteenth century, we started with one formula, the famous Secret Coke formula. This was a bit like Henry Ford and his Model-T. One could get a Ford T in any color, as long as it was black. Over time however, step-by-step, we have developed this one Secret Formula into what I would call a »MySecretFormula.com« idea. In the twenty-first century, our aim is one-to-one customization and personalization. Ideally we deliver each consumer a fully tailored choice, and communicate accordingly.

What does it mean for marketing if we see our consumer as the real »chief marketing officer?« We still have classical marketing functions in place, but we're looking at them in a broader way. For example, we are seeing R&D more and more as a function within marketing. We believe it can drive differentiation with new beverages, unique flavors, fresh packaging, and different sizes. We also develop and innovate our go-to-market models, meaning the way we serve our customers and consumers. To deliver against the MySecretFormula.com model, we are trying to provide a 100 percent tailored solution. Our ultimate destination is serving every single customer with a special go-to-market approach. Mass marketing to one. Or if »one« is not possible yet, at least to the smallest manageable cluster.

Jesko Perrey: Getting all these things done sounds like a big challenge. How do you manage a global brand without losing perspective on local tastes and preferences?

Chris Burggraeve: Over the years, we have moved from a more global approach based on our franchise system to what I think is a reasonably balanced global versus local approach. We call it »Freedom within a Framework.« While we need to leverage our scale in global processes, we also need to be as local as possible. In our multiple international R&D centers, for example, we focus on the D in R&D, tackling local/regional innovation challenges, whereas the global center focuses more on the R. In Germany, this might be dealing with the specific issue of returnable packages. In Japan, we have to think carefully about vending machines. But you saw recently the new global Coke campaign »The Coke Side of Life«: one idea, executed locally, but globally recognizable.

Jesko Perrey: Despite any controversy today about the proper way to measure brand equity, Coke has been the most valuable brand in the world for many years. How important is this strong brand equity, and how do you leverage it for further growth?

Chris Burggraeve: Our brand valuation is pretty high, yes. This is a well-deserved reflection of our collective work on this brand over the past 120 years. However, the past is the past. We need to generate shareholder value for the coming 120 years as well. That's why we're asking ourselves how to translate brand strength into a convincing growth story in the context of the next decades. We need to help the capital markets understand that Coke's core business is still growing and that we have lots of other growth opportunities.

When we look at total worldwide liquid consumption, we see that Coke's volume accounts for only about 3 percent. So, in terms of upside, Coke still has 97 percent of the market to conquer. That's an enormous opportunity, and every drop counts! We are developing to become truly a total beverage company, beyond Coca-Coca and soft drinks. We are thinking through the MySecretFormula.com approach with offerings in different beverage categories, for different times of the day, in different packages, different occasions, new distribution models, across 200+ markets. This is a fabulous growth story, and one we need to communicate clearly to investors.

Jesko Perrey: That sounds very interesting! Is this shift also a reason for the first corporate communication campaign that you recently launched?

Chris Burggraeve: Exactly. Marketers of today need to look beyond classic brand management. Today, somebody who offers choice is perceived as more relevant and more positively. In our marketing of today, we need to consider all relevant target groups. Of course, some key targets do not change: our customers, our retailers, and so on. But we also have to reach our shareholders and stakeholders. We need to mention that we are selling not only Coke but also light drinks, juices, teas, sport drinks, water; choices for almost every occasion. We also have a huge responsibility for our employees and are heavily engaged in the field of health care; we continue to support an active lifestyle at large.

So, if you look at the company as a pyramid, as marketers we now deal with corporate branding, category branding and category perception management, shopper/channel marketing, and then brand management at the top. It used to be that marketers in Coke were only doing pure brand management. That was the way I was also trained at Procter & Gamble. We spent a lot of our time with classic product research and creating TV ads. Today, I want our marketers to think much wider. The same hundred dollars of marketing could be reasonably invested not just in brand management or between brand portfolios or between the various media, but also in all other related functions and areas. For example, we may be losing consumers who don't want to buy Coca-Cola because they have a problem with the corporation. If you don't solve that problem first, what is the point of having sexy ads on TV? Marketers need to think holistically about the business issues and opportunities at hand and allocate resources accordingly.

Jesko Perrey: As you consider communications strategies, how do you deal with the variety of media and their proliferation?

Chris Burggraeve: Media is usually where most of the marketing money is invested. Some people still think it's an easy decision; they say: »I need 52 weeks of television, good-bye.« And then twelve months times two million dollars walk out the door. But a year of Internet for a million or even a hundred thousand dollars in other forms of word-of-mouth campaigns can make a bigger impact and deliver a better RoI – if you hit the right chord. From my perspective, one of the biggest changes in classic brand management is the move from analog to digital. It's still happening. Three or four years ago, a German magazine reported that fewer than 6 percent of the marketing directors in Germany were even thinking about digital marketing. Most didn't even *want* to think about it.

I've been told that the number now reaches 80 percent, yet for many that just means buying some banner ads and opening a Web site. The percentage of people who *really* leverage the promise of digital in their marketing mix and invest accordingly are probably in the single digits or low double digits. To us at Coke that's great, because it gives us more time to stay ahead and be different with the Coke brand portfolio. Coke decided to be a pioneer in the »new media« and, since then, has never looked back. Coke does not want to be a pure-play digital brand like the Googles or Yahoos or YouTubes of the world. We sell »dreams in bottles,« after all. But we owe it to ourselves as the number one global brand to do what we can to remain a leading brand in the digital age.

Jesko Perrey: How do you think about media strategy and marketing mix at Coke? What's the difference?

Chris Burggraeve: Today, media strategy is about touch points or, more precisely, identifying the relevant touch points and then having one creative core idea »conjugated« over all of them. So, to avoid proliferation, you need one idea that you can flex across all those touch points. You'll find »The Coke Side of Life« expressed on the Internet, in print media, and on TV, and you find it in the sales folder when you enter this building. Everything should give you that »Coke Side of Life« experience and messaging. Every touch point tells you: Coke is about optimism. You buy »happiness in a bottle.«

More than ever, when we work with our outside agencies and inside communication experts, we need the iron discipline to stick to what Coke wants to communicate from a message point of view. We created a framework for that, with clear rules about how to use the degrees of freedom inside the boundaries of the framework. And we invested a lot of time in creating the capabilities in the system across our teams and with our agencies to bring this approach to life globally.

Jesko Perrey: Consumer touch points or, more precisely, stakeholder touch points are very different. How do you actually measure marketing RoI, considering these differences?

Chris Burggraeve: In the end, marketing is really about finance. The objective is to grow brand contribution sustainably over time. We do measure our equity scores. Equity helps to justify premiums, and we are getting a bit more sophisticated in the way we are measuring them. And faster. But in the end, the essence of brand management to me has not changed in terms of what you want to achieve. So, although some measurement techniques may have become more sophisticated, for us it is still about helping our system create sustainable premiums on each one of our brands. Since one can manage best what one can measure, we constantly look for new measurement methods that increase our ability to increase the premium. Is that premium increasing or decreasing? Is my brand well known? Is it well liked? Do people recommend my brand? What percentage is sold »on deal« versus at full price. Given proliferation, we are conducting a lot more analyses than we used to, and it makes the job a little harder again.

Jesko Perrey: We agree with the idea of thinking about customer touch points, and we are investing heavily in how to measure the effectiveness and efficiency of communication across different touch points. Do you already have such a tool or approach in place, or is it still a combination of trial and error or step-by-step learning?

Chris Burggraeve: If I had the final answer, I would probably not be at Coke (laughs); I'd have my own consulting firm and be a billionaire. But seriously, I have had to accept this area as more of a journey than I would have liked. We have developed proprietary models to identify the touch points, and we are finding ways to correlate touch-point impact management and share. We're certainly making some progress, and we have already made significant media reallocation decisions based on the new insights.

Jesko Perrey: So, you're looking for a systematic approach to compare, for example, word-of-mouth or viral marketing with TV? But aren't you finding that it's still hard to convince other people in marketing who still live in a branding world that's pure television?

Chris Burggraeve: Yes. Recently, at the Munich Media Days (*Münchener Medientage*) the theme was »Is Coke getting out of TV?« The answer is, not really. But we will use TV in a different way than before. If consumers are flocking to TV for football games, we will be there, too; but in very new ways; combining TV with more media more than ever, as you began to see in the World Cup 2006. Our World Cup media strategy really worked. Despite hundreds of companies advertising, Coke clearly broke through the clutter in many ways. Our equity indicators during that big event were, for the first time, as strong as in the Christmas season, traditionally one of our periods of greatest strength.

Jesko Perrey: When we are talking about a new measuring system or a new currency, from our point of view, there are two challenges: one is about understanding the real or net cost of media, since there are so many »lost« or useless contacts. And the second one is what you were calling »brand experience.« What is the quality of a medium in terms of the contacts it generates? At Coke, how do you get insight into these topics?

Chris Burggraeve: We are experimenting more than ever with new allocation models and measurement systems. In fast-changing times, experiments with new models and measurement systems are critical for survival, and to secure continued effectiveness and efficiency of investment. For a brand like Coke Zero, for example, less of the mix will be in TV, and then we'll begin to see how that actually impacts the equity indicators. While we are approaching Coke Zero in a very different way, TV's still a part of the mix. On some other brands, such as Sprite, some countries started »clean testing« (mono-media) to see how other approaches might work. And that's the way we're going to learn, to develop our database and our knowledge base around the world. Moving away from traditional approaches can be hard, especially for the brand manager wanting to »make that next big TV ad,« and for the media manager who keeps believing budgeting for next year is »this year plus a little more.« That's not the way of the future, but in huge corporations, changes take some time.

Jesko Perrey: That brings me to one of our last questions: How is the entire organization feeling and thinking about the brand? How far are your thoughts from the middle ground or the mainstream thinking at Coke?

Managing Brands

Chris Burggraeve: Sometimes closer than I think. Sometimes farther away than I would want. It really depends on the topic. But I do carry the informal title of Chief Evangelist (Laughter). I evangelize about what we ought to do and then back that up with facts, figures, learnings, and so on. In marketing, face-to-face conversations with consumers and teams are key. I listen to new learnings. I demonstrate what we're learning in other markets, and I always encourage my teams to visit markets where something great is happening. The way you evangelize is important. I was educated a Jesuit college. Jesuits were the marketers of religion, going deep into the jungle to convert souls. No change happens by hiding in an ivory tower.

Jesko Perrey: Do you think Coke will be as successful in the future?

Chris Burggraeve: Absolutely. We will only have ourselves to blame if we are not. A senior manager at Coke once said, »When you work at Coke, you carry the burden of greatness.« Nobody else has the number one brand. Nobody has the distribution power and sales capabilities that we have. Nobody has the magic to pull in so many partners. Nobody knows beverages as well as we do. But everybody is out there trying to get you out of that number one spot. It is like any sport. Getting to number one is one thing. Staying there for a long time is a very different kind of challenge.

Yet I see no reason why Coke cannot come out winning over the next 120 years. We were a leading brand of the industrial age. With the right winning culture, with the right belief in the power of the Coke brand and its portfolio, all while reinventing our Secret Formula where needed, there is absolutely no reason for Coke not to remain the absolute number one in the digital age.

Jesko Perrey: One more question for you as a consumer. What brand do you start the day with?

Chris Burggraeve: With my BlackBerry – my alarm clock.

Notes

1 »Werbung ist out«, *manager magazin*, Mar 1999, p. 98.
2 James, Allen, Frederick F. Reichheld, Barney Hamilton, and Rob Markey, »Closing the delivery gap,« Bain & Company, 2005, www.bain.com.
3 Mitchell, Colin, »Selling the Brand Inside,« *Harvard Business Review*, 1 Jan 2002.
4 LaClair, Jennifer A., »Helping Employees embrace change,« *The McKinsey Quarterly* 4, 2002, www.mckinseyquarterly.com.
5 Corporate Web sites, McKinsey research (Nov 2007), *Harvard Business Review*.
6 Parsley, Andy, »Employee Engagement: the What, Why and How,« *Management Issues*, 6 Dec 2005, www.management-issues.com.
7 Chandrasekar, Mythili, »Internal branding«, *Business Line*, 7 Sep 2006.
8 Simonian, Haig, »Three Letters Gain a Personality: UBS, Europe's Biggest Bank, has Collapsed its Multiple Brands to Focus on a Single Global Name,« *Financial Times*, 18 Apr 2005, p. 12.
9 Panke, Helmut, Speech at the Paris Motor Show, 2002.
10 www.bmw.com (November 2007).
11 Beuttel, Bianca, »Muji – markenlose Qualitätsprodukte,« Hochschule für Gestaltung, Offenbach am Main, Feb 2004.
12 Klein, Naomi, *No Logo: Taking Aim at the Brand Bullies*, New York: Picador, 1999.
13 Beuttel, Bianca, »Muji – markenlose Qualitätsprodukte,« Hochschule für Gestaltung, Offenbach am Main, Feb 2004.
14 Dooley, Roger, »Sensory Marketing to Jolt Espresso Sales,« posted under *Neuromarketing* at blog.futurelab.net, Nov 2007.
15 www.philips. com.
16 Saal, Marco, »Riesige Fokusgruppe; Philips-Marketingchef Andrea Ragnetti über eine ungewöhnliche Form der Ideenfindung,« *Horizont*, Jul 2007.
17 Coumau, Jean-Baptiste, (with J.F. Gagne and E. Josserand), »Manager par la Marque,« *Editions d'Organisation*: Paris, 2005.
18 Procter & Gamble and Adidas AG *Annual reports*, 2007.
19 Werbemarkt Report, SevenOne Media, 2008; »Key statistics for 2005 and comparison to previous years,« UK Advertising Association, 2006; »UK Internet advertising expenditure grows 38 percent year on year to reach £2.8 billion in 2007,« Internet Advertising Bureau, 2008; »US advertising expenditures grew 0,2 percent in 2007,« TNS Media Intelligence, 2008, www.tns-mi.com.
20 Duyn, van Aline, »Online advertisers may gain from downturn,« *Financial Times*, 23 Sep 2007; Fenton, Ben »TV industry faces financial crisis,« *Financial Times*, 27 Aug 2008.
21 European Audiovisual Observatory, various years; *Werbung in Deutschland 2007*, ZAW, 2007.
22 Media Consumption Study, various years, EIAA Mediascope Europe.
23 Privates Institut für Marketing und Kommunikation (IMK).
24 Sponsorship Vision 2008, Pilot Group.
25 Nöcker, Ralf, »Für Trittbrettfahrer kann es teuer werden,« *Frankfurter Allgemeine Zeitung*, 14 Jul 2005, p. 16.
26 Deutscher Direktmarketing Verband e.V., www.ddv.de.
27 PQ Media Global Product Placement Forecast Series 2006–2010.
28 Schiller, Gail, »Volkswagen bugged about NBC Universal deal,« *Hollywood Reporter*, 16 Jul 2007.
29 »Product-Placement im Film *I, Robot* großer Erfolg: Der Audi RSQ beflügelt die Image-Werte der Marke,« in: *Digitale Pressemappe*, Audi AG (ed.), www.presseportal.de.

30 Trendbarometer Amient Media, Fachverband Ambient Media, 2008; MindSet 2007, Jost von Brandis, 2007.

31 Nieschlag, Robert, Erwin Dichtl and Hans Hörschgen, *Marketing*, Berlin: Duncker & Humblot, 1997; Meffert, Heribert, *Marketing: Grundlagen marktorientierter Unternehmensführung*, Wiesbaden: Gabler, 2000.

32 *Vernetzte Kommunikation*, SevenOne Media, 2003; *Handbuch Crossmedia Werbung*, VDZ, 2003; *WerbeWirkungsWeisen*, RMS, 2003.

33 »Ein großer Schritt,« *Werben & Verkaufen*, 12 Jul 2007.

34 American National Association, several publications, 2005–2007.

35 Neff, Jack and Lisa Sanders, »It's broken; Procter & Gamble's Stengel takes industry to task for clinging to outdated media model,« *Advertising Age*, 16 Feb 2004.

36 Gupta, Sunil and Thomas J. Steenburgh, »Allocating Marketing Resources,« *Harvard Business School*, Mar 2005.

37 Knudsen, Trond, »Confronting proliferation: A conversation with four senior marketers,« *The McKinsey Quarterly 8*, 2007, www.mckinseyquarterly.com.

38 See also »Boosting Returns on Marketing Investments,« *The McKinsey Quarterly 2*, 2005, pp. 36–47, www.mckinseyquarterly.com.

39 Bloom, Jonah, »Ogilvy, Dove miss chance to turn bad press into ›debate‹,« *Advertsing Age 42*, Vol. 79, No. 19, 12 May 2008, © Crain Communications; Collins, Lauren, »Pixel Perfect – Pascal Dangin's Virtual Reality,« *The New Yorker*, 12 May 2008.

40 »Better ROI from YouTube than Super Bowl ad,« *Advertising Age*, 29 Oct 2006.

41 *Advertising Age*, Apr 2008.

42 Case study, PlayStation, Contagious Magazine, Issue 4, 2005, www.shop.contagiousmagazine.com.

43 Schultz, Don E., »Measuring Brand Communication ROI,« *Association of National Advertisers*, 1997.

44 2003 ATL data compiled by AC Nielsen, EHI, M+M Eurodata, DPAG, and McKinsey.

45 Nielsen Media Research, Kraftfahrtbundesamt, 2005–2007.

46 The RCQ model, described in section 4.2, provides an excellent basis for structuring these types of questions.

47 Schäffer, Utz, »Eine Zwischenbilanz der Balanced Scorecard,« *Frankfurter Allgemeine Zeitung*, 3 Mar 2008, and Gerhard Speckbacher, »A Descriptive Analysis on the Implementation of Balanced Scorecards in German-Speaking Countries,« *Management Accounting Research*, Vol. 14, No. 4, Dec 2003.

48 Maddox, Kate, »Special Report: Tech Marketing – The Dashboard Dynamos,« *B to B*, 4 Apr 2005, © Crain Communications, Inc.

49 Swanson, Sandra, »Marketers: James Richardson,« *B to B*, 24 Oct 2005, © Crain Communications; Mayeda, Andrew, »Cisco's brand master sets the pace,« *NT Money Central* (now *MSN Money*), 18 Nov 2004.

50 Peters, Thomas J. and Robert H. Waterman, *In Search of Excellence: Lessons from America's Best-Run Companies*, New York: Warner Books, 1982.

51 Low, George S. and Ronald A. Fullerton, »Brands, Brand Management, and the Brand Manager System: A Critical-Historical Evaluation,« *Journal of Marketing Research 31*, No. 2, 1994, pp. 173–175.

52 Decker, Charles, *Winning with the P&G 99: 99 Principles and Practices of Procter and Gamble's Success*, London: Harper-Collins, 1998.

53 Low, George S. and Ronald A. Fullerton, »Brands, Brand Management, and the Brand Manager System: A Critical-Historical Evaluation,« *Journal of Marketing Research 31*, No. 2, 1994, p. 173.

54 According to the »Marktzahlen« (market data) area of the Bofrost website, www.bofrost.com, as of 3/2008.

55 de.wikipedia.org/wiki/nespresso.

56 Smith Peter and Jim Pickard, »Permira wins Birds Eye auction,« *Financial Times*, Aug 2006.

323

57 »At a glance – The story of Adidas,«
Adidas corporate information, see
www.adidas-group.com.

58 Sony corporate information,
www.sony.net.

59 Hein, Kenneth, »Sony (under repair),«
Brandweek, 2 Jan 2006.

60 »The 100 Top Brands 2006,« *Business
Week*, 7 Aug 2006, www.businessweek.
com.

61 »Coca-Cola hofft auf Wachstum durch
Mineralwasser,« *Financial Times
Deutschland*, 18 Mar 2002, p. 5; »Stille
Wässer pushen Branche,« *Lebensmittel
Zeitung*, 17 Jan 2003, p. 14; Teather,
David, »Coca-Cola Reduces Profit Tar-
gets,« *The Guardian*, 12 Nov 2004, p. 24.

62 Zepelin, Joachim, »Turm im Sturm. Die
Softwarebranche ist in einer Krise wie
nie zuvor,« *Financial Times Deutschland*,
9 Jul 2002, p. 25.

63 »Agenturbeziehungen: Kinder aus
gutem Haus,« *Horizont*, 26 Jun 2003,
p. 30; »Werbepartnerschaften: der Bund
fürs Markenleben,« *Horizont*, 8 Oct
2001, p. 82.

64 Elliott, Stuart, »McDonald's Campaign
Embraces a Loving Theme,« *The New
York Times*, 12 Jun 2003.

65 Smith, Rob, »Wieden talks about Nike
relationship,« *Portland Business Journal*,
29 Jan 2004.

66 Clef, Ulrich, *Die Ausgezeichneten*,
München: Clef Creative Communications, 2003.

67 Oehler, Klaus Dieter, »Auch Autover-
mieter setzen auf billig,« *Stuttgarter Zeitung*, 15 Oct 2003, p. 9; Köhn, Rüdiger,
»Hertz lassen die Billigstrategien der
Konkurrenten kalt,« *Frankfurter Allgemeine Zeitung*, 2 Feb 2004, p. 16.

68 »ADC-Visions, Kongress für den kreati-
ven Nachwuchs: Auf der Jagd nach Kunden,« *Horizont*, 14 Mar 2002, p. 35.

69 Peymani, Bijan, »Kult und Kultur,«
Werben & Verkaufen, 7 Mar 2003, p. 34.

70 Richter, Kerstin and Peter Hammer,
»Der Kampf wird härter,« *Werben & Verkaufen*, 5 Apr 2002, pp. 42–45.

71 WPP press release, 12 May 2004.
Regarding Coke's agency model, see for
example, Guy Brighton, *Coke Avoids
Agencies To Make New Campaign*,
www.psfk.com, 31 Oct 2006. Also see
Chris Burggraeve's comments on »one
idea, executed locally, but globally recognizable« in the interview with Jesko Perrey at the end of the section.

72 Nobel-Sagolla, Sybille, »Der Chef-Jäger-
meister,« *Süddeutsche Zeitung*, 14 Oct
2003, p. 26.

73 Vossler, Manfred, »Mast-Jägermeister
AG berichtet über erfolgreichstes
Geschäftsjahr,« *Lebensmittel Zeitung*,
25 Apr 2003, p. 12; Wörmann, Barbara
and Ute Müller, »Jägermeister –
Höherer Absatz,« *Die Welt*, 27 Jan 2005,
p. 15; Mast-Jägermeister AG, Jahres-
abschlüsse, various years.

74 Taylor, Jim, *Space Race: An Inside View of
the Future of Communications Planning*,
Chichester: John Wiley & Sons, 2007.

75 Feldmeier, Sonja, »Wie korrupt ist die
Mediabranche,« *Werben & Verkaufen* 16
Jan 2008; also see Heil, Christian, »Der
Sturz des Sonnenkönigs,« *Frankfurter
Allgemeine Zeitung*, 24 Aug 2008,
No. 34, p. 54.

76 According to Frank-Michael Schmidt,
head of J. Walter Thomson, and Tom
Felber, financial manager of BBDO, »In
die Enge getrieben,« *Werben & Verkaufen*, 16 May 2003, pp. 42–45. Also see
GWA, »Frühjahrsmonitor 2007« and
Association of National Advertisers
(ANA), »Trends in Agency Compensation 2007.« For a more in-depth discussion of agency compensation, see
Gordana Uzelac, »Vergütungsmodelle
von Werbeagenturen« (academic
paper), Karlsruhe, 2007.

77 See e.g., Krenn, Ulrich, »Großer Friede,
keine Freude,« *Werben & Verkaufen*,
30 Jan 2004, and Amirkhizi, Mehrdad,
»Streit landet unterm Teppich: Jung von
Matt und BBDO vereinbaren Waffen-
stillstand,« *Werben & Verkaufen*, 29 Jan
2004.

5.
Power Brands: Ten Perspectives

With this book, the authors have attempted to present a model for more effective marketing management. Our aim was to describe the model as clearly and comprehensively as possible for readers in a wide range of disciplines. We believe that users can succeed in measuring, making, and managing their brands better than ever before, provided they apply the right set of instruments. Is that all there is to it? No, the bar is a little higher than just that. Indeed, it is so high that many managers may be reluctant to try to clear it. Do companies that have achieved a perfect mastery of all of the techniques and processes exist? Can companies ever apply all of the instruments in an optimal way? Even if such companies do exist, their number will certainly remain very small. But this is no reason to hang back. As always, when success is the goal, one principle remains true: begin with a small step and don't waste too much time contemplating the big picture! For this reason, instead of a classic closing summary, we have synthesized ten points that show brand managers who are motivated and determined the way to advance along the path to creating and managing a power brand.

1. More systematic approach, less gut feeling

As in all business functions, a systematic approach should become a given. Those who apply the available tools will significantly reduce the number of mistakes they make in brand management and will rely less on gut feeling or hunches and more on rational findings: more system, less intuition.

2. Facts count, guesswork confuses

No other discipline relies as much on supposed expertise and experience as marketing. Nowhere else do facts and figures count for so little. For successful brand management, this has to change. Marketing must stop flying

Power Brands. H. Riesenbeck and J. Perrey
Copyright © 2009 WILEY-VCH Verlag GmbH & Co. KGaA, Weinheim
ISBN: 978-3-527-50390-2

blind and start using the instruments at its disposal. For many marketing managers, using facts and figures for orientation requires a real change in mindset – and also represents an enormous opportunity to secure greater success in the marketplace.

3. Focus on one target group; forget trying to be everybody's darling

Many companies still find it hard to focus their brands on one target group only and to optimize their value proposition for this core group alone. Neglecting customer groups you previously served can be painful. But those who seek to be everybody's darling run the risk of selling run-of-the-mill products that can only succeed in the market with a huge investment in sales push.

4. Create a clearly differentiated brand promise; pay less attention to competitors

Many companies are reluctant to give their brands a sharp profile, that is, to deliberately compete on just a few points of value. They fear that neglecting other important aspects will allow competitors to exploit the gaps and gain the upper hand in terms of market share. This explains why many companies implement and communicate their brands by stressing every last one of their advantages and believe it is important to have as many advantages as possible. They forget that such an »everything-to-everyone« profile has little or no credibility in brand communications and results in a relatively fuzzy profile versus rivals. Such a strategy can stabilize a company's market share – but only when competitors are equally weak and the company has a relatively strong sales force.

5. More science, craft, and targeted creativity; *less l'art pour l'art*

In marketing management, the artistic element – above all in advertising and communication – has played too large a role for far too long. It is time for a change of direction. Scientific insights and excellent craftsmanship should dominate in the future. Using BrandMatics® will not make the world of advertising duller. Rigorously applied, it will make advertising more effective, and the effects can be counted sooner in euros and cents.

Specifically, ramping up science and craft does not entail any cut-backs on creativity. Creative thinking and original execution will always be cornerstones of successful branding. The challenge is to use science and craft to define a frame in which creativity can unfold its full potential in a targeted way – as a means to an end, not an end in itself.

6. For consistency; against incessant change

Strong brands are characterized by consistency and continuity in management. In practical terms, companies that want to secure and strengthen their success in this field have to reduce job rotation in order to prevent their brands from bouncing among different decision makers and different philosophies. If new people are absolutely essential in the given decision-making roles, it is still critical to ensure the continuity of the brand. Changes should be made very cautiously and not for the sake of a newly minted manager's self-marketing campaign.

7. Ensure top management responsibility for the brand, not fragmented decision-making authority

The brand is a playing field for nearly everyone in the company. Practically no other asset is as affected by as many decision makers in as many different parts and at as many different levels of the company as are brands. Product development, production, sales, marketing, public relations, and even the legal department may be making important decisions about the brand independently of one another. Only a few companies assign all decision-making authority to one specific brand manager. And only a few have consistently implemented Procter & Gamble's original brand management model. Most companies clearly assign responsibility for other important assets such as patents, factories, machinery, and inventories to one functional unit. Corresponding centralization of brand decisions is an important initial step on the way to better brand management.

8. Treat external providers as partners, not as subworkers

It is only when companies take external specialists seriously and involve them in brand management as competent sources of knowledge that senior executives can expect to see better results. As long as product managers treat advertising agencies, market research institutes, and branding consultants merely as subworkers and do not involve them in important decisions, they will fail to tap critical stimuli and promising ideas. Only open and occasionally critical discussions among specialists, plus the brand manager's ability to synthesize the various viewpoints into a clear resolve, will ensure success.

9. Brand equity as a component of the balance sheet: Put an end to guessing games

Brands will automatically command more of senior management's attention and receive greater consideration in shareholder value analyses when they are treated as assets in the balance sheet. Their value has to be objectively measured by third-party accountants, and not with unclear models applied by external branding service providers who juggle dangerously high and unverifiable brand values. After brand equity becomes generally accepted as an important asset on the balance sheet, it will also be discussed regularly at the meetings of management and supervisory boards – and will thus become an important driver for greater professionalism in brand management.

10. Marketing knowledge for all: Down with the ivory tower

Why are the instruments for effective brand management not taught as a part of the core curriculum in university business administration courses? Why are these methods not included in companies' trainee programs for up-and-coming management talent, along with the fundamentals of balance sheet accounting, finance, and business law? Because marketing is still perceived as a specialized discipline that only a few can master, and thus it is also commonly viewed as only a qualitative semi-science. Yet today, as growth becomes ever more important for all companies, well-informed brand management – knowing how to create and extract value from an existing brand – is becoming more critical. This knowledge – making, measuring, and managing power brands – should therefore be broadly anchored in management.

Table of illustrations

Power Brands. H. Riesenbeck and J. Perrey
Copyright © 2009 WILEY-VCH Verlag GmbH & Co. KGaA, Weinheim
ISBN: 978-3-527-50390-2

335

Table of
illustrations

Table of
illustrations

Selected bibliography

Aaker, David A. *Building Strong Brands*. New York: The Free Press, 1996.

Aaker, David A. *Brand Portfolio Strategy – Creating Relevance, Differentiation, Energy, Leverage, Clarity*. New York: The Free Press, 2004.

Aaker, Jennifer L. »Dimensions of Brand Personality,« *Journal of Marketing Research*, Vol. 34, August 1997, 347–356.

Backhaus, Klaus. *Industriegütermarketing*. Munich: Vahlen, 2003.

Bekmeier-Feuerhahn, Sigrid. *Marktorientierte Markenbewertung – eine konsumenten- und unternehmensorientierte Bewertung*. Wiesbaden: Gabler, 1998.

Bonoma, Thomas V. and Benson P. Shapiro. »Evaluating Market Segmentation Approaches.« *Industrial Marketing Management*, Vol. 13, 1984, 257–268.

Bruhn, Manfred. *Handbuch Markenführung*. 2nd edition. Wiesbaden: Gabler, 2004.

Carlotty, Stephen, Mary Ellen Coe, and Jesko Perrey. »Making brand portfolios work.« In: *The McKinsey Quarterly*. No. 4, 2004, 25–35.

Caspar, Mirko and Patrick Metzler. »Entscheidungsorientierte Markenführung. Aufbau und Führung starker Marken.« In: *Arbeitspapier Nr. 3*. Düsseldorf: McKinsey & Company, Inc./Marketing Centrum Münster (Publisher), 2002.

Caspar, Mirko, Achim Hecker, and Tatjana Sabel. »Markenrelevanz in der Unternehmensführung: Messung, Erklärung und empirische Befunde für B2B-Märkte.« In: *Arbeitspapier Nr. 4*. Düsseldorf: McKinsey & Company, Inc./Marketing Centrum Münster (Publisher), 2002.

Collins, Allan M. and Elizabeth F. Loftus. »A Spreading Activation Theory of Semantic Processing.« *Psychological Review*, Volume 82, 1975, 407–428.

Copeland, Tom, Tim Koller, and Jack Murrin. *Valuation: Measuring and Managing the Value of Companies*. 4th edition. New York: Wiley, 2005.

Coumau, Jean-Baptiste (with J.F. Gagne and E. Josserand), *Manager par la Marque*, Paris: Editions d'Organisation, 2005.

Power Brands. H. Riesenbeck and J. Perrey
Copyright © 2009 WILEY-VCH Verlag GmbH & Co. KGaA, Weinheim
ISBN: 978-3-527-50390-2

Court, David, Jonathan Gordan, and Jesko Perrey. »Boosting returns on marketing investments.« *The McKinsey Quarterly*. No. 2, 2005, 36–47.

Court, David et al. *Profiting from Proliferation*. New York: McKinsey & Company, Inc., 2006.

de Chernatony, Leslie and Malcolm McDonald. *Creating Powerful Brands in Consumer Services and Industrial Markets*. 2nd edition. Oxford: Butterworth-Heinemann, 1998.

Decker, Charles. P&G *99: 99 Principles and Practices of Procter and Gamble's Success*. London: HarperCollins Publishers, 1998.

Echterling, Jens, Marc Fischer, and Marcel Kranz. »Die Erfassung der Markenstärke und des Markenpotenzials als Grundlage der Markenführung.« In: *Arbeitspapier Nr. 2*. Düsseldorf: McKinsey & Company, Inc./ Marketing Centrum Münster (Publisher), 2002.

Esch, Franz-Rudolf. *Moderne Markenführung. Grundlagen. Innovative Ansätze. Praktische Umsetzung*. Wiesbaden: Gabler, 1999.

Fanderl, Harald and Fabian Hieronimus. »Consumer Driven Redesign – Capturing New Potential Through Customer Insight«, *Recall No. 1*. Düsseldorf: McKinsey & Company, Inc., 2008.

Fischer, Marc. *A Brand Value Metric for Balance Sheets*. Working Paper, Anderson School of Management, University of California at Los Angeles, 2003.

Fischer, Marc, Fabian Hieronimus, and Marcel Kranz. »When do brand investments pay off? – The relevance of brands in B2C markets.« In: *Arbeitspapier Nr. 1*. Düsseldorf: McKinsey & Company, Inc./Marketing Centrum Münster (Publisher), 2002.

Freeling, Anthony, Trond Riiber Knudsen, Hajo Riesenbeck et al. *McKinsey BrandMatics – Systematically Improving Brand Economics*. Düsseldorf: McKinsey & Company, Inc., 2003.

Galamba de Oliveira, Raul, Fabian Hieronimus, and Martin Huber. *Brand-Driven Retail Banking*. Frankfurt: McKinsey & Company, Inc., 2006.

Gregory, James R. and Donald E. Sexton. »Hidden Wealth in B2B«, *Harvard Business Review*, March 2007.

Haley, Russell I. »Benefit Segmentation: A Decision-Oriented Research Tool.« *Journal of Marketing*, 32, July 1968, 30–35.

Hölscher, Ansgar. »Customer Insights.« In: Hajo Riesenbeck/Jesko Perrey (eds.), *Marketing nach Maß*. Heidelberg: Redline, 2007.

Keller, Kevin L. »Conceptualizing, Measuring, and Managing Customer-based Brand Equity.« *Journal of Marketing*, Vol. 57, January 1993, 1–22.

Keller, Kevin L. *Strategic Brand Management: Building, Measuring, and Managing Brand Equity*. Upper Saddle River: Prentice Hall, 1998.

Klein, Naomi. *No Logo: Taking Aim at the Brand Bullies.* New York: Picador, 1999.

Knudsen, Trond Riiber, »Confronting proliferation: A conversation with four senior marketers.« In: *The McKinsey Quarterly*, No. 3, 2007.

LaClair, Jennifer A. »Helping Employees Embrace Change.« *The McKinsey Quarterly*, No. 4, 2002.

Low, George S., and Ronald Fullerton. »Brands, Brand Management, and the Brand Manager System: A Critical-Historical Evaluation.« *Journal of Marketing Research*, Vol. 31, 2/1994, 173–175.

Low, George S. and Charles W. Lamb Jr. »The Measurement and Dimensionality of Brand Associations.« *Journal of Product and Brand Management*, Vol. 8, 6/2000, 350–368.

McKinsey & Company, Inc./Marketing Centrum Münster (Publisher). *So lohnen sich Investitionen in die Marke – Aufbau und Führung starker Marken.* Düsseldorf: McKinsey & Company, Inc., July 2002.

Meffert, Heribert, Christoph Burmann, and Martin Koers. *Markenmanagement.* 2nd edition. Wiesbaden: Gabler, 2005.

Meffert, Heribert. *Marketing – Grundlagen marktorientierter Unternehmensführung.* Wiesbaden: Gabler, 2000.

Meffert, Heribert and Manfred Bruhn. *Dienstleistungsmarketing: Grundlagen – Konzepte – Methoden.* Wiesbaden: Gabler, 2003.

Perrey, Jesko. *Nutzenorientierte Marktsegmentierung. Ein integrativer Ansatz zum Zielgruppenmarketing im Verkehrsdienstleistungsbereich.* Wiesbaden: Gabler, 1998.

Perrey, Jesko, Nicola Wagener, and Carsten Wallmann. *Kreativität + Content Fit = Werbeerfolg.* Düsseldorf: McKinsey & Company, Inc., 2007.

Peters, Thomas J. and Robert H. Waterman Jr., *In Search of Excellence – Lessons from America's Best-run Companies.* New York: Warner, 1982.

Sattler, Henrik (ed.). *Praxis von Markenbewertung und Markenmanagement in deutschen Unternehmen.* Publisher: PricewaterhouseCoopers Deutsche Revision. Frankfurt, 2001.

Sattler, Henrik (ed.). *Praxis von Markenbewertung und Markenmanagement in deutschen Unternehmen: Neue Befragung 2005.* Publisher: PricewaterhouseCoopers Deutsche Revision. Frankfurt, 2006.

Schellekens, Maarten. »Segmentierung.« In: Hajo Riesenbeck/Jesko Perrey (eds.), *Marketing nach Maß.* Heidelberg: Redline, 2007.

Schiller, Z. »The Marketing Revolution at Procter & Gamble,« *Business Week.* 1988, 72–76.

Schultz, Don E. *Measuring Brand Communication ROI*. Association of National Advertisers. 1997.

Taylor, Jim. *Space Race: An Inside View of the Future of Communications Planning*. Chichester: John Wiley & Sons, 2007.

Companies and brands

343

Companies and
brands

Power Brands. H. Riesenbeck and J. Perrey
Copyright © 2009 WILEY-VCH Verlag GmbH & Co. KGaA, Weinheim
ISBN: 978-3-527-50390-2

About the authors

Hajo Riesenbeck joined McKinsey & Company, Inc., in 1979 as a consultant in Düsseldorf. He was elected to Principal in 1985 and to Director in 1991. He advises international clients in the consumer goods, financial services, branded industrial products, retail, transportation, and chemicals industries. He is one of the leaders of McKinsey's global Marketing & Sales Practice.

Dr. Jesko Perrey is a Partner of McKinsey & Company, Inc., and based in the Düsseldorf office, which he joined in 1999. He leads McKinsey's German Marketing & Sales Practice and McKinsey's European Branding & Marketing RoI service line, and serves clients in the consumer goods, retail, financial services, and logistics industries. The functional focus of his work is on branding and marketing spend effectiveness.

Power Brands. H. Riesenbeck and J. Perrey
Copyright © 2009 WILEY-VCH Verlag GmbH & Co. KGaA, Weinheim
ISBN: 978-3-527-50390-2

About the illustrations

Jens Lorenzen provided an artist's interpretation of the brand names, company logos, and company products gracing the pages of our book. With his fresco-like paintings and collage work, Lorenzen, who was born in Schleswig in 1961 and now lives in Berlin, has made a name for himself in the past ten years both in the art world and in the world of business. After his studies at the Academy of Art in Braunschweig, Lorenzen exhibited his works at galleries, museums, and major corporations. His pictures are included in collections belonging to Commerzbank Berlin, Volkswagen Bank Braunschweig, Norddeutsche Landesbank Hannover, and the Axel Springer Verlag Hamburg.
(www.jens-lorenzen.com)

This book is due for return on or before the last date shown below.